Abandoned

Abandoned

Foundlings in Nineteenth-Century New York City

Julie Miller

NEW YORK UNIVERSITY PRESS
New York and London

NEW YORK UNIVERSITY PRESS
New York and London
www.nyupress.org

© 2008 by New York University
All rights reserved

Library of Congress Cataloging-in-Publication Data
Miller, Julie, 1959–
Abandoned : foundlings in nineteenth-century New York City /
Julie Miller.
p.   cm.
Includes bibliographical references and index.
ISBN-13: 978-0-8147-5725-3 (cl : alk. paper)
ISBN-10: 0-8147-5725-1 (cl : alk. paper)
ISBN-13: 978-0-8147-5726-0 (pb   )
ISBN-10: 0-8147-5726-X (pb   )
1. Abandoned children—New York (State)—New York—History—
19th century.   I. Title.
HV885.N5M55 2008
362.76—dc22   2007043280

New York University Press books

Manufactured in the United States of America

c 10 9 8 7 6 5 4 3 2 1
p 10 9 8 7 6 5 4 3 2 1

This book is dedicated in memory of Estelle Miller.

Contents

Tables

Acknowledgments

I would like to thank the people who welcomed me in from their doorsteps, both literally and figuratively, during the many years that I worked on this book. Foremost among them is Gerald Markowitz, who nurtured the book from beginning to end. I appreciate his wisdom and kindness. Thomas Kessner also played an important role; I appreciate his close reading and value the many conversations we had over the years.

Other faculty members of the history department at the Graduate Center of the City University of New York also read and commented on this book at various stages. They include Bonnie Anderson, Ann Fabian, Margaret King, David Nasaw, and Barbara Welter. I am grateful to them for their enthusiasm and guidance. At New York University Press I am also grateful to Deborah Gershenowitz, Salwa Jabado, Despina Papazoglou Gimbel, and the anonymous readers.

I am also grateful to the colleagues who listened to and commented on portions of this work that I delivered at conferences over the years. These include the Conference on New York State History, the European Social Science History Conference, the Gotham History Conference at the Gotham Center for New York City History, the Nineteenth-Century Studies Association conference, and the Society for the History of Children and Youth's biennial meeting.

At different stages of this project I was assisted by several awards: the Nina E. Fortin Memorial Fund Dissertation Proposal Award of the Women's Studies Certificate Program of the CUNY Graduate Center, a dissertation fellowship from the Jewish Foundation for Education of Women, The Dixon Ryan Fox Manuscript Prize of the New York State Historical Association, and the Bernard and Irene Schwartz Postdoctoral Fellowship of the New-York Historical Society. These awards provided funds, encouragement, and the essential gift of time. I would like to express my gratitude to the donors and administrators of these awards for their great generosity to me.

New York City's libraries and archives are among the city's great treasures; I could not have written this book without them. I would like to thank the staff of the New York Public Library, who retrieved innumerable books, manuscripts, and boxes of microfilm for me; Ken Cobb and Leonora Gidlund of the Municipal Archives, who have performed essential work in preserving and making available the records that document New York City's history; the Municipal Reference and Research Library, particularly Devra Zetlin, now retired; Adele Lerner, also retired, formerly the archivist of the New York Weill Cornell Medical Center Archives, and her successor, James Gehrlich; the New-York Historical Society library; Sister Rita King, archivist of the Sisters of Charity Archives at Mount St. Vincent College; Sister Marilda Joseph, archivist at the New York Foundling Hospital; the New York Academy of Medicine library; and the libraries of Hunter College, Lehman College, New York University, the New School, and Columbia University. I am especially grateful to James Folts of the New York State Library, and Peter Lee and Kay Mackey of the library of the Benjamin N. Cardozo School of Law, for guiding me through the complexities of nineteenth-century law.

Other friends, colleagues, and family members provided help and encouragement during the years it took to write this book. They include G. David Brumberg, Joan Jacobs Brumberg, Laura Chmielewski, Vincent DiGirolamo, Rebecca Jacobs, Barbara and Martin Miller, Phil Pappas, Madeline Rogers, Iris Towers, Jack Wertheimer, my colleagues at Hunter College, and my friends at the Alderbrook Pool. I would also like to thank the many friends who over the years pointed out to me the presence of innumerable foundlings in novels, movies, cartoons, and myths. In everything I do I remember my brother, Paul Miller.

I was lucky to have a wonderful aunt, Estelle Miller. She was a great reader and she devoted herself to making me one too. This book is dedicated to her with love and gratitude.

Abbreviations

AH Almshouse or Almshouse Department, as it was called 1832–59.

AFV Almshouse Foundling Volume, 1838–41, New-York Historical Society. This volume is cataloged as Foundling Hospital Indentures, 1838–40. It is in two parts. The first contains data on women who registered with the almshouse to work as wet nurses; the rest is a chronological record of foundlings received.

AICP Association for Improving the Condition of the Poor

NCH Nursery and Child's Hospital*

NYFA New York Foundling Asylum

NYFH New York Foundling Hospital

NYHS New-York Historical Society

NYIA New York Infant Asylum*

NYNCH New York Nursery and Child's Hospital*

PC Department of Public Charities (the result of a split of the Department of Public Charities and Correction, 1895)

PCC Department of Public Charities and Correction (succeeded the Almshouse Department in 1860)

SCAA State Charities Aid Association

* Unless otherwise specified, records of the Nursery and Child's Hospital, New York Infant Asylum, and New York Nursery and Child's Hospital are at the New York Weill Cornell Medical Center Archives.

Introduction

On a May evening in 1841, a widow named Charlotte Sears discovered a day-old boy abandoned in the entry of her house on Fourth Street near Avenue D in New York City. She carried the baby to the offices of the almshouse in City Hall Park. There she told the clerk who recorded her story that she did not know "who left it there nor to whom it belongs." The commissioners of the almshouse, whose responsibility it was to care for the city's infant castoffs, placed the foundling with a wet nurse and gave him a name. The name they chose was Oliver Twist, after Charles Dickens's fictional street urchin, who first appeared in print in 1837.

Dickens himself arrived in the United States for an American tour in January 1842. By February he was in New York, where—as was to be expected of a novelist of social conscience—he toured the city's charitable institutions, its prisons, and its slums. But he did not get the chance to meet his character's namesake. The New York–born Oliver Twist had spent less than two months with a wet nurse on Sullivan Street and then, like most of the city's foundlings, he died.[1]

Today everybody knows of the fictional Oliver Twist, but nobody remembers the real one. When we think about foundlings, we are likely to think of biblical, mythical, and literary examples: An infant set adrift in a little boat, a newborn deity cast out on a hillside, a baby in a basket on a stranger's doorstep. Moses was a foundling; so were Oedipus, Hercules, Tom Jones, and, most recently, Harry Potter. Nineteenth-century New Yorkers such as Charlotte Sears knew this literary legacy too. But, unlike us, they lived in a world in which foundlings were as embedded in everyday life as they were in literature. As early as Shakespeare's time, foundlings were associated at least as much with poverty and unmarried motherhood as with the mythical and magical.[2]

Nineteenth-century New Yorkers first interpreted the phenomenon of infant abandonment with a set of ideas borrowed from Europe.

Foremost among these was that the foundling was the baby of an unmarried mother impelled by poverty, shame, or both to give up her child soon after birth. The stigma attached to illegitimacy meant that Europeans made a sharp distinction between foundlings and orphans. Orphans, children who had lost one or both parents through death, were simply unfortunates. Foundlings, discarded by living parents, were stained with sin.

This was the prevailing characterization of the foundling in nineteenth-century New York; the focus on the sinning mother shaped the way New Yorkers treated their foundlings. While illegitimacy did often lie behind infant abandonment, in reality, mothers and a few fathers abandoned their babies for a wider range of reasons. Poverty was nearly always one of them, and the case of Drusilla Smith provides one example. In the winter of 1839, Smith brought her five-week-old boy, Charles Smith Pugsley, to the commissioners of the almshouse. The baby was illegitimate. His father, Jesse Pugsley, had taken the route followed by so many young men before the Civil War: he went west, to Illinois, where a man could have a farm of his own and cast off forever the binding ties he'd left back East. The almshouse accepted baby Charles from his mother "on a/c [account] of her poverty."[3]

New Yorkers abandoned their babies for a variety of reasons, and the city's institutions for foundlings defined their charges in a variety of ways. In this book, a foundling is an abandoned baby, regardless of the marital status of the mother or the method of abandonment, and the term includes children born in the foundling asylums. Children identified as foundlings in this book were aged from newborn to no more than two years old, since that is the way most people and institutions in nineteenth-century New York defined them the great majority of the time.

Antebellum New Yorkers, drawing on their European and in particular their British heritage, not only scorned foundlings as illegitimates, but also took them for granted, understanding them as a sad but fundamentally normal part of the social order. Before the Civil War, when New York had no foundling asylums, none of the city's private charities, including its orphanages, admitted abandoned babies. The taint foundlings bore as presumed illegitimates created one barrier; their physical fragility and the difficulties involved in finding adequate supplies of breast milk for them created another. As a result, the only institution in antebellum New York that would accept foundlings was the public poorhouse, or almshouse, which was mandated by law to care for the city's destitute and homeless. Yet it had a reputation for terrible squalor.

The charitable men and women who ran New York's antebellum orphanages, many of whom had been deeply influenced by the religious revivals of the first decades of the nineteenth century known as the Second Great Awakening, surely knew that the foundlings they refused were likely to die.[4] Twenty-first-century Americans might find this apathy toward the young and vulnerable very difficult to understand. But the ability of these apparently compassionate people to turn their backs on foundlings, to, in a sense, doubly abandon them, marks them as bearers of a worldview that held that the fate of sinners and the very young was in the hands not of compassionate men and women but of God.[5]

Of all young children who lived in nineteenth-century New York, foundlings were the most vulnerable, and their problems and those of their mothers the most closely associated with the social disorganization of large cities. This book is an attempt to understand New York's experience with foundlings in the nineteenth century, and to show how that experience was shaped by New Yorkers' interpretation of the foundling not only as an endangered child, but as a symbol of female sexual transgression and urban social breakdown. The book shows how New Yorkers took a set of European ideas and reshaped them (and in some cases were forced to reshape them) to fit the contours of a social landscape formed by immigration, machine politics, Catholic-Protestant conflict, and the physical and moral anxiety induced in urban leaders by urban growth so rapid that it turned their once-familiar city into a dangerous and unfamiliar place.

New York and Its Foundlings

While in the first decades of the nineteenth century the city was content to let the almshouse cope with its foundlings, after the Civil War four institutions opened to serve them. In the late 1850s, alarmed by the physical and moral dangers they saw developing in their city, a group of city councilmen and almshouse officials began planning the city's first foundling asylum. The Civil War interrupted the progress of their plan.

But in December 1865, after the war ended, they opened their found-ling asylum, which they called the Infant's Home. Instead of running it themselves, city officials delegated its supervision to Mary Du Bois, "first directress" of the Nursery and Child's Hospital, an institution that had opened in 1854 to provide twenty-four-hour care to the often-neglected children of wet nurses, which expanded into a children's hos-pital in 1858. Within less than a decade after the war, three more foundling asylums opened in New York. The New York Infant Asylum, like the nursery a Protestant institution, also opened in 1865, sputtered and failed, then reopened in 1871. The New York Foundling Asylum, run by the Catholic Sisters of Charity, opened in 1869. And in 1869 the city built another foundling asylum, this time keeping it entirely under public auspices. Located on Randall's Island in the East River, the three-story, stone-winged edifice was called the Infant Hospital.

The people who organized the city's foundling asylums were a fasci-nating and contentious group. Some were religiously motivated. These included Mary Delafield Du Bois of the Nursery and Child's Hospital and Abigail Hopper Gibbons, a Quaker reformer and a leader of the New York Infant Asylum. While the leaders of the nursery and the New York Infant Asylum came from the Protestant community, Sister Irene Fitzgerald, a member of the Sisters of Charity and the longtime head of the New York Foundling Asylum, was an advocate for the city's Catho-lic, immigrant poor.

Others held the scientific and bureaucratic perspective that began to dominate thinking about the poor after the Civil War. Physician and sanitarian Stephen Smith, a leader of the New York Infant Asylum and a founder of New York's first permanent board of health, had a foot in each camp: as a physician and advocate of sanitary reform, he was a man of science, but he also brought religious tracts to distribute when he worked in army hospitals during the Civil War.[6] Physician Abraham Jacobi, a refugee from the German revolution of 1848 and a leader of the emerging field of pediatrics, brought his radical interpretation of medicine as a means for uplifting the poor to his work with New York's foundlings. City politicians who supported institutions that served foundlings included "Slippery Dick" Connolly, who was at the center of the Tweed Ring, the corrupt band of politicians that stole millions from the city treasury through bribery and graft. His wife, Mary Connolly, was a lay benefactor of the New York Foundling Asylum. Erastus Brooks, a state senator and the anti-immigrant Know Nothing Party's candidate for governor in 1856, supported the Nursery and Child's Hospital through his family connection to Mary Du Bois. Also among this group of organizers of foundling asylums was almshouse governor Isaac Townsend, a dreamer who had been impressed by the London Foundling Hospital's programs of music and art. He hoped to replicate London's example in New York by elevating the city's cultural tone along with its moral behavior. The press, too, was a factor in the creation, and the operation, of the foundling asylums, judging, prodding, shedding sentimental tears, and always watching.

New York's experience with foundlings was on a different scale from that of other American cities. During the first half of the nineteenth century, New York overtook Philadelphia as the country's largest city. Its port, the best on the East Coast, drew in not only the commerce that filled the city's banks, but the poor immigrants who filled the city's slums in massive numbers.[7] New York, more than other American cities, was filled with the needy. During the antebellum years, its streets and stoops began to fill with foundlings.

While its problems were on a larger scale, New York was neither the first nor the only American city to encounter foundlings and open foundling asylums. The first foundling asylum in New York State was incorporated in 1852 in Buffalo.[8] During and after the Civil War, foundling asylums opened in Boston, Chicago, San Francisco, and Washington, D.C.[9] But New York City had more foundlings and built more foundling asylums than any other American city ever did.[10] Thus New York's experience with foundlings was more like that of London or Paris than that of Boston or Chicago. It served as a testing ground for solutions to what many perceived as a European problem in an American context, and the city's significant engagement with foundlings makes it the best place in which to study the problem of foundlings in the United States.

Foundlings in Europe

To date, there have been only a few, limited efforts to examine the history of American foundlings.[11] European historians, in contrast, have produced a wealth of scholarship about European foundlings, and in doing so have unearthed a forgotten problem of enormous proportions.[12] Their work has shown how governments, religious groups, charitable organizations, and individuals conceptualized the foundling as a product of poverty or sexual transgression. They have also investigated the related issue of social control of women and families by church and state. The policies and practices of the foundling asylums that appeared in European cities from the Middle Ages onward were expressions of their societies' values concerning family honor, female sexuality, and the state's obligations to the poor.

Europe faced the problem of foundlings much sooner than the United States did. When America's British settlers stepped off their boats in the early seventeenth century, Europe already had cities large enough to create the social conditions that produced significant numbers of foundlings, as well as the religious and governmental structures with which to help them. By then, Europe already had foundling asylums that were several centuries old. By the eighteenth century, when the United States was just starting and its cities were still small, infant abandonment was a mass phenomenon in places like London and Paris. It took until the nineteenth century for New York to overtake London as a center of Dickensian urban ills, including the presence of large numbers of foundlings.[13]

In the Catholic countries of Europe, and also in Russia (with variations depending upon time and place), local and national governments, often together with religious bodies, assumed full responsibility for foundlings. Accidentally conceived infants were anonymously absorbed into large, urban foundling asylums. These asylums were at the center of great networks of wet nurses, transporters of babies, physicians, religious officials, and bureaucrats. This was the so-called Catholic System. Its goal was to preserve the honor of unmarried women and families by making babies born outside of marriage disappear.

In the contrasting "Protestant System" there were no central foundling asylums supported by networks of functionaries. In England, foundlings, along with the rest of the destitute, were relegated to the care of the parish, the local governmental unit designated to care for those poor who had established residence within its boundaries. In keeping with the Protestant emphasis on individual responsibility, local authorities sought parents out in an effort to wrest payment from them for their children's care, while the children themselves lived in the almshouse until they were old enough to apprentice.[14] Dickens's description of the early life of his fictional Oliver Twist comes very close to the reality experienced by English foundlings.

Foundlings in New York's Almshouse

American poor laws were originally modeled on those of England. In New York, as in English cities, the almshouse was responsible for abandoned babies. Even after the Civil War, when private groups opened three foundling asylums in the city, the almshouse continued to care for foundlings, by this time in its Infant Hospital on Randall's Island. For most of the antebellum period, however, the methods New York's almshouse used to care for its foundlings remained essentially static. Foundlings retrieved from streets and doorsteps were carried to the almshouse by finders such as Charlotte Sears, by the police, or by passersby. In addition, many babies were brought by baby farmers, women who cared for groups of young children in their homes for pay. Single women who lived in middle- and upper-class households as domestic servants often placed their infants, who were unwelcome in the homes of their employers, with baby farmers. If these working mothers were unable to keep up with the payments for their children's board, baby farmers resorted to the almshouse. Once children had been brought to the almshouse, officials placed them with homeless women living in the almshouse, some but not all of whom were able to breastfeed. Whenever they could, almshouse officials sent foundlings to the homes of poor women who worked for the almshouse as wet nurses.

Most foundlings raised in the almshouse did not survive their infancies. A physician paid by the almshouse to care for its foundlings in the 1860s remembered that "all of them died."[15] The almshouse's own grim statistics from the same period report that the mortality of motherless infants in the almshouse, a category that included foundlings, "has always been eighty-five per cent by the records . . . it is believed that not an infant survived a year."[16] Some did survive, but prenatal neglect; the exposure some had suffered on stoops and streets; lack of individual care; exposure to infectious illness in the close quarters of the almshouse, which was packed with the sick and dying; and the difficulties the almshouse had in feeding motherless babies—all of these factors lay behind the appalling death rate. They also suffered from the environmental dangers that all young children in nineteenth-century cities experienced. The overall survival rate of children in American cities at the time was also shocking; according to the estimate of New York's Metropolitan Board of Health, one third of children in American cities died during their first year, a rate the health board described as "frightful."[17]

Not only were almshouse officials responsible for the care of abandoned infants, but they often had to assign them names. Some foundlings arrived at the almshouse with notes attached to their clothing that bore their names, but in many instances they did not. The names chosen by the commissioners of the almshouse—Oliver Twist, for example, or Phineas T. Barnum, Henry Foundling, or William Unknown—seem careless, a reflection of the reality that they did not expect these children to live long enough to need usable names.[18]

Those foundlings who survived their infancies remained in the almshouse or were returned to it by their nurses. The almshouse was then responsible for raising them. In the mid-1830s, the almshouse opened Long Island Farms, a nursery for its foundlings and other destitute and parentless children. It was located on what is today the Queens shoreline, opposite Roosevelt (then Blackwell's) Island. In 1847 the almshouse replaced Long Island Farms with a new set of nursery buildings on Randall's Island. Foundlings remained at these almshouse nurseries until they were old enough to be apprenticed, usually before their teens. Then, unlike French, Italian, or Russian foundlings, who were marked by their association with large-scale church and state-run foundling systems, American foundlings disappeared into the population. This makes them difficult to trace, but it demonstrates how the decentralized, patchwork, and sometimes chaotic nature of American charity, particularly before the Civil War when the federal government played no part in social welfare other than the distribution of military pensions, had an unintended benefit: it allowed those foundlings who managed to survive the extraordinary dangers of their childhoods to escape the stigma that blighted the lives of their European counterparts.

The Discovery of the Foundling

This system—infancy in the almshouse or with a hired wet nurse, childhood in the almshouse or, by the 1830s, at one of the almshouse nurseries, then indenture—was in place when New Yorkers began planning their first foundling asylum. By the 1850s, public officials and reformers had begun to identify infant abandonment as a pressing problem, and the almshouse system, in place since the end of the American Revolution, no longer seemed adequate. These urban leaders, who had previously been content to ignore the high death rate of foundlings, were moved to action, most immediately by a rise in their numbers. They were also forced to act by the press, which, eager to feed the sentimental and pathetic story of the foundling to its broadening readership, published the work of urban investigators who turned up foundlings in the city's darkest corners.

There were also larger religious, political, scientific, and social forces at work. During the first half of the nineteenth century, most of New York's charities, which had not, as yet, turned their attention to foundlings, were infused with religious enthusiasm stimulated by the Second Great Awakening. By midcentury, however, as the material needs of waves of poor immigrants became overwhelming and as sanitary reformers began to bring scientific values to urban problems, pragmatic goals began to take precedence over spiritual ones among the city's charitable community.[19] Traditional indifference toward the welfare of young children, born out of religious submission as well as the inability of science and medicine to do much for the very young, was gradually replaced by a more attentive and compassionate perspective. People who lived in the nineteenth-century United States saw the welfare of children move out of the private domain of families and closer to the center of public debate.

This momentous change did not begin in the United States, nor did it start in the nineteenth century. It is a Western phenomenon that began perhaps as early as the seventeenth century, and it took on speed during the eighteenth-century Enlightenment. It can be seen as a dimension of the age of reform, a product of the same focus on humanitarianism and individual rights that also produced the movements to free the slaves, to grant equal rights to women, and to make the love of wives and mothers—not the power wielded by fathers and husbands—the force that held families together.[20]

The awakening of New York's reformers and public officials to their responsibility toward the foundlings who died on the streets and in the care of the almshouse was also a product of their alarm about the physical and moral dangers that young children faced in large, crowded, industrial cities. Their city was growing with bewildering rapidity, and by the 1840s reformers and city officials had begun to worry about the growing numbers of poor and vagrant children in the city: little match-sellers, rag-pickers, boot-blacks, newsboys, crossing sweepers, thieves, and prostitutes. Would foundlings who managed to struggle past infancy join these "embryo courtezans and felons," as New York's first chief of police called them? Or, if they reached adulthood, would they join the "dangerous classes"?[21] Charles Loring Brace, the founder of the Children's Aid Society, thought so.[22] The Children's Aid Society began collecting poor city children, some of whom lacked homes or parents, and sending them west on so-called orphan trains to be resettled in the homes of rural families.[23] The first orphan train left the city in 1854, just before almshouse officials began to worry about foundlings. In later years, the foundling asylums themselves sent foundlings west on Brace's trains or patterned their own western placement programs on Brace's model.

The creation of New York's foundling asylums was equally stimulated by anxiety about the behavior of foundlings' mothers at a time when American society, particularly the urban middle class, was elevating the innocence of children, the purity of women, and the sanctity of motherhood to new heights.[24] Foundlings were seen as the embodiments of illicit sexuality and also, seemingly, were evidence of an explicit rejection of maternal values. For reformers, to whom the sexuality of abandoning mothers loomed larger than their poverty, the foundling was the hidden made visible and, as such, was both symptom and symbol of the moral, cultural, and physical decay this group of leaders associated with big cities. All of the foundling asylums except the publicly run Randall's Island Infant Hospital made the moral reform of the so-called "fallen woman" their central goal, an expression of their administrators' belief that the foundling was, above all else, evidence of the mother's wrongdoing.

Focused on the fallen woman, foundling asylum administrators wanted to use their institutions not just to save children from the street, but to combat abortion and prostitution, both of which were on the rise at midcentury. Reformers argued that by relieving women of the products of their sin and keeping their secrets, foundling asylums could rescue fallen women from what they saw as an inevitable downward spiral into prostitution. At the same time, physicians associated with the American Medical Association's midcentury antiabortion crusade argued that foundling asylums could combat abortion by giving women a place to deposit their unwanted babies.

Despite their commitment to moral purity, the foundling asylums quickly became enmeshed in the city's interreligious tensions and reliant on the largesse of its corrupt machine politicians. This was, in part, the result of New York's peculiar system of social welfare. During the nineteenth century, overwhelmed by poor immigrants, New York City and New York state developed the practice of delegating public funds to private religious charities, including the foundling asylums. New York's Catholic and Protestant charities competed bitterly for these public dollars, and the Catholic and Protestant foundling asylums were vigorous participants in these interethnic battles. The New York Foundling Asylum discovered just how dangerous this dalliance with power could be in 1871, when city comptroller Richard Connolly, husband of its benefactor Mary Connolly, was implicated in the scandal that brought down the Tweed Ring. The ring's stolen dollars had benefited the Foundling Asylum, along with many other city institutions. The resulting public reluctance to spend public money on private religious institutions made funding unstable for all of the foundling asylums for the remainder of the century.

Some of Europe's foundling asylums lasted for hundreds of years; New York's, for no more than a few decades.[25] This was partly a function of when they were founded. Infant abandonment was generally a byproduct of life in large cities. New York only began to see foundlings in significant numbers when it began to resemble a European city in size, density, and squalor. By the time New York opened its foundling asylums, Europe's were starting to close. By the late nineteenth century, and particularly by the first decades of the twentieth century, New York's foundling asylums began to close, too, because they had learned what European foundling asylums had learned before them: that gathering large numbers of infants together in an institution led to many deaths.

During the first decades of the twentieth century, three out of New York's four foundling asylums closed. At a time of rising expectations for children, their tragic failure to keep their infant charges alive was central to their failure. They were doomed also by the city's rising population, by their inability to attract stable sources of funding, and by the obsolescence of their goals and methods. By the early twentieth century, the Victorian vision of the fallen woman was fading fast. Physicians and professional social workers had taken over the care of the sick and poor. And as foster care became the norm, the foundling asylums' crowded wards became obsolete.

The epidemic of foundlings receded, too, in the face of such developments as the popular acceptance of adoption and the passage of laws to facilitate it, better educational and occupational opportunities for women, and the creation of a federal social safety net during the Progressive and New Deal eras. From World War II to the present, birth control, abortion, and the recent society-wide destigmatization of illegitimacy have led to fewer Oliver Twists.[26] The occasional baby is still abandoned today in the United States, but—while infant abandonment persists in China and other parts of the world—there is no epidemic of foundlings in the West as there was in the nineteenth century.

If there are voices missing from this story, they are those of the foundlings themselves. Most died before they were old enough to speak. Their voicelessness, combined with the mystery of their origins, made them blank templates on which anyone could project their direst anxieties. To New York's reformers and public officials the appearance of foundlings, physically fragile, morally compromised, and tragically unwanted, in growing numbers on the city's streets meant that social disorder, sexual squalor, and disease were rising in their city. The work that follows is an attempt to see what an epidemic of abandoned babies meant to New Yorkers at an anxious time.

1

"Children of Accident and Mystery"

Foundlings in History and Literature

On a December evening in 1838, a group of well-to-do New Yorkers sat down to dinner at the home of Philip Hone, a former mayor of the city. As the group tucked into their game and oysters, they were interrupted by an unexpected ring of the doorbell. When Hone's servant answered the bell, he found no one there—until he looked down at the doorsill and saw a baby boy, about a week old, packed in a basket. The servant carried the baby in his basket into the dining room for Hone and his guests to see. Hone was captivated by the baby, whose appearance he meticulously recorded in his diary: "It had on a clean worked muslin frock, lace cap, its underclothes new and perfectly clean, a locket on the neck which opened with a spring and contained a lock of dark hair; the whole covered nicely with a piece of new flannel, and a label pinned on the breast on which was written, in a female hand, Alfred G. Douglas. It was one of the sweetest babies I ever saw."

Hone and his guests abandoned their dinner and launched into a discussion of what to do. Hone was tempted to keep his charming guest, but his guests advised against it, warning that if he took the foundling in, he "would have twenty more such outlets to my benevolence." Furthermore, Hone reflected later that evening in his diary, "if the little urchin should turn out bad, he would prove a troublesome inmate; and if intelligent and good, by the time he became an object of my affection the rightful owners might come and take him away."

The anonymous author of the note pinned to Alfred's wrapping identified herself as the mother of the baby and a "poor friendless widow." Hone, knowing nothing more of his mother's marital or sexual history, presumed that, like most foundlings, Alfred was illegitimate. "Poor little innocent," Hone sympathized, "—abandoned by its natural protector, and thrown at its entrance into life upon the sympathy of a selfish world, to be exposed, if it should live, to the sneers and taunts of uncharitable illegitimacy!" In the end, Hone took his guests' advice and decided not to keep the foundling. He repacked Alfred in his basket and sent him to the almshouse with a servant.[1]

When confronted with a foundling, Hone and his guests knew just what to think, to fear, and to do. Their familiarity was partly the result of experience. Infant abandonment, while not yet present on the scale familiar to those in European cities such as London and Paris, was relatively commonplace in early nineteenth-century New York City. In the year when Alfred Godfrey Douglas landed on Philip Hone's doorstep, the almshouse collected a total of eighty foundlings. Three of these, including Alfred, were retrieved on Hone's street alone.[2] But New Yorkers of this period did not need to encounter foundlings directly in order to decide what they signified. As descendants of European immigrants and inhabitants of a port city where they were the recipients of a continuous flow of transatlantic information, New Yorkers such as Hone and his guests belonged to a culture in which infant abandonment was entrenched. They believed it was tragic, even deviant, but they also understood it as an ineradicable part of life. To them, the presence of foundlings seemed at once terrible—and normal.[3]

"Helpless Indigent Beings": European Foundlings and Their New York Counterparts

New York's experience with foundlings can be understood as a New World manifestation of a problem long familiar in the Old World. Infant abandonment was widely practiced in the ancient Mediterranean, for instance. In Rome, fathers were legally entitled to abandon (and also to sell or kill) any babies born in their households whom they did not choose to keep.[4] Institutions devoted exclusively to the care of foundlings appeared first in Italy, with possibly the very first appearing in Milan in 787. Foundling asylums spread through Italy, and then through the rest of Europe in the fourteenth and fifteenth centuries.[5] By the eighteenth century, infant abandonment had become a mass phenomenon in European cities; as many as one out of every three or four children was abandoned in French, Italian, and Spanish cities at that time.[6] In 1785,

Abigail Adams, while accompanying her husband on a diplomatic mission to France, visited Paris's foundling hospital, the Hôpital des Enfants Trouvés. She was appalled to learn that it took in six thousand foundlings per year. Britain, too, was hit with a blight of infant abandonment in the eighteenth century. In London, retired shipwright Thomas Coram saw "young Children exposed, sometimes alive, sometimes dead, and sometimes dying" as he walked through the city in the early mornings. Coram, a charitable and childless man, was so shocked by the sight that he organized the London Foundling Hospital, which opened in 1741.[7] In 1756, when the London Foundling Hospital initiated an experimental policy of open admissions, it was at first inundated with a flood of more than one hundred foundlings per week, and it accepted a total of fifteen thousand over the four years the policy was in effect.[8]

Abigail Adams believed that foundlings, "helpless Indigent Beings brought into existence by criminality; and owned by no one," were to be particularly expected in France, "a Country grown old in Debauchery and lewdeness." She predicted that in the United States, newborn and flush with republican virtue, "wherein Mariage is considerd as holy and honourable, wherein industry and sobriety; enables parents to rear a numerous offspring," foundlings would never proliferate as they did in Paris.[9]

In the 1780s, foundlings were very few in American cities, but they were not unknown, as the following story from a brief notice in the *New-York Packet* demonstrates. Early on a spring morning in 1788, a market woman, accompanied by her dog, was traveling through the fields and farms of Manhattan's northern hinterland on her way to sell her produce in the city. When the dog disappeared into a field by the side of the Bowery, the same street that angles through the crowded metropolis today, she left her cart in the road and went to see what had attracted its attention. Beneath the dog's excited muzzle she found "a living infant lying on the ground, apparently but a few hours old, with a bundle of clothes, and a purse containing 50 guineas."[10] The *Packet* recorded the market woman's reaction to her discovery as "astonishment" and to her experience as "an uncommon adventure." In 1796, New York's almshouse officials counted twelve infants in their care. Most of the twelve, they noted, were "orphans and foundlings," maintained together because the infants' numbers were still too few to require the specialized institutions that the city would later build.[11]

In contrast, by the nineteenth century, nearly all major European cities had foundling asylums, and thousands of infants were abandoned to them every year.[12] It is difficult to know exactly why there were so many foundlings in European cities, particularly since infant abandonment was typically carried out in secret by poor people whose motivations went unrecorded. But several factors make it possible to speculate. One is the rise in illegitimate births that occurred all across Europe beginning in the eighteenth century and continuing into the nineteenth. In mid-nineteenth century Paris, where the rate of infant abandonment was particularly high, approximately one third of all births were illegitimate.[13]

Although not all illegitimate babies were abandoned, most foundlings in most times and places have been illegitimate, and generally they were assumed to be so. For hundreds of years, Europeans defined foundlings as infants who had been conceived outside of marriage, delivered in secret, and abandoned by their mothers in order to conceal the evidence of sexual downfall. When the shepherd in Shakespeare's *A Winter's Tale* finds the foundling Perdita in a chilly desert, he speculates lewdly: "this has been some stair-work, some trunk-work, some behind-door work: they were warmer that got this than the poor thing is here." When the housekeeper in Henry Fielding's popular 1749 novel *Tom Jones* finds the infant Tom abandoned in her employer's bed, she exclaims: "it goes against me to touch these misbegotten wretches, whom I don't look upon as my fellow-creatures. Faugh! how it stinks! It doth not smell like a Christian. . . . it is, perhaps, better for such creatures to die in a state of innocence, than to grow up and imitate their mothers; for nothing better can be expected of them."[14]

The association of foundlings with illegitimacy, along with the stigma that was traditionally attached to unmarried mothers and their accidental children, traveled across the Atlantic to New York. It is behind Philip Hone's reflexive assumption that baby Alfred's mother's claim to widowhood was untrue and that her child was illegitimate.

The rise in illegitimate births and the consequent rise in the number of foundlings was the product of a collection of social, demographic, and economic factors.[15] The nineteenth century was a time of massive migration of unattached young people to cities. Many of these people experienced poverty in the rapidly growing yet fragile wage-based economies they encountered. Young women on their own had few occupations open to them other than the poorly paid ones of domestic service, the needle trades, and factory work; thus they were particularly vulnerable to poverty and single motherhood—the two factors that contributed most to infant abandonment.[16]

The occupation that absorbed the greatest number of working women in nineteenth-century New York was domestic service. And in New York, as in London, observers noted that the mothers of many foundlings were domestic servants. During the first decades of the nineteenth century, domestic servants were typically young, unmarried, American-born women. By the 1840s, these servants were replaced largely by Irish immigrant women. Domestic servants typically lived in the households of their employers, and since Irish immigrant women were typically young, single, and on their own, the room and board the job provided were welcome. But domestic service was hard work. Nineteenth-century servants had to haul water, keep fires going, boil vats of laundry, dispose of the contents of chamber pots, cook, clean, and tend children. Sequestered in middle-class households, with very little time or space to themselves, they were vulnerable to sexual involvements, wanted and unwanted, with their employers or fellow servants. Unmarried servants who became pregnant were rarely allowed to keep their children with them. Without family members and church and community leaders to drag laggard or unwilling lovers to the altar, these women sometimes found themselves in desperate circumstances that led them to abandon their babies.[17]

Just as growing cities were magnets for the migrating poor, urbanization itself was closely linked to infant abandonment. This was particularly true in America. In Europe, rural women could take advantage of urban foundling asylums, whose tentacular systems of porters, midwives, doctors, and priests stretched into the countryside, allowing them to send their babies off to the city.[18] The absence of a central government meant that these were not available in colonial America. In the nineteenth century, the federal government played little role in social welfare, making extensive systems like these unavailable in America.

Although America experienced the same late-eighteenth-century rise in illegitimate births as Europe did, the result was not massive infant abandonment but marriages enforced by parents and communities, as well as some infanticide. In the small communities of early America, it was evidently too difficult to leave a baby on a doorstep and get away unseen. Infanticide was practiced more often than abandonment in small American communities, since the murder and secret burial of an infant thoroughly, and tragically, eliminated all traces of the mother's sexual wrongdoing.[19] Only when large cities developed in the United States did infant abandonment become common. During the first half of the nineteenth century, New York's population grew explosively, creating unprecedented possibilities for personal privacy. In the "city of strangers" that New York became, it was possible for unmarried women to form secret sexual relationships, as well as for women from the countryside to come to the city to hide their accidental pregnancies.[20] This same urban anonymity provided the cover under which an unmarried woman was able to deposit an infant on a stranger's doorstep.

Urban anonymity, however, could not hide all sins, particularly given the intimacy of some New York neighborhoods. The residents of these neighborhoods, particularly before the period of mass immigration from Ireland and Germany that began in the 1840s, were sometimes just as observant as their village counterparts. As a result, some women were not only observed abandoning babies, but also were known to their observers and reported by name to the authorities. This urban intimacy is evidenced by the case of a baby boy found "on the foot walk in Division Street" by a woman named Mrs. Ashdone in May 1809. The baby was delivered to the almshouse, which learned, possibly from Mrs. Ashdone herself, that he was the illegitimate son of a man named William Lambert and a widow named Eliza Ledworth, who worked as a domestic servant for a distillery. Throwing the last scrap of secrecy to the wind, the almshouse clerk recorded the baby's name as William Lambert, after the father who would presumably have preferred to remain anonymous.[21]

It is possible that the very presence of foundling asylums in European cities also helped to contribute to the epidemic of foundlings there, because they systematized the practice of infant abandonment. In locations where foundling asylums were the least restrictive, neither quizzing mothers about their sexual histories nor dunning fathers for upkeep, many babies were abandoned. Nineteenth-century Milan is perhaps the most extreme example of this. The Pia Casa degli Esposti, Milan's foundling asylum, had a wheel, or turntable, in the niche of the exterior wall of the building. This turntable allowed abandoners to rotate babies to the inside without being seen themselves.[22] Milan's Pia Casa was one of many foundling asylums throughout Catholic Europe to use a wheel. But the Pia Casa, unlike other foundling asylums, allowed parents to reclaim their children later on, without asking parents to pay for the cost of their children's care. The result was that the institution accepted a staggering number of Milanese babies: virtually all illegitimate ones and some legitimate ones, too. In the 1840s, for instance, 30 to 40 percent of all babies born in Milan entered the Pia Casa, even though the rate of illegitimacy in the city was only around 16 percent.[23]

In eighteenth-century Paris, entry to the Hôpital des Enfants Trouvés was also automatic and anonymous.[24] Jean-Jacques Rousseau gives something of the flavor of this culture of abandonment in his *Confessions*. Rousseau abandoned all five of his children to the Paris foundling home, the Hôpital des Enfants Trouvés. His *Confessions* reveal just how easy and normal infant abandonment seemed to Rousseau and members of his Parisian social circle. When Therese Le Vasseur, the servant who was Rousseau's companion for many years, first became pregnant in 1747, Rousseau learned about the service provided by the Hôpital des Enfants Trouvés from some dining companions. Among this group, in which sexual boasting was the common currency of conversation, "the man who best helped to stock the Foundling Hospital was always the most applauded." Rousseau decided to adopt this method of getting rid of his unwanted baby. " 'Since it is the custom of the country,' I told myself, 'if one lives there one must adopt it.' " Le Vasseur, whom Rousseau never married, accepted his decision resignedly. "She obeyed with a sigh," Rousseau told the readers of the *Confessions*. Le Vasseur's mother, on the other hand, fearing "embarrassment in the form of a brat," actively helped Rousseau in his project.[25] Rousseau left an identifying monogram with this first child, but not with any of the others, and he never attempted to retrieve them. When a friend tried to do so years later, the foundling asylum was unable to find them.[26] Although Rousseau later came to regret his actions, at the time the "arrangement seemed so good and sensible and right to me that if I did not boast of it openly, it was solely out of regard for their mother."[27]

The surprising ease with which Rousseau was able to discard each of his five babies, and the fact that many others did the same, ought to be understood as having occurred in a context in which infants and young children were frequently separated from their families. The methods for doing this were institutionalized and routine. One of these was the practice of sending infants to live in the homes of rural wet nurses, sometimes for several years. Foundling asylums flourished in countries such as Italy and France, where wet nursing was common practice. In societies in which families were in the habit of sending their infants away to the countryside to nurse, the idea of separating infants from their parents was not alien.[28]

Even in countries such as England and America, where families did not routinely send their babies away to rural wet nurses, there were still many common practices that separated young children from their parents. Young boys were sent away to sea as cabin boys or sailors-in-training.[29] English families of the upper classes sent their young children to boarding schools. Young apprentices lived and worked in the homes of their masters. In Britain and in early America, children were placed in the homes of others to work as servants. This was a customary practice for comfortable as well as poor families, who evidently saw it as a way to instill discipline in their children. More often, town authorities in colonial American placed children from destitute or shattered families as indentured servants in the homes of more economically viable ones. The practice of indenturing homeless or orphaned children continued into the late nineteenth century.[30]

Some practices that separated young children from their families, while customary, also formed a part of more troubling, exploitative practices. The children of American slaves were vulnerable to separation from their families by sale.[31] Domestic service also resulted in the separation of babies from their mothers. Baby farmers—women who cared for the young children of poor parents; single, working mothers; and poor widowers—took in such children in a twenty-four hour boarding arrangement. Mothers working as servants surely visited on their days off, but the separation of mother and child was nearly total.[32] Some of these children ultimately became foundlings when their mothers were no longer able to keep up their payments to the baby farmer. In the nineteenth century, many of the infants received by New York's almshouse were brought there by unpaid baby farmers.[33] In other cases, mothers working as domestic servants abandoned their babies themselves, as did as the distillery servant Eliza Ledworth, who left her infant son on a half-completed New York City street in 1809.

Ledworth was caught up in a transatlantic culture in which infant abandonment, though heartbreaking, was a normal practice. She was also among the increasing number of New York women who, during the nineteenth century, would be driven by poverty, unmarried mother-hood, and the conditions of domestic service to recreate in New York the epidemic of foundlings that had begun developing a century earlier in Europe.

The Taint of Illegitimacy

Whatever the reasons for the increased numbers of foundlings in eigh-teenth- and nineteenth-century Europe, and despite the fact that many, perhaps most, foundlings died in infancy, one result of the proliferation of their numbers was the creation of a caste of social marginals. Since abandonment was associated with illegitimacy, and illegitimacy was as-sociated with shame, to be identified as a foundling was to live with stigma all one's life.

Conscious of this association, and seeking to spare their infant in-mates from lifelong stigma, foundling asylums sometimes tried to avoid using the word "foundling." In the 1760s, the London Foundling Hos-pital considered changing its name to Orphan Hospital because of "the general notions of the common people that the name Foundling carrys with it the Idea of contempt, and that of Orphan of compassion."[34] A French law of 1795 forbade the use of the name *enfants trouvés* (found-lings), recategorized its foundlings as *orphelins* (orphans) and, in the spirit of the French Revolution, it lumped orphans and foundlings to-gether under the heading *enfants de la patrie,* the nation's children.[35] Ultimately, this effort to reduce the stigma foundlings faced was un-successful. Remi, the foundling protagonist of Hector Malot's popular, late-nineteenth-century French children's book *Sans Famille* (translated as *Nobody's Boy*), lives with a foster family in a French village. He ex-plains the drawbacks of the condition he shares with the children of the foundling hospital: "I felt ashamed to admit that I was a foundling,—a child picked up in the streets! I knew how the children from the Found-lings' Hospital had been scorned. It seemed to me that it was the most abject thing in the world to be a foundling."[36]

In the United States too, foundlings were associated with the stigma created by illegitimacy. The Charleston, South Carolina, Orphan House attracted the scorn of a Scottish visitor, James Stirling, for deciding to admit foundlings. "To treat thus magnificently the progeny of the reckless and sinful," Stirling thundered, "is to encourage improvidence and hold out a premium on prostitution."[37]

The large-scale, government-sponsored systems of foundling care typical of Catholic countries such as postrevolutionary France literally marked foundlings in permanent and quasipermanent ways. They gave foundlings distinctive, even derisory names; issued them identifying clothing; and even inscribed them with permanent marks on their bodies. These made them painfully noticeable and impeded their successful assimilation into society.

Foundlings in these systems were typically placed as infants with wet nurses in the countryside and then remained there through their childhoods. To keep track of them and to prevent fraud, several kinds of identifying marks were used. Eighteenth-century Irish and Sicilian babies were branded—a practice more typically associated with slaves, criminals, animals, or, in Puritan New England, adulterers. In Italy and France, in select times and places, small gold earrings with identifying markings were permanently soldered into the ears of infant foundlings. Necklaces bearing identifying tags were used in Italy, Ireland, France, and Russia. In France and Italy, these were permanently fastened with marked lead seals. Hector Malot has his foundling protagonist, Remi, describe what it was like to be marked by a necklace from the foundling home: "In the village there were two children from the Home. . . .They had a metal plaque hung round their necks with a number on it. They were badly dressed, and so dirty! All the other children made fun of them and threw stones at them. They chased them like boys chase a lost dog, for fun, and because a stray dog has no one to protect it."[38]

European foundlings who survived their early childhoods often, although not always, became members of a despised underclass.[39] Those raised in rural villages in France were limited to agricultural day labor in the surrounding areas. Undesirable as marriage partners, without even the minimal property and protection a poor family might have been able to provide, some of these *"petits Parisiens"* became vagrants and thieves. In 1766 a French noblewoman complained to the authorities about a community of foundling outcasts in her rural region: "These children start by watching the flocks, and when they grow up they marry other bastards, girls whom they call their sisters. This tribe, with no property and precious little savings, get themselves cottages on the commons. . . . They all apply themselves to ravaging the communal woods . . . and if you complain of such behavior they only threaten you with arson."[40] Officials in charge of foundlings throughout Europe and in Russia worried that these children would grow up to be prostitutes and criminals and, with no firsthand knowledge of family life, would only create more generations of foundlings.[41]

John Adams, in Europe, witnessed the social marginalization European foundlings experienced. Like his wife, he visited the Hôpital des Enfants Trouvés in Paris, and the experience gave rise to musings. "I have seen," he wrote,

> in the Hospital of Foundlings, the *"Enfans* [sic] *Trouvés,"* at Paris, fifty babes in one room;—all under four days old; all in cradles alike; all nursed and attended alike; all dressed alike; all equally neat. I went from one end to the other of the whole row, and attentively observed all their countenances. And I never saw a greater variety, or more striking inequalities, in the streets of Paris or London. Some had every sign of grief, sorrow, and despair; others had joy and gayety in their faces. Some were sinking in the arms of death; others looked as if they might live to fourscore. Some were as ugly and others as beautiful, as children or adults ever are; these were stupid; those sensible. These were all born to equal rights, but to very different fortunes; to very different success and influence in life.[42]

Adams's musings were probably colored less by his pity for the plight of French foundlings than by an issue that concerned him as the United States was embarking on its republican experiment. In their identical circumstances but varying capacities, these Parisian foundlings provided for Adams a paradigm for the limits of opportunity in the newborn United States. Equal opportunities might be extended to all, but all were not equally able to make the most of them. Adams's insight, which manages to be both bleak and hopeful, comes close to the truth of what foundlings would experience in nineteenth-century New York. In the United States, foundlings would not be marked as European foundlings were, or as American slaves were marked by race. Unlike Europe, there was no central system to both rescue and label abandoned babies. Instead, those few that survived their infancies would be free, rather like immigrants or settlers on the frontier, to either succeed or fail on their own.

Art Imitates Life/Life Imitates Art: Foundlings in Literature

New Yorkers were heir to the European historical background—particularly the British, to which they were most closely attuned. They were also heir to a very significant literary background, as the foundling story permeates Western literature. Nineteenth-century New Yorkers who were themselves immigrants carried the foundling story across the Atlantic with them; those native to the city inherited it from their forebears. Versions of the story continued to sail across the Atlantic and into the city's bookstores, lending libraries, and theaters, remaining alive in the minds of New Yorkers of all classes in the nineteenth century.

In 1809, theater-going New Yorkers savored a version of this tale when *The Foundling of the Forest,* a play by the prolific, now-forgotten English dramatist William Dimond, opened simultaneously at the Theatre Royal in London and at New York's Park Theater.[43] The play is about Florian, a foundling whose noble birth is forgotten when he is abandoned in a forest as an infant. Florian, who proves his merit by his actions, refers to himself modestly as "the child of accident and mystery —a wretched foundling." But as an admirer observes: "the brave man's laurel blooms with as fresh an honour in the poor peasant's cap as when it circles princely brows."[44] Only at the end is Florian's noble birth revealed through a plot twist often used in foundling tales.

For an audience that would have included older people for whom the American revolution was within memory, a story about a "natural aristocrat," in this case a foundling, would have stirred republican sentiments. Certainly the play's melodramatic elements—an "entangled and intricate" forest, a violent storm during which key parts of the action take place, the virtuous and handsome foundling hero, an evil baron, a madwoman, a love affair—also helped to make it popular in New York. It was produced there nine times between 1809 and 1826.[45] In 1810, a critic writing for *The Columbian,* a New York newspaper, noted how *The Foundling of the Forest* thrilled the audience at the Park Theater, where it was once again being staged. The critic reported that the play produced tears, agitation, and "the fainting of a lady in one of the boxes." Indeed, he remarked, the play "electrified the house with all the delicious luxury of woe."[46]

The Foundling of the Forest was only one of many retellings of the foundling story that nineteenth-century New Yorkers knew. Foundlings have populated the imagined world of the west as far back as the literary record reaches. Moses is the most famous of the biblical foundlings. The hillsides and waterways of mythical Greece and Rome were littered with multitudes of foundlings, with Hercules, Oedipus, Atalanta, and Romulus and Remus among the most well known.[47] Folk and fairy tale traditions around the world include foundlings in their rosters of standard characters. In some of these tales, such as Hansel and Gretel, cruel or impoverished parents or stepparents abandon their children. In other stories, abandoned babies are rescued by animals, angels, fairies, princesses, kings, shepherds, goatherds, cowherds, and swineherds. Some turn out to be royalty; others function as underdog tricksters or heroes.[48] *Beowulf* opens with the funeral of a foundling, whose burial at sea resembles his earlier experience as an abandoned infant set adrift in a boat. These folk traditions also influenced "high" culture: Shakespeare used foundling characters in several of his plays, and Mozart's *The Magic Flute* is a foundling story. Stories about orphans and foundlings are also central to eighteenth- and nineteenth-century novels. Henry Fielding (*Tom Jones*), Charles Dickens (*Oliver Twist*), Eugene Sue (*Mysteries of Paris*), George Sand (*The Country Waif*), Herman Melville (*Billy Budd*), George Eliot (*Adam Bede*) and Oscar Wilde (*The Importance of Being Earnest*) are among the authors who played the predicament of the abandoned baby for either pathos or farce.

In this interconnected body of literary work about foundlings, some story elements no doubt originated in the hopeful or fanciful imaginations of their tellers, but many others are rooted in historical reality. There have always been doors between the worlds of fact and fiction.[49] If fact appeared to echo fiction, it was because fiction had borrowed a page from fact. The foundling stories in Greek and Roman mythology, for instance, reflect the pervasive practice of infant abandonment in the ancient world. In the story of Hansel and Gretel, elements specific to a historical time and place shape what appears to be a wholly imagined story. The tale includes that notorious archetype, the cruel stepmother, but it is also about hunger, specifically the hunger of premodern, northern European peasants. Only after the woodcutter worries over how he can feed his family during a time of famine does his cruel wife suggest abandoning his children in the forest. Images of food abound in this story: the breadcrumbs Hansel and Gretel leave behind, the edible house that the famished children find in the woods, the witch's threat to make a meal out of them.[50]

Some of the stories that nineteenth-century New Yorkers knew from fictional works are plausible enough to have happened, and events close to those in the stories did happen in New York. Here is one: early on a June morning in 1838, a woman named Ann Van Berg crept into the Norfolk Street house of Eliza Ann Oliver and left her illegitimate two-week-old girl, Hannah Gilmore. There were no witnesses to this event, since Oliver was not at home and her eleven-year-old son, William, "lay asleep on the floor." Two years later, the same sort of scenario happened again. This time Bridget Brisshan, who made her living selling fruit, left work and returned to the room on Water Street that she shared with her three children. There she found a three-week-old girl "lying in her bed crying." Bridget's children, the oldest of whom was seven, reported that "some strange woman had entered the room and left it there."[51]

The experiences of these two real women are similar to that of the fictional Mr. Allworthy in the first pages of Henry Fielding's popular novel *Tom Jones*. Mr. Allworthy, returning late from a trip to London, "was preparing to step into bed, when, upon opening the clothes, to his great surprise he beheld an infant, wrapt up in some coarse linen, in a sweet and profound sleep, between his sheets."[52]

Fictional and factual stories about foundlings sometimes crossed paths in the press, providing further evidence of the foundling story's deep interpenetration into both worlds. In the fall of 1843, the New York workingman's newspaper *The Subterranean* published an excerpt from Eugene Sue's novel, *The Mysteries of Paris*. Sue's *Mysteries*, which was serialized in the French *Journal des Debats* in 1842–43, took readers on a tour through a Parisian underworld populated by castoffs of society—thieves, thugs, prostitutes, and foundlings, including the novel's heroine, Fleur de Marie. Fleur de Marie, like William Dimond's Florian and Shakespeare's Perdita, turns out to be an abandoned child of noble birth.[53] The *Mysteries* was extraordinarily popular in New York. The staff of *The Subterranean*, however, knew something about foundlings, not only from this well-known literary source but from their own experience: the previous summer, a member of *The Subterranean*'s staff opened the office one morning to find a newborn boy lying on a counter.[54] Something similar happened in 1859, when the *New York Tribune* ran a prominent advertisement on its front page for a serialized story, *Azael Kain; Or, the Fortunes of a Foundling,* which was scheduled to run in the *New-York Weekly.* A few pages in, readers of the *Tribune* saw the following notice of a real discovery: "FOUNDLING.—A healthy female infant, two weeks old, found at 7 o'clock, Tuesday evening, and taken to the Governors of the Alms House."[55]

Exposed to this mix of real and imaginary foundlings, New Yorkers sometimes confused the two. Philip Hone, for instance, turned to an imagined artistic rendering from the Bible to describe his own foundling experience. After admiring the baby in the dining room, Hone had him carried into the kitchen. Guests, family, and servants followed, surrounding the kitchen table where the foundling lay in his basket. Observing this group, Hone, who was a collector of paintings, mused that the scene "would have furnished a capital subject for a painter." A canvas on a biblical theme assembled itself in Hone's mind as he imagined "my wife and daughters, standing like the daughters of Pharaoh over the infant Moses in the bulrushes" and his servants and guests arranged picturesquely around the table, each in a characteristic attitude, "all interested, but differently affected."[56]

Educated members of society such as Philip Hone were likely to be familiar with the ubiquitous foundling stories in novels, plays, the Bible, and other written sources. But were poor women, the group most likely to abandon babies, familiar with these written tales? Some of the people who left foundlings around antebellum New York enclosed notes, and these notes demonstrate that their writers were also familiar with the literary conventions of their time. The woman who left Alfred Godfrey Douglas on Philip Hone's doorstep in 1838, for instance, was familiar with literary formulas. Her note reads, in full:

> Have compassion upon my poor <u>orphan</u> child its father was lost in the Pulaski—I am a poor friendless widow in a strange city had I kept it—it would have lingered and died with starvation: oh it will drive me frantic—to think I must part with my first and only pledge of my departed Husband but God will forgive me—oh! I do it for the best—but —if God restore my health I would seek for it and labor for its maintenance but it will never be I am fast hurry to my *grave*—let it bear the name of its Father—Alfred Godfrey Douglas
> I can write no more[57]

This note may be a formulaically rendered work of fiction. The *Pulaski* was a steamboat that left Savannah on June 13, 1838, and exploded off the coast of North Carolina the following night, killing seventy-seven of its 155 passengers. In the published lists of passengers, there was no one named Douglas. It is possible that the author of this note was not a widow at all, but an unmarried mother, perhaps a New Yorker who was aware of Hone's wealth and local renown, who believed that a story of poverty and widowhood by steamboat explosion would be more acceptable to a potential benefactor than one of furtive sex and illegitimate birth. If Alfred's mother read the newspapers, she would have seen the extensive coverage of the *Pulaski* disaster, which occurred early in her pregnancy. She could also have counted on Hone to know about it. Like financial panics and cholera epidemics, steamboat accidents were a characteristic and much discussed danger of the age. Whether or not her story was true, one fact that can be relied on is that the woman who left Alfred Godfrey Douglas on Philip Hone's doorstep was unable to cope with a baby and that she tried to assure him—unsuccessfully, as it turned out—a soft landing in a new life.[58]

Another note from this period ends with almost the same despondent, trailing phrase—"I can write no more." This note, also unsigned, was left with John Green, a month-old boy abandoned in the Sixteenth Ward on Twenty-Fourth Street near Tenth Avenue in 1840. The note indicates that this baby was left with his father's father, evidently by his mother. Like Alfred's mother, the mother of John Green claims to be suffering from poverty, husbandlessness, and an inability to nurse:

> Mr Green sir this is your sons child[.] it is not but what I love [not] the child that I part with it[,] I have no milk for it[,] I am too poor to put it to nurse and to see it taken from my armes to the alms house I cant stand[.] looke on this little suffer in Mercy and I hope god will bless[.] God I wish you would get it chrisend[,] call it After its father[.] Looke at it and Looke its father[.] it was born the febbuary 22[.] I hope god bless it and forgive me[.] you must give it [laudanum][.] I had to do so to keep it quiet[.] I cant [write] ane more[.][59]

Did the father of this baby drift away, perhaps west or to sea, leaving this woman behind? Did he retreat to the safe haven of his family after a fleeting dalliance in the slums? In 1840, the newly established Sixteenth Ward, on the west side of Manhattan and north of the built-up section of the city, was still only sparsely inhabited with a mixture of market gardeners and the country retreats of the well-to-do.[60] The grandfather on whose doorstep the baby was left apparently had not seen the baby previously, and the author of the note asked him to note the resemblance between father and child, indicating that he may have been the product of an illicit love affair unknown to the father's family.

The author of this note is less adept at writing than the author of the one left with Alfred Godfrey Douglas. The note's artless pathos, particularly the special instructions about how to care for the baby, gives it the scent of authenticity. Yet its last line, so similar to the last line of the note left with Alfred, smells like a convention of literary melodrama, the sort of phrase that might have oozed from the pen of a swooning heroine of a romantic novel.

It appears that "I can write no more" was a rhetorical convention used in both fiction and real letters to signify emotion. In Fanny Burney's epistolary novel *Evelina,* first published in 1778, the eponymous heroine, in a moment of excitement and haste, writes: "I can write no more now. I have hardly time to breathe—." In 1826, the Virginia congressman John Randolph ended an emotional letter in which he recalled his deceased brother with a variation: "I can no more." In 1835, Helen Jewett, a New York prostitute whose 1836 murder resulted in a sensational trial, wrote the man who would soon be accused of killing her: "But I am weak and can write no more."[61]

The familiarity of desperately poor women with literary conventions used in novels and the letters of the well-to-do is not surprising. The literacy gap between men and women that prevailed in colonial America gradually closed between the last decades of the eighteenth century and the middle of the nineteenth. This was the result of greater efforts to educate women, not so much for their own pleasure or practical use, but to prepare them to become mothers of the informed and responsible male citizens required by the new republic.[62] Newly literate women became avid consumers of novels, and novels of the time were often written by women and directed at women readers. The eighteenth and early nineteenth century was the period of the gothic novel, whose language is echoed in the notes left with Alfred Godfrey Douglas and John Green. Seduction themes, used in English novels such as Samuel Richardson's *Pamela* and *Clarissa* and American ones such as the popular *Charlotte Temple* by Susanna Rowson and *The Coquette* by Hannah Webster Foster, were directly relevant to the circumstances of the unmarried mothers of foundlings.[63]

This was also the era when the penny press was bringing popular literature to a widening audience.[64] Novels were typically serialized in newspapers or magazines before they were published as books. Charles Dickens's *Oliver Twist* first appeared in serial form in *Bentley's Miscellany* in 1837–38. The penny papers made fiction available to those who could not afford books. The serialization of Eugene Sue's *Mysteries of Paris* in the New York worker's paper *The Subterranean*, and of the now forgotten *Azael Kain; Or, The Fortunes of a Foundling* in the *New York Weekly* are two local examples.

The fact that an increasing number of women had access to the rich storehouse of literary information about foundlings and fallen women, and that some borrowed the literary language of their day in the notes they left with their babies does not take away from the authenticity of the notes. The very act of abandonment is proof enough of real desperation. But it does mean that when a woman who wanted to abandon a baby took up a pen to write a note, the wealth of stories about seduced heroines and abandoned babies gave her abundant literary models to copy. She might have been comforted to know that she shared her predicament with many imaginary foremothers.

"Unmarketable Freight": How to Abandon a Baby

While the written word provided many New Yorkers with stories about foundlings, other people no doubt shared such stories too. Information and even instructions about how to abandon a baby were most likely shared in conversations among neighbors, relatives, and friends, particularly in the densely packed, poor neighborhoods of the city. Proof of this lies in the fact that New Yorkers appear to have had a distinct repertoire of methods for abandoning babies. These methods were used over and over throughout the nineteenth century and into the twentieth. Clearly, there was a normative tradition of infant abandonment in New York. While the whispers that passed from one woman to another have evaporated, written documentation of the methods New Yorkers used to abandon babies has survived in the records of the almshouse.

These methods ranged from the careful to the hasty and included both methods that approached infanticide and infanticide itself. Some babies were warmly dressed, packed in baskets, and placed on carefully chosen stoops.[65] These abandoners sometimes slammed doors or rang doorbells to be sure that the baby would be picked up quickly.[66] Other foundlings were left near houses, on busy sidewalks, near police watch stations, or in other well-frequented places where police officers or passersby would be sure to find them quickly. Thus George Church was abandoned in a "clamb-basket" at a night watchman's station in 1808, and on a February evening in 1839, Sarah White was found by a night watchman "on the side walk in a willow market basket." The watchman was assisted by a "coloured maid" who called his attention to the baby. In 1859, the *New York Times* referred coyly to the "unmarketable freight" baskets such as these contained.[67] Less fortunate foundlings were left naked or barely covered with dirty rags on sidewalks, in alleys, in the entries of tenement houses, and in fields in thinly populated areas of the city.[68] Some were thrust into the arms of strangers. Many were left with the midwives, wet nurses, baby farmers, and other poor women paid to care for children by parents who stopped payment, then disappeared.[69]

Those abandoners who wanted not just to rid themselves of their babies but to provide them with better lives than they themselves could offer, took great care over the locations they chose. The woman who selected Philip Hone's doorstep was one of these. In 1838, when Alfred Godfrey Douglas landed on his doorstep, Hone had earned a fortune in the auction business and lived in a new house at the corner of Broadway and Great Jones Street, near genteel Washington Square. His finances had been shaken by the Panic of 1837, but his situation would still have looked secure enough, even sumptuous, to someone desperate enough to abandon a baby. If this woman had peeked in the window before laying the baby on the stoop, she would have seen firelight, new furnishings, books and paintings, and servants hovering around a table set with food and surrounded by family and friends.[70]

In 1822, a woman named Mary Anderson made a similar calculation when she abandoned her four-month-old girl. Anderson told a companion that she was looking for a "gentleman's door" because she believed that, if she laid the baby there, "it would be taken care of." Anderson was a Baltimore-born black woman who had come north after her husband's death. By the time she abandoned her baby, she had been living in New York for five years. The baby's father, a black man named J[o]no[than] Battis, made childbirth arrangements for her but supplied no further help. A fair bit is known about her because Anderson failed in her attempt to abandon her baby and was brought before a court.

Anderson's life in New York appears to have been unsettled. A witness told the court that she lived with a Dr. Jacques on Broadway, probably as a domestic servant, while Anderson claimed that she was living at Mechanic Hall, as was Battis. Her baby had also led an itinerant life, boarding at different times with a "yellow woman" named Amelia Dawson and with "two black girls" named Susan Mann and Milley. (The witness who identified Milley did not give her last name.) Anderson's lack of assistance from the baby's father and her inability to create a permanent home for herself in New York might help explain what led her to abandon her baby.[71]

Two years earlier, at ten o'clock on a spring night in 1820, Bridget McGlone left her baby, Alice, on the doorstep of John Connolly, the Catholic bishop of New York. After putting Alice down, she knocked on the door and ran away. Her method of abandonment also demonstrates concern about Alice's physical welfare, while her choice of doorstep reflected her worries about the baby's spiritual well-being. McGlone, who was caught in the act, told the police court that as a Catholic she did not want her baby to go to the almshouse, "as I would not like it to be brought up to the religion the[y] have there." In the note she addressed to Bishop Connolly, McGlone describes the circumstances that led her to abandon her child: "kind Sir," she wrote, "it is poverty and hardship that occations my intruding on you." Alice's father (McGlone does not indicate whether she was married to him or not) disappeared before the baby was born, she had no place to live, and she could not "earn a living for myself and the baby." She had four other children, three of whom were living in the almshouse at the time she abandoned Alice. In addition, a crisis of some kind—whether it was the aftereffects of childbirth, the accumulated crush of circumstances, or something else—had overtaken her. Before she was arrested, she had intended to go to the country, where she hoped "in the course of a few months" to recover. She concluded her note: "I hope the Almighty will pardon me as it was severe hardship that compels me to take this step." Statements appended to McGlone's note by court officials confirm her state of destitution. One official wrote: "this woman appears to be reduced to the extreme of wretchedness." They also hint at what may have been the trouble behind her to wish to go to the country to recover: "She got a little drunk yesterday on Beer."

Interestingly, it was not against the law to abandon a baby in 1820. Another note on McGlone's court documents, presumably written by a court official, explains that simply leaving the baby on the Bishop's stoop was not an indictable offense—only "if any injury had happened to the child it might be."[72] Neither McGlone's nor Anderson's babies were injured. Why, then, in the absence of any law against abandonment were these two women arrested? It is difficult to say, but their arrests indicate a discomfort with abandonment that was addressed in 1829, when the New York State legislature passed a law that made the abandonment of a child punishable by imprisonment. The law was a part of a broader revision of New York's statutes rather than of any larger effort on behalf of foundlings at that time.[73]

Despite the passage of the law, abandonment continued, and the strategies people used persisted as well. In a humbler version of the strategy used by those, such as Mary Anderson, Bridget McGlone, and the mother of Alfred Godfrey Douglas, who carefully chose their stoops, some abandoners, perhaps because they were less knowledgeable about who was who beyond their immediate neighborhoods, left babies on the doorsteps of people who did not necessarily possess fame, wealth, or civic power, but who were managing capably for themselves and their families. In 1838 and 1839, for instance, babies were left on the doorsteps of two grocers, a milkman, a dealer in duck for sailmaking, and two lawyers. Thomas Glover, the secretary of the Eagle Insurance Company on Wall Street, was the recipient of two foundlings in the space of three months in 1838.[74]

One of the lawyers was Hugh Maxwell, who had been district attorney for a period of two decades ending in 1829. In 1838 a one-month-old baby was deposited on his stoop on St. Mark's Place (the almshouse commissioners named the baby Agnes Maxwell to commemorate the owner of the stoop on which she was found). In 1836 Maxwell had defended the man alleged to have murdered the prostitute Helen Jewett. The Jewett trial was heavily attended and reported widely, but without more evidence it is hard to know what Maxwell's notoriety would have meant to someone who wanted to abandon a baby. His status as a lawyer and former district attorney or even his residence in a reasonably prosperous area might have been enough.[75]

Dressing babies in good clothes appears to have been another strategy used by abandoners to draw attention and, they must have hoped, favor. Month-old Hannah Frost was abandoned at the door of a former city alderman in 1809. The almshouse officials who recorded her case noted that she was "wrapped up in a mantle, well dressed and in every respect well provided with clothes."[76] Whoever dressed Hannah Frost with such care was probably making use of the powerful and well-known myth of the well-to-do or well-born foundling whose identity is made apparent by its expensive clothing. This strategy, with its fairytale overtones, persisted into the twentieth century as long as abandonment as a normative practice itself persisted. During the second half of the nineteenth century and into the twentieth century, when newspapers and magazines were richly illustrated and packed with sentimental stories, editors exploited the story of the foundling, and particularly the well-dressed foundling, to the fullest.

An inordinate number of babies, the press suggested, were abandoned in sumptuous clothing.[77] One article from 1896 described the clothing of a six-week-old girl found in the entry of a house on West Forty-third Street: "She wore a silk cap, a white cashmere cloak, embroidered and trimmed with cream silk ribbon. Her little frock was of lawn trimmed with lace and embroidery. The waif's clothing and appearance led the police to think that it is the offspring of wealthy parents."[78] The *New York Herald,* which thrived for decades on sentimental foundling tales, implied on more than one occasion that foundlings were normally found in expensive clothing. Thus, when in 1897 a two-month-old boy was left in a hotel room on Broadway dressed in flannel underwear, a muslin dress, a "daintily embroidered" white cashmere coat, and a silk cap with a lace ruffle, a reporter asserted that "the baby's clothing was fine, as that of foundlings often is."[79]

People who saw foundlings day in and day out discounted the notion that abandoned babies wore expensive clothing. During the last decade of the nineteenth century, all of the city's foundlings passed by Superintendent Blake of the Department of Public Charities, one of the institutions that succeeded the almshouse. Blake, known as the "godfather" of the city's foundlings, debunked the theory firmly. The stories "about handsome raiment and evidences of having come from wealthy surroundings are the flimsiest phantoms," Blake told a reporter. "The cases of waifs in swansdown and embroidered flannels, stiff with crests were nonexistent."[80] Swansdown and crests aside, the tactic of dressing foundlings in fine clothing was really used, but stories about it had clearly taken on lives of their own.

Another hands-on witness from the late nineteenth century was Police Matron Webb, whose nursery in the police department's central office on Mulberry Street housed foundlings in the 1880s. "You can always tell something about foundlings by the way they are dressed," the straight-talking Webb told a reporter from the *Herald*. "Rich people don't leave babies in the street. If they want to bring 'em up they pay for their keeping somewhere. All the babies that come here have cheap clothing on. Some may have more than others, but it is all cheap. Some have needle work on their dresses that a gentleman might say was worth $5, when it wasn't worth five cents."[81]

Just such a misinterpretation occurred in September 1888, when a servant stumbled on a foundling near the basement door of the West Twenty-fourth Street home of the Rev. Dr. Cookman. "The most singular point in the case," the press account claimed, "is the varied description of the clothing which enveloped the stranger." Mrs. Cookman said that the baby was dressed in "clothing of delicate material, costly and of excellent workmanship." But once the baby had been delivered to Matron Webb, she argued that, to her more experienced eye, the clothing was "of common material, badly made and not at all expensive."[82]

The journalist and photographer Jacob Riis, whose camera and pen took him into the slums on a regular basis during the last decades of the nineteenth century, sided with Superintendent Blake and Matron Webb on the quality of foundlings' clothing. He commented bluntly: "The stories of richly-dressed foundlings that are dished up in the newspapers at intervals are pure fiction."[83]

This aspect of foundling stories may have been exaggerated, or even invented in some cases, but its evocations of mystery, fate, and quick turns of luck interested readers, as the *Herald* understood, and it may also have given ideas to people about how to dress babies they planned to abandon. In 1896, in a case reminiscent of Oscar Wilde's *The Importance of Being Earnest,* a six-week-old boy was abandoned in the waiting room at Grand Central Station. The *Herald* devoted a long piece to the incident in its Sunday paper. The article dwelled rapturously on what the baby was wearing: "The clothing consisted of a blue durah silk cloak, trimmed with lace; a white silk embroidered cap, also trimmed with lace; a large blue flannel silk embroidered cap, and blue kid shoes."[84] In response to this publicity, hundreds of people went to visit the baby at Bellevue, where foundlings were taken routinely in the 1890s. Within the week, one of these visitors was allowed to adopt the "Blue Silk Baby." Many visitors had wanted to adopt him, but

Superintendent Blake chose a "prosperous merchant, owning considerable real estate, interested in religious and charitable affairs and of good social standing."[85]

This successful outcome may have influenced the tactics of another abandoner. On the same day as the adoption was reported, another baby dressed in blue silk was abandoned, this time in a department store. His clothing, the *Herald* noted in its Sunday edition, "was of the finest make," and he seemed to be a "child gently reared and apparently of good family."[86]

Of course, creating this impression may have been a deliberate tactic, as had been suggested by some women who went to visit the Blue Silk Baby at Bellevue. According to the *Herald,* opinions were divided by gender. While the Bellevue doctors believed that the baby probably had been abandoned accidentally by "some agitated mother" rushing to catch a train, the women visitors granted the mother greater guile. They argued that the child's dress was "an attempt to make the little waif as attractive as possible before throwing him on the mercy of the world."[87]

Hereditary aristocracy was a fairy tale in the United States, but the legal and social status that came with inherited racial identity was not. It appears that in at least one case a black mother tried to bypass this reality by presenting her infant to the almshouse in the guise of a white foundling.

In 1808, a baby named John Luke was brought to the almshouse; the clerk who took down the information described his deliverer as "a Mulatto Woman." The woman told almshouse officials that the baby had been "left at her house by a white woman." The almshouse accepted the baby and placed him with a wet nurse, as it routinely did with foundlings.[88] Almshouse officials typically indicated when the babies or nurses they dealt with were black, but almshouse records include no such indication next to the names of either John Luke or his nurse. When the almshouse received black foundlings, they were placed with black nurses when they were available. The facts here appear to show that they believed the mulatto woman's story and accepted John Luke as white. The infant John Luke remained with his nurse for at least fifteen months, and there is no record that he died, as there is in so many other cases.

If the "mulatto woman" was, in fact, John Luke's mother, and if she succeeded in passing him off as white in infancy, her ruse did not survive into his adulthood. Thirty years later a black man named John Luke was living at 49 Laurens Street. Laurens Street, located on the site of today's West Broadway north of Canal Street, housed many African Americans in the late 1830s and early 1840s. Public School No. 2 for black children was located at 51 Laurens Street, and three black women who worked as nurses for the almshouse lived there too. John Luke, assuming the racial identity his mother tried to take from him, had also found his way there. Further, it appears that he fathered a foundling of his own.

On a spring night in 1838 a black woman named Sarah Jones discovered an abandoned week-old boy in the entry of 49 Laurens Street. On his clothes was pinned a note that said simply "John Luke." We can only guess what the mother was thinking when she delivered this baby, labeled like a package, to his putative father's door. The name the almshouse commissioners bestowed upon this baby, Lawrence Black, is a record of the street where he was left, Laurens (which the almshouse clerk spelled "Lawrens"), and their impression of his color, which in his case, unlike John Luke's, was unmistakable.

When New Yorkers abandoned babies they typically borrowed methods that would have been familiar in any European city. But New York's heritage of slavery, which only came to an end in 1827, and the caste-like status of African Americans in New York as elsewhere in the United States, led to this addition (if John Luke's story is as it appears) to the repertoire of methods traditionally used to abandon a baby.[89]

"Misplaced Confidence": Scams

Desperate mothers were not the only group to make use of the almshouse's mandate to care for unwanted babies or to come up with ingenious schemes for abandonment. Some cases in which baby farmers and other caretakers brought infants to the almshouse for nonpayment of board were really fraudulent collusions with mothers. In 1838, mother Elizabeth Andrews attempted to involve caretaker Jane Spear in such a collusion. Andrews, mother of Alexander Clements, who was "supposed to be illegitimate," tried to enlist Spear in a plan to take advantage of the almshouse's usual practice of accepting babies from unpaid baby farmers.

After spending several weeks with her son at Mrs. Spear's, Andrews departed for the country, "promising to pay the child's board." When Andrews could not pay, she wrote asking Spears "to take the child to the Alms House—conceal all the circumstances appertaining to the case —and give it a new name." With this ruse Andrews would have received free care from the almshouse for her child; whether or how she meant to retrieve Alexander she did not say. In return for carrying out her plan, Andrews offered to pay Spear in dresses, cherries, and "winter butter." But the plan backfired. Spear went directly to the almshouse, showed the almshouse commissioners Andrews's letter containing her plan, and told them what she wanted in return for her betrayal of Andrews: permission to keep Alexander and receive pay from the almshouse for his care. The commissioners agreed; any repercussions for Andrews are not recorded.[90]

In another scam, mothers may have worked with caretakers to share the fee that the almshouse paid to those who cared for abandoned babies. When nurse Ann Murray reported to the almshouse commissioners that Mary Ann Davis had left a child with her and then disappeared, they believed her—until Murray returned and took the baby back. They wrote: "It was presumed that the mother and Mrs. Murray were leagued for the purpose of extortion money for the child's board from the commissioners." Murray's rapid return to retrieve the child evidently made the commissioners question the truth of her original story. The commissioners were apparently so concerned about such cases of fraud that as early as 1830 they made those who brought in foundlings swear an oath in an attempt to guarantee the truth of their stories.[91]

These attempted collusions between abandoning mothers and the nurses hired by the almshouse demonstrate that these women had shared concerns. Both came from the ranks of the city's most impoverished women, and together they participated in a quasi-underground urban economy facilitated by the almshouse, an economy in which the desperate misfortunes of some resulted in abandoned children who provided a barely adequate income to others. By subverting this system through cooperation, they tried to extract from the almshouse as much as they could.

Others strove to maintain their privacy. Of all the ways to abandon a baby, perhaps the oddest and most dramatic was the method of anonymously depositing a baby with a stranger, whether in the street, a store, or a home. Bridget Brisshan's experience of finding a baby in her bed—so similar to Mr. Allworthy's in *Tom Jones*—provides one example. Bridget's children were passive—and probably amazed—observers of this event, but in several other cases, older children took active parts as intermediaries. In 1840, a little girl made use of the pandemonium at the almshouse office to hand a crying baby—a sibling? a neighbor? a stranger?—to a woman she did not know. Then, as the woman testified to the commissioners, the girl "pushed her way through the crowd and deponent has not seen her since."[92] In a similar case, a woman approached a small boy and asked him to take her year-old baby to the almshouse. A "gentleman" later discovered the boy with the baby, heard his story, and brought the baby to the almshouse himself.[93]

Such fleeting yet momentous encounters with abandoners must have been disorienting, even frightening reminders of the vulnerability of one's neighbors, their children, and, by extension, oneself. Imagine the bafflement of Catherine Reed, who, in 1840, complained to the almshouse commissioners that a woman who gave her name as Mary Mitchell had come to her house and asked her to hold an infant for a short time. Mitchell then left and did not come back. Reed, the commissioners recorded, "really believes [Mitchell] does not intend to return she now prays that the child may be taken to the Alms House to be taken care of." Or consider the experience of William E. Johnson one autumn evening in 1840. Johnson was at the home of a friend at the corner of Hudson and Charlton Streets "when a female came up to him, and asked him to take her child which he did, when she immediately absconded, and he has not seen her since." Johnson protested that he had only agreed to take the child temporarily and that he was "wholly unacquainted with the mother of the said child."[94]

The method of abandoning a baby to a third party who could be relied on to bring it to the almshouse or perhaps even keep the baby may have been used by poor and desperate mothers who wished to avoid exposing their babies to the dangers of streets or doorsteps, as well as to avoid exposing themselves to prosecution under New York's 1829 law against abandonment. In 1841, for instance, Clarissa Davis agreed to watch ten-month-old Laura Miranda Bowerhorn for an hour, but a week went by and the mother did not return. As she told the commissioners, "information" she gathered, possibly from neighborhood

In this illustration titled "A Sad Case of Misplaced Confidence," a "Sympathetic Gent" tells a police officer how a woman duped him into holding a baby. Two hours later, he was still holding it. The practice, familiar before the Civil War, persisted after it, as this illustration demonstrates. Thomas Worth. *Wild Oats* [1874]. Collection of the New-York Historical Society, 79725d.

informants, revealed "that it was her [the mother's] intention to abandon it, and for Mrs. Davis to have it sent for its support to the Commissioners of the Alms House." The baby's father was in prison, and her mother, a former almshouse resident, presumably did not want to return there herself.[95]

Infanticide

While many people who abandoned babies in antebellum New York chose methods that did not immediately threaten their babies' lives, others did not. Sometimes the line between abandonment and infanticide was very thin; sometimes it was nonexistent. In fact, some babies discovered on the street were not foundlings but murder victims. These were discovered with their heads bashed in or their throats cut; some were thrown over the walls of cemeteries, drowned in ponds, or tossed into the city's encircling rivers, from which, their killers must have hoped, they would be washed out to sea with the rest of the city's flotsam. Victims of such violence included a week-old girl, who was found in 1839 in the entry of a house with her legs tied together and a string around her neck, still alive. The condition of Maria Moulton, a newborn found in an entry in 1841, made the man who found her suspect that she had "been thrown in there this morning as its head appears bruised."[96] Maria, found alive, died a few months later.

Other babies were left in lonely places where their abandoners could not have been certain they would be found, such as the sparsely inhabited region of Eighth Avenue between Forty-fifth and Forty-sixth Streets, where in June 1838 two boys found a baby abandoned "in the grass," or between Fifteenth and Sixteenth Streets "close to the east river," where newborn Maria West was found at three o'clock on a May morning in 1841. The dismal luck of a newborn boy left in a vacant lot on Third Street at the city's eastern margin on a January night in 1840 was acknowledged perversely by the commissioners when they named him John J. Astor.[97]

All three were found alive. Maria West died a few months later, but young Astor defied the commissioners' expectations. He not only lived, but was adopted by a Harlem family.

Babies were occasionally left thinly wrapped in brutally cold weather. Five-month-old George Davis was found "during a snow storm under a cart" on a November night in 1838. During the same cold month, a passerby rang the bell at 12 Batavia Street to alert the house's inhabitant, a rigger named Robert Reader, to the presence of a "child lying on his stoop entirely *naked* (altho the morning is excessively cold)." The almshouse commissioners aptly named this baby William Frost. James Spring was found at the front door of a house on Spring Street on a January evening "almost naked—having nothing [on] but [a] petticoat and laid on the bricks." George Davis died the morning after he was found. William Frost, placed by the almshouse with a neglectful nurse, lasted one week, then died from "debility."[98]

In general, contemporaries understood abandonment and infanticide to be two faces of the same phenomenon and blamed both on the desperation of unmarried mothers. In the spring of 1820, a newspaper columnist who called himself Howard noticed an unusual number of cases of infants "born alive but cruelly exposed to die in some neglected part of our city and suburbs." One of the cases he cited was that of a newborn infant found "on the upper end of Essex-street" who, the coroner reported, had been born alive but afterwards exposed. In another case, a newborn boy was "found floating in the slip and wrapped up in rags." In a third, a baby boy was found in a pond on the corner of Chapel and Canal Streets. Howard commented in horror that these acts were the work of "inhuman mothers" who had destroyed their children rather than suffer the shame of unmarried motherhood.[99]

Yet in many cases, what appeared to have been deliberate infanticides may in fact have been accidental ones, the result of hasty or careless abandonments. They may demonstrate panic or heartbroken desperation rather than cruelty. This may have been the state of mind of whoever left a year-old boy "on the pavement near a stable gate" on Sullivan Street between Bleecker and Houston in 1838. The baby, named William Bleecker by the commissioners, died of syphilis—possibly the source of his parents' misery—seven weeks later. In another case, a newborn, "naked and unwashed," was "laid on an old piece of blanket" and left in the entry of a house on Doyer Street in 1839, most likely a testament to his mother's poverty, loneliness, and fear. A butcher walking near Fulton Market on a June night in 1838 saw a "tall Irish woman" dressed in a "light calico frock and Tuscan hat" lay a child on the pavement and run away. Perhaps she, too, felt beyond hope of being able to do anything for her child.[100]

In 1838, the country was in the midst of the depression spurred by the Panic of 1837. Philip Hone, who had felt the effects of the Panic himself, noted the high cost of food in Fulton Market while shopping for his family. Marveling at the high prices, the soft-hearted capitalist wondered: "What is to become of the laboring classes?"[101] The desperate act of the tall Irish woman in the calico dress and Tuscan hat provides one answer to his question.

"In Consequence of Her Poverty": Who Abandoned Babies, and Why?

It is difficult to know very much about the people who abandoned babies in antebellum New York. Seeking to avoid laws that would either make them pay for the upkeep of their children or jail them for endangering their welfare, most people who abandoned babies did so as secretly as they could manage. When they were seen, as with the tall Irish woman in the calico dress and Tuscan hat, it often was only fleetingly. In a similar case in 1839, a baby was discovered on the balcony of a house and two "suspicious women were seen in the immediate neighbourhood and were pursued but not overtaken." The owner of the house suspected that the child belonged to a former servant, who had been pregnant when he had fired her not long before.[102]

The letters left with foundlings provide a bit more information about the people, mainly women, who abandoned babies.[103] However, as we have seen, these letters communicate as much about what their writers thought those finding their babies wanted to hear as about the circumstances that led them to abandon their babies. The methods people chose to abandon babies and the condition in which the babies were found also reveal something about their circumstances, but overall the available knowledge is frustratingly slight.

More substantial is the information mothers, nurses, and others revealed about themselves when they brought babies directly to the almshouse's reception office in City Hall Park. When Eliza Pride's husband left her three months after their marriage, she had to resort to living in the almshouse and gave birth to her baby there. Eliza subsequently left the almshouse and got a job as a servant, placing her daughter with a wet nurse or baby farmer. The nurse brought the six-month-old girl into the almshouse after Eliza failed to pay her even though "she now receives $5. per mo. wages." When the almshouse official who recorded the nurse's story said he could take the child the following day, the nurse, evidently disgusted with the wait, left the baby "on the pavement" in the park outside the almshouse commissioners' office on her way out. The commissioners, who took the baby in, named her Josephine Park to commemorate this event. She died the following March.[104]

Jane Johnston left her illegitimate year-old son, John Rome, with a man she met in the street, who in turn brought the baby to the almshouse. The father, whose name and address almshouse officials knew, was "too sick to be arrested." This child died within five months.[105]

On October 1, 1840, Miss Ann Mulligan of Twelfth Street, possibly a nurse or baby farmer, brought nine-day-old Catherine Rogers and her two-year-old brother, John, into the almshouse. The baby had been born on the military installation on Governor's Island to a woman who died in childbirth. The father, a soldier, was leaving for duty that day. Neither Mulligan nor the almshouse commented on her motive. Perhaps the pay the father had offered her to care for his children wasn't high enough; perhaps she brought the children to the almshouse at his direction.[106]

A particularly sad case is that of Eliza Waile, "a poor idiot" who re-fused to feed her illegitimate daughter, who was a week old by the time she was admitted to the almshouse. Eliza's married sister, with whom she lived, was "too poor to maintain it," and Eliza would not reveal the father's identity. This baby died a few months later.[107]

In rare cases, mothers and some fathers brought their babies to the almshouse themselves and were thus able to tell their own stories. In these cases, they appear to have been so broken and destitute that they felt they had no choice but to throw themselves on the mercy of the almshouse. Ann Reeder, an abandoned wife, brought her four-month-old son, Charles Mortimer Reeder, to the almshouse "in consequence of her poverty." Charles died within three months.[108] Another abandoned wife, Eliza Eugenia Haviland, brought her "ruptured son" to the alms-house so that she could take a job as a domestic servant. This boy, for whom no age is given in the almshouse records, died in under four months.[109] William McClinchia brought his eight-month-old son to the almshouse after his wife abandoned the baby in an uninhabited house. For two nights after the abandonment, he "walked the streets with the child in his arms having no home." The almshouse delivered the boy back to his mother, who denied the father's statement.[110] In October 1840, Michael Lynch brought his eight-month-old daughter to the alms-house; his wife had been run over by a horse and cart near Washington Market and killed the previous August. The lapse of months demon-strates Lynch's effort to keep his daughter. By the time he came to the almshouse, he had concluded that he "is unable to support it."[111]

These stories, all of which come from a record book the almshouse maintained between 1838 and 1841, reveal information about the per-sonal lives of people who abandoned babies. There was the single par-enthood of men as well as women, which resulted not only from birth outside of marriage, but also from marital breakdown through death or abandonment; homelessness; illness; the unwillingness of the employers of female domestic servants to house their children; and women's lack of employment options. Greed, indifference, even cruelty may have played a role in some cases. Poverty appears to have been the condition common to all.

When the city and its private, religious charities came around to organizing foundling asylums, they made the reform of fallen woman central to their programs. These reformers and public officials were not incorrect to presume that unmarried motherhood lay behind most abandonments. But as our stories demonstrate, poverty was paramount.

One way of understanding the importance of poverty to cases of abandonment is by looking at the ages of babies when they were abandoned. According to the accepted understanding, illegitimate babies had to be whisked immediately out of sight at birth in order to preserve their mothers' honor. Yet of the 143 cases for which ages are available in this 1838–41 record book, only 10 were newborns; 84 were between 2 days and 3 months old; 39 were between 3 months and 1 year old; and the remaining 11 were older than a year. The oldest was 2 years old. These ages were frequently guessed at by almshouse officials, and they did not always know or record legitimacy status. The data is further clouded in the case of babies brought to the almshouse by baby farmers. In those cases it is difficult to know whether the parents intended to abandon their child when they brought the child to the baby farmer, or whether they intended, but were unable, to keep up their payments. In either situation, the child grew older while with the baby farmer. These numbers nonetheless demonstrate that most people who abandoned babies, including illegitimate babies, attempted to keep them, most for up to three months, a few for over a year, either at home or with a baby farmer, despite the social force of shame that must have been operating in many of these cases.[112] Implicit in these stories is the importance of poverty in the decision to abandon, and the failure of urban communities to support or absorb errant or suffering members.[113]

"Streams of Accumulated Knowledge"

Just one week after Philip Hone's dinner party was interrupted by the unexpected arrival of Alfred Godfrey Douglas, Hone dined among friends again, this time at the home of Abraham Schermerhorn (a great-uncle of Edith Wharton).[114] Hone looked around the table and made an observation that he later recorded in his diary: "I noticed a fact at the dinner table to-day which proves the increased intercourse between the people of the United States and Europe. Of a party of twenty seated at the table every person has been to Europe." This was a change, he noted, from previous years, and the result was that Americans were increasingly well informed about European trends. "Now," Hone added, "the streams of accumulated knowledge may be obtained at innumerable fountains; the Abraham Schermerhorns, the James J. Joneses, the Gibbses, the Primes do pour forth streams of intellectuality . . . sufficient to assuage the thirst of the most ardent untraveled seeker of knowledge."[115]

This knowledge of European affairs may explain why Hone and his dinner guests of the previous week seemed so unsurprised by the arrival of a foundling and so well informed about the consequences of taking one in. Antebellum New Yorkers, rich and poor, and regardless of their own experience with foundlings, knew about them as a result of their contact with Europe either through visits there, through contact with imported European cultural productions such as novels, plays, paintings, and prints, or as immigrants or descendants of immigrants from the other side of the Atlantic. As the city grew during the first half of the nineteenth century, New Yorkers would have been more likely to experience foundlings on their own turf as readers of newspapers, as hearers of the stories that must have traveled around neighborhoods where babies were left on streets and doorsteps, or, like Hone and his guests, as direct participants in the discovery of abandoned babies. Their very familiarity with both real and imaginary foundlings made them overlook them as a cause for alarm. They appeared to believe that foundlings were an inevitable part of the urban landscape and that the almshouse, where Philip Hone sent Alfred Godfrey Douglas, was an adequate refuge for the city's unwanted waifs.

2

"New York as a
Nursing Mother"
Foundlings in the Antebellum City

During the first half of the nineteenth century, private charitable institutions for the poor multiplied in New York. This proliferation became even more pronounced by midcentury as immigration intensified. Overwhelmed, the state developed a practice of delegating the care of the poor to private, often religious, charitable institutions to which it allocated public funds.[1] Many of these institutions were established specifically for the care of poor women and children. By the eve of the Civil War, New York had accumulated no fewer than nine orphan asylums, but these were meant for children missing one or both respectably married parents; none accepted the abandoned babies of unmarried mothers.[2] Later in the century, the New York Foundling Asylum recalled this benighted period: "one class of sufferers seemed to be overlooked,—the most pitiful of all,—silent sufferers, incapable of pleading for their own relief, —innocent, yet paying the penalty for the sins of others,—the Foundlings alone were unprovided for."[3]

Many of New York's antebellum orphan asylums served very specific constituencies, depending upon the interests or religious affiliations of their founders. There were orphan asylums for Protestants, Catholics, and Jews; for whites and blacks; for half orphans (children missing one parent) and full orphans. These institutions were not prepared to be receptive to foundlings of indeterminate origin. Some, including New York's first orphan asylum (the New York Orphan Asylum, founded in 1806), admitted children only after they passed through an application process overseen by the asylum's executive committee, a process that necessarily precluded the admission of a nameless baby abandoned on a doorstep.[4]

But the two principal reasons behind orphan asylums' refusal of foundlings were their presumed illegitimacy and the fact that they were infants. None of the orphan asylums accepted any children, foundlings or otherwise, under the age of two or three, fearing what Dr. George T. Elliot, Jr., called the "fearful ratio of mortality" of young children. In 1859, when Dr. Elliot made this characterization, he was an attending physician at the Nursery and Child's Hospital, the only institution in the city that did take infants (but not foundlings or illegitimates) at that time. He angrily suggested that the other children's institutions in the city refused infants because they would elevate these institutions' mortality statistics. In this era when infant death was common and expected, particularly for poor and neglected children, what angered Dr. Elliot was not only that masses of poor infants died, but that his institution alone had to bear the burden of a high mortality rate, with all of its implications of poor public relations and difficulty in raising funds.[5]

Illegitimacy was the other barrier that kept foundlings out of New York's orphan asylums. The orphan asylums, like other antebellum charities, only assisted those they judged deserving. While idleness or alcoholism could block a man from receiving help from a private charity, women were excluded if they failed to observe the era's strict codes of sexual morality. The Society for the Relief of Poor Widows with Small Children, founded in 1797, and the New York Asylum for Lying-In Women, a maternity hospital founded in 1823, only assisted women who could prove that they were "respectable."[6] As illegitimates, the children of unmarried mothers bore a moral taint, with the result that, in the words of one administrator of a post–Civil War foundling asylum, "some may say that, because they were the offspring of guilty parents, it were better that their existence in this world should be extinguished at its dawn."[7]

Not everybody shunned illegitimate children and unmarried mothers, however. The reading habits of American women communicate something about the heartfelt empathy many felt for these female unfortunates and their children. Samuel Richardson's *Pamela* and *Clarissa,* Hannah Webster Foster's *The Coquette,* and Susanna Haswell Rowson's *Charlotte Temple* were all seduction novels published first in the eighteenth century that (like Fielding's *Tom Jones*) remained very popular in the nineteenth. At least one early nineteenth-century Maine family named its daughters Pamela and Clarissa after Richardson's heroines. Their mother was pregnant at marriage, as was one of the daughters later on. *Charlotte Temple,* an American novel whose eponymous heroine was seduced by a British soldier and then abandoned, along with her baby, in revolutionary-era New York, was America's first bestseller. Its readership was very broad, extending across regions and classes and including men as well as women. Devoted readers even made pilgrimages to the fictional Charlotte's supposed grave site at Trinity Church in New York.[8]

Apparently, then, many American women of the antebellum years could empathize with the fallen. Yet the women who ran charitable organizations in New York in the first half of the nineteenth century were largely products of the evangelical revivals of the Second Great Awakening. It was their moral sense that guided the city's charities and excluded foundlings. It was left to the almshouse, then, to take them in.

Making Fathers Pay

Because the city's private charities erected barriers against foundlings, the only New York institution that would accept them during the antebellum years was the city's public poorhouse, or almshouse, the refuge of last resort for the destitute and homeless. New York's poor laws, modeled on those of England, made the almshouse responsible for illegitimate and abandoned babies. The almshouse took in solitary foundlings; it housed destitute mothers along with their babies; it paid wet nurses to care for babies that mothers could not care for on their own; and it paid mothers to care for their own babies at home, an alternative that was not open to women who worked as domestic servants. To fund the care of foundlings and illegitimates, the almshouse pursued their fathers; when they could be found, sometimes through local informants, these men were required to pay "bastardy bonds,"[9] sums of money made over to the almshouse to pay for the care of their children.

A woman who took advantage of an unusually generous bastardy bond was Sarah Jane Hannah, the unmarried mother of William Henry Niblo. William's father, William Niblo, was very likely the same William Niblo who established his fame and made his fortune at Niblo's Gardens, the complex of restaurants, theaters, and hotels that opened in 1828 at the corner of Broadway and Prince Streets. Baby William Henry was born in 1816 when his father was twenty-seven years old, newly arrived from Ireland, and working at a coffeehouse on Pine Street. He may have arrived in New York with cash in hand, or else he began demonstrating his talent for making money early. In 1818, he paid the almshouse the large sum of three hundred dollars to care for his illegitimate son. Niblo married a woman named Martha King (whether he was already married to her or not at the time the baby was born is unclear). The baby's mother, Sarah Jane Hannah, may have been the same "Miss Hanna" who, an advertisement in a New York newspaper states, was performing in the circus in 1827; as such performances were standard fare at Niblo's Gardens, this may explain how young William Henry came to be conceived. Hannah was evidently committed to her work, since the unusual size of the bastardy bond she received from the almshouse did not stop her from placing her baby with a nurse.[10]

Most unmarried fathers were not as prosperous as William Niblo, so when fathers could not raise the money, the almshouse allowed sureties to stand in for them. This happened in the case of William Lambert, the baby abandoned by distillery servant Eliza Ledworth on the Division Street footwalk in 1809. Notes on William Lambert Senior in the almshouse records indicate that he did not have the money for the bond and do not mention any occupation for him, which probably indicates that he did not have one. Another man posted the bond for baby William, and the money was used to pay a wet nurse to care for him. After a few years, the wet nurse relinquished him to the almshouse, as evidently neither parent was able to take him back.[11]

Mothers who were able and willing to keep their babies could apply for funds from the almshouse to do so. The nursing paybooks that the almshouse kept to record its biweekly payments to nurses show that in many cases the babies' nurses were their own mothers.[12] This was the choice made by Mary Harned, whose "natural daughter," Ann Louisa Harned, was the product of a liaison with the appropriately named Philander Worden. Ann, born in 1814, was at nurse with her mother on Mulberry Street.[13] Baby Elizabeth Levy, born in 1828, the "natural child" of Abner Levy and Mary Ann Tway, was also at nurse with her mother. New York's small Jewish community typically took care of its own poor, but by forming an alliance with a Christian woman and fathering their child outside of marriage, Abner Levy, whose name indicates that he was a Jew, violated his community's norms and lost his right to its charity.[14]

For these parents, the almshouse, despite the sordid accommodations it provided and the limited funds it was typically able to supply, was the only refuge available.

The Almshouse Empire

New York's first almshouse (after the one build by the Dutch in 1653) was built in 1736 on a triangular plot of meadow at the northern edge of the city, an area that was known then as the common, and today is City Hall Park. It was initially a multipurpose institution, housing not only destitute paupers—who included the ill, elderly, blind, and insane —but also vagrants, prostitutes, and criminals. Children with and without their mothers were included in this mix. In 1816, the almshouse left City Hall Park, which by then it shared with City Hall, and moved to new buildings at Bellevue, then a hilly, wooded, riverside site at First Avenue and Twenty-sixth Street. When Bellevue was completed, it was the biggest building in the city—a statement about the substantial dimensions of poverty in New York at that time.

Bellevue, First Avenue and Twenty-sixth Street. When Bellevue opened on this site in 1816, it consisted of an almshouse, a hospital, and a penitentiary. Collection of the New-York Historical Society, 79727d.

In order to house its ever-swelling populations of the destitute, abandoned, diseased, and wayward, and in a generally unsuccessful attempt to keep the virtuous and criminal elements in these populations separate from each other, the almshouse pursued a continuous building program throughout the eighteenth and nineteenth centuries. In 1832 the city redesignated the almshouse as the Almshouse Department, in recognition of its expanded responsibilities. By the eve of the Civil War, the Department of Public Charities and Correction, as the Almshouse Department had by then been renamed, administered a grim empire that consisted of the almshouse itself, nurseries for destitute children, hospitals, a lunatic asylum, a work house, a prison, a penitentiary, a cemetery, and the Department of Outdoor Poor.[15] The "outdoor poor" were people who were capable of caring for themselves in their own homes but still required assistance, which they received in the form of alms from the city. The Department of Outdoor Poor distributed money, food, coal, and other supplies to these people; another of its responsibilities was to serve as the intake office for foundlings.[16]

After the almshouse moved to Bellevue in 1816, the group of exhausted old buildings it left behind in City Hall Park was taken over by the city for use as offices and courts. Some almshouse offices remained behind in the park as well. One of these was the Department of Outdoor Poor. By 1848 the Department of Outdoor Poor was housed in the Rotunda, a domed, columned, brick structure, which was built in 1818 by artist John Vanderlyn to display his panoramic paintings. The Rotunda, whose high-domed, skylit interior once housed Vanderlyn's illusionistic scenes of the gardens of Versailles, was divided by the city, after it took the building over, into a warren of poorly ventilated offices. In 1851, George Kellock, Jr., the Superintendent of Outdoor Poor, complained that "in inclement seasons, when it is most thronged," his office required "the constant use of disinfectants."[17]

As Kellock suggested, the office was a chaotic place. A typical mid-century scene there consisted of "dense crowds of human beings, of various countries, colors, and ages, filling the rooms and passage ways, to the extent of nearly preventing ingress and egress." The applicants for alms who crushed into the office of the almshouse's Department of Outdoor Poor included the "sick and exhausted . . . fretting out the term of life in the most piteous poverty." People brought in by cart because they were too weak to walk sometimes "died on the floor from the sheerest exhaustion." The insane wandered the office "in the wildest in-

Waiting to collect alms at the almshouse's Department of Outdoor Poor. By 1868, the department had moved from the Rotunda to 1 Bond Street, but the chaotic scene had changed little from the one described by Commissioner Leonard in 1848. Stanley Fox. *Harper's Weekly,* February 15, 1868. Collection of the New-York Historical Society, 79753d.

coherence of *mania,"* while pregnant women, "waiting their turn to obtain the alms sought for, are seized with the pains of parturition, and, ere they have time to leave, *give birth to their offspring."* Included in this crowd were "infants abandoned—just breathing their first moments, unclothed in some instances, in others conveyed hither as found in the public streets, in the rudest enclosures."[18] The scene, according to then almshouse commissioner Moses G. Leonard, was "harrowing to the heart."[19]

The Almshouse as Parent to the City's Foundlings

The methods used by the almshouse to care for foundlings changed very little between the late eighteenth century, when New York's poor laws were revised in the aftermath of the Revolution, until 1860, when the Almshouse Department underwent another major overhaul to become the Department of Public Charities and Correction.[20] The almshouse commissioners (or almshouse governors, as they were called between 1849 and 1859), prided themselves on the special care they provided for the city's cast-off infants. In 1856, almshouse governor Isaac Townsend lauded his colleague, Simeon Draper, who was retiring from the presidency of the almshouse Board of Governors: "The poor miserable abandoned child—the worse than orphan outcast, whose parents have been to it a curse rather than a blessing—has found in him a thoughtful protector, a guardian possessing a *heart* as well as a head. These have constituted special objects of his sympathy; and, gentlemen, the proper and judicious management of 1,200 infants is no trivial responsibility."[21]

When the almshouse first decorated the cover of its annual report with an illustration, the picture it chose was an allegorical figure of a mother with a baby at her breast, surrounded by young children. Objects symbolizing learning, plenty, justice, patriotism, and other wholesome values were strewn around the scene. During the 1850s and 1860s, the almshouse used no fewer than three versions of this implied portrait of itself as a nursing mother. In choosing this image, the almshouse elevated its role as a surrogate parent above all its other roles. Compared to the paupers, criminals, and vagrants crowding their buildings or beseeching them for aid, children, even foundlings, looked eminently worthy to almshouse officials.[22]

The officials of New York's almshouse were typical of the officials of charitable institutions of their era in their equation of destitution with immoral behaviors such as drinking, idleness, and, in women, sexual promiscuity. To those who were thriving in the burgeoning market economy of the United States, the "crime of pauperism" seemed even more unforgivable. Almshouse commissioner Moses G. Leonard protested: "in our highly favoured country, where labor is so much demanded and so liberally rewarded, and the means of subsistence so easy and cheaply obtained, poverty need not and ought not to exist." The almshouse commissioners, like other charitable administrators of this era, made clear which groups they considered worthy: "The child, (unprotected), the lunatic, the aged, the infirm, and the demented may be, and many are, unfortunately paupers: —worthy subjects of our charity, entitled to all the sympathies and provisions, now made for, and exercised toward them. But beyond these, *none.*"[23]

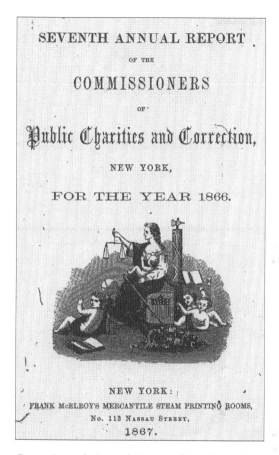

Cover, Seventh Annual Report of the Commissioners of Public Charities and Correction, 1866. In this illustration, the almshouse's successor, the Department of Public Charities and Correction, presents an allegorical image of the city as a nursing mother to its destitute and abandoned infants. Collection of the New York Public Library.

The almshouse was a parent to the city's foundlings out of necessity, but it was not necessarily a good parent. The luckiest foundlings were probably the ones adopted directly from the Department of Outdoor Poor, who thus managed a quick escape from the almshouse. Adoption, as practiced by the almshouse in the first half of the nineteenth century, was not true, legal adoption as it is practiced today. At that time in the United States there was no legal adoption by which all parental rights were transferred from the birth parents to the adoptive family. This did not develop in New York State until the passage of an adoption law in 1873. Prior to 1873, families wanting to adopt foundlings as full family members could use the only legal instrument available: the indenture agreement used for apprenticeship—even though, as one contemporary critic expressed it, the practice as applied to "children in the cradle, becomes absurd and repulsive."[24] Even so, most infant adoptions in this period, even when they were solidified with an indenture agreement, were probably guided more by sentiment than by venal motives, since an infant, unlike an older child, could not work and would require unremunerated care for years to come.

The experience of infant John Ferguson demonstrates just how narrow an escape adoption could offer to a foundling. John's mother was a housekeeper in the home of Archibald Pohock. John's father was absent from the scene when he was born in the spring of 1840. After his birth, John's mother also disappeared. Pohock placed John with a nurse, and it was the nurse, Elizabeth McCarthy, who brought seven-week-old John to the almshouse, presumably because Pohock had failed to keep up his payments to her. The almshouse quickly placed him with one of its own nurses, with whom he remained for almost twenty months. After being abandoned by both his parents, his mother's employer, and his original nurse, John was adopted from the almshouse by George B. Wooldridge, a hatter with an address on Duane Street. The hatter provided him with a secure nest and the first lucky break of his life.[25]

Infant adoptions could also prove precarious. Martha Clarissa Night, who was picked up off a stoop in 1807, was the subject of a flimsy adoption. When Martha was approximately thirteen months old and had been with the nurse assigned to her by the almshouse for a year, a French family offered to adopt her. The almshouse commissioners were enthusiastic about this interesting foreign family. Monsieur Etienne Thuron ("The english of Etienne is Stephen," the almshouse clerk offered helpfully) had "expressed a desire to have this child to bring her up as his own," and since the almshouse commissioners judged him to be a "Man of humanity," they handed over Martha, the "helpless & abandoned female Infant." Thuron and his wife kept Martha for five-and-a-half months, but when the family decided to return to France, they dis-

TABLE 2.1
New York City Almshouse Department, Children at Nurse, 1849–1859

	1849[a]	1850[b]	1851[c]	1852[d]	1853[e]	1854[f]	1855[g]	1856[h]	1857[i]	1858[j]	1859[k]
At Nurse, Start of Year	165	109[l]	130	164	183	173	174	178	—	196	199
Received During Year	349	[290][m]	295	339	303	330	299	274	—	386	367
Total	514	399	425	503	486	503	473	452	—	582	566
Adopted	50	20	40	61	43	48	46	47	—	46	51
Discharged to Parents or "Friends"	97	77	69	76	69	77	78	51	—	73	67
Died	258	172	152	183	201	204	171	174	—	264	266
At Nurse, End of Year	109	130	164	183	173	174	178	180	204	199	182

[a] AH, annual report, 1849, 192. There was a cholera epidemic in New York in 1849, which may account for the relatively high numbers of babies recorded as received and dead. See Charles Rosenberg, *The Cholera Years: The United States in 1832, 1849, and 1866* (Chicago: University of Chicago Press, 1987). Because there was great corruption in city government, and because record-keeping was not practiced with exactitude in this period, these figures, which come from the annual reports of the almshouse, should be regarded as approximations.

[b] AH, annual report, 1850, 120. This year George Kellock, Superintendent of Outdoor Poor, specified: "90 have been received as foundlings or abandoned," p. 119.

[c] AH, annual report, 1851, 130.

[d] AH, annual report, 1852, 111.

[e] AH, annual report, 1853, 104.

[f] AH, annual report, 1854, 214.

[g] AH, annual report, 1855, 193

[h] AH, annual report, 1856, 281.

[i] AH, annual report, 1857, xiv, xv. This year, the almshouse did not provide the usual figures, just the end-of-year figure, which was taken not on the last day, but on the last Saturday of the year, which may account for the discrepancy in the number recorded at nurse at the start of the following year. This was the year of the Panic of 1857, which may account for both the disorganization and the large number.

[j] AH, annual report, 1858, 280.

[k] AH, annual report, 1859, 294.

[l] AH, annual report, 1849, 192.

[m] This is my calculation, as no figure is supplied in the 1850 AH annual report.

appointed the commissioners' expectations and returned the baby to the almshouse.[26]

Perhaps more fortunate were the babies, some of them foundlings, who were returned to their families or "friends" (a term the almshouse used the way Jane Austen did, to refer to a close circle that included family members as well as unrelated neighbors and friends) who stepped up to claim them. Two-week-old Hannah Gilmore, for instance, the baby left by a stranger at Eliza Ann Oliver's house on a June morning in 1838, was sought out and reclaimed by her mother three months later.

Nearly thirty years earlier, Thomas McConnell, a three month old who was abandoned by his "drunken parents," was reclaimed by them. In a twist, these evidently feckless parents did not remove their baby from the nurse with whom the almshouse had placed him, but instead moved in with her and the baby.[27]

The majority of foundlings, who were neither adopted nor reclaimed by their families, remained subject to the care of the almshouse. The first parental responsibility the almshouse commissioners carried out toward infants brought in from the street was to name them. The commissioners borrowed the European practice of assigning distinctive names to many foundlings.[28] While some foundlings, including Hannah Frost, Alfred Godfrey Douglas, and John Luke, came with notes indicating their names, many did not. To lack a surname was to lack a connection with a family, and a child's namelessness signaled to the world that no father had acknowledged paternity. To "have no name" was to be illegitimate. All of this made the bestowal of names a particularly serious responsibility, yet the almshouse commissioners often treated it with surprising carelessness. In 1859, the *New York Times* described how foundlings received by the almshouse were subject to the "fancy and invention" of almshouse officials and "labeled as the Property Clerk labels a piece of stolen goods."[29] The *Times*'s criticism may seem colorful, but it was also correct. The naming methods used by the almshouse commissioners were often as serendipitous as the one described by Charles Dickens in *Oliver Twist*. "We name our fondlins in alphabetical order," declared the workhouse beadle, Mr. Bumble. "The last was a S, — Swubble, I named him. This was a T, — Twist, I named *him*."[30]

The foundling discovered in Mrs. Sears's doorway, who the commissioners named Oliver Twist after Dickens's character, died on July 4, 1841, after less than two months of life.[31] The commissioners' choice of a name for this ephemeral New Yorker looks like evidence of a kind of careless brutality, an indulgence in black humor based on what they knew about the abbreviated lives of most foundlings. What difference, after all, did it make if they named a baby Oliver Twist? He would not live even to be old enough to be teased about it. Neither, they correctly believed, would Com[modore] Vanderbilt, who died in January 1861 at the age of about two months, nor Phineas T. Barnum, entered in the almshouse's admissions books in July 1863 at two months old and dead less than two weeks later.[32]

Just as satirical, probably, were names such as Martha Washington, awarded to a baby found on a stoop in March 1807, five years after the death of the real Mrs. Washington, and George Washington, an infant admitted to the almshouse in 1861. Alexander Burr was named by the almshouse commissioners after he was brought in by a night watchman in 1808, four years after the Burr-Hamilton duel.[33] The Civil War era produced two Abraham Lincolns; a Lydia Maria Childs, named after the abolitionist author Lydia Maria Child; and Jeff Davis, a "colored" baby who lived a little more than two months.[34]

Sometimes the imaginations of almshouse officials faltered. Between 1819 and 1821, they saddled seven babies with the brutally descriptive surname "Foundling," including Henry, Adrian, Ann, James, Mary Ann, and William Henry. The last member of the invented Foundling family was called Spruce Foundling, probably named after Spruce Street in lower Manhattan. The commissioners must have been having an especially bleak day when they named William Unknown, a boy whose babyhood flickers briefly on the books between February and April of 1820.[35] With these names, the almshouse commissioners were echoing their European counterparts, who gave foundlings names such as Esposito (meaning exposed, a word used to mean "abandoned" in Italian) or Trouvé ("found" in French).[36]

The commissioners also used names to memorialize information about the circumstances under which babies were found and the people who played some role in their early lives, such as those who found them or the nurses who cared for them. The boy found on a stoop on a cold morning in November 1838 was named William Frost. The baby girl who was afterwards briefly adopted by a French family was found in 1807 on a stoop "between the hours of ten and eleven at night" was named Martha Clarissa Night.[37]

The names of some babies recalled the days of the week on which they were found. These include Clarinda Friday (1807); Caroline (1807), Leonora (1821), and Mary Monday (1822); and Juliana Saturday (1807). Even adults, if they were unable to tell the commissioners their names, could be named after days of the week. The Rev. Ezra Stiles Ely, who began preaching in the almshouse in 1810, told of a grown man, "a poor idiot, who was found in the yard of the hospital. Whence he came, no one knew; but, since he was found on Friday morning, like Robinson Crusoe's man, he has been called by that name."[38] As we have seen, many descriptive names chosen by almshouse commissioners commemorated the places where babies had been found. This was a practice also used in Europe. In England, France, and Ireland, for instance, abandoned babies were named after the streets and places where they were discovered. Anyone could guess the origins of an Irish girl named Ann Queenstreet or of the English Henrietta Garden. If they lived, these women would never be free of the shame of having started life as foundlings.[39] In New York, the almshouse commissioners named foundlings James Secondstreet (1821), William Bleecker (found on Bleecker Street in 1838), Elizabeth Houston (found in 1841 at the corner of Elizabeth and Houston), Peter Dey (left on a stoop on Dey Street in 1839), Emily Charlton (handed by a woman to a stranger on the corner of Hudson and Charlton Streets in 1840), James Bowery (1860), and Jane Broadway (1863), to mention only a few. These place names reconstitute a virtual map of nineteenth-century New York foundlingdom.[40] For babies found near their offices in City Hall Park, the commissioners used the surname Park; Mary, Elsie, Josephine, and Henry Park were all found in the park in 1838. Given the prevalence of this practice, we can guess where Ann Alley and Perry Alley were found.[41] The usual process in which streets are named after people was reversed here, making foundlings—at least one of whom dotted nearly every corner in lower Manhattan at one time or another in the nineteenth century—the city's own namesakes.

Another of the almshouse commissioners' common practices was to name babies after people. We have seen how the names of famous people were occasionally coopted; yet, people closer to hand—public officials, nurses, and people who discovered foundlings—sometimes lent their names, some knowingly, some probably not. Among those who knowingly offered their names to foundlings, in New York as in Europe, were asylum, almshouse, and city functionaries.[42] Jane Palmer, abandoned at about six months old on Ridge Street in 1835, was named after Alderman Palmer, who sent her to the almshouse. Special Justice Miles Parker, who participated in the cases of foundlings Mary Parker and Maria Parker in November 1840, contributed his name. In the late 1850s, foundlings were named for almshouse governor Simeon Draper, and mayor (and former almshouse governor) Daniel Tiemann.[43] Foundling Martha Clarissa Night was sent by the almshouse commissioners to a nurse called Martha Tice, which might account for young Martha's first name. Her middle name, so unnecessarily fancy for a poor, abandoned baby, brings to mind the eponymous heroine of Samuel Richardson's *Clarissa*. Melissa Frances Whittey was found in 1809 in the entry of a house on Hudson Street where a cartman named Nicholas Whittey lived and was subsequently placed by the almshouse with a nurse named Melissa Francis.[44] Martin Pringle was named after the two boys, John Martin and Alex Pringle, who found him in the grass on Eighth Avenue between Forty-fifth and Forty-sixth Streets on a June day in 1838. Agnes Maxwell, as we have seen, was named after the man on whose stoop she was found, Hugh Maxwell, the lawyer in the Helen Jewett case. Bridget Waters was the name given to the baby whom Bridget Brishhan was startled to find in her room on Water Street in 1840.[45]

In Italy, foundlings who kept names like Esposito, Innocenti (the name of the foundling hospital in Florence, also used in other Italian cities), Colombo (after the dove on the emblem used by the foundling asylum in Milan), or the devastating but less frequently used Incogniti (unknown) would have suffered from stigma all their lives. Yet in New York, some evidence suggests that foundlings who survived and grew up did not keep revealing surnames such as "Foundling," "Unknown," "Secondstreet," and "Friday," all of which advertised their bearers' sad, even illicit beginnings, particularly in a city full of European immigrants who could have guessed what these names signified. In this respect, foundlings were not unlike slaves, another American group burdened with foolish or otherwise distinctive names. On emancipation, freed slaves often shed their "slave names" and adopted new ones that better expressed their own family histories.[46] The absence in the city directories of the more egregious foundling names distributed by the almshouse during this period indicates that some grown foundlings shed the names the almshouse commissioners had bestowed on them.[47] And of course foundlings adopted in infancy had the chance to avoid the whimsical naming practices of the almshouse commissioners altogether; thus a two-month-old girl left on a stoop on Mott Street in 1838 was given the name of her adoptive father, Jacob Furman of Brooklyn, and became Mary Jane Furman. Among the gifts that adoption provided was the opportunity to start over with a fresh name.[48]

Foundlings and Their Nurses

Another one of the almshouse's critical responsibilities toward foundlings—some of whom had been lying on broiling or chilly stoops, unfed, for hours—was to place them with wet nurses as quickly as the almshouse commissioners could find them. From the late eighteenth century until 1860, the commissioners placed foundlings with any women resident in the almshouse who happened to be lactating, and they also kept a roster of women available to work at a moment's notice as wet nurses in their own homes.

For the most part, the lactating women who lived in the almshouse served as a kind of captive, unpaid workforce for the almshouse commissioners. Yet as possessors of a desperately needed commodity, they sometimes found themselves in a position to argue for terms beneficial to themselves. This was what almshouse inmate Margaret Davis did in 1792. Davis, who was acting as wet nurse to a foundling, decided to leave the almshouse to take a wet-nurse job on her own in the lucrative private market. The commissioners, lacking any "other proper person in the house to suckle the said infant," asked Davis to keep the child and agreed to pay her.[49] In 1838, another almshouse inmate, Eliza Forbes, was less successful when she attempted a similar tactic. When she left the almshouse, Forbes simply took the baby she was nursing with her. Hoping to be paid because she was on the outside, she brought the ten-week-old girl to the almshouse commissioners and applied to work as an independent wet nurse. The commissioners not only rejected her application and assigned the baby to another nurse, but they added insult to injury when they named the child Mary Lyons after her new nurse, Phebe Lyons.[50]

Life for foundlings who lived in the almshouse with their inmate-nurses—together with the rest of the institution's population of the elderly, ill, blind, insane, criminal, and desperately poor—was unwholesome at best. The Rev. Ezra Stiles Ely, the almshouse preacher, kept a diary recording his experiences there, and most disturbing to the evangelical Ely was the sexuality he sniffed in the stale air of the almshouse. The "greater part of the wards abound with the vile," he protested, "and here and there a solitary believer is vexed with the filthy conversation of this second Sodom." Not only was the house inhabited by prostitutes and other "fallen" women, some suffering horribly (and in Ely's view deservedly) from sexually transmitted diseases—"wretched females . . . on beds of disease, planted with thorns"—but the crowded physical arrangements of the almshouse promoted promiscuity. "In some rooms," he recorded in dismay, "husbands and wives, with children, and even unmarried persons sleep together . . . it cannot be prevented under existing circumstances, to procreate a future race of paupers. These things should not be."[51]

In the midst of all this were young children. In 1811, Ely tried to deliver a sermon in "a ward which was full of poor mothers with little children. They would cry," he complained, "and required attention continually. It was no favourable place for thought and speech, and I was not a little interrupted by fifty babes."[52] Some of these may have been foundlings with their pauper caretakers. Older children were also underfoot; Ely noted that seventy or eighty of these, all living in one room "in which all the beds touch . . . are allowed to ramble through the apartments."[53] Some of these children may once have been babies picked up on the street who were living out their childhoods in the almshouse.

Despite the almshouse's continual expansions, moves, and attempts to separate the different "classes" of paupers, conditions remained unpalatable throughout the nineteenth century. In 1853, the warden empathized with the "many old, feeble, and respectable women, who are obliged to seek an asylum here" because they were forced to live with "women who have lived a life of prostitution and debauchery, and who, even here, cannot be restrained from indulging in their old habits of using obscene and profane language."[54] The sordid conditions at the almshouse throughout the first half of the nineteenth century may have been what led the Common Council to pass an ordinance in 1838 requiring that, when wet nursing could be done "out of the [alms]house, it shall be preferred."[55]

Outside of the almshouse, the "lacteal ladies" (as the *New York Tribune* dubbed independent wet nurses in 1859) employed by the almshouse were generally poor mothers whose own babies had died or been weaned.[56] Some were needy enough to take in foundlings while their own infants were still at the breast. Frances McCarty, who applied to the commissioners to nurse in 1838, already had a week-old child. The commissioners noted "husb[and] sick—poor" to explain McCarty's need to take in an abandoned baby for pay.[57] From at least the 1820s to the 1840s, the wet nurses collected their pay biweekly at the Department of Outdoor Poor's office, amidst the crowd of applicants for alms. The majority signed for their pay with marks, an indication that they could not write.[58] In this era when literacy was increasing for women in the United States, the fact that these women could not write—which probably also meant that they could not read—is an indication that they were indeed poor.[59]

Almshouse commissioner Moses G. Leonard described the women hired by the almshouse to nurse foundlings as widows. The sums paid them, according to Leonard, were "the main support of many a widowed woman, who, by this means supports herself and family, at any rate, in part, and saves herself from having her name enrolled on the pages of the pension book."[60] This may have been an idealized representation of the identities of most of the nurses. The hard-working, deserving widow was a character commonly conjured up by charitable organizations seeking to prove that their alms went only to the worthy. In reality, many and possibly the majority of the independent wet nurses hired by the city were not widows but poor, married women whose husbands' pay was inadequate or single mothers who lied to the almshouse officials about their marital status in order to get their jobs.[61]

The majority of the women who applied to work as wet nurses between 1838 and 1840 claimed to be married, probably a sign of the commissioners' insistence that they must be.[62] The nurses who had husbands gave their occupations as laborers, artisans, and small tradesmen, including cartmen, house and ship's carpenters, a blacksmith, a ropemaker, a shoemaker, a waiter, a vegetable-seller, a mason, and a boatman.[63] Even though they had husbands, these women still needed to earn a living.

Some women told the clerk who took down their information that, although they were married, their husbands were not living with them and not supporting them. A few of these women really were widows; a few husbands were sailors, away at sea; at least one husband was a soldier. A few women, like Frances McCarty, reported husbands who were sickly or otherwise down on their luck. Some simply stated that their husbands were "away" and gave the clerk and everyone else in the crowded office a topic for gossip. One woman stated outright that her husband had abandoned her.[64]

The clerk who recorded the information given by women applying to work as wet nurses noted each woman's appearance. Shorthand comments such as "Amer[ican] ap[pearance] good," "ap[pearance] tol[erable]," "ap[pearance] very good for Irish," and "Amer[ican] widow, ap[pearance] respectable" are typical.[65] He also noted race, as in the case of Mary Ann Bunce, who applied in 1838 and about whom the clerk wrote: "Coloured woman husb[and] ship carp[enter] in Brown and Bulls yard, ap[pearance] good." Slavery ended in New York in 1827, so Bunce and her carpenter husband must have been free and self-supporting, though evidently they were poor.[66] In the antebellum South, it was customary for enslaved black women to nurse white babies, but in northern cities such as New York, cross-race wet nursing was not the norm. A free black woman would have had difficulty finding work as a wet nurse in a white family. This local bias, constructed out of the evil complexities of southern slavery and northern racism, apparently extended to the almshouse authorities, who matched black babies with black nurses when they could. In the process, with no particular benevolence intended, they created jobs for black women.

Thus when a "female coloured child about four weeks old" was found early one April morning in 1840, she was named Letetia Finder by the commissioners and put to nurse with Margaret Sickles, the black woman who had found her. Elizabeth Houston, the two-week-old "female coloured child" found at the door of a black man identified as Mr. Leveridge (at the corner of Elizabeth and Houston Streets, an African-American neighborhood in this period), was put to nurse, successively, with Jane Martin, Julia Ann Smith, and Sophia Gibson. All three were black. Charles Smith, a black neighbor of Mr. Leveridge, had brought Elizabeth into the almshouse. The concentration of African Americans in the early life stories of Elizabeth Houston and Letetia Finder, and in that of John Luke and his putative son Lawrence Black, indicates more than the efforts of the almshouse to provide black babies with nurses of their own race. It also shows instances of African-American mutual aid, facilitated by the almshouse, in the city's black residential pockets.[67]

When there were no lactating women available, either inside or outside the almshouse, the commissioners were forced to place babies with "dry nurses," women (often older) who would feed the babies in any way they could.[68] Dry nursing was a perilous business for babies. For most of the nineteenth century, there was no safe, effective substitute for human breast milk. The city did not have a reliable supply of clean water until 1842, when Croton water was piped into New York for the first time. Even then, this new source of fresh, clean water did not reach every home, and even when it did, artificial food for infants was not available until the late 1860s. Pasteurized, chilled, and antiseptically bottled cow's milk was not available in New York City until the 1890s and not widely available until after the turn of the century; it was the result of knowledge gained from the bacteriological discoveries of the

1880s and the dogged efforts of milk reformers, which extended back to the middle of the century.

Before these innovations, both cow's milk and water were infested with bacteria, particularly in hot weather, and could be lethal to infants and small children. Each summer, hundreds of New York babies died from cholera infantum, an intestinal disorder colloquially known as "summer complaint." Even when milk started off clean it was difficult to use and easy to contaminate. Artificial feeding implements of the time, which included bottles, spoons, and objects such as rags and sponges soaked in milk, were profoundly unhygienic. Job Lewis Smith, a physician who worked with foundlings in the almshouse (and who was associated with several of the city's foundling asylums after the Civil War), wrote that "infants under the age of six months, who are entirely bottle-fed, in any hospital or asylum within the limits of New York, almost invariably die during the hot months, whatever the care and treatment which they receive."[69] It was this specter of certain death that the antebellum orphanages had in mind when they refused to accept foundlings.

Those foundlings who survived their infancies with outside nurses typically stayed with them for one or two years, until they were weaned.[70] From the eighteenth century until the 1830s, nurses returned their charges directly to the almshouse, where the children lived until they were old enough to be indentured. Sometimes, however, nurses evolved into foster mothers with whom foundlings remained for substantial lengths of time. For some of these women, nursing for the almshouse—whether it was wet nursing, dry nursing, or fosterage—served as an ongoing cottage industry.

One such woman was Martha Skaats, who cared for three almshouse babies over a period of more than six years. Beginning as early as December 1819, when she first appears in the almshouse records, Martha appeared at the almshouse office at every biweekly pay period and signed for her pay with a mark. On one rare occasion when she did not come, Elizabeth Skaats, presumably a relative, signed for her. The child she cared for longest was Henry Foundling, a member of the ad hoc Foundling family created by the almshouse commissioners. The almshouse pay books show that Martha returned Henry to the almshouse—whether with or without sorrowful regret we cannot know—in May 1826. She also cared for another boy intermittently during those five-and-a-half years. In 1827, after Henry was gone, the pay books show Skaats receiving payments for the care of a girl named Margaret Watters.[71]

More typical were nurses who cared for several babies in quick succession—generally because so many of these ill and neglected infants died so quickly.[72] One such nurse was Johanna Hill. Hill's own baby was three months old when she applied to the almshouse commissioners on April 20, 1838, to work as a nurse. On May 1 she took foundling Mary Park to nurse. The week-old infant had been left the previous afternoon "by an unknown woman in the kitchen of the Old Alms House" in City Hall Park. She died on August 1 of cholera infantum. On July 27, while she still had Mary Park and her own baby in hand, Hill took in another foundling, eleven-month-old Ann Clark, who died on August 22. Three days later, Hill took in six-month-old Charles Cox, who lived only until October 19.

Hill cared for three babies in the space of four months in 1838, and every one of them died. Almshouse officials did not leave any notation, as they had in other cases, to indicate that they considered Hill to be particularly at fault.[73] In March 1839, after a hiatus of five months, Hill took in another foundling, Charles Smith Pugsley. Five-week-old Charles was the illegitimate baby whose father had decamped for Illinois and who was brought to the almshouse by his mother, Drusilla Smith, "on a/c [account] of her poverty." Hill returned him to the almshouse less than two weeks later, noting that he was "sickly." Perhaps she was unwilling to have another baby die on her hands, or else she feared an illness that could spread to herself or her own child.[74]

Johanna Hill's experience demonstrates the danger these often sickly babies could pose to wet nurses and their families. In order to avoid becoming infected, some women simply chose not to take foundlings that looked sick. Worrisome diseases included smallpox and syphilis, which carried the stigmatizing taint of sexual wrongdoing in addition to its physical ravages.[75]

Baby farmers, whether they took in almshouse foundlings or the young children of poor, working mothers, developed an unsavory reputation in both English and American cities by the 1850s. These women were often accused of neglecting the children they were paid to care for, or even of making unwanted infants disappear through underground adoptions or fatal neglect.[76] Martha Skaats's efficiency in picking up her pay and habit of accepting several babies at once identify her as a baby farmer, although given her success with Henry Foundling, she was evidently a fairly competent and responsible one. Nursing for the almshouse was a job for poor women like Martha Skaats. Ironically, it was a job that was only made possible by the hard luck of other poor women. It did not require any particular skills, only that the applicant be female and, preferably, lactating. As the case of Johanna Hill demonstrates, it carried serious risks for the nurses and their families. Yet it was a way for poor women to make money in a world in which very few occupations were open to them.

Some foundlings were endangered not by their nurses but by the indifference of physicians who wrote them off as hopeless. In 1857, an almshouse nurse named Phebe Powell asked the local dispensary (a neighborhood clinic that treated poor patients and dispensed medicine) to send a doctor to look at one of the six children she was caring for. The doctor refused to visit. "The poor rotten things," he told Powell, "they ain't worth raising." Powell claimed that "the physicians at the Dispensary talk and act so about these children" that she could not "bear to go there at all." Margaret Edwards Dormand, another almshouse nurse, similarly reported that when she attempted to take her "diseased pauper infant" to the local dispensary, the doctor there told her "they would do nothing for it, as it was not her own child; but she must take it where she got it if she wanted it helped."[77]

There was another side to this story that was less flattering to the nurses. George T. Elliot, a physician later associated with several of New York's foundling hospitals, implicated the nurses in the dispensaries' failure to help foundlings: "How many black-hearted guardians of motherless babes await, with ill-concealed anxiety, the end of the little life; and I know, from my personal observation, that the Dispensaries are thus often prostituted to people who bring the little sufferer but once, that its disease may be recognized, and a certificate of death from natural causes be obtained, without ever availing themselves of those advantages which the Dispensaries were designed to offer."[78]

Some of the nurses the almshouse hired may have been criminally neglectful; in most cases they were simply poor women doing one of the few jobs available to them as best they could. In at least one instance it seems that sorrow and altruism, not money, motivated a woman to take a baby from the almshouse to nurse. In the winter of 1839, a woman named Augusta Alexander, whose newborn baby had died, applied to the almshouse to work as a wet nurse. The almshouse gave her Sarah

White, the baby girl found by one of the city's night watchmen "on the side walk in a willow market basket." The almshouse clerk noted in his records: "Takes it without charge."[79]

The Almshouse Nurseries: Long Island Farms and Randall's Island

Before the 1830s, when the almshouse built its first nursery, foundlings were returned by their nurses to the almshouse once they were weaned. (As the case of Henry Foundling demonstrates, however, some children spent longer with their nurses. Almshouse rules were not always strictly followed, especially when there was money to be made.) Those who had spent their infancies in the almshouse remained there.[80] In the almshouse foundlings from about two through ten years old had only the ad hoc supervision provided by a transient population of female pauper inmates and mingled with prostitutes, ailing sailors, vagrants, the insane, the aged, the blind, the ill, and the destitute. They also met other children, with whom they attended the almshouse school.[81] The almshouse, as the legally mandated receptacle of last resort for all New York's homeless and destitute, housed not only foundlings but also children who were admitted with their families; children who had been removed from unfit families by the city; children sent by their families or the authorities to the almshouse for disciplinary reasons; blind and disabled children; children who had been born in the almshouse to destitute mothers; lost children, who remained only until their families could pick them up; orphans whose ages, conditions, or backgrounds did not match the requirements of the city's private orphan asylums; and a few solitary, homeless children. One of these was six-year-old Richard Shannon, who walked into the almshouse alone one day in 1827. Richard was an immigrant whose family had set sail from Liverpool in 1825. He told the almshouse officials who admitted him that his mother was dead and his stepfather, an alcoholic, could not or would not care for him.[82]

By combining foundlings with the other children, the almshouse was departing from the European practice of separating foundlings from orphans so as to avoid "contaminating" legitimate children. Officials of the almshouse sometimes even described foundlings in ways that obscured their origins so as to lessen the stigma against them as illegitimates. In 1849, almshouse clerk George B. Gilbert kindly attempted to designate the infants abandoned with baby farmers as "paupers" rather than "foundlings," so that they could avoid what he evidently felt was the greater stigma of illegitimacy. When describing the infants whom the almshouse was maintaining at nurse, he carefully defined his terms:

> About forty-six children are classed as paupers . . . also those left at board [with baby farmers] in the city and abandoned; as many are included in this class as possible, to avoid the stigma of being illegitimate.
> The infants found in the streets are called foundlings.[83]

Thus, paradoxically, one result of the sordid confusion of New York's antebellum almshouse was that it served to lighten the stigma historically assigned to foundlings.

In the 1830s, the almshouse began separating its children from the other almshouse inmates by establishing a separate "nursery." In taking this step, the almshouse was bending to the prevailing winds of opinion regarding the care of poor and dependent children. By the 1830s, the idea that children were being raised in almshouses along with prostitutes and criminals dismayed a wider number of people than it had when New York's first almshouse was built a century earlier. In the 1830s, Americans began removing wayward, parentless, destitute, abused, and abandoned children from all-purpose institutions such as almshouses and creating special children's institutions. Some of New York City's eight orphan asylums were part of that trend. Yet because of their association with fallen women, foundling asylums were not part of the first wave of children's institutions. New York City had no foundling asylums until after the Civil War. Even then, the fact that foundlings were not simply allowed into orphanages but were considered to require separate institutions is evidence of considerable stigma.

Overall, this new attention to the needs of children reflected the beginning of an understanding that had been building in Europe and the United States since at least the eighteenth century and possibly earlier: that children were essentially innocent and good and that childhood ought to be a protected time of life unsullied by work, sex, and other adult dangers and concerns. The experiences of Charles Dickens's workhouse child, Oliver Twist, whose incandescent goodness glows even in the grit of the London slums, captured the heightened sentiments of this era in regard to children.

Despite the almshouse commissioners' burgeoning sensibilities about children, their first nursery, Long Island Farms, was a disaster from beginning to end, a victim of neglect and bad management. In approximately 1831, the city purchased Long Island Farms, a 230-acre tract of farmland located on the shoreline of present-day Queens, opposite Blackwell's Island. In the spring of 1835, it began constructing a building to house children there.[84] This building, meant to serve as a "school house, nursery, &c." was "materially injured by the neglect of proper filling in round the foundation, and other attentions towards its completion," despite an appropriation of funds in 1836 by the Common Council's Committee on Charity and Almshouse to complete and furnish it. As a result, by 1837, even though the children had already moved in, conditions were poor. According to the superintendent and the matron, Jane Ley, the children also suffered from inadequate supplies of clothing, shoes, food, water, and fuel. Ley further complained that the meat received at the Farms was of inferior quality, the lack of fuel compelled the women and children to gather twigs in the woods, and the superintendent of the almshouse had not visited in nine months. Another official had in that time "visited the *Farmer,* but not the *children,*" Ley complained.[85]

From about the mid-1830s, when it opened, until 1847, when it closed, about six hundred children lived at Long Island Farms at any given moment.[86] These were accompanied by a smaller number of adults, dependents of the almshouse, who absorbed the elevating benefits of hard labor while helping to feed themselves and their fellow almshouse dependents by working the farm. Jane Ley, the matron, was accompanied by an assistant matron, a superintendent, a steward and his assistant, a physician, and a nurse. The children attended a school at Long Island Farms that was run by the Public School Society, the Protestant-dominated, privately run school organization that later evolved into New York's public school system. Black children were excluded from Long Island Farms, which, given the conditions there, could have been considered just as well for them, except that conditions in the almshouse proper, where they remained, were equally awful.[87]

During the 1830s and 1840s, when America's asylums were still new and hopeful experiments, they were a popular destination for visitors.[88] Although Long Island Farms was never a model institution, as was the penitentiary at Auburn in upstate New York or the insane asylum at

Bloomingdale in northern Manhattan, it had its share of visitors. While the farms' personnel seem to have been capable of putting on a good show, visitors generally perceived the bleakness that lay just beneath the surface. The abolitionist and author Lydia Maria Child, visiting in 1842, remarked: "The oppressive feeling is, that there are no *mothers* there." While noting that the children seemed to be clean, well-dressed, and well-housed, she objected to the regimentation of life in a children's institution. "The sleeping-rooms were clean as a Shaker's apron," she observed. "When I saw the long rows of nice little beds, ranged side by side, I inquired whether there was not a merry buzz in the morning. 'They are not permitted to speak at all in the sleeping apartments,' replied the superintendent. The answer sent a chill through my heart."[89]

Other visitors unearthed deeper evidence of demoralization and disarray. The physician and city inspector John Griscom found ophthalmia, an inflammation of the eye common among institutionalized children, at Long Island Farms.[90] Quaker abolitionist James Gibbons, who established with his wife, Abigail Hopper Gibbons, a tradition of visiting the children at Long Island Farms every July Fourth (later, every Christmas), was particularly cutting. The children at Long Island Farms, he observed, "need everything and have nothing; and whose initial lesson, on going there, is to learn practically that they are the most miserable little wretches in all creation, that obedience to hirelings is their first duty, and to expect nothing. Secondly, gratitude for bad treatment; and thirdly, any quantity of the same stuff continued."[91]

By 1846, the year in which James Gibbons recorded his caustic comment, the situation at Long Island Farms had deteriorated dangerously. Almshouse officials belonging to the administration that came in with almshouse commissioner Moses G. Leonard in 1845 looked back on the unsatisfactory work of their predecessors and complained that the "miserable group of hovels" there were "more than crowded," and "so dilapidated and ill-arranged" that the Farms "may now be termed the *opprobrium* of the Alms-house Department."[92] In 1847, with new nursery buildings under construction on Randall's Island, the children were removed from the "old and wretched 'Long Island Farms' hovels," as Commissioner Leonard termed them, and placed temporarily in one of the recently completed but still vacant almshouse buildings on Blackwell's Island. Abigail Hopper Gibbons and her friend, author and reformer Catharine Sedgwick, were present the day the children were removed and traveled over to Blackwell's Island with them. "We crossed

Almshouse buildings on Blackwell's Island (today's Roosevelt Island), 1853. The building at left, facing south, was for women; the other was for men. In 1847, the children of Long Island Farms moved into these buildings. The children, along with Abigail Hopper Gibbons and Catherine Sedgwick, landed at the dock at left or one like it. The Manhattan shore, still bucolic, is visible at right. George Hayward. Courtesy of the National Library of Medicine.

over in a scow," Gibbons recalled, "and a sadder sight than these blind and crippled children, sick in body, crushed in spirit, my eyes never witnessed."[93]

Long Island Farms was such a dilapidated eyesore that as soon as the children moved out, local people set it on fire. Since Long Island Farms represented the efforts of his predecessors, Commissioner Leonard approved of the work of the Long Island vigilantes. "Has not the city of New York for years been disgraced in the possession of the unsightly barracks of Long Island Farms?" Leonard inquired. "The neighbors on Long Island thought so, and having more regard for us than we had ourselves, eventually burned them to the ground."[94] The destruction of Long Island Farms foreshadowed a similar action taken by the citizens of Staten Island a decade later.[95] Fearing the spread of yellow fever to the local population, the Staten Islanders burned down a quarantine station where ship passengers were taken before being allowed to enter the city. The Long Island locals who burned Long Island Farms must have similarly feared contagion—in this case moral as well as physical—from poor, sick city children.

In 1848, after the demise of Long Island Farms, the almshouse completed the construction of a new and much improved "Nursery Establishment" on Randall's Island. The deterioration and overcrowding of Long Island Farms was the immediate impetus behind the new buildings, but the new nursery was also part of a larger program of construction and renovation that the department was undertaking on Randall's and Blackwell's Islands in the East River. In the same year that the Randall's Island nursery was completed, much of the grounds of Bellevue were sold. The convicts, vagrants, and paupers formerly living there were sent to the penitentiary, almshouse, and insane asylum buildings on Blackwell's Island. Bellevue became Bellevue Hospital, finally losing its multipurpose character.[96]

Central to this program were the notions of separating the different "classes" of paupers and criminals from one another and of isolating many of them from the city proper. Commissioner Leonard even proposed erecting walls between the different institutions on Blackwell's Island in order to separate the penitentiary, workhouse, and almshouse buildings there.[97] The new almshouse had separate buildings for men and women, in contrast to the old one, where men, women, and children freely—and, Ezra Stiles Ely thought, promiscuously—mingled. The "poison of the contact" between criminals, vagrants, respectable elderly women, and vulnerable children would, Commissioner Leonard hoped, finally be eliminated.[98]

It was in this spirit of classification and separation that Randall's Island was devoted solely to institutions for children. (The only institution on the island other than the city's nursery was the privately run House of Refuge for juvenile delinquents, which was moved there from Manhattan in 1854.)[99] The Randall's Island nurseries, in keeping with this era's sharpening focus on the welfare of children, was an enormous improvement over Long Island Farms—at least in its original conception. It consisted of twelve buildings on an elevation at the island's center. Facing southeast, the buildings enjoyed "a view of Flushing bay, the intervening islands and adjacent country—one of the finest prospects in the vicinity of New York."[100] The nursery's central structure was a stone schoolhouse. Arranged around the school building were a reception house where new arrivals were quarantined, a kitchen building, four dormitories, and an Infants' House for small children who were

"GIMME PENNY, POPPY?"

Children at the window of the Infants' House, part of the Randall's Island nurseries. When this illustration was made, children under three, including foundlings, were housed in the Infant Department in the almshouse on Blackwell's Island. At about age three, they were sent to the Infants' House on Randall's, where they joined other destitute young children. W. H. Davenport. *Harper's New Monthly Magazine,* December 1867. Collection of the New-York Historical Society, 79756d.

too old to nurse but still too young to go to school. The nursery hospital, a public children's hospital, consisted of two hospital buildings, a kitchen, and a separate structure for the mentally disabled, or idiots, as they were pitilessly called. The nursery hospital received charity cases from the city as well as patients from the island. The island's resident staff, many of whom lived in these buildings, consisted of a superintendent, matrons, teachers, a chaplain, a physician, and nurses, as well as adult paupers, dependents of the almshouse who worked as cooks, servants, boatmen, and farm laborers.

The children's dormitory buildings—two were originally planned, but two more were added immediately due to overcrowding—were designed for comfort, health, and even pleasure. Each had porches on

Washing the small boys at the Randall's Island nurseries. W. H. Davenport. *Harper's New Monthly Magazine,* December 1867. Collection of the New-York Historical Society, 79757d.

every floor, a hot-air furnace in the basement, and large, high-ceilinged rooms for eating and sleeping. The dormitories supplied that commodity so hard to come by in the packed slums: fresh air. Croton water, still a novelty only six years after it had been introduced to the city at large, was piped in. Commissioner Leonard, aware of the eye diseases that were commonly passed from child to child in large institutions, was particularly proud of the new "apparatus for bathing." It was a circular tub, ten feet in diameter, in which a dozen children could splash at once. Between bath times, the children could wash their hands and faces with hot and cold water spraying from the tub's pipe. The separate sprays of water were meant to guard against eye infections—but the communal baths probably undid the benefit.

For health as well as fun, the children swam in the rough, cold, salty water that raced around the island. To protect them from the "turbidness of the water and the strong currents of the river," a bath house for boys was built in 1851 on the eastern side of the island (Hell

Gate threatened navigators on the western side). Another for girls was planned for the following year.[101] In rainy weather, the children played in two brick playhouses, and gymnasium equipment was set up in the boys' playroom and in the so-called idiot's house. Randall's Island boasted landscaped grounds planted with "hundreds of ornamental and useful trees." An almshouse farm, worked by paupers, supplied milk and produce.[102]

During the hours when they were not at school, the Randall's Island children worked. The boys worked on the farm or learned to make men's clothing under the direction of a master tailor. The girls were also kept busy at sewing, producing clothing, towels, and other items for use by the populations of the almshouse institutions. Even girls in quarantine and in the hospital were put to work making "eye-towels" (probably what we would call wash cloths) for the use of inmates of almshouse institutions, a frightening demonstration of the still-limited understanding of contagion.

The products of the children's labor, like those of the paupers working on the farm, brought monetary returns to the almshouse, but the labor itself was also meant to serve as an inoculation against future pauperism. In 1855, the warden of Randall's Island noted approvingly: "The habits of industry impressed on their minds . . . will, in my opinion, be quite as beneficial to them in mature years as their educational improvement while here."[103]

According to Commissioner Leonard, Randall's Island was no less than paradise. "We can certainly now," he wrote in 1848, when the buildings were just completed, "after having been incommoded with miserable and unsightly hovels for many years, boast with a becoming pride, of possessing the most thoroughly complete, convenient and elegant establishment for the rearing of the young orphans of the City's care known in the world—here, true humanity can fulfill its ennobling mission."[104]

But Randall's Island also had its problems. These included overcrowding and epidemics of scarlet fever, measles, and other diseases.[105] Another problem identified by critics was the use of men and women from the workhouse, penitentiary, and other almshouse institutions as a source of free labor on the island. At first, Commissioner Leonard was optimistic about even this. Arguing in favor of the use of convict and pauper labor on the Randall's Island farm, he stressed the "entire practicability of employing pauper labor in agricultural and horticultural pursuits." Not only would the unpaid labor of almshouse dependents produce farm products for the children of Randall's Island, but it would also serve to "bring forth the latent industry of a destitute dependency." Farm labor, he believed, could serve as a "prop" to "broken down constitutions," such as those that belonged to the city's paupers.[106] Soon enough, though, the use of convict and pauper labor on Randall's Island, not only on the farm but in every area of its operation, would prove to be a plague that each new set of almshouse officials would try to remove. In 1854, after the warden of the almshouse succeeded in limiting the amount of convict labor used, at least for the moment (the almshouse never could quite bring itself to entirely relinquish this ever-replenishing supply of free, captive labor), he expressed his pleasure at removing a "great source of trouble, and also relieving the children from the corrupting influence of that class of persons."[107]

Visitors came to Randall's Island just as they had to Long Island Farms and the rest of the city's public and private charitable institutions. Delegations of politicians, fire and police companies, and other groups regularly made their way over the East River to be serenaded by the children, observe them at meals and at play, and present them with flags, Christmas treats, and other gifts. The journalists who reported on these visits, even those from the *New York Times* and *Harper's* (which by the end of the century would turn on the almshouse and its treatment of children), made favorable comments. "There were no 'Olivers' asking for 'more' " declared a reporter for the *New York Tribune,* describing a visit of the newly elected state legislature to Randall's in 1853. "In no other institution of this kind do we remember to have ever seen such a general appearance of contentment with their lot—such a home-like happiness as these poor children exhibited on our visit yesterday."[108] A decade later, the *Times,* reporting on the visit of another group, noted that the "excellence of all the arrangements and the proficiency of the boys called forth many expressions of satisfaction and gratification."[109] Abigail and James Gibbons had transferred their annual Christmas visits from Long Island Farms to Randall's Island and continued to bring friends with them, including Catharine Sedgwick; Sedgwick commented on the "wise and generous provisions the city has made for its young pensioners, by which they are to become a crown instead of a curse to us."[110]

In the nineteenth century, visitors were welcome at institutions.
In 1867, the Caledonian Club, in kilts, visited the Randall's Island
nurseries and watched the children at play. Note the uniform dress
and short haircuts of the girls skipping rope. The building is one of
the dormitories. H. L. Stephens. *Harper's Weekly,* November 2,
1867. Collection of the New-York Historical Society, 79752d.

Growing Up

Once the children of the nurseries were old enough, at ages twelve, ten, or even younger, they were apprenticed to farmers, artisans, sea captains, and factories, as almshouse children had always been.[111] From colonial times, localities used indenture, also known as "binding out," as a way to place illegitimate, orphaned, or poor children in households. In the 1790s, the binding out of children was so routine a practice in New York that the almshouse commissioners ended nearly every one of their weekly meetings with the phrase "after binding out a boy . . . they adjourned."[112] Even well into the nineteenth century, as the system of live-in apprenticeship declined in favor of wage labor and immigrants began to take the jobs once held by children and young adults, the practice of binding out survived as a way for public authorities to place poor and parentless children. New York's almshouse commissioners bound out orphans and foundlings to provide them with housing, supervision, vocational training, education, and, if they were lucky, a substitute family.[113]

In 1846, the Almshouse Department appointed John McGrath to the position of "visitor"; his task was to check on the whereabouts and well-being of children who had been bound out or placed in adoptive homes by the department since the early 1830s. McGrath paid visits to the homes of many children, including foundlings Catharine Carr Chapman and Catharine Jane Petit, who were living as adopted children in new families. Each had taken the name of her adoptive family, and both appeared to be doing well. Of Catharine Chapman, who was living in Harlem, McGrath reported: "begins to read, with him 7 years; adopted, very good child, is a foundling." After seeing her again in 1847, he added that she "goes to school; is a very good child." Three-year-old Catharine Petit was five months old when she was taken in by William Petit, who lived on Avenue C. About her, McGrath noted that she was "a foundling, gets on very well."[114] Another girl he visited who may have been a foundling was three-and-a-half-year-old Jane Dey, who was an infant when placed in the home on Sixteenth Street where McGrath found her in 1847. Her name also indicates a foundling origin, as Dey Street in Manhattan had supplied a surname to at least one known foundling, Peter Dey, in 1839.

Some of the older children and young adults McGrath visited may also have been foundlings, but he did not note this, perhaps because that history was best forgotten. Many of these were also doing well. Twenty-one-year-old Thomas B. Mathers, for instance, had been with his master on Water Street for five years. McGrath reported that he had "done well during his apprenticeship, reads, writes and cyphers; now working for him [his master] as a journeyman, and receives eight dollars per week." Thirteen-year-old Margaret McGowen also satisfied McGrath's expectations. She was a "very good girl, reads and writes," and was learning to make artificial flowers, which, like piecework for the garment trade, was one of New York's home-based occupations for women.[115]

Sometimes the arrangements did not take. McGrath found children who were treated badly and cases in which masters failed to educate the children or fulfill other agreed-upon obligations toward them. When McGrath found that Elisha Corwin had failed to educate his apprentice, Elizabeth Smith, McGrath "told him I would call and see her again, and if not attended to would take her away." A boy apprenticed in the Catskill region north of the city was "very ill treated by his master." McGrath was also very doubtful about the effect that labor on the Erie Canal might have on an almshouse boy. Joseph Kelly, bound to a master in Rochester, worked on the canal, which, according to McGrath, "is considered a very bad school for boys."

In other situations it was the child who did not live up to the expectations of his or her master. McGrath saw fit to caution twelve-year-old Catherine Fauzer "severely about her habits." One master complained to McGrath that his twelve-year-old apprentice, Henrietta Valentine, was "not industrious" and said that he wanted to return her to the almshouse, even though she had been living in his home for six years. And Jane Wright was apparently the cause of constant problems; McGrath found her unable to read or write at the age of fourteen and commented: "this girl has been in other places, and found fault with—she needs looking after much."

When the relationship between master and servant broke down, children—including a significant number of girls—sometimes took matters into their own hands and ran away. One example is fifteen-year-old Margaret Bell, who had been with her master since she was nine. Even though her master advertised for her after she ran away, according to McGrath she was "not heard of." Three boys, all placed with the same evidently impossible master, remained with him a short time, then ran away. In some instances, McGrath found that masters had simply lost track of their charges. Ellen McCluskey's former mistress told McGrath that she was "supposed to have gone to New Haven." Ellis Rushton, similarly, was "supposed to have gone to New Jersey." A few boys broke their indentures and ran away to sea.[116]

While many of the children McGrath visited in 1846 and 1847 were living in New York City or its immediate environs, others were living farther afield, in places such as Westchester County, Long Island, the Catskills, and even as far away as New York's Finger Lakes region. The almshouse had been placing children in the rural regions surrounding the city since at least the 1790s. But rural placement was no guarantee of health or happiness for almshouse children. In 1792, the almshouse commissioners acknowledged that there had been frequent complaints made on behalf of children "placed at a distance in the country." These children, it appeared, had been "very illy treated by the persons with whom they live."[117]

Despite this history, by the mid-1850s almshouse officials began to express their belief that country life was best for almshouse children. Boys on Randall's Island were assigned to work in the island's farm and garden. Labor on the land, albeit on a waterbound, city-surrounded sliver of land, was supposed to teach them "industrious habits, as well as make them familiar with a farmer's life."[118] Once it was time for them to be indentured, the almshouse tried to place them "as far from the City as practicable" with "respectable farmers and mechanics, in the country towns of this and adjoining States." Placement with farmers, an almshouse official reported in 1856, "is preferred by the Alms-house Department."[119]

In 1854, the almshouse began a program of sending children as far away as Iowa, to the Rev. Charles C. Townsend's Orphan's Home of Industry in Iowa City. Some of these children lived in the Iowa City Home, while others were placed with nearby families. Among the fifty children Townsend took from the New York almshouse were two or three infant foundlings. In 1858, Townsend reported that he had three foundlings, but in 1859 he claimed to have only two. In this era of vague record keeping, Townsend evidently did not feel it necessary to explain what had happened to the missing foundling.[120]

Almshouse officials' enthusiasm for the countryside at a time when there was massive immigration into New York both from the surrounding countryside and from the farms and villages of northern Europe, is an expression of the nostalgia many country-born urbanites felt for rural places. It is also an echo of the eighteenth-century pastoralism of Thomas Jefferson. New York in the mid-nineteenth century was crowded, noisy, dirty, unhealthy, and socially and geographically complex in a way that was alarming to the city's middle class, among them the public officials, reformers, physicians, and others who had power over poor and parentless children.

The irony was that the poor themselves—many of whom had come from the country in the first place—were notoriously unwilling to leave the city. Virginia Penny, a social investigator who published a study of women's work in 1857, noticed that women who worked as domestic servants much preferred the city to the country, even though the glut of servants in the city drove down their wages. "The majority of female domestics would rather starve in New York than go to the country, or even little towns around for fair wages. I think it arises from the fear that they will not find associates," Penny observed.[121] Later in the century, a journalist made a similar, if more cynical, observation about men "who might have healthy country homes [but instead] choose rather the tenement, with its facilities for indulgence in ward politics and bad whiskey."[122] In 1859, an urban missionary was bewildered by the unwillingness of New York's poor to leave the slums, even though he had long ago left a farm in New Jersey for the more satisfying challenges of the city. This missionary wondered, "The question often occurs, Why do the needy thus crowd together in our over-populated towns? How is it that they do not find their way into the broad and fertile districts, where labor is to be obtained and food is plentiful?"[123]

Horatio Alger answered this question in 1868 in his novel *Ragged Dick*. Describing a street boy who is sent to live on a farm, then runs away and resumes his life on the streets of New York, Alger explained: "it is often the case that the young vagabond of the streets . . . gets so attached to his precarious but independent mode of life, that he feels discontented in any other. He is accustomed to the noise and bustle and ever-varied life of the streets, and in the quiet scenes of the country misses the excitement in the midst of which he has always dwelt." Alger's fictional boy expressed his feelings more succinctly: "I got lonely," he explained. "I like New York best."[124]

In sum, the antebellum almshouse and its nurseries provided foundlings with a childhood that was sometimes satisfactory, sometimes deadly, but always precarious. It was able, however, to provide them with one advantage over the institutions serving their European counterparts. Because the almshouse did not separate foundlings from its other children, largely because in this period they were still relatively few in number, it did not stamp them with anything resembling the lifetime membership in a despised caste that was the legacy of foundlings from countries with large, well-organized foundling systems. Just as the minority of New York foundlings that managed to survive their infancies could blend in with the other children in the almshouse, so, evidently, did they manage to blend in with the population as adults. The paper trail of most antebellum almshouse foundlings ends with apprenticeship. Like immigrants or outlaws, they may have even changed their names and moved west, concealing their origins and growing new roots for themselves.

3

"The Murder of the Innocents"
New York Discovers Its Foundlings

Foundlings were a part of the landscape in antebellum New York. They were to be pitied, but also to be expected in a city as large and complex as New York was coming to be. Private charities felt helpless to do anything about them, and the almshouse coped with them as it was mandated to do. And then in the 1850s, infant abandonment— always a subterranean problem, a problem of night time and the streets —broke the surface of public consciousness. Public officials, private reformers, newspaper reporters, religious leaders, and others who had previously turned their backs on foundlings began to worry about them, and, for the first time, to act specifically on their behalf. In the spring of 1857, the Board of Governors of the almshouse formed a committee to consider the possibility of building New York's first foundling asylum. The following summer, the city's Board of Councilmen, which together with the Board of Aldermen made up New York's legislative branch, appointed its own committee for the same purpose. In November 1858, the councilmen resolved to build the foundling asylum, and a year later the cornerstone of the new institution, which the councilmen decided to call the Infant's Home, was laid.[1]

This group of urban leaders was the first to take substantial action on behalf of New York's foundlings, but they were not the first to address the problem or to ponder the possibility of a foundling asylum. "Howard," the newspaper columnist who commented on the rise of infanticides, raised the idea of a foundling asylum in 1820, but only to oppose it. Howard argued that foundling asylums in Europe had helped to stem the murder and exposure of unwanted infants, but he also argued that they had encouraged "habits of infidelity, immorality and dissoluteness" by making abandonment too easy. Instead of a foundling asylum, he jocularly recommended "virtue to women, prudence and honesty to bachelors, continence to married men, and as for the old gentlemen who haunt Broadway at night and assail every female, I would prescribe for them a *shower bath,* to be administered by every friend to morality."[2] More serious was the passage of New York's 1829 law criminalizing infant abandonment.[3] Yet neither Howard's half-serious suggestion nor the 1829 law appear to have been the result of widespread public anxiety about foundlings. By the 1850s, however, foundlings were attracting serious notice, resulting in the construction not only of the Infant's Home but also three more institutions like it after the Civil War.

What made the men who composed the committees of councilmen and almshouse governors, along with their supporters, come to the realization that infant abandonment was a pressing problem that needed an immediate solution? The answer can be found somewhere in the middle of a conglomeration of demographic changes, shifting cultural values, private and professional interests, and incidents of the sort that attracted the interest of the press. Contemporary observers marveled at the rapidity of the change in sentiment that made the creation of this and all of New York's foundling asylums possible. After the Civil War, the *New York Herald* remarked how "years ago public sentiment in this country appeared to be decidedly averse to such an establishment [a foundling asylum], but that same public sentiment has undergone a wonderful change of late, until now there seems to be but one opinion on the subject."[4]

The shift in sentiment that made New York's foundling asylums possible was part of the broader sentimentalization of family life, motherhood, children, and childhood in the West. Evident at least by the eighteenth century, it was in full force by the nineteenth.[5] Older ideas, which ranged from apathy toward the welfare of young children to the Puritan belief in infant depravity, were evaporating in favor of a new belief in infant innocence. The abandonment of infants to their deaths in the street, while always a horror, seemed particularly galling to nineteenth-century New Yorkers, newly sensitized as they were to the concept of the innocent child—a concept that by the 1850s had stretched to include even foundlings. They were galled, too, by the rejection of maternal sentiments that infant abandonment seemed to represent. Thus when the city's legislators began to plan their foundling asylum, the old and widely held view that these asylums promoted illicit sexuality by accepting its results was overtaken by an even stronger concern for the welfare of babies—even illegitimate babies.[6]

Foundlings caused particular concern because they formed the lead-
ing edge of a rising death rate among urban infants. By the middle of
the nineteenth century, physicians, sanitary reformers, and public officials had come to realize that as cities grew infant mortality rose also.
The dilapidated housing into which immigrants crowded, the inability
of the city's water and sewage systems to keep up with growing demands, and the easy spread of disease from one household to another,
facilitated by the close proximity in which urban dwellers lived and
worked, led to dangerous conditions for the city's youngest and most
vulnerable citizens.[7]

The Metropolitan Board of Health was founded immediately after
the Civil War, and two of its founding members were Stephen Smith and
Elisha Harris, both physicians and leading public health reformers who
also took leadership roles in several of the city's foundling asylums.[8]
Members of the board noticed that the effects of the city's dirt and disease were most intense for infants and young children. According to the
board of health, infant mortality in American cities was "frightful"; one
third of American urban children died before the age of one, and half
died before they had the chance to turn five. That these deaths were
caused by human neglect seemed intolerable to Smith, Harris, and the
other reform-minded physicians of the Metropolitan Board of Health.
"All must be humiliated at their great mortality," they remarked re-
morsefully. "It would seem that we can succeed in raising domestic animals but fail in rearing our own children."[9]

In this context, the catastrophic death rate of foundlings, once accepted by physicians, city officials, and the public as inevitable, emerged
as an issue that could no longer be ignored. Their vulnerability even
worked its way into the public discourse as a source of civic or national
shame. In 1859, the *New York Times* lamented that the miserable condition of the city's foundlings gave the lie to the glories of "our boasted
social organization" and compared the almshouse to an Aztec temple
"on which infants are weekly sacrificed by the score to the demons of
ignorance and incapacity."[10] The councilmen's foundling committee asserted similarly, if less colorfully, that "much more must be done to save
the lives of foundlings before we, as a christian community, can be satisfied."[11] The phrases "the slaughter of the innocents" or "the murder of
the innocents" began to appear over and over in reference to foundlings, whether in the press, the reports of public officials, or the writings
of reformers, as these people came to feel that the massive death rate of

foundlings was not inevitable but the result of human failings. And the councilmen and almshouse governors, even as they continued to understand foundlings primarily as the byproducts of the guilty acts of fallen women, also understood that the wholesale deaths of these infant castoffs reflected badly on their own qualifications as city fathers.

Though a changed public sentiment meant that it was no longer acceptable to allow foundlings to die unnoticed, that did not give public officials any better ability to save their lives. In this era, in fact, few believed that much could be done to save the lives of foundlings, the frailest of all young children, given the degree of danger that all infants faced. Physician George T. Elliot, who served the Nursery and Child's Hospital as an attending physician from its opening in 1854 until the outbreak of the Civil War, used the flowery rhetoric of the Victorians to describe the fragility of all infants: "these little ones, innocent and pure, [who] drift by us like the snow-flakes, and melt away in the warm breath of disease." Arabella Mott, secretary of the Nursery and Child's Hospital and the wife and daughter-in-law of physicians, spoke more plainly, referring to the sickly foundlings and illegitimate babies the nursery received. "A common idea prevails," she wrote in her 1859 report, "that if infants are placed in so fine a building, with ladies to watch the nurses, and good food provided, the children would not get sick or die. . . . The issues of life or death are not in our hands; we pretend to do no more than this: we keep them clean, warm, well-fed, and provide well-ventilated apartments." But those infants admitted to the nursery in poor physical condition, she stated firmly, "*must* die." As late as 1882, Mary Du Bois, the founder and "first directress" of the nursery and a moving spirit behind the Infant's Home, argued that despite the difficulties involved in keeping foundlings alive, it was still the nursery's duty to receive them because at least there, "they *must* get better care and attention, and can die in comfort."[12]

The people who gathered to plan the Infant's Home in the 1850s hoped their new institution would at least keep babies from languishing on the streets, and they hoped that the modernizing practices of sanitation and nutrition would help to save some foundlings, but for the most part they believed that their Infant's Home could provide a clean, comfortable, and humane place for sickly and unwanted babies to die.

"Embryo Courtezans and Felons": Foundlings Increase in Number

Probably the most potent impetus behind the new concern about foundlings in New York at midcentury is that their numbers were increasing. The city's population rose dramatically during the first half of the nineteenth century. From 60,489 in 1800, it swelled to 805,000 by 1860.[13] As New York's population rose, its population of foundlings rose, too.

Yet while the number of foundlings moved upward in the nineteenth century, the rise followed a jagged path. Economic and other crises contributed to the rising numbers of foundlings and other destitute infants, and more prosperous times allowed those numbers to decline. In December 1807, at the end of his second term as president, Thomas Jefferson imposed an embargo on shipping in an effort to avoid conflict with Britain. The result was a depression. In 1809, during that depression, the almshouse counted 190 babies (an undifferentiated group of solitary infants, not all of whom were foundlings) during its annual census, a substantial rise from the twelve "orphans and foundlings" it recorded in 1796.[14] By 1823, even as the population of the city pursued its march upward, the number of almshouse infants subsided from the embargo height of 190 to 129.[15] In 1840, when the city was suffering from the depression caused by the Panic of 1837, the almshouse counted 142 infants during its annual census.[16] Health crises also took their toll. In 1849, during one of the three great nineteenth-century cholera epidemics, the almshouse reported receiving "about three to four infants" daily.[17]

Before the Civil War, the almshouse did not distinguish systematically between the foundlings and the other infants it cared for in the statistics it presented in its reports, making an exact count of foundlings over a sustained period impossible.[18] The figures just cited are for all of the infants, including foundlings, that the almshouse was responsible for. But in the late 1840s, almshouse officials began to single out and comment with alarm on the number of foundlings it received. In 1848, almshouse commissioner Moses G. Leonard described the number of foundlings as "numerous" and estimated that his department cared for between 160 and 200 "and upwards" yearly.[19] In 1851, the Superintendent of Outdoor Poor worried, "The number of children abandoned by their parents at a very tender age is increasing yearly, and calls for prompt and energetic measures on the part of the police authorities for the detection and punishment of those who, even in the most inclement season expose their children to almost certain death."[20]

In 1857, during the depression caused by that year's economic collapse, known as the Panic of 1857, the number of infants slid up again.[21] It was during this crisis that the councilmen passed their resolution in favor of a foundling asylum. The number of foundlings in New York was not even close to the number collected in European cities in the same period. Between 1849 and 1859, when New York's almshouse accepted an average of 323 infants, including foundlings, each year, the Hospice des Enfants Trouvés in Paris took in a yearly average of 3,704 foundlings. Yet the upward trend in their numbers was enough to cause New York officials serious alarm.[22]

This alarm was composed not only of fear for the well-being of New York's foundlings, but also of what they might become if they lived to adulthood. The nineteenth century, a time of economic transformation and changing political expectations, was also an age of urban political disorder and crime, in Europe as well as in the United States. In the tight spaces of crowded industrial cities, the working classes and the well-to-do rubbed together daily and often irritated each other to conflagration. In New York, there were election-day riots and violence, race riots, flour riots during the Panic of 1837, the Astor Place riot in 1849, a crime wave in the 1850s (which one historian refers to as a "decade of disorder"), the severe draft riots of 1863, and more. The lawyer and diarist George Templeton Strong saw and heard the draft riots from his Gramercy Park windows, and the experience inflamed his disdain for the Irish immigrants who took part.[23]

For George W. Matsell, the first chief of New York's professional police department (founded in 1845), the army of poor and vagrant children that crowded the city's docks, alleys, and street corners at midcentury seemed primed to join the dangerous urban mob. In 1849, Matsell devoted a substantial section of one of his early reports to the issue of vagrant children. He complained about the increasing number of "embryo courtezans and felons" who "infest our public thoroughfares, hotels, docks, &c.; children who are growing up in ignorance and profligacy, only destined to a life of misery, shame and crime, and ultimately to a felon's doom." A decade later, almshouse officials were echoing Matsell's concerns, brooding over the "large number of children in the city of New York that are constantly running at large with no one to look after their moral or intellectual culture . . . the expense of supporting for a few years the children, will be as nothing compared to the expense of supporting in prisons when grown, if they are not educated and taken care of when young."[24]

Charles Loring Brace, the Congregationalist minister who founded the Children's Aid Society in New York in 1853, believed similarly that the city's vagrant children would grow up to populate the "dangerous classes," mobs of criminals and revolutionaries that would overwhelm the city.[25] Soon after Brace's book *The Dangerous Classes* was serialized in *Appleton's Journal*, the Paris Commune of 1871 erupted as if to further prove his point. Brace associated the condition of being a foundling specifically with criminality in later life. He found evidence for this view from France, where foundlings and law-breaking were closely associated. Looking at "some striking statistics from France," Brace found that a disproportionate percentage of the French prison population was composed of foundlings.[26] The warnings of urban observers like Brace and Matsell, both of whom were steeped in the city's street life, only heightened the awareness of other reformers and city officials of the dangers posed to society by a growing number of foundlings.

The Vision of a "Mere Politician": Isaac Townsend and the London Foundling Hospital

All of these factors and more motivated almshouse governor Isaac Townsend, who was the chair of the three-man foundling asylum committee appointed by his colleagues on the Board of Governors of the almshouse. According to Mary Du Bois, who knew him, he was the committee's moving spirit.[27] Townsend was fifty-two in 1857, when he took the chair of the foundling asylum committee, and he was a prosperous member of the city's business community with an interest in civic affairs. He had served as a vice president of the Bank of the State of New York and a director of the Panama Railroad Company. *Harper's Weekly* singled him out, describing him as "one of the most respectable of the Ten Governors" (the nickname applied to the Board of Governors). On his death in 1860, the *New York Evening Post* described him as a "well-known resident of this city" with an address on West Twenty-fifth Street. He had been an almshouse governor since the board's formation in 1849 and had served as the almshouse board's president for one year. In 1857, Townsend and the two others on the foundling asylum committee, Anthony Dugro and Washington Smith, also composed the permanent committee that oversaw the Department of Outdoor Poor, which was in charge of foundlings, so their reconstitution as the almshouse foundling committee must have been almost automatic, but Mary Du Bois believed that it was Townsend's "kind heart" that led him to make this special effort to help the city's abandoned babies.[28]

Townsend was motivated by a more quixotic set of interests than the other foundling asylum supporters in the city. While in London to investigate the London Foundling Hospital as a possible model for New York, the "mere politician," as he referred to himself humbly in his committee's report, was evidently bedazzled and a little cowed by the splendor of the hospital's concerts and art collection, the legacy of its early association with artist William Hogarth and composer George Frederick Handel.[29] He devoted eight pages of his sixty-two page report to his encounter with European high culture at the London Foundling Hospital. (In contrast, the councilman's report was only eight pages in its entirety.) These pages on the London Foundling Hospital record Townsend's deep feelings about the related problems of foundlings, female responsibilities, urban social breakdown, and even national inadequacy.

Townsend was impressed by the hospital's chapel with its stained glass windows, its paintings (including the American-born Benjamin West's *Christ Presenting a Little Child*), and its chorus of foundlings singing works composed for them by Handel, accompanied by an organ donated by the composer. The chapel, he wrote, "is large, light, elegant, and airy in its appearance. Stained glass sheds its rich glories upon the floor." But "the fascination," he continued avidly, "is that slope of youthful faces descending from the ceiling to the front of the gallery . . . the boys, in their dark dresses on the right, on the left the girls, all neatly attired in white, and the noble organ, Handel's munificent gift, rising between them."[30] The combined effect, according to Townsend, made the London Foundling Hospital "one of the most popular places of metropolitan resort" for London's "mingled crowd of the thoughtful, the wealthy, or the fashionable."[31]

But there was a thorn in the heart of Townsend's pleasure. Like many Americans, Townsend was stung by European criticisms of American cultural inferiority, such as this famous one made by Sidney Smith in the *Edinburgh Review* in 1820: "Who reads an American book," Smith inquired snidely, "or goes to an American play, or looks at an American picture or statue?"[32] Criticisms such as this one hurt because they were largely true. The United States did not provide sufficient training, patronage, or venues for its own artists.[33] The result was that American artists went to Europe. Townsend was miffed to find Benjamin West's painting in the London Foundling Hospital's chapel. The painting, he wrote, "is treated in West's best manner. Why is not that picture in New York?"[34] He despaired that American artists such as West and John Singleton Copley were "painting works for European palaces" instead of for the public buildings of the new republic.[35]

Townsend may or may not have realized that the Rotunda, the building that housed his own Department of Outdoor Poor, was itself a testament to the failure of art in New York. When the Rotunda, which had once served as a gallery to house artist John Vanderlyn's panoramic paintings, failed in 1826, the paintings were carted away and the city took back Vanderlyn's lease and converted the building into offices. (Vanderlyn's *The Gardens of Versailles* is now in a round room of its own at the Metropolitan Museum of Art.)[36] The English author Frances Trollope, who visited the United States soon after the failure of Vanderlyn's gallery, with the superiority assumed by Europeans in these years, noted New Yorkers' indifference to art: "I visited all the exhibitions in New York. The Medici of the Republic must exert themselves a little more before these can become even respectable. The worst of the business is, that with the exception of about half a dozen individuals, the good citizens are more than contented, they are delighted."[37]

But Townsend was not one of those satisfied "good citizens"; he wanted to be a republican Medici. In his report he observed indignantly: "We are not destitute of artists who would gladly hang historical pictures upon the wall of a similar national institution in New York. . . . We are not devoid of composers, and if due encouragement were offered, the character of their productions would rise. But the institution is yet unbuilt that might receive the memorials of their patriotism."[38]

Inspired by his visit to London, Townsend hoped that the foundling asylum his committee was planning would be that institution. Then, according to Townsend, "the genius of another COPLEY—the inspiration of another WEST—will fall like the mantle of the prophet upon sons of the soil domiciled amongst us."[39] Culture, he believed, could elevate the morals of a society, and Townsend regarded foundlings as evidence of a society in a state of moral decline; he worried that civilization was in danger of breaking down in New York. "New-York is a city of strangers accidentally thrown together," he observed. In such a city of immigrants, there was no community life of the sort that could enforce marriages and prevent illegitimate births, and infant abandonment was one result. "Not only is the idea of *home* one that fails to be realized, but there is the absence of the realization of all the duties and obligations to society which the establishment and maintenance of a home requires, imposes, and secures," he believed.

A foundling asylum filled with art, in his view, would fulfill two functions: it would save unwanted babies from the street, and it would provide New York's citizens with an "alliance with the loftiest manifestations of PAINTING, SCULPTURE, and MUSIC," thus helping to prevent a "second barbarism."[40]

The Nursery and Child's Hospital, to which the Infant's Home was attached, did not become a cultural center according to the model of the London Foundling Hospital and Townsend's vision, although it did hold cultural events to raise money. These, however, provided more monetary than spiritual satisfaction. A decade after Townsend's death, the secretary of the Nursery and Child's Hospital complained that fairs, concerts, art exhibitions, and the nursery's annual charity ball, while remunerative, were "fatiguing." "We would gladly be relieved of this method of raising funds," she complained, since "the contrast between our daily labors among wailing infants and sorrowing mothers, and the brilliant and merry ball-room is too startling."[41]

Urban Investigators: Samuel Byram Halliday and William F. Mott

Other characters behind the city's plan to build a foundling asylum were urban missionary Samuel Byram Halliday and Quaker philanthropist William F. Mott. Shortly before Townsend's committee and the councilmen's committee began their investigations, probably during the winter of 1856–57, these two men descended into the crowded tenement districts to investigate the foundlings and other babies the almshouse placed with the city's poorest women.[42] Mott and Halliday discovered foundlings and their nurses tucked into every corner of the city where poor people lived—"the vicinity of the Five Points not excepted," Halliday noted darkly, referring to the city's most notorious slum. Many of the harried, impoverished women who took infants home from the almshouse for a dollar per infant per week were, to Halliday's eyes, "persons of slovenly and almost filthy habits, and plainly wholly unfit to be employed as nurses for the dependent infants of the great city of New York."[43] Halliday was the chief instigator of the investigation, and the elderly Mott soon dropped out of the picture. Halliday brought his report not only to the Board of Governors of the Almshouse, but also to the press. The release of these findings to the newspapers—at a time when the penny press was eager for scandals with which to entertain its expanding readership—stung public officials into action.

Mott and Halliday's focus on the effect of the urban environment was typical of the trend that charity was taking at midcentury. As the city filled with floods of destitute refugees from the Irish potato famine, charities turned their attention away from the failed moral reform efforts of the first decades of the century and toward the more pragmatic goal of alleviating the physical distress of the poor.[44] Their method was the urban investigation. As squalor increased in poor neighborhoods such as London's East End or New York's Five Points, social reformers, physicians, journalists, novelists, and government investigators began to explore these places. And not unlike the reports of British scientific expeditions to far-flung colonial outposts, these individuals and groups began reporting back to a curious and frightened public. The novels of Charles Dickens, with their colorful descriptions of the London slums, are perhaps the most famous literary example. In New York, journalist George Foster, author of *New York by Gas-Light* (1850), delineated that city's underworld for an anxious public. New York city inspector John Griscom's 1845 *The Sanitary Condition of the Laboring Population of New York* was modeled on the *Report on the Sanitary Conditions of the Laboring Population of Great Britain* (1842) by the British social investigator Edwin Chadwick. Friedrich Engels's *The Condition of the Working Class in England,* which was based in part on his tour of industrial Manchester in 1844, is another example of a genre that spanned literary, political, and scientific disciplines to reflect a broad interest in growing cities, industrialization, and the increasingly separate and (to its middle- and upper-class observers) foreign world inhabited by the poor in the nineteenth century.[45]

The backgrounds of these two men led them naturally to their subsequent efforts as urban investigators. William F. Mott was a Quaker who found success in business but believed that "Christian moderation forbade large accumulations by individuals." Thus he retired from business to devote himself to charity.[46] Early in 1857, Mott brought his concerns about the almshouse babies to the American Female Guardian Society, where they attracted the interest of Samuel Halliday, the society's missionary. While Mott was the one who brought the problem to Halliday's attention, he played a minor role ultimately, and Halliday took the lead in their investigation.

Samuel Halliday was born on a farm in New Jersey in 1812. He began his working life as a grocer's clerk in New York. When eyestrain and bouts of "nervous prostration" interrupted his theological studies and early efforts in missionary work, he left New York and took up a business career in Providence, Rhode Island. By 1839, Halliday was apparently recovered enough to return to New York and begin missionary work for the American Female Guardian Society. He documented his work there in the books *The Lost and Found; or, Life Among the Poor,* which was published in 1859, then reissued in 1860 as *The Little Street Sweeper; or, Life Among the Poor.* Halliday was ordained in 1863, and in 1869 he went to Brooklyn Heights to work as Henry Ward Beecher's assistant at the Plymouth Church of the Pilgrims. Halliday appears to have been so devoted to the reformist preacher that "nothing gave him greater satisfaction than to tell him that he was getting to look like Mr. Beecher." After Beecher's death, Halliday became the pastor of the Beecher Memorial Church in Ocean Hill, Brooklyn, where he remained until his own death in 1897.[47]

When they began investigating almshouse babies and their nurses, the first problem the two men encountered was that they could not locate some of the nurses, even though they carried a list supplied by George S. Kellock, the Superintendent of Outdoor Poor. This should not have come as a surprise, however, as New York's poor were notoriously mobile. Many decamped yearly on the city's traditional moving day, May 1. Others lived in ephemeral boarding arrangements and probably moved even more often.[48] When Mott and Halliday found the nurses on their list, most of the time they did not like what they saw, and their comments are often colored with class disdain. While a few almshouse babies were living in "really comfortable situations" with competent nurses, they noted, in most cases the two investigators found the poor women the almshouse relied on to nurse infants dirty and "sluttish." "It would be a legitimate inference," the two men remarked of the nurses, "that they regarded dirtiness as being chief of the cardinal virtues." At times they did show a bit more sympathy for the conditions in which the largely immigrant poor were made to live by gouging and neglectful landlords and a city government as yet unconcerned with urban planning; they noted that the nurses' homes were "in the worst portions of many of the worst streets in the city—on lots crowded full of tenant-houses, and these houses completely stowed with families, from sixteen to thirty-five or forty on each lot." All of this, they noted, was "exceedingly unpropitious for the promotion of their [the babies'] health."[49]

With an attention to sordid detail worthy of Dickens, Mott and Halliday described the dark, damp, airless, filthy, smelly living conditions in the shanties, basements, and crowded neighborhoods of the poor. At one "miserable shanty," Halliday beat aside "flocks of fowls, hogs, goats, cats and dogs" in order to enter. Inside the dark hovel, which had a dirt floor and unplastered walls, he found "a protégé of the Ten Governors in the shape of a little urchin some 2 1/2 or 3 years old, running round the room, with no earthly covering than an inconveniently short shirt, his hair sticking out every way for Sunday, like porcupine's quills, with almost dirt enough on his little hide to set potatoes in, and to cap the climax, the skin peeled off his mouth and nose by a butt he had received from the young goat" that Halliday found inside the shanty along with other children, the nurse, a cat, and a dog.

At one home they visited, a neighbor reported that two almshouse children living with a Mrs. McCabe "suffered dreadfully from simple neglect." Mrs. McCabe left the children alone for hours, and when the neighbor went in to check on them, she found them "lying in wet places on the bed." The neighbor told Mott and Halliday that she did her best to move them to dry spots on the bed, but "from these neglects they became sore, and even in almost a rotten state." In spite of this, the neighbor seemed to pity Mrs. McCabe rather than blame her, perhaps out of empathy born from shared experience. She noted that Mr. McCabe was an occasional resident of the city's penitentiary and, when he was home, was abusive to wife and children. It was he, the neighbor implied, who was ultimately at fault.[50]

Mott and Halliday also found instances in which the nurses favored their own children over the almshouse infants whose weekly dollars supported the household. They described a "stout Irishwoman" whose son was a "fat burly little fellow," noting that this child's well-fed appearance "told better than language could, that the presence of the

Almshouse babies had not lessened the quantity or quality of the fodder that might help him along to aldermanic dimensions."[51] In this era of the urban political machine, the distended belly of the bribe-fattened alderman, often pictured in political cartoons, was a visceral representation of political corruption.

Like other urban investigators, Mott and Halliday looked to see how the dirty, overcrowded urban environment damaged not only the health, but also the morals of the poor. "Temperance and chastity," Halliday observed, "are as fond of pure air, and clean beds, and plenty of room as any *millionaire* on the Fifth Avenue, and shun the fetid attics and the stifling alley with fastidious speed." In the promiscuously overcrowded conditions of the tenements, Griscom argued, "can it be doubted that the nice moral distinctions so necessary to a life of virtue, will be gradually subdued, or overthrown, the heart hardened against the teachings of the moralist, and the wave of lustful passion become of increased power?"[52]

Almshouse babies, who shared the threadbare circumstances of the city's poorest families, had no access to the pure air, clean beds, and spacious dwellings that nurtured virtuous citizenship. If better conditions were not provided, Mott and Halliday warned, "*this large* and *over* flowing accession to its [the city's] population shall come to take their places among us in active life with vitiated, damaged constitutions" and "depraved and rotten moral propensities." Like Police Chief Matsell and Charles Loring Brace, Mott and Halliday believed that neglected almshouse children—those who lived to grow up—were as much to be feared as feared for.

Halliday emerged from the tour convinced that the almshouse's system was "radically defective," riddled with systemic flaws that caused the suffering and deaths of children. The fault lay with the almshouse governors, they wrote, who had failed to keep track of these infants or of the conditions in which they were living. "There can be no question that scores and scores of these children were murdered," Halliday accused, "and are not these men to be held responsible for the consequences of their neglect?"[53] When Halliday spoke before the councilmen's committee in 1858, he was a bit more polite, blaming the condition of the infants on "the system" rather than on the men he stood before, but his recommendation was the same: to remove almshouse babies from their nurses and house them together in an institution, which he suggested they call the Infant's Home.[54]

The Infant's Home and the Antiabortionists

The councilmen seeking to create a foundling asylum found a more sympathetic set of helpers in the city's physicians. There was, they wrote, "on the part of the medical profession of this city, a very general desire to aid them in their labors."[55] Physicians believed that a foundling asylum, by absorbing unwanted babies, would reduce abandonment and infanticide. Significantly, they also believed that a foundling asylum would cut off the practice of abortionists. Abortionists belonged to the tribe of irregular medical practitioners that began to proliferate during the first half of the nineteenth century, threatening both the authority and the livelihoods of regularly trained physicians. Further, as guardians of the physical well-being of the home at a time when domestic life appeared threatened, midcentury physicians had begun to object to abortion on the grounds that it prevented married women from fulfilling their biological destinies as mothers.

In the spring of 1857, a Boston physician named Horatio Robinson Storer, backed by the American Medical Association, began the first significant crusade against abortion in the United States.[56] Storer's crusade took place at a time when American women were resorting to abortions in increasing numbers, and most were obtaining them from irregular medical practitioners. Until the 1820s, there were no laws regulating abortion in the United States. During the antebellum years, the American public did not commonly believe that a fetus was a person or that abortion was a crime; most Americans understood abortion as a reasonable, if shameful, solution for unmarried women who became pregnant. Law and public opinion normally allowed folk practitioners and midwives to wield their ancient arsenal of abortifacients—plants such as black hellebore, ergot, tansy, and the aptly named rue—unmolested.[57]

The first antiabortion laws, enacted by states between 1821 and 1841, were really poison control laws, passed to protect women against dangerous abortifacients. These laws typically punished the purveyors of abortifacients rather than the women who used them. Also at stake was the status of physicians; the so-called "regular" physicians of this era favored laws that limited the movements of "irregular" practitioners, including abortionists, because their own professional status was faltering.

Antebellum physicians were threatened by the proliferation of those they called "irregular" medical practitioners and the establishments that trained them. Homeopaths, proprietors of water-cure establishments, vendors of pills and patent medicines, and so-called specialists in every ailment, including "female complaints"—the heading under which abortion hid—all flourished during this period, and the regular physicians considered the others to be operating at their expense. In truth, the regulars, whose repertoire consisted of painful, often ineffective, and frequently harmful treatments such as cupping and bleeding, as well as toxic drugs such as calomel (mercury), had little better to offer.[58]

Physicians paid the price for their high-pain, low-cure regimens. Between about 1830 and 1850, state legislatures, losing faith in the expertise of the regular physicians, began to repeal medical licensing laws, thus stripping them of their legal sanction. But the disappearance of medical licensing laws made it possible for anyone to set up shop as a healer.[59] In 1847, physicians founded the American Medical Association and began to fight back. The AMA combated physicians' loss of status by drawing firm boundaries around what they defined as "regular" medical practice and protecting those boundaries against those they considered interlopers without credentials.

In the 1840s, physicians were battered by yet another phenomenon —the habitual use of birth control and abortion by married, white, middle-class, Protestant women. The birth rate among white, married women in the United States declined by about half over the course of the nineteenth century. While in 1800 such a woman could be expected to give birth to slightly more than seven children, by 1850 she had between five and six, and by 1900 this figure had dipped to between three and four. The sharpest decline took place in the decade between 1840 and 1850. Historians agree with physicians of the time that this drop in the birthrate was the result of the deliberate use of birth control and abortion by married women.[60]

This trend signaled a change in attitude about what and whom birth control and abortion were meant to serve. The traditional associations of birth control with prostitutes and of abortion with the unmarried was fading. In this era of the first movement for women's rights, married women were starting to use birth control and abortion to control their reproductive lives. For physicians, however, this trend opened up a new front in their war against abortion, and one that was painfully close to home, since now they were fighting women of their own social milieu.

From the colonial period onward, married women prevented conception by resorting to such traditional methods as abstinence, coitus interruptus, and prolonged breastfeeding. By the middle of the nineteenth century, as a result of advances in the production of rubber, they could also buy condoms and diaphragms. Sponges, spermicides, and mechanisms for douching were also available in the nineteenth century. It appears that married women of means, the ones whose fertility rate declined over the nineteenth century, were more likely to use these methods and devices than poor, single women. Lacking the same degree of money, knowledge, and power over men, as well as the domestic space necessary for privacy and storage, poor, single women may have found birth control more difficult to get and use.[61]

When married women found themselves pregnant unwillingly, they turned to unlicensed abortionists. Poor, single women used abortionists, too, but expense may have been a barrier in this case as well.[62] By the 1840s, abortion had moved outside the domain of herbalists and midwives and become a business—a province of the "irregulars." Women could visit the discreet parlors of abortionists, or they could purchase products with names such as "Female Regulator," "Periodical Drops," or "Woman's Friend" to take privately at home.[63] Abortion, whether induced by preparations or implemented at the hands of abortionists, could prove risky. In the parlors of New York abortionists such as Madame Restell, whose lucrative business made her famous, women subjected themselves to dangerous, sometimes fatal probing by untrained technicians using primitive tools.[64] Women may have been willing to take these risks because at this time doctors did not know how to prevent infection, so childbirth, too, could pose mortal dangers.

To the dismay of the regular physicians and others, abortionists, like other businesspeople in this era of expanding economic opportunity, placed thinly disguised advertisements in the newspapers. By the middle of the nineteenth century, northeastern women were literate in numbers equal to men, so they were a part of the newspapers' expanding audience and could read newspaper advertisements placed by abortionists in the privacy of their parlors.[65] Thus women routinely, and without the advice or assistance of their physicians, sought out a service the regular physicians scorned. To add insult to injury, they paid high fees to abortionists such as Madame Restell, who in the spring of 1857 purchased a plot of land opposite St. Patrick's Cathedral, on which she would erect her brazenly magnificent house.[66]

At this moment in the history of the medical profession in the United States, Townsend and the councilmen formed their foundling asylum committees, and physicians gathered to advise them that a foundling asylum would provide an alternative for women who would otherwise patronize abortionists. One physician who made this point was the young surgeon Alexander Brown Mott. Dr. Mott was thirty-two in 1858 when he testified before the councilmen. He had received his M.D. just the year before, although he had already been practicing for several years at several New York hospitals. He had studied medicine in France, and he displayed a knowledge of French foundling hospitals to the councilmen. His father, with whom he practiced, was the prominent surgeon Valentine Mott. His wife was Arabella Phelps Mott, a founding member of the Nursery and Child's Hospital's board of lady managers and its secretary from about 1857 to 1863. Both must have been sources of information for him about the circumstances and states of mind of unwillingly pregnant women, both poor and well-to-do.

Later Mott would make a satisfying career for himself. As an army surgeon during the Civil War, he was present at General Lee's surrender at Appomattox. At his death an obituary described him as "one of the most noted of American surgeons." But even as early as 1858, Mott was on his way to full membership in the medical establishment's upper ranks. As his testimony demonstrates, he saw it as his responsibility to defend those ranks against those perceived as intruders.[67]

Mott presented the councilmen with a vivid picture of masses of women forthrightly, anxiously, but unsuccessfully seeking abortions from their doctors. (Many had bypassed doctors altogether and gone straight to abortionists.) In his testimony to the councilmen, Mott emphasized this theme: *There was hardly a physician in the City to whom application was not made every week to induce abortion.* Some of these appeals, Mott added, "were of a very pathetic and energetic character." When regular physicians turned women away, he said, they went to "quacks" instead. Mott described these "quacks" for the councilmen in terms that revealed his personal and professional biases. "There are many men in this city, chiefly foreigners," Mott explained, "uneducated men, who are professed abortionists. They are unable, from their ignorance of medicine, to remedy the dangerous consequences they frequently inflict." Mott also sidestepped a reality that he was surely aware of—that many abortionists, both traditional purveyors of potions and services and modern, entrepreneurial purveyors of essentially the same products—were women. When a member of the councilmen's committee asked Mott how a foundling asylum would "lessen the unnatural crime so frequently attempted by *married* women in the desire to subject themselves to the abortive process," Mott told him that if the city had a foundling asylum where women could leave their unwanted babies, they would not resort to abortion. A foundling asylum, Mott explained, was a "facility which rendered child-murder unnecessary."[68] Mott's colorful definition of abortion as child-murder, juxtaposed against his picture of masses of women seeking abortions, demonstrates the rift that had opened between doctors, who disdained abortion, and their patients, who like other Americans of this period, did not. It was physicians, not the general public, who drove the antiabortion movement that began in the 1850s.

Another physician who testified before the councilmen was David Meredith Reese. Dr. Reese had established a reputation as a warrior against medical "quacks." He was the author of an 1838 book titled *Humbugs of New York: Being a Remonstrance Against Popular Delusion; Whether in Science, Philosophy, or Religion* in which he protested against the "ultraism" of the reform-crazy Jacksonian period in all its forms. Most of Reese's irritation was provoked by the medical and psychological practices that threatened his own profession. "Any clown," he protested, "may succeed in acquiring popularity, and even wealth, by announcing himself a quack doctor!"[69]

Reese was also the author of an 1857 report on infant mortality in large cities.[70] According to Reese, half of all the deaths that occurred in large American cities during the first half of the nineteenth century were of children aged five and under. Looking at New York City, and comparing 1843 (the first year that the city inspector was required to record deaths) with 1853, Reese found that the ratio underwent an "appalling increase . . . vastly beyond the proportional increase of the population of the city."[71]

Reese included stillbirths, which included intentional abortions, in his figures for infant mortality, and therefore identified abortion as one of the factors contributing to the rise.[72] "[T]hat very many 'premature births and stillborn children' are the result of mischiefs inflicted upon mother or child or both, by awkward or unskillful attempts at abortionism," Reese asserted, "can neither be denied nor doubted."[73] Reese, like Alexander Mott, argued that one function of a foundling asylum would be to "remove the temptations to the unnatural crime of abortionism."[74]

Drs. Mott and Reese were anxious to make the point that it was not only poor, unmarried women who wanted to rid themselves of unwanted babies—married, well-to-do women did, too. Abortion, which required access to information and the means to pay a fee, was more commonly resorted to by women with means than by poor women. But the physicians read into the visible evidence produced by poor, single women—abandoned babies and victims of outright infanticide—the less easily spied misdeeds—abortion—of middle-class, married women. In his report on infant mortality, Dr. Reese commented angrily and at length at the failure of married women to embrace motherhood wholeheartedly, claiming that they chose "late hours; crowded assemblies; the excitements of the opera, the theatre, or the ball-room" over responsible maternal behavior.[75] At their worst, according to Reese, such women avoided giving birth at all by going to abortionists: "Would that it were only the profligate, or even the unfortunate of their sex, whose guilty fear or shame thus seeks to hide the evidence of their illicit amours. But the proof is overwhelming, and everywhere known to the profession, that even the married, to postpone the cares of a family, the perils of parturition, the privations and duties of maternity, and sometimes in view of the pecuniary burdens they apprehend as intolerable, consent to the use of drugs, and even the employment of instrumental and other means, to arrest early pregnancy."[76]

In his testimony to the councilmen, Alexander Mott warned: "A married woman capable of sending her child to a foundling hospital, was very capable, if not prevented, of doing worse. She would commit murder, she would procure abortion." The city councilmen agreed, asking, "who will dare even to guess at the hundreds and thousands of cases occurring every year, which are known only to the woman and her physician—occurring not in squallid haunts of poverty, but among the so-called better classes, where exposure would be infamy?"[77]

The councilmen and almshouse officials who deliberated over the possibility of building a foundling asylum understood that it would be mostly poor women, many of them domestic servants, who sought the services of their proposed institution. They sympathized with the plight of poor women, citing "sudden emergency," "the pressure of immediate and unprotected poverty," and "the desertion of a husband" as among the factors that caused them to abandon their babies.[78] Yet they were susceptible to the physicians' argument that a foundling asylum could also help to stem the epidemic of abortion among the married and comfortable. Isaac Townsend and his colleagues argued that abortion had been nearly eradicated in cities such as London and Paris, where found-ling asylums were available to take in unwanted babies. In New York, where foundling asylums were lacking, they argued, the "vile occupa-tion of the 'abortionist'" flourished.[79]

The Infant's Home versus the "Yawning Hell of Prostitution"

The city officials and their advisors had yet another use in mind for their proposed foundling asylum: they hoped it would help lead fallen women away from the brink of what Townsend's report referred to as the "yawning hell of prostitution" and back onto the safer path of sex-ual respectability. The idea that the fallen woman was permanently ru-ined was a nineteenth-century idea, one that was widespread and deeply felt.[80] Charles Loring Brace, the founder of the Children's Aid Soci-ety, gave voice to this belief when he argued that prostitution "seems to sap and rot the whole nature." Women who engaged in prostitu-tions, according to Brace, were soiled "beyond all human possibility of cleansing."[81]

The people involved in New York's foundling asylums, like many others, believed that the victim of seduction was sucked into a down-ward spiral that led to a host of terrible possibilities, including aban-doning or even killing her infant, killing herself out of shame, or turning to prostitution, which virtuous Victorians believed was the only possible employment for a woman revealed to have lost her virtue. Isaac Town-send's report described such a scenario as it was enacted by the "friend-less Irish or German emigrant girl in New York," who is seduced and abandoned and gives birth in secret: "We next read that she has taken poison, or if nothing be afterwards known, is it unfair to suppose, that, devoid of all assistance and shelter, the yawning hell of prostitution ab-sorbs, as a fatal necessity, thousands who go down to the pit, despairing of all reclamation and past all hope?"[82] Townsend's pity for the fallen woman is evident in this passage. He, as well as the other planners of the Infant's Home, believed that their proposed institution would be able to reclaim hope for virtuous women victimized by unscrupulous men, women who, according to Victorian standards, were no less ru-ined than those who knowingly participated in illicit sexual relation-ships. By accepting illegitimate babies from their mothers at birth, the Infant's Home would allow fallen women to keep their sexual histories secret and rejoin society as honorable women. The taint of sexual down-fall, which would have cast them out of honorable society and doomed them to careers as prostitutes, as the common understanding had it, would be erased.

The dangers of prostitution seemed particularly vivid to Townsend and his colleagues at the time their committee was meeting, as prostitution had entered what one historian refers to as a "halcyon period."[83] By the 1850s, prostitution had become particularly widespread and visible, spreading beyond the waterfront districts and into the heart of the city. Streets running alongside the commercial spine of Broadway contained blocks that included as many as eight houses of prostitution. Broadway itself was sprinkled with them.[84] Ordinary citizens going about their business could no longer avoid the spectacle of prostitutes going about theirs. Prostitutes who strode boldly through the city's bustling business district were perceived as being like the abortionists who mimicked the methods of businessmen by placing advertisements in the newspapers; both mocked the developing, middle-class ethic of a deliberate, watertight separation between the world of private life, women, and the home and the public life of men, commerce, and the street. Furthermore, the public displays of abortionists and prostitutes, like unwanted babies lying in the street, were public evidence that private sexual protocols were disintegrating.

The first paragraphs of the report produced by the councilmen's foundling asylum committee were not about foundlings but about prostitutes, a demonstration of the link in their minds between these two issues. Prostitution, they wrote, "intrudes everywhere, and will no longer be named in whispers, or elbowed or frowned out of sight—it is as open and as patent as drunkenness or pauperism."[85] William Sanger, the resident physician of the city-run almshouse and hospitals on Blackwell's Island and the author of the 1858 book *The History of Prostitution: Its Extent, Causes, and Effects Throughout the World*, was horrified at its new ubiquity. Prostitution, he observed, "no longer confines itself to secrecy and darkness, but boldly strides through our most thronged and elegant thoroughfares, and there, in the broad light of the sun, it jostles the pure, the virtuous, and the good."[86]

One of the most important factors contributing to the expansion of prostitution at midcentury was the presence of legions of ill-paid, underemployed, unmarried young women in the city, both immigrants and migrants from the countryside. Journalist George Foster was only one

among many who commented on the vulnerability of desperately under-
paid seamstresses to the pecuniary temptations of prostitution. "Here
are thirty thousand women and young girls," he wrote, "who work ten,
twelve, fourteen hours a day for that which scarcely, with the strictest
economy, procures them the merest necessary food and cheapest rags to
cover them." It was little wonder that these impoverished women, seeing "the daughters of infamy flaunting along in idle and fantastic splendor," asked themselves, "why shall I be thus a martyr to that virtue that
will not even bring me bread?"[87]

Sanger's book included the results of a study he had conducted of
two thousand New York prostitutes, women like the ones he met regularly in the hospitals on Blackwell's Island. He concluded that underemployment leading to poverty was one factor that made women turn to
prostitution.[88] He regretted that there were not more occupations open
to women, as well as occupations that were steadier and better paid. He
asserted "unhesitatingly and without fear of contradiction, that were
there more avenues of employment open to females there would be a
corresponding decrease in prostitution."[89] He made this case forcefully:
"The most prominent fact is that a large number of females, both oper-
atives and domestics, earn so small wages that a temporary cessation of
their business, or being a short time out of a situation, is sufficient to
reduce them to absolute distress. Provident habits are useless in their
cases; for, much as they may feel the necessity, they *have nothing to
save,* and the very day that they encounter a reverse sees them penniless.
The struggle a virtuous girl will wage against fate in such circumstances
may be conceived: it is a literal battle for life, and in the result life is too
often preserved only by the sacrifice of virtue."[90]

The almshouse governors on the foundling asylum committee turned
to William Sanger when they wanted to learn more about prostitution, a
natural step, since Isaac Townsend and William Sanger were already acquainted. It was Townsend who, as president of the Board of Governors
of the almshouse, had suggested several years earlier that Sanger get to
work on his study of prostitution. Sanger's *History of Prostitution* was
ultimately commissioned by the almshouse. When Townsend became
president of the almshouse governors' foundling asylum committee, he
borrowed Sanger's research material for his committee's report.[91]

Like the physicians who testified before the councilmen, Sanger believed there was an integral link between prostitution and the abandonment of infants. He concluded that a country's rate of infant abandon-

ment was, like its amount of prostitution, an indicator of its level of sexual morality. But he argued in favor of foundling asylums, noting that in countries such as Italy where they existed, the rate of infanticide went down, while in countries without them, such as Peru, unwanted infants were, he claimed, "cast on dunghills, to be devoured as carrion by obscene animals and birds of prey." With such evidence in hand, Sanger warned doubters to "suspend a hasty judgment on Foundling Hospitals." Townsend and his almshouse colleagues appropriated Sanger's message and also his gruesome example: "In Lima," they wrote, "where no such institution [a foundling asylum] exists, it is not unusual to notice the dead bodies of infants cast out by unfeeling mothers, and what reason have we to avert the fact that our own Hudson and the East River carry with them to the Atlantic, with the returning tide, annually, a number of equally hapless victims."[92]

The councilmen also suspected that at least some of the foundlings for whom they were considering building an asylum were the children of prostitutes.[93] Further, the girl inmates of foundling asylums were traditionally thought to be in more than ordinary danger of growing up to become prostitutes. The foundling asylums in Dublin, Cork, and Paris, for instance, were reputed to be incubators for prostitutes. This possibility worried Townsend's committee, but the members contended that, if this was true for Paris, it was probably due to the "lax morality of Parisian society." In any case, they argued, "is the accidental misuse of a humane institution any valid argument against its existence?"[94]

The connection between infant abandonment and prostitution that seemed the most treacherous to these city officials was their belief that the mothers of foundlings, as fallen women, were in danger of falling further into what they believed was the inescapable trap of prostitution. They hoped that their proposed foundling asylum would be able to rescue women from that fate, but by offering to provide a place for fallen women to rid themselves of their babies, they opened themselves up to the accusation that they were promoting sin. The members of the two committees and their supporters argued vigorously against the accusation that foundling asylums smoothed the way for sexual sinners by providing them with a place to rid themselves of the evidence of their misdeeds. James Wynne, a medical statistician who testified before the councilmen, wielded his statistical tables to prove that "the causes of illegitimacy lie beyond the influence of foundling hospitals, and are in no way affected by the existence or absence of these establishments." Townsend's committee claimed combatively that "in demolishing the assertion that Foundling Hospitals have a tendency to encourage licentiousness, one fact is worth a thousand theories." They then presented not one, but a string of facts and asked "whether even the records of that noble institution, the Sunday School, can produce a more cheering picture" than a foundling asylum for promoting virtue. It was the absence of foundling hospitals, not their presence, Townsend and his colleagues concluded, that led to "the commission of graver offences; intentional abortion, child murder, and all the evils, frequently death itself, resulting to the woman, who has no asylum to hide her shame and amend her life."[95]

Mary Du Bois and the Nursery and Child's Hospital

The unforgivable transgressions of women, the men on the committees believed, rather than the excusable missteps of men, were at the heart of the foundling problem. Both committees, believing that foundlings were a female problem, felt that women ought to be in charge of the proposed institution.[96] Isaac Townsend went further. For the temple of art and charity he envisioned, women were to be the priestesses, since "for them music, painting, sculpture, every art, every science of civilized life, start into activity at the tap of the wand of that potent beneficent fairy, that irresistible enchantress—WOMAN."[97] Yet despite Townsend's enthusiasm for female involvement, the only woman either committee invited to participate in its deliberations was Mary Du Bois, founder and "first directress" of the Nursery and Child's Hospital.

Mary Delafield Du Bois was born in London in 1813 of a prosperous New York family. Her banker father, John Delafield, and later her husband, attorney Cornelius Du Bois, provided her with important ties to the city's mercantile elite; her uncle, the prominent physician Edward Delafield, tied her to its medical community. Dr. Delafield was a consulting physician at the nursery from its founding in 1854 until his death twenty years later. These years overlapped with his tenure as president of the prestigious College of Physicians and Surgeons. The children and parturient women of the nursery benefited from Delafield's medical specialties in obstetrics and ophthalmology. They may also have gained from whatever compassion he learned from the catastrophes of his first marriage; all six children born during that marriage predeceased him, as did his wife.[98]

Mary Du Bois was raised in New York after the family returned from England in 1820 and was educated at the Litchfield Female Academy in Connecticut. The Litchfield Female Academy was one of the many new schools, including schools for girls, that were founded after the American revolution to create educated citizens for the new republic. In addition to feminine training in needlework, painting, and dancing, the school offered girls such as Mary Delafield a relatively rich offering of academic subjects. This was the sort of education that could make an intelligent and ambitious girl like Mary Delafield (and author Catharine Beecher, another Litchfield alumna) restless and dissatisfied in a world that could only imagine a future consisting of wifely duties, motherhood, and domestic seclusion. The academy also offered proximity to the marriageable young men of the Litchfield Law School. It was there that she met her husband, Cornelius Du Bois, also a member of a New York mercantile family. After their marriage, the Du Boises settled in the genteel neighborhood of Gramercy Park, where they raised their three children.[99]

In 1854, Mary Du Bois founded the Nursery for the Children of Poor Women (which in 1857 was renamed the Nursery and Child's Hospital) for the children of wet nurses and other poor working women.[100] Women who made ends meet by hiring themselves out to work as live-in wet nurses for well-to-do families often had to place their own babies with even poorer women. The result was that wet nurses' babies often died of malnourishment, mistreatment, or disease. At least one physician of this period believed that, "As a rule, all infants of wet nurses die, and generally from neglect."[101] As the nursery itself needed wet nurses, early on it began admitting mothers with their babies and required them to feed one additional baby along with their own.

Mary Du Bois modeled the nursery on New York's many existing woman-headed charities, and she had ties through two of its charter managers to at least one of them, the New York Asylum for Lying-In Women, a maternity hospital for poor married women that had been founded in 1823. These charities, influenced by the evangelical revivals of the first decades of the nineteenth century, typically aided poor women and children. Their chief officers were women, some of whom also took the title "first directress," and like the nursery they were administered by all-female boards of managers.[102]

The managerial and executive roles that women took on at such charities were an antidote to the civil impotence that law and custom imposed on women in a public world run by men. During the nineteenth century, women could not vote, serve on juries, run for political office, or train for and practice the great majority of professions. When a woman married, her property passed into the control of her husband. Any money she earned belonged to him. And if she was divorced or widowed, she frequently lost custody of her children to her husband or a male guardian. Over the course of the nineteenth century, states passed married women's property acts that addressed these inequities gradually. These acts allowed women to revive somewhat from the "civil death" that marriage had traditionally condemned them to. But while the bonds were loosened, they were not fully untied, and both law and custom continued to limit women's actions in the public realm.[103]

The world of antebellum female charity, in whose traditions the nursery was rooted, could be a liberating environment for the (mostly) married women who ran these organizations. When women founded charities and had them chartered by the state, they acquired rights as members of a genderless corporation that they did not have as individuals. They could buy land, sign leases, order the construction of buildings, manage personnel, and control funds. They also gained the confidence to claim their constitutional right to petition legislators. Representatives of New York's women's charities traveled regularly to Albany to convince members of the state legislature to charter their organizations, grant them funds, and pass laws that favored their goals.

The charities organized by women in cities during the antebellum years evolved over the course of the century into virtually a national welfare system, the country's first. These organizations, fueled by the unpaid labor of married, middle-class women, took on work left undone in a country with no established church and no national tradition of charity. In New York City, where there were so many poor strangers, the city and state were particularly willing to delegate the work of succor to private, religious charities. In this environment, ambitious, educated women such as Mary Du Bois took on their duties like a force unleashed.[104]

In 1856, the nursery added a children's hospital. After being housed in temporary quarters for two years, the renamed Nursery and Child's

The Nursery and Child's Hospital, corner of Lexington Avenue and East Fifty-first Street, ca. 1868. Courtesy of the National Library of Medicine.

Hospital, with assistance from city and state, moved to new buildings on Fifty-first Street and Lexington Avenue in 1858.[105] The nursery also sprouted some auxiliary functions. By 1859 it had established a free, public dispensary that was attached to the hospital. And for the benefit of the poor mothers living in its wards (as well as for the city's middle- to upper-class women, who were continually in search of household help), the nursery opened a "servants' school" (which also trained girls from the Children's Aid Society), as well as a placement service for wet nurses.[106]

The nursery was pathbreaking in that it was the first private institution for children in New York to admit infants and young children under two or three. Yet Du Bois was conservative in her attitude toward foundlings and other illegitimate babies, whom at first she refused to admit. She found, however, that wet nurses, the very women she wanted to help, were often single mothers, and that these women appeared with their babies at the nursery's door. According to Du Bois, the "pitiable condition" of their babies caused her to relax her restriction against illegitimates and to join with Isaac Townsend in his plan to build a foundling asylum.[107]

Du Bois later regretted the nursery's initial decision to exclude foundlings. "Can it be believed," she wrote at her institution's twenty-fifth anniversary, "that when the Nursery was founded, our minds were so narrow, our hearts so numb, that we turned away the 'waifs and strays,' so much more to be pitied than those who had mothers—however poor and destitute. . . . The very thought of that time of strict rule, is the only blot which causes a blush to rise as we review our record of charity."[108]

Mary Du Bois's experience of running New York's only institution that accepted infants was probably what made the city officials tap her for advice. The three-man councilmen's committee even left their rooms at City Hall to pay a visit to the Nursery and Child's Hospital on St. Mark's Place and were pleased with what they found there.[109] But it was not her own experiences that Mary Du Bois presented when she testified before the councilmen. Instead, Mary Du Bois, like Isaac Townsend, looked to the London Foundling Hospital as an important model for her work. It was not art and music that attracted her, but the hospital's moral values. She tried to make these a part of the policies of the nursery, and she hoped the councilmen would do the same at their proposed foundling asylum.

Unlike foundling asylums in Catholic countries, which accepted all foundlings offered anonymously and indiscriminately until the second half of the nineteenth century, the London Foundling Hospital never had enough room or money to support all of the babies that women in London and its surrounding area would have liked to abandon. The difference had to do with funding and government commitment. While foundling asylums in countries such as France and Italy were funded by governments, the London Foundling Hospital was privately run and funded, except for a few years in the mid-eighteenth century when the government stepped in to support it as an experiment.

Initially, the London Foundling Hospital relied on chance, rather than moral discrimination, in its admissions process. In 1742, one year after it opened, the London Foundling Hospital put in place a lottery-like admissions procedure in order to limit the number of children admitted. Part of the procedure involved a system of ballots in the form of black, white, and red balls. Women seeking to be relieved of their babies assembled at the hospital on an appointed day, sat on benches placed around the walls of a reception room hung with paintings, and chose a ball at random. Those who chose white balls were allowed to hand over their babies (if the babies could pass a medical examination); those who chose black balls were sent away; and those who chose red balls could draw again if any spaces were left at the end of what must have been an excruciatingly suspenseful process.

In 1763, the governors of the London Foundling Hospital added a layer of complexity to their already uncomfortable admissions process. Now they began making applicants petition for the right to have their babies admitted before they were allowed to advance to the balloting phase. Women had to answer a series of questions on a printed form and appear for an interview with a committee of hospital governors. Applicants, most of whom were poor young women working as domestic servants, were required to provide the hospital's governors with information about their babies' fathers and, humiliatingly, details about the sexual relationships that had produced the babies. They had to demonstrate that they felt an appropriate degree of shame over what they had done (a woman could demonstrate her shame by proving that she had striven to keep her pregnancy secret). And they had to prove —testimonial letters were submitted for this purpose—that they had enough support from families or employers to get back on their feet again. The collection of this kind of information signaled a shift in the hospital's goals. Instead of simply seeking to save the lives of infants abandoned on the street, as Thomas Coram had originally intended, the London Foundling Hospital adopted the new mission of reforming fallen women. With only limited space available, the hospital chose its babies based on their mothers' ability to prove to the governors that they could be restored to "a course of Industry and Virtue." When in 1801 the hospital ruled that only illegitimate babies would be received henceforth, it further cemented its commitment to the reform of fallen women. At the same time, the hospital administration made clear that its members believed that the only "proper" foundling was an illegitimate baby.[110]

Mary Du Bois eschewed the ceremony and paraphernalia of the London Foundling Hospital. Her institution also accepted mothers, while the London Foundling Hospital separated mothers and babies. But Du Bois retained the London Foundling Hospital's spirit in the admissions policies she formulated for the nursery. To be admitted with their babies, women had to be of "previously good character" and penitent.

Women pregnant with a second illegitimate child were not admitted. Mary Du Bois defended this policy with an acknowledgment that not every woman could be reformed: "[W]hen we refuse (as we *must*) to open our doors to unmarried women in their second confinements," she wrote, "we see that there is 'in the lowest deep, a lower deep.'"[111]

Shame was important to Mary Du Bois and the lady mangers of the nursery, just as it was to the governors of the London Foundling Hospital, since she and the others believed that it was the quality that made these women worth saving. Alice T. Barlow, an officer of the nursery, went farther by suggesting that only the unmarried mothers with the finer sensibilities, those capable of feeling shame at their condition, were driven to murder their illicitly born children. "[I]t is well known," she wrote, "that it is not by the lowest or most degraded that the crime of infanticide is oftenest committed: it is those in whose breasts the sense of shame is not only not wholly dead, but on whom it inflicts its keenest pangs, that this temptation so often haunts and finally overpowers." Mary Du Bois claimed that the almshouse was good enough for those women "who have no shame or modesty left which would prevent their seeking refuge in a public charity."

Du Bois referred here to unmarried mothers who chose to openly present themselves to the almshouse so that they could take advantage of its assistance. In order to make this system work for them, however, women had to expose their plight to the almshouse authorities and name the fathers of their babies so the almshouse could pursue them for bastardy bonds. Many did so rather than sink into the destitution that might have forced them to abandon their children. Others may have had more personal and complicated motives for wanting to seek help from the almshouse. A committed member of the city's demimonde such as Sarah Jane Hannah, for instance, the circus performer who may have had a son with theater-owner William Niblo, would certainly not have been the kind of woman Mary Du Bois was interested in helping. The women Du Bois sought to receive at the nursery were a different breed, not, she suggested, the common run of immigrant slum dwellers, and certainly not acrobats in tights, but virtuous country girls who had come to hide their accidental pregnancies in what she called "the vortex of the city." Only these American-born women, in her opinion, possessed the moral sensitivity needed to understand the blackness of the crime they had committed. They were women whose "dread of discovery is greater than their love of life."[112]

When Mary Du Bois appeared before the councilmen's foundling asylum committee, she presented them with an "interesting statement of the Foundling Hospital in London, an institution similar to which she deems will be adapted to the city of New York," the councilmen reported. Du Bois described the "strict discrimination" practiced in London, and argued that in New York, as in London, there "must be a strong probability the reception of the child will be the means of rescuing the mother from that course of sin and shame on the brink of which she stands."[113]

Two of the councilmen's advisors did not agree with Mary Du Bois's easy conflation of foundlings with illegitimacy. One of these was Samuel Halliday. In his testimony, Halliday told the councilmen that he believed, based on his observations, that not more than one-quarter to one-third of almshouse infants were illegitimate. In light of that estimate, he recommended calling the new institution by the neutral name of Infant's Home rather than Foundling Hospital. David Meredith Reese maintained similarly that legitimately born children should not be housed in an institution that was openly identified as a foundling asylum. He argued that the city should establish two institutions, one called the Foundling Hospital and the other the Infant's Home, so that the legitimate children could be, in effect, quarantined from the illegitimate. He made both medical and moral arguments to support this suggestion. Half of all illegitimate children, he claimed, "were born constitutionally diseased, and it would be imprudent to allow healthy children to live with them." Not to speak, he added, "of the odium which would attach through life to any one who should emanate from a Foundling Hospital."[114]

In the end, the councilmen were less interested in the semantic debate —they called the institution they decided to build the Infant's Home but gutted the distinction of meaning by making it serve only illegitimate children—than they were in the cause of fallen womanhood, which they indicated when they decided to hand over the proposed institution to Mary Du Bois. In late November 1858, the councilmen recommended building its Infant's Home on city-owned lots adjacent to the nursery's own newly erected building on Fifty-first Street between Lexington and Third Avenues, in the northern, still sparsely populated reaches of Manhattan. They allocated twenty-five thousand dollars for the project. Administration of the publicly funded Infant's Home was to be handed over entirely to the Nursery and Child's Hospital. The Infant's

Home would be the city's first foundling asylum. There, mothers would learn to mend their ways by emulating the moral example set by the lady managers—middle- to upper-class women such as Mary Du Bois and Arabella Mott. As at the London Foundling Hospital, the Infant's Home would admit only those babies whose mothers could demonstrate their candidacy for "entire reform."[115]

The planned Infant's Home had many expectations to fulfill, from the curbing of abortion and prostitution to the promotion of high culture. But at a time when New York was increasingly compared to London as a center of urban squalor and vice, the London Foundling Hospital, whose entrance policies were meant to curb the sexual misbehavior of poor women, looked like the best possible model to copy, according to the councilmen on the foundling asylum committee and their influential advisor, Mary Du Bois.

The Dangers of "Mercenary Maternity": The Mary Cullough Scandal

Only a few months after the councilmen resolved to build their Infant's Home, the press decorated the city's breakfast tables with a scandal involving almshouse nurses and their foundling charges. The incident that attracted the papers' attention occurred in late January or early February 1859. A gentleman named J. W. Barker took a policeman and went to visit the home of a servant, Mary Cullough, to retrieve some stolen household items.[116] Yet what Barker saw at Cullough's apartment on East Thirty-fourth Street made him forget his lost bedclothes and shirt collars: on dirty beds in Cullough's apartment lay three ill and starving babies apparently at the point of death. All three were almshouse babies, and Mary Cullough, in addition to performing domestic day labor in Barker's home, was an almshouse nurse.

Horace Greeley's *New York Tribune* made the most of the story. Under the headline "Murder of the Innocents," the *Tribune* described the children's condition: "They were found in a dark room! They reeked with filth, strangers to fresh water! Their beds, and their rags stank with foulness! They had not strength to cry! Not even if pinched! They were motionless with exhaustion! Their limbs were shrunk to an inch in diameter, and their hands looked like bird's claws! One of the little innocents, in the agonies of starvation, had sucked its arm to an unnatural shape! They had evidently been drugged! Their eyes were idiotic and ghastly! And all within a stone's throw of the palaces! Do you hear, mothers, who live in the great houses—close beside you—systematized child-murder by slow degrees!"[117]

"And now," the *Tribune* concluded, "shall we have a reform, or only a spasm of horror?" The *Tribune,* as well as the other papers that reported on the incident, made much of the baby who sucked on its arm. The heavy symbolism of this was not lost on *Harper's Weekly,* which reported that the resulting "excrescence" could be compared to a "female nipple," access to which was the very thing this baby lacked.[118]

The governors of the almshouse—who had just devoted so much effort to rectifying this very problem—were furious at the *Tribune* for exposing this lapse. Less than a week after the article came out, the governors met and heard affidavits gathered from witnesses to Mary Cullough's good character. The witnesses included neighbors; a fifteen-year-old girl who worked for Cullough, caring for the children; Aletta Frost, a "visitor" the almshouse governors had appointed to check up on the babies at nurse around the city; William Bevins, a doctor who had visited the apartment to see the babies; and a woman who kept cows in the still relatively pastoral Yorkville section of the Upper East Side of Manhattan who supplied Cullough with milk.

Almshouse governor Washington Smith, who had been a member of Isaac Townsend's three-man foundling asylum committee and was now the chair of the almshouse committee that oversaw the Department of Outdoor Poor, passionately defended his department. Referring to the *Tribune*'s description of the baby who sucked its arm and raised what looked like a nipple, Smith attacked the paper for its sentimental manipulation of this gruesome manifestation: "Now, how perfectly figurative this is, how perfectly figurative!" he raged, "It is a beautiful theme to go to the tender-hearted mother and kind parent and harrow up the feelings of each and every one of them, and of every person who has a sympathy for these little suffering ones of the city." Smith argued that if the babies the almshouse farmed out to city nurses were sickly, that was how they were received, and it was not the fault of the nurses or the department. "Every member of this Board knows," he ranted, "and every gentleman who visits this department, if they will observe, knows that we have many children brought here who are constitutionally diseased; many of them are almost perfectly destroyed with scrofula or with syphilis from their parents; so that when you take them up into your hands you have nothing but a putrefying mass of sores; I have witnessed that myself."

Dr. William Bevins, the doctor who had visited Mary Cullough, seconded Smith's impression. He testified that he believed that Cullough was so trusted a nurse that the city gave her the most hopeless children to care for. Most of the children in her charge died, he revealed, but "I did not consider it her fault," he told the governors, because "her children were *debilitated*."[119]

Governor Smith suggested angrily, and his colleagues concurred, that the *Tribune* publish the proceedings of their meeting with its testimony on behalf of Mary Cullough. The *Tribune* did so, but they also assembled their own witnesses for the other side, resurrected William Mott and Samuel Halliday's report of two years earlier (which the two investigators, on reading the *Tribune*'s first article about the case, visited the paper's office to deliver on their own initiative), and published the whole thing under this blaring headline: "The Murder of the Innocents. Revenge of the Governors. Abusive Tirades Against the Press. The Other Side. Children are Crucified. Disease, Dirt and Death."[120] The witnesses assembled by the *Tribune* included a group of neighbors less friendly to Cullough than those the almshouse governors had found as well as some the governors had already heard, including the almshouse visitor Aletta Frost and Catharine MacMahon, the Yorkville dairywoman, who this time gave somewhat different stories. The collective portrait of Cullough these witnesses painted was of a woman who drank, had a violent temper, entertained bad company late at night, and mistreated the children she took from the almshouse.

One of Cullough's neighbors reported that she had bragged about being able to get as many children to nurse from the city as she wanted. Cullough accomplished this with bribery. The neighbor, Mrs. McCartee, claimed that Cullough had bought a scarf with a "bad two dollar bill" and used it to pay off "some one who had something to do with giving out the children." This practice was not limited to Mary Cullough; Mrs. McCartee testified that another woman who lived in the building also worked as a nurse for the almshouse and that she, Mrs. McCartee, had loaned this woman fifty cents, which she saw the woman give "to the person who carries out the children from the Hall."[121] It would be a decade before the Tweed Ring reached the height of its power, but bribery's greasy give and take was already oiling the wheels of New York's municipal machinery. The testimony of Mrs. McCartee suggests that the almshouse's system for boarding its foundlings with poor women depended, like so many other city systems, on graft.

The *Tribune* also heard from Cullough herself. In the midst of the accusations made against her, Cullough's statements are oddly unemotional, suggesting either the practiced poise of the habitual malefactor, skilled at dodging uncomfortable questions, or the exhausted apathy of a woman beaten down by life. She made no effort to defend herself against her accusers, but instead offered that she was separated from her husband, a drunkard, and that she had one child of her own. In addition to her work for the almshouse, she explained, she did washing for Mr. Barker and other households. She made no effort to refute Barker's accusation that she had robbed his house.

Amid this tangle of testimonies, it is difficult to know if Mary Cullough was the murderer her accusers said she was or if she was doing the best she could in difficult conditions, according to her own less-than-genteel standards. That her life was difficult is made evident by the fact that she was poor enough to take in babies from the almshouse for the paltry fee of one dollar per week (a rate, the *Times* bitterly remarked, "at which it would not be easy to keep a thoroughbred pointer in perfect condition") and to give in to the temptation to steal odd items of clothing from Mr. Barker's laundry.[122]

On the Saturday after "The Murder of the Innocents" appeared in the *Tribune,* Washington Smith, still not satisfied that the reputation of his department had been restored, led a small delegation of almshouse officials and newspaper reporters on a tour of some of the homes of the women hired by the almshouse to care for its abandoned babies. Yet the tour did not give visitors the rosy view that Smith perhaps intended, as what they discovered was very much the same as what Mott and Halliday had found two years earlier. Some children were even as ill and neglected as those found in Mary Cullough's apartment. On Third Street, the delegation entered a building whose ground floor was occupied by a liquor shop—a marker, to any urban reformer of this era, of the evil of intemperance. They climbed to the top floor, on the way up becoming increasingly overwhelmed by the stenches "altogether too complicated to be analyzed" and unnerved at the sight of the "dirty and curious faces" peeking out from behind doors to see them ascend. At the top they were greeted by what the *Times*'s reporter called a "dirty Irishwoman." She showed them into her dimly lit and imperfectly cleaned room, where the group found two almshouse babies in advanced stages of illness. Horrified, the group fled back down the stairs. "The sight," the *Times*'s reporter wrote, "with the close, damp air of the room, was sickening, and the pure atmosphere outside, which was reached as speedily as possible, was the best and surest relief."[123]

In other homes, however, it was apparent that the babies were as healthy, happy, and comfortable as these poor families could make them. Mrs. Ward, a "woman of very respectable appearance," kept her home on Avenue C tidy and "tolerably clean." Her oldest child cried when the visitors lifted almshouse baby Rachel Logan out of her cradle to be inspected, as the child had grown attached to Rachel and feared that the visitors would take her away. On East Thirteenth Street, twenty-month-old John McMahon was "dirty and fat; eating beefsteak and screaming between mouthfuls. Well enough off," the *Tribune* observed dryly.

A Mr. Goss, whose children's hair was uncombed and whose table was piled with dirty dishes, was proud of the progress made by the baby his wife had taken from the almshouse a year earlier. When the delegation asked what the baby was called, the Goss children yelled out, "Horace Greeley," causing the visitors to explode in laughter, certainly their only opportunity to do so that day. " 'We've taken as good care of it as we have of our own childers,' " Goss told them, bouncing the baby up and down. The *Times* described this baby as "stupid" and "sickly-looking," but the *Tribune*'s reporter, perhaps in tribute to his employer, described young Horace as "thriving and fat," and commented that he was "as well cared for as the average of children in that condition of life."[124]

This spate of press attention not only uncovered for a wider public the welfare of the abandoned babies the almshouse sent out to nurse, but also the mire of conflicts and animosities stirred up by the practice of farming out babies in class-divided, ethnically antagonistic, politically corrupt New York. For example, Aletta Frost, the visitor paid by the almshouse to inspect babies in the homes of their nurses, was viewed as an enemy by the women who nursed for the almshouse. Almshouse nursing was a business for these women, and Mrs. Frost had, and used, the power to take away infants and the money they brought. The fact that she redistributed some of these infants to herself and her own mother doubtless also detracted from her popularity. A widow still wearing mourning for her husband, Mrs. Frost was assailed with taunts of "the d[amne]d black b[itc]h" when she went into the nurses' neighborhoods. She feared to go there after dark, she said, as the women threatened her life.[125]

Press accounts also hinted at threats and suggestions made to the witnesses for Mary Cullough. Mary Hyde, one of Cullough's neighbors, reported that "a person" visited her to say that if she spoke on behalf of Cullough—which she did—all of the other neighbors would go against her and that it would be "the worse" for her. Her unidentified visitor elaborated that he "did not like to see American women taking part with the low Irish." Aletta Frost received a visit from Samuel Halliday, who demonstrated a surprising facility with the tactics of forceful persuasion by warning her against testifying on Cullough's behalf, arguing that since the almshouse governors had "got themselves into a scrape . . . let them get out of it the best way they can."

The doctor's statements had also been tampered with; almshouse governor Benjamin Pinckney admitted that Dr. Bevins had been "made to say" that he visited more almshouse children than he really had. Along with the other threats made over the course of this incident, and the apparently routine bribes that Cullough and others were said to have offered to almshouse officials, this reveals that intimidation and corruption were a part of the process of placing out almshouse babies.[126]

Tensions between reformist newspapers such as the *Times* and the *Tribune* and the city government also came into play during this incident. Aletta Frost embodied these tensions when she gave a "blowing up," or angry piece of her mind, to a *Tribune* reporter she happened to meet in the Jefferson Market courthouse.[127] So did the anti-Irish feeling that was integral to this conflict between the reformist press and the municipal machine, which was driven by immigrants' votes. The anti-Irish tone of the Mary Cullough scandal is made explicit by the illustration that appeared in *Harper's Weekly* with an article on the topic. In it, Cullough appears gorilla-like, stooped and heavy browed, with clawlike hands, while Mr. Barker and the policeman look entirely human. The artist was employing a standard anti-Irish caricature of this era: the simianized Irishman.

English cartoonists and caricaturists first began drawing the Irishman as gorilla in the 1840s, but the practice reached a height in England and the United States in the 1860s and lasted into the twentieth century. Illustrated magazines such as *Harper's* were full of drawings of ferocious Irish men and women with low brows and prognathous jaws. These drawings were the product of a combustible mixture of science, pseudo-

Mr. Barker discovers starving almshouse babies in the home of
baby farmer Mary Cullough. Note her simianized features and the
spartan character of her room. *Harper's Weekly,* February 19,
1859. Collection of the New-York Historical Society, 55120.

science, and anxious social conditions. Darwin's *Origin of Species* was
published in 1859, and even prior to its appearance scientists had begun a debate about the beginnings of life. British scientific expeditions
abroad had made the English aware of the existence of the gorilla,
among other things, and they combined this knowledge with new ideas
that linked race with cranial dimensions, as well as with older ideas
about the relationship of physiognomy to character. All of these factors
contributed to the atmosphere that made the development of such a caricature possible. The proposal that humans were descended from apes
rather than from Adam and Eve was, in a century of unsettling change,
one of the most unsettling things for many people to accept. In New
York, where genteel native-born Protestants saw the immigrant Irish as
a dangerous element (as in Britain, where the "wild Irish" were agitat-
ing for home rule), it was more comfortable for readers of magazines
such as *Harper's* or *Frank Leslie's Illustrated Weekly* to believe that the
Irish, rather than they, were descended from apes.[128]

Harper's also slandered the city's poor women, many of them Irish

NEW YORK AS A NURSING-MOTHER TO HER FOUNDLINGS.
(See the Evidence in the CARLOCK *Case.)*

In this conceptualization of Mary Cullough, she wears a dress edged with dollar signs to indicate her mercenary character. Baby farmers were accused of using laudanum, a preparation made from opium (bottle at left), to drug babies into silence. *Harper's Weekly,* February 26, 1859. Collection of the New-York Historical Society, 77823d.

immigrants, when it editorialized, "It is absurd to expect sagacious nursing or liberal treatment from the class of women who, in the city, take Almshouse children to nurse at a dollar a week. They would be false to their condition, and exceptions to their class, if they exhibited a kindliness, generosity, or care to the infants hired out to them. It is natural that they should neglect, and, in most cases, maltreat the poor little creatures." Such "slovenly, besotted, wicked women," the *Tribune* added, could not be trusted to nurse the city's tender infant charges. The *Times* was more sympathetic toward the "poverty-stricken souls upon whom this great Metropolis has thrust the awful responsibilities of a mercenary maternity" but, like the others, it concluded that the system was irreparably broken. The solution, the papers argued, was to remove the city's foundlings from their nurses and place them in a foundling asylum such as the one the councilmen had just agreed to build.[129]

Building the Infant's Home

On a stormy day in December 1859, a group assembled at the corner of Lexington Avenue and Fifty-first Street to witness the laying of the cornerstone of New York's first foundling asylum, the Infant's Home. Mary Du Bois was nominally in charge of moving the stone into place but, the *New York Times* informed its readers, the hefting was done "really and truly by two laborers." The Rev. Henry Montgomery of the Church of the Incarnation presided over the ceremony, and his address echoed the themes Du Bois had presented to the councilmen. The soon-to-be built Infant's Home, he told the sparse, shivering group gathered around the cornerstone, was "designed for the illegitimate children of fallen women of previous good character, whose reception into such an asylum would in all probability, be the means of replacing the mother in the course of virtue and in the way of an honest livelihood." These goals were "precisely the same," according to Montgomery, as those professed by the London Foundling Hospital. The *Times* blamed the poor turnout on the stormy weather. Much worse weather for the new institution was soon to threaten.[130]

The first disaster to befall the Infant's Home was the loss of two of its most visionary supporters. In April 1860, Isaac Townsend died. Mary Du Bois eulogized him, remembering his "kind heart" and lamenting that "he died before his desire [of opening a foundling hospital] was accomplished." Even if Townsend had lived, however, it is not clear what his role at the Infant's Home might have been, since in 1860, the year of his death, the city abolished the Almshouse Department, the administrative body that oversaw the almshouse, and dismissed its Board of Governors. In its place the city created the Department of Public Charities and Correction, which was headed by four commissioners appointed by the city comptroller. One of the earliest acts of the new administration was to remove all of its foundlings and other babies from the homes of the poor women who served as their nurses. Since the Infant's Home was still under construction, the babies were all taken to the almshouse on Blackwell's Island. This step appears to have been a response to the depredations uncovered during the Mary Cullough scandal of 1859. Certainly it was a realization of the worst fears of the child who cried when threatened with the possibility of losing her foster sister, almshouse baby Rachel Logan. It must also have been a blow to the many poor women who had been used to counting on the almshouse for work.[131]

In any case, the death of Townsend deprived the future Infant's Home of a steadfast supporter. Then, in January 1861, Mary Du Bois resigned from her post as "first directress" of the nursery.[132] She gave ill health as a reason, and the diarist George Templeton Strong, who was her neighbor in Gramercy Park and also the husband of one of the nursery's managers, Ellen Ruggles Strong, made this insightful observation in his diary: "Had that lady ordinary health and physical vigor instead of being, as she is, a mere embodiment of 'Neurology,' a bundle of active diseases and morbid changes of structure, unable to speak but in a whisper, and paralyzed suddenly at intervals by disease of the heart, she'd found a dynasty and die Imperatrix of the United States with a secured succession to her issue, therein probably beating Louis Napoleon. I look with absolute awe on her."[133]

Other observers made similar comments about Du Bois's powerful but damaged personality. Abraham Jacobi, a physician who came to work at the nursery during the Civil War, and who came to know Du Bois afterward, described the "power of that strong and reckless mind, whom so many either know too little or fear too much."[134] Jacobi may or may not have known about an 1855 incident in which a group of the nursery's lady managers accused Mary Du Bois of high-handedness. Soon after the nursery opened, a faction on the board protested that they were "never consulted," that "the meetings are only held, that the ladies may approve, but are in no way to express a contrary opinion," and "the Ladies are reluctant to express an opinion at the meeting lest they should be considered *personal* or lest they should be *put down* or made to feel uncomfortable and therefore, though the ladies disapprove, they never speak." Du Bois, who penned this account of the controversy, reacted to the criticisms with blind bravado. "I think I can look around me with confidence," she replied to her accusers, "and feel there must be very *few* who *imagine* I could wish to put *any* one down or make any one uncomfortable."[135]

Strong's description of Mary Du Bois's condition brings to mind what neurologist George M. Beard would term "neurasthenia" after the Civil War. Neurasthenia was the name applied to the vague yet debilitating collection of physical and psychological symptoms experienced by many women beginning around the middle of the nineteenth century. Neurasthenics had fainting fits, headaches, bouts of weakness, and other incapacitating symptoms that could not be explained by the presence of any disease that physicians of that era could identify. When it occurred in women such as Mary Du Bois, neurasthenia might have been a physical manifestation of the frustration that resulted when forceful, ambitious personalities collided against contemporary expectations of silence and passivity in women.[136]

Even though she was what her neighbor George Templeton Strong called an "embodiment of 'Neurology,'" and despite the whispery voice that Strong evokes for us, Du Bois founded and ran an institution and wrested funds for it from the state legislature. She accomplished all of this with what Strong described as "the application of her indomitable will." Du Bois's colleagues at the nursery also used the word "indomitable" to describe their leader; they recalled how "all obstacles to the success of the nursery she has founded and firmly established were crushed beneath the indomitable determination to work out this problem of helping tender, neglected infancy to live."[137] Yet Du Bois fled into infirmity. Du Bois unsteadily tread the line between *being* powerful and effective and *seeming* fragile and helpless. She alternated between action—a particularly female kind of caring action on behalf of needy others—and the fragility that was positively associated with Victorian femininity.

Most damaging to the future of the Infant's Home was the outbreak of the Civil War. The war was all absorbing, drawing away both the funds and the personal energies of the reformers of previous decades. The war also affected the poor, easing poverty for destitute men, who were absorbed by the army, while increasing it for the women and children left behind. The lady managers of the nursery were burdened and distracted by the war. They took in children whose parents were "rendered destitute" as a result of the conflict, and they complained about the "new and unusual trials" the war imposed.[138]

Interestingly, the foundling issue played a very small part in the sectional debate that took place before the war when a few proslavery voices sought to make New York's foundlings a part of their argument against what they believed was the depravity of the urban north. The proslavery polemicist George Fitzhugh, for instance, raised the specter of Jean-Jacques Rousseau to condemn what he considered to be the moral laxity of the North. "John James Rousseau, from whom Mr. Jefferson, Mr. Franklin, and all of our new lights, learned their philosophy, sent all his children to the foundling hospital so soon as they were born, and never inquired about them afterward. Now, all Yankee philosophy and morality (there is no Yankee religion) tends to this end."[139]

In the same vein, a New York organization that called itself the "Pro-Unionist, or Anti-Abolitionist Society" advertised a pamphlet gleefully titled *Abolitionism Unvailed! Hypocrisy Unmasked! And Knavery Scourged! Luminously Portraying the Formal Hocusses, Whining Philanthropists, Moral Coquets, Practical Atheists, and the Hollow-Hearted Swindlers of Labor, 'yclept the "Northern Abolitionists,"* which they promised would contain "a graphic account of a foundling hospital in this city for black and colored girls." When the pamphlet was published it contained no such description, and, in fact, there was no such institution, but for this group New York's foundlings created an irresistible opportunity to charge northern society with immorality.[140]

The Infant's Home was completed just before the war broke out and was quickly requisitioned as a hospital for wounded soldiers. So it remained for the duration.[141] But the plan, although suspended, remained clear. The new asylum, by accepting the babies of fallen women with and without their mothers, would help not only to combat infant abandonment and infanticide, but also to address abortion, prostitution, and even baby-farming. All of these were disturbing female behaviors that were on the rise, and each represented a threat to evolving ideas about the sanctity of motherhood, childhood, and the home. As for the foundlings themselves, Mary Du Bois, the city officials, and their physician advisors realized that there was not much they could do to keep them alive, but the Infant's Home represented their will to try.

4

"The Basket at the Door"
The Foundling Asylums Open

The Civil War put the plan to open the newly built Infant's Home on hold. Two of its principal advocates, Isaac Townsend and Mary Du Bois, were gone from the scene. The war monopolized all the money, time, and attention that charitable and reform-minded New Yorkers had to give. The new building was being occupied not by needy babies but by wounded soldiers. And immediately after the war, since the building and the lots it sat on were owned by the city, the nursery had to fight to get the building back. Later Mary Du Bois recalled that "many had seen how admirably this building was arranged, and it was only after many contests, that it was finally restored and occupied as originally designed." At war's end Du Bois rose from her sickbed to reclaim her place as head of the nursery and lead these "contests," the prize for which was a perpetual lease for the building.[1]

In December 1865, the Infant's Home finally opened its doors to foundlings and their mothers. The new building included a lying-in asylum, or maternity ward, which "enabled us," the nursery's secretary wrote, "to strike still deeper at the root of the evil . . . our earnest hope and endeavor being to save women from the ghastly crimes of infanticide and suicide, by first bringing them succor, comfort, and hope in their agony and trial, and then to commence the work of reformation."[2]

By 1865, the nursery had moved well beyond its original mission of assisting wet nurses and their children. In addition to its children's hospital, new foundling asylum, and lying-in asylum, Du Bois's nursery also had a dispensary, a servant's school, and a wet-nurse placement service. And as time went on and the parentless children in its care grew older, the nursery established relationships with placement and training organizations, including Charles Loring Brace's Children's Aid Society. In 1870, the nursery opened a "Country Branch" on Staten Island, to which Mary Du Bois and her family had moved.[3]

But it was the opening of the foundling asylum (the name "Infant's Home" was dropped as soon as the new building opened, a sign of its full incorporation into the nursery) that defined the nursery's new goal.[4] After the Civil War, the nursery fully committed itself to the salvation of fallen women. As at the London Foundling Hospital, the nursery chose babies, including those still in utero, based on the moral qualifications of their mothers. To enter, unwed mothers had to be "previously virtuous" and penitent. Women who were able to pay were charged for their board and were permitted to leave when they pleased. In 1875, this fee was twenty-five dollars. In an era in which domestic servants, who dominated the ranks of abandoning mothers, earned between four and ten dollars per month, this was a significant sum. Women who could not pay were required to stay at least three months after their babies were born to nurse their own children and one other each.[5] The resident mothers also contributed their labor to making the institution run, cleaning, sewing, and doing all the hot and heavy chores involved in nineteenth-century housekeeping, such as tending stoves, carrying water up and down stairs, beating rugs, and boiling, wringing, and ironing laundry.

Thus, the nursery's admissions policies defined its clientele: women who could prove their essential virtue by having "fallen" only once and their babies. The poor and penitent women who remained at the nursery were those deemed best able to benefit from the moral example set by the well-to-do and socially respectable managers who administered the wards. During their months at the nursery, they were required to "strictly conform to all the rules of the Establishment, and yield implicit obedience to the authority of the Matron and Physician," and bear the nursery's heavy load of daily chores. In addition, the "erring, penitent" mothers were also supposed to look to the nursery's managers for models of proper feminine behavior. Mary Du Bois and her colleagues took it as their mission to "surround them with purifying and elevating influences, and by thus doing, furnish them a stimulus to overcome, by their future lives, the effects of their previous misfortune and crime."[6] By running their new asylum for foundlings as an institution for the reform of fallen women, Mary Du Bois and her lady managers demonstrated their belief that the sexual misbehavior of women, more than poverty or the social inequities women faced, was the root cause of infant abandonment.

The New York Infant Asylum, 1865

The nursery's Infant's Home was the first foundling asylum planned, but it was neither the first nor the only one to open. Immediately after the Civil War, four foundling asylums opened in New York: The nursery's Infant's Home; the New York Foundling Asylum, organized by the Sisters of Charity; the Infant Hospital, a city-run foundling asylum on Randall's Island, which was added to the almshouse children's institutions already there; and the New York Infant Asylum, which, like the nursery, was a Protestant-run institution. All of these institutions were brought into being by the same concerns that motivated the founders of the Infant's Home, but they were also responding to the number of foundlings and infanticides in the city, which had risen further due to the hardships of the Civil War. Mary Du Bois recalled how "in 1865 the crime of child murder had increased to such an extent, that our police reports were filled with accounts of new born infants found in open lots, the public docks, and not infrequently in the most thickly populated streets of our city." The Sisters of Charity similarly remembered, "Each morning's paper brought its lengthened record of infanticide. The necessity of an asylum for the poor waif was evidently increasing."[7]

Usurping the Infant's Home's place as the city's first foundling asylum was the New York Infant Asylum. The New York Infant Asylum opened its building on Morningside Heights in the spring of 1865, failed, then reopened in November 1871. Its founder was Sarah Richmond, who was the founder and "directress" of the House of Mercy, a Protestant Episcopal residence for "fallen women" located in Inwood, at the northern tip of Manhattan. Her husband was the Rev. William Richmond, rector of St. Michael's Protestant Episcopal Church at Amsterdam Avenue and Ninety-Ninth Street on Manhattan's Upper West Side. Both Richmonds worked with poor women who had been sexually compromised or were in danger of becoming so. The Rev. Richmond's subjects were the poor, unmarried women he met in the maternity wards of Bellevue Hospital on his ministerial rounds. To these pious, charitable reform workers, the link between the catastrophes of sexual downfall and infant abandonment was evident.[8] William Richmond died before the couple's project to open a foundling asylum took shape, so it was Sarah Richmond who traveled to Albany in the winter of 1865 to have the new asylum chartered by the state.

Among the members of the New York Infant Asylum's board of managers were physician and sanitarian Stephen Smith, its first secretary. Smith had spent the war years serving as a surgeon in military hospitals in Virginia and New York and working on the bill that would create New York's Metropolitan Board of Health.[9] Also involved were the same Rev. Montgomery who presided over the cornerstone laying of the nursery's Infant's Home and another man with a close link to the nursery, Edward Delafield, Mary Du Bois's uncle. Dr. Delafield was the New York Infant Asylum's first president even as he served as a consulting physician at the nursery.

The New York Infant Asylum's original board of managers also included several public officials with links to the city's Democratic machine. These men included John T. Hoffman, a Tammany leader who was later elected mayor of New York and then governor of the state, and John T. Keyser, a plumber and close confederate of the Tweed Ring who became a millionaire on inflated city contracts. Keyser's wife served on the infant asylum's board of lady managers. Also listed is a "Tweed," though the records do not indicate if this is the great Boss Tweed himself or a relative. In any case, none of these politicians lasted long on the New York Infant Asylum's board.[10] By the time the New York Infant Asylum had regrouped after its closing, the Tweed Ring was on the verge of collapse, and these men were no longer able to be helpful.[11]

The New York Infant Asylum was in many ways similar to the nursery. Both were Protestant institutions. Both believed that the way to limit foundlings was to redirect the sexual behavior of poor women. Both established residential programs for unmarried mothers. And the two institutions were linked by their ties to Henry Montgomery and Edward Delafield. There was one important difference, however: while the nursery was run entirely by women, the New York Infant Asylum, although founded by Sarah Richmond, was led initially by an all-male board of managers. Sarah Richmond's title was superintendent, probably a reflection of her hands-on role.

Upon its opening, the New York Infant Asylum was immediately attacked by disasters. The asylum's rented building was a former hotel called Woodlawn, located at 104th Street and West End Avenue, just a few blocks from St. Michael's Church. It was "an old wooden structure and scarcely fitted for occupation," and "utterly unfit . . . during inclement weather." Furthermore, funds were in short supply. Worst of all, the foundlings taken in by the new asylum did not thrive. Of the

182 babies admitted between its opening on May 11, 1865, and its closing on December 15 of the same year, ninety-seven died. Stephen Smith remembered that the "patients died in such numbers as to completely thwart the purposes of the organization." Elisha Harris recalled that the "pious Mrs. Richmond" "watered with her tears for the fearful death-rate that prevailed" in the asylum's early days.[12] Then Sarah Richmond's own health failed, and she died on January 1, 1866. In a memorial minute, the managers of the New York Infant Asylum praised Mrs. Richmond's work "for the forlorn and fallen of her own sex, and more recently for the outcast children." She was "so truly," they enthused sadly, "the Florence Nightingale of New York."

The New York Infant Asylum closed its doors when Sarah Richmond departed for her deathbed in December, and the surviving children were transferred to the nursery's newly opened foundling asylum. The only relic of the failed institution they brought with them was their names. Following the practice of European foundling asylums, the New York Infant Asylum had named some of its foundlings after its building and its founders. An infant Henry Montgomery and Josephine, Alice, and Clara Woodlawn were among the children transferred from the failed New York Infant Asylum to the nursery. A baby Walter Scott was also among the number, but given the death rate among this group of foundlings, it is unlikely that he lived to follow in the popular novelist's footsteps.[13]

The New York Foundling Asylum, 1869

The third institution to open was the New York Foundling Asylum, which was opened in October 1869 by the Sisters of Charity, an order of Catholic nuns that specialized in teaching and nursing. The New York Foundling Asylum was urged into existence by Archbishop John McCloskey, who suggested the idea to Mother Mary Jerome, the order's mother superior. Like others who recognized the difficulties involved in caring for sickly infants, and "doubtful of public sympathy and support" because of the morally problematic nature of foundlings' origins, the Sisters of Charity hesitated at first.[14] They acquiesced eventually, however, and Mother Mary Jerome plucked Sister Mary Irene Fitzgibbon, then in her forties, from her job as head of the school associated with St. Peter's Church on Barclay Street and appointed her the head of the new foundling asylum. Sister Irene, as she was known, remained in this position until her death in 1896. Like Mary Du Bois, Sister Irene was the dominant personality at her institution. But unlike Du Bois, Sister Irene appears to have been charismatic, beloved, and possessed of real executive skill. Most of the letters left by desperate mothers with their babies were addressed directly to her.[15]

The archbishop and the Sisters of Charity were motivated by many of the same factors that influenced others who opened foundling asylums in the city. But as Catholics they also realized that the presence of two Protestant foundling asylums suggested that a need had arisen in their own constituency. The New York Foundling Asylum was a part of a great wave of Catholic institution-building that had begun with the arrival of impoverished refugees from Ireland's potato famine of the mid-1840s. Churches, schools, colleges, orphanages, reform schools, hospitals, and homes for women (both "fallen" and of "good character") were among the projects that provided alternatives to the city's Protestant-dominated system of education and charity, a system that was less than respectful toward the faith of the Catholic poor.[16]

In New York, schools and charities were often on the frontline of interreligious struggle. New York's Catholic leadership sought to rectify a situation in which their poor, young, and vulnerable were cared for by Protestant charities whose active proselytizing was typically an important part of the program.[17] Nativist disdain sometimes colored relations between administrators of Protestant charities and their often largely Catholic clientele, as well. A spat over hiring practices at the nursery demonstrates how the simmering anger over Protestant treatment of the Catholic poor could boil over. In 1856, a letter appeared in the Catholic *Freeman's Journal* describing the nursery as a "Proselytizing Nursery Trap" that had the "hidden object" of getting hold of Catholic children and making them attend Protestant Sunday schools, where "their holy faith will be calumniated." The author of the letter was moved to write when he saw an advertisement for help placed by the nursery that specified "Protestants preferred." Mary Du Bois's response to the letter makes her anti-Catholic, anti-immigrant bias clear. She protested that she sought help "with that solicitude and intelligence which (as regards food and medicine pardon me for saying it) which we had not found in Catholics of that class, who for the most part are foreigners and uneducated."[18]

In designing a Catholic foundling asylum, the Sisters of Charity turned to Catholic models. Unlike their Protestant counterparts, the Sisters of Charity found some examples in the United States. The summer before they opened the New York Foundling Asylum, a group of Sisters of Charity took a tour of roughly comparable institutions in Philadelphia, Baltimore, and Washington, D.C. Although none of these was devoted solely to the care of foundlings, they all took in infants, and one, St. Vincent's Infant Asylum in Baltimore, also took in "poor unfortunate girls" who had fallen and provided them with "shelter from the scoffs of a wicked world."[19]

More important to the New York Sisters of Charity as models were the foundling asylums of Catholic Europe. But the national and regional systems of rural wet nurses, midwives, transporters of infants, doctors, priests, and bureaucrats, all in the pay or under the direction of government-run foundling asylums, could not be duplicated in the nineteenth-century United States. In this era, American charity was carried out by private organizations, which were typically Protestant, and by local governments. With the exception of pensions for war veterans, the federal government played no role in social welfare, and it would not do so until the Progressive era of the early twentieth century.[20]

The separation of church and state mandated by the United States Constitution was less of an impediment to New York's foundling asylums than one might think. While the profound entwinement of church and state that made Europe's foundling asylums possible was alien to the United States, both New York City and New York State routinely funneled public money to private, religious charities in the nineteenth century. As the Catholic population grew, and as the Democratic machine fattened on immigrant votes, Catholic charities became significant beneficiaries of public funds, typically outstripping Protestant and Jewish ones.[21]

Despite the limitations specific to the American charitable and political landscapes within which American Catholic charities had to work, the European Catholic model of charity still provided a rich lode of practices for Sister Irene to mine. One that she modified for the New York Foundling Asylum was highly characteristic of the Catholic system: the wheel, or turntable, that was embedded in the outer walls of Catholic foundling asylums and that allowed babies to be abandoned secretly. Mary Du Bois referred disdainfully to this practice, remarking

A woman leaves a baby in the basket at the New York
Foundling Asylum, 17 East Twelfth Street. This illustration
accompanied a story that, like many stories about found-
lings, was published on Christmas. *Frank Leslie's Illustrated
Newspaper,* December 25, 1869. Collection of the New-York
Historical Society, 79754d.

that the Protestant nursery operated "(with wise discrimination) only
on the English plan condemning 'the basket at the door.' "[22]

Yet it was exactly this "basket at the door" that Sister Irene adopted.
In the entry of the New York Foundling Asylum, the sisters placed a
large wicker cradle. Over the years, thousands of babies were laid in
this basket.[23] Some twenty years after the New York Foundling Asylum
opened, missionary and author Helen Campbell hid herself near the
asylum's entryway one night to see how the basket worked. She observed a woman approaching the building with a baby in her arms, and
saw that,

with a burst of tears she laid it in the basket and silently hurried down the steps. Crouching again in the friendly shadow she waited, her face turned toward the door-way, till a baby's wail followed by a sharp little cry was heard, and she half sprung up and stretched her arms toward the basket. The door opened even as the cry came. A woman with a calm gentle face stood for a moment, the flood of light from the hall bringing out every line of her face and figure, then stooped and lifted the bundle to her shoulder, pressing the little face close to her own. The baby nestled to her as she passed into the hall; the door closed, and the woman crouching in the darkness stole away, bearing her secret with her.[24]

The New York Foundling Asylum opened on October 11, 1869, in a rented house at 17 East Twelfth Street. The Sisters of Charity received their first foundling on October 12; by the end of the month, they had taken in eleven babies; by the end of the following month, forty-nine; and by October 1, 1871, they had accepted 2,560 foundlings. This high figure may have been induced by the pent-up need of parents for whom only a Catholic foundling asylum was acceptable. The pace picked up as the months went on, at least at first. Between the opening date and October 1, 1870, the asylum received 1,183 babies, or an average of about 103 babies per month. The flow increased between October 1, 1870, and October 1, 1871, when the asylum accepted 1,377 babies, or an average of about 115 per month. By 1875, however, the asylum reported receiving no more than thirty-five infants each month.[25]

Even though most of the babies were placed with outside wet nurses, the asylum's first building overflowed, necessitating a move in the fall of 1870 to a larger one on fashionable Washington Square, where the foundlings had the benefit of taking the air in Washington Square Park.[26] As babies continued to pour in, Washington Square also grew tight. So in 1873, the New York Foundling Asylum moved to its first permanent building, located on the block enclosed by Lexington and Third Avenues and Sixty-Eighth and Sixty-Ninth Streets on the Upper East Side of Manhattan. The Sisters of Charity's new foundling asylum was built on plots provided by the city, with funds granted by the state. The nursery, which was less than a mile to the south, had pursued the same geographical trajectory, starting in crowded lower Manhattan, then moving north to the still thinly built center of the island.[27]

Sisters of Charity record the arrival of a foundling at the
New York Foundling Asylum. *Frank Leslie's Illustrated
Weekly*, December 25, 1869. Collection of the New-York
Historical Society, 79755d.

Unlike the Nursery and Child's Hospital, which accepted mothers
along with babies from the start, the Sisters of Charity planned to accept only babies at first. They changed their minds very soon after opening, when they were faced with a mother who threatened suicide if she
was turned away and who offered to breastfeed her own infant and another if the Sisters would allow her into the asylum with her baby. The
Sisters realized the valuable service lactating mothers could provide, and
they began to accept mothers along with their babies. Once they made
this shift in policy, the Sisters, like the managers of the nursery, hoped
to teach unmarried mothers "to walk in the way of virtue."[28]

The Sisters of Charity at first tried to follow the Catholic model and accept as many babies as they could with no questions asked, but limitations of space and funds made this challenging. One way the Sisters coped was to farm out babies with independent nurses. Another was to limit their admissions. As at the London Foundling Hospital and the Nursery and Child's Hospital, the rules of admission the New York Foundling Asylum developed reveal the Sisters' understanding of the qualities that made a baby deserving, so to speak, of abandonment.

As at both of those Protestant institutions, the Sisters of Charity admitted babies based on the moral qualifications of their mothers, when mothers presented themselves for admission along with their babies.[29] But the Sisters differed from the Nursery and Child's Hospital on the question of accepting the children of wet nurses, and in this difference was embedded a paradox. The Sisters refused to accept wet nurses' babies because they believed that women who chose to breastfeed other women's babies for pay were neglecting the path of true motherhood in favor of monetary gain and the pampering that wet nurses received in the homes of their employers. Such behavior, the Sisters believed, "exhibits a heartlessness and an absence of maternal duty which we feel ourselves obliged to oppose, and against which our moral sense revolts."[30]

This was just the reverse of the tactic adopted by Mary Du Bois at the nursery. Like the Sisters of Charity, Mary Du Bois suspected that some poor, lactating women chose to put their own comfort and gain above the well-being of their babies by hiring themselves out as live-in wet nurses to middle-class families, in whose homes they typically received better pay, better food, and better lodging than other domestic servants. This was all for the benefit of the employing family's baby, but the image of the live-in wet nurse as an excessively powerful and demanding figure who threatened to walk out (thus threatening the life of the baby) if her material needs were not met circulated among middle-class homes in the nineteenth century. The fact that wet nurses were typically poor, unmarried mothers made their demands appear irritatingly outlandish, and the whiff of street and slum they brought into the comfortable homes of their employers created further discord.[31]

Like the Sisters of Charity, the women of the nursery could be scathing about what they took to be a selfish choice. Arabella Mott remarked on the nursery's difficulty in convincing the women it admitted, many of them wet nurses, to remain with their own babies in the institution: "women in the station they occupy are seldom found with the maternal instinct strong enough to induce them to remain and nurse their own infants," she sniffed. The comfortable quarters and relatively high wages that private wet nurses commanded were enough, she suggested, to tempt poor women to abandon their own babies, even to death.[32] Despite all this, the nursery interpreted its responsibility toward wet nurses in precisely the opposite way as the Sisters of Charity did; indeed, the nursery had been founded specifically to help the children of wet nurses. Perhaps Mary Du Bois believed that nothing could change the behavior of these women, while the Sisters had greater hopes for their reformation.

Both Mary Du Bois and the Sisters of Charity were attempting to address the neglect of wet nurses' children, which shocked all who were concerned about the welfare of poor babies in the city. Yet both institutions, focused as they were on what they believed to be the degraded state of maternal feelings among poor, immigrant women, overestimated the degree of choice these women were able to exercise. Families who hired wet nurses typically did not allow them to bring their own babies with them, since they did not want to share the milk they were paying for. Thus it was the policy of the employing families, rather than the greed of poor mothers, that led to the abandonment and, in many cases, the deaths of wet nurses' babies.

Another rule that illuminates the Sisters of Charity's definition of an "appropriate" foundling, this one enacted by the early 1880s, specified that babies would be accepted only from their mothers: "It is a rule with the Sisters to take no child from other parties than the mother, as she is the rightful person to abandon it." One of the tragedies of infant abandonment, the Sisters believed, was that it was, among other things, a demonstration of a failure of maternal devotion. Yet, paradoxically, the rules of the New York Foundling Asylum decreed that if any abandoning was to be done, it was the mother who should do it. This rule did not take into consideration the possibility that the impetus to abandon may have come not from the mother but from a widower or the angry father of an unmarried young woman. The Sisters also ruled against the admission of legitimate babies, arguing that "this is not the place for such cases, and kindly assure them that it is their parental duty to care for their children themselves."[33] This rule thus enshrined the notion that a foundling was an illegitimate. The Sisters, while recognizing that poverty was one of the causes of infant abandonment, maintained their focus on illegitimacy, threatening to turn away poor parents who played by the rules and bore their children within the boundaries of marriage.

In reality, the Sisters were more generous than their rules, accepting many babies that did not fit their specifications.[34] Furthermore, the presence of the New York Foundling Asylum's wicker reception cradle made their admissions rules at least partially moot, since they only applied to people who presented their babies for admission openly. As a result, the Sisters of Charity continued to accept more babies than they could house even in their large new building on Lexington Avenue. They coped with this by adopting the tactic of sending babies out to live in the homes of wet nurses, the practice abandoned by the almshouse following the well-publicized Mary Cullough scandal. Despite that scandal, the New York Foundling Asylum chose to place babies with independent wet nurses, some of whom may have been the same poor women who had been put out of work by the almshouse in 1860, because it simply lacked the room to keep all the babies in its building without dangerous overcrowding.[35]

The Sisters learned to package their "out-door department," as their external nursing program was called, in a positive way for public consumption. They required the nurses to make monthly visits to the asylum to present their foundlings for inspection and receive their pay, and they turned these into occasions at which the press was welcome. The journalist and social reformer Jacob Riis called this event "one of the sights of the city."[36] On pay days, the New York Foundling Asylum boasted, "There may be seen gaily-dressed Italians, thrifty-looking Germans, smiling Irish matrons, and a few colored folk." But the boast was edged with wariness, an expression of the unease these rough, slum-dwelling women aroused in the Sisters as well as in most reformers who dealt with New York's tumultuous poor: "Order reigns in spite of the constant influx," they added, "for two police-officers are in attendance, and marshal the nurses by groups to the pay-office."[37] On several occasions the *New York Daily Graphic* sent an artist to capture the scene. He, too, pictured the monthly gathering of these poor and ethnically various women as a colorful big-city spectacle, yet from the discontented faces he gave many of them it appears that, like the Sisters, he believed that these women of the tenement districts were capable, if not restrained, of bringing chaos to the Sister's scrubbed and orderly institution.[38]

Dr. James B. Reynolds, the foundling asylum's physician, had his doubts about the healthfulness of the placing-out program. "The great mass of our infants are boarded out about the city and in the surrounding country," he wrote in 1871, but although many did well, "a proportionally greater number at wet nurse outside fail and are returned to us in a dying condition." The reasons he gave for the unsatisfying mortality rate both inside and outside the asylum were the same as those given by everyone who wrote about the terrible fragility of foundlings. "It would be unfair," Dr. Reynolds argued, "to attribute the larger mortality in Foundling Hospitals, chiefly to causes found within the hospital. We should consider the condition in which they are received." Exposure to cold, infection with syphilis, parents from the "lowest walks of life, with constitutions exhausted by disease, excess, and want": all of these factors, Dr. Reynolds believed, made the physical rescue of foundlings a nearly hopeless task.[39]

Even with the restrictions on entry it was forced to enact, the New York Foundling Asylum was still a far more welcoming institution (for Catholics and also for others, since it did not discriminate by religion) than the Nursery and Child's Hospital or, after 1871, the resuscitated New York Infant Asylum. The administrators of the Nursery and Child's Hospital and the New York Infant Asylum ministered to their largely destitute, immigrant clientele from behind the barrier of class and ethnic divisions, while the Sisters of Charity created their foundling asylum for their own poor, rather than for a population of what they might have deemed alien others.

As a significant benefactor of the Irish Catholic immigrant poor whose votes fueled the Democratic machine, the New York Foundling Asylum attracted the support of the leaders of Tammany Hall. The person through whom much of this support flowed was Mary Schenck Townsend Connolly, a member of the foundling asylum's Ladies' Society, a group of lay women who supported the foundling asylum by organizing fundraising events and who met there regularly to sew for the children.[40] She was also the wife of Richard Barrett Connolly. Connolly, known to his enemies as "Slippery Dick," was the city's comptroller and a central figure in the spectacular rise and fall of the Tweed Ring, the bribe-fueled cabal led by the Tammany leader William M. Tweed.[41]

Mary Schenck Townsend, a Protestant and "the daughter of an old New Yorker," according to the *New York Herald,* made a most unusual choice when she married the Irish immigrant and political climber Connolly around 1837.[42] During the early years of their marriage, the Connollys lived at a succession of addresses in the rough immigrant districts east of the fashionable squares inhabited by the likes of Philip Hone, Mary Du Bois, and George Templeton Strong. Once Richard Connolly gained access to the spoils of the comptroller's office, however, the family's addresses began to reflect its improved fortunes. The Connollys moved first to a house at 42 Park Avenue and then began building themselves a mansion at Fifth Avenue and 130th Street, farther north even than what Edith Wharton called the "inaccessible wilderness" of the area around Central Park.[43]

Mary Connolly put both her husband's money and his political connections to work for the New York Foundling Asylum. In December 1869, less than two months after the foundling asylum had opened, and when it was still operating in rented quarters, she wrote Sister Irene: "Mr. Connolly and I have been talking over the matter to night and feel that you must have an *Institution*." The list of the New York Foundling Asylum's earliest benefactors was headed by the central figures of the Tweed Ring. William M. Tweed, then at the height of his powers as "Grand Sachem" of Tammany Hall, was at the top with a gift of a thousand dollars. City chamberlain Peter B. Sweeney—often referred to as the brains of the Tweed Ring—gave five hundred dollars, and Mayor A. Oakey Hall contributed a hundred. Others gave smaller sums.[44] For one of these, Smith Ely, Jr., an interest in the foundling asylum may have arisen from personal experience. On December 6, 1839, exactly thirty years before he handed in his donation of ten dollars to the foundling asylum, a servant living in the house of merchant Smith Ely (presumably Ely Jr.'s father), discovered a two-day-old boy left in a basket on Bond Street at two o'clock in the morning. The almshouse named the boy Alexander Bond, and it may have been the recurrence of the anniversary date of his discovery that stimulated Ely's gift.[45]

Early in 1870, as Sister Irene was approaching the state legislature for funds for a building to replace its rented house on East Twelfth Street, Mary Connolly assured her that "Mr. C. will do all he can in Albany to forward your Petition."[46] That year, the state legislature awarded the New York Foundling Asylum a hundred thousand dollars for the construction of its building on Lexington Avenue. The state granted the money with the proviso that the asylum come up with matching funds in an equal amount. When the proceeds of a fair fell short by almost thirty thousand dollars, Mrs. Connolly set to work making up the difference among her friends. Once again, these included her husband, Mayor Hall, Tweed, Peter Sweeney, and such Democratic tycoons as financier August Belmont and department store magnate A. T. Stewart.[47]

The Sisters of Charity were not alone in gaining assistance with their institution from unsavory elements in government. Mary Du Bois formed a similar alliance with a no more savory politician, but one who was specifically opposed to Catholic interests. This was the newspaper editor and nativist politician Erastus Brooks. In 1853, shortly before Du Bois's nursery was founded, Brooks was elected to the New York State Senate as a member of the Know Nothing or American Party, which espoused an anti-immigrant policy. He was the Know Nothing Party's unsuccessful candidate for governor in 1856. In the state senate, Brooks clashed with Archbishop John Hughes over the Church Property Act, a bill that sought to take away the property tax exemption from New York's Catholic church.

Du Bois was linked to Brooks through her son, Eugene, who was married to Brooks's daughter. They were also neighbors on Staten Island, where Du Bois lived after the Civil War. When Du Bois applied to the state government for funds, Brooks helped to smooth the way. He also delivered addresses at the cornerstone laying and inauguration of the nursery's children's hospital, and he was a member of the small crowd that braved the cold to attend the Infant's Home's cornerstone laying in December 1859. Brooks helped Du Bois regain the new Infant's Home building after the Civil War, first interceding with the city to have it cleared of wounded soldiers, then helping to beat back the other groups that coveted it. According to Du Bois, one of these groups was "the Roman Catholics [who] wanted it for a school."[48] By the early 1870s, Brooks was a member of the nursery's advisory board.[49]

Though he was very helpful to Du Bois's institution, Brooks was not universally liked. George Templeton Strong, Mary Du Bois's neighbor when she still lived on Gramercy Park, recorded his acute disdain for Brooks in his diary. As a member of the city's Republican elite, Strong was also anti-Irish, but he was far more genteel than Brooks. Gramercy Park neighborliness was such that Strong sometimes found himself in unwilling company with "Rat Brooks," as he called him, and on an October evening in 1856 Strong complained that he had to spend "an hour in a dresscoat at Mrs. Du Bois'." "Dirty little Erastus Brooks there," he reported, "looking quiet, stealthy, and malignant. . . . If men are to develop into animal forms, each according to the law of his individual be-ing, Erastus will be a very ugly, cunning and vicious rat."[50]

The Sisters of Charity got substantial help with their foundling asy-lum from a source outside government, too: the *New York Herald*. The *Herald* had been founded by Scottish immigrant James Gordon Bennett in 1835. It was part of a new trend in newspaper publishing—the penny press. These cheap newspapers were aimed at a wide, working-class au-dience. Bennett's *Herald* led the pack—by 1865 it had become the lead-ing daily newspaper in both New York City and the United States.[51] To attract these readers, papers such as the *Herald* relied on sentimental, titillating, or sensational stories. This made the New York Foundling Asylum a natural part of the *Herald*'s regular beat. Bennett devoted space in his paper to New York City news, and his sympathies were generally on the side of the poor. He was also a Catholic and an oppo-nent of Protestant reform efforts. All of these factors made the Catholic foundling asylum a subject of his paper's interest and sympathy.

Soon after its opening, the New York Foundling Asylum became the darling of the *Herald*. The *Herald* began assisting in its fundraising ef-fort, reminding its readers that "there are so many ways in which the Sisters can be assisted, and which will readily suggest themselves to every charitable heart. . . . The poor can contribute their mite as well as the rich their hundreds." The *Herald* congratulated itself on its efforts on behalf of the foundling asylum, reporting that its "frequent notices of the establishment caused contributions to flow in rapidly." These contributions included gifts of milk, medicine, cribs, and bedding, in addition to funds.[52] The relationship between the New York Foundling Asylum and the *New York Herald* was a symbiotic one; the *Herald* publicized the foundling asylum's need for support and funds, while the foundling asylum was a bottomless source of sentimental stories about the "poor little waifs of sin and shame."[53]

Reporters from the *Herald* visited the foundling asylum periodically. Their stories provide vivid word pictures of life there. "Now that the lenten season has commenced," a *Herald* reporter remarked in the spring of 1871, "one cannot do better than pay a visit to the New York Foundling Asylum and take a peep at the babies that the good Sisters of Charity have taken under their motherly protection." The "spotless marble steps" of the asylum's house on Washington Square made the reporter hesitate before marring them with his muddy boots. Inside, he found everything "airy, cheerful and clean." Upstairs, in "the domain of the babies," he found rooms full of cribs, each with its "appointments of snowy whiteness." The sights and sounds of the children reminded him "strongly of the nursery at home" and reminded him that "these babies and your own darlings are equally near to God."[54] In 1881, a *Herald* reporter asked Sister Irene for a description of the foundlings' day:

> "Oh," she replied, her dimpled face beaming with pleasure as she glanced toward the children in her own ward, "we keep them occupied all the time. Each day has its regular routine of exercises and is passed before we know it. The children are accustomed to it and expect it. They rise and retire at six o'clock. It is so arranged that each nurse [these were the unmarried mothers who lived at the Asylum with their children] has her cot bed at the side of the crib containing her charges. These are either two infants or an infant and one able to run about, who sleep at each end of the cribs, covered with a canopy of white net. The nurse dresses both of the little ones. Breakfast is followed by morning prayers for those old enough to lisp the words, the play hour and singing for the youngest, and lessons in the schoolroom for the older ones, occupy the time before the dinner hour. Then comes the favorite kindergarten hour, with its employments so fascinating for the little ones. The singing of simple songs, play in the yard or playroom, with lessons for the older ones, prayers before supper—they are too sleepy afterward—and then preparations for the night.

The reporter agreed that the hour when the kindergarten was in session was the best time of the day. "Then those of two, three, or four years of age are seated at tables arranged around the room, and when the little ones are all busy it resembles a fairy workroom."[55]

Other newspapers were also susceptible to the charms of the New York Foundling Asylum and Sister Irene's evidently considerable personal magnetism. Two years after the aforementioned article appeared in the *Herald,* a reporter from the *New York Tribune* described his tour through the foundling asylum's new building on Lexington Avenue in similar terms. By this time, a maternity hospital had been added, where the reporter found "an odorless purity of consummate cleanliness."

> Through ward after ward of the same snowy whiteness and unimpeachable sweetness and cleanliness the reporter threaded his way from floor

to floor and from wing to wing, past great wardrobes filled with all manner of seasonable clothing carefully selected and daintily made on the premises—sixteen sewing machines on the top floor going all the time and mainly under the hands of "mothers" and penitents being reclaimed—past great lavatories, and inviting dining and store rooms with burnished tins and culinary ware; through the quiet hospital wards where the same gentle, skilled solicitude was manifested, through great store-rooms, with judicious supplies of all needful things, through the great kitchen with its mammoth ranges and reservoirs, where great piles of fragrant loaves are in waiting.

This reporter's extravagant admiration for the New York Foundling Asylum—his description borrows the language of fairy tale to make this institution for abandoned babies sound like a magical castle run by industrious elves—was not shaken by Sister Irene's frank admission that the institution's mortality figures were "appalling." "It must be borne in mind," Sister Irene reminded him, "that offspring of crime are unwelcome, often ante-natal sufferers,—born of wretched and distracted mothers, who often are both ignorant and brutal; that they are frequently consumed with disease, are brought here exposed to all kinds of inclement weather scantily clothed, improperly cared for and sometimes, almost stricken with death." "This," Sister Irene summed up, "is the fatality hanging over all foundlings."[56]

The New York Infant Asylum Resurrected, 1871

The Protestant-run New York Infant Asylum, which had closed in the winter of 1866 after the death of founder Sarah Richmond, propelled itself back into action very slowly, and then only when it was prodded. In 1868, a grand jury met to investigate the same post–Civil War rise in the number of infant abandonments and infanticides that had worried the Sisters of Charity and Mary Du Bois. The conclusion of the grand jury was that New York ought to have a foundling asylum. (The grand jury ignored the existence of the Nursery and Child's Hospital, whose restrictive policies radically limited its effectiveness, and the New York Foundling Asylum and Randall's Island Infant Hospital did not open until 1869.) The grand jury discovered the state charter that had been issued three years earlier to Sarah Richmond to establish the New York

Infant Asylum, and implored the defunct institution to reassume its responsibilities. A member of the New York Infant Asylum's board, who identified himself only as "One of the Trustees," defended his moribund institution in a letter to the *New York Times* by reminding readers of the great disaster that the New York Infant Asylum had been and arguing gently that even though the trustees were willing either to act or to "resign the trust to those who might possibly execute it better than they," the New York Infant Asylum would not be able to get back onto its feet unless "the community are prepared for such an institution" and "the benevolently-disposed are willing to contribute of their means to the object."[57]

For the moment, that was the end of that. Despite the embarrassing furor, the board of the infant asylum did not meet to address the grand jury's call to action. Finally, in February 1870, the trustees of the New York Infant Asylum did meet, for the first time in almost two years— but only to discuss the possibility of merging its remaining assets with those of the Nursery and Child's Hospital. After a month during which unsuccessful talks were held with the nursery, this plan was abandoned, and the New York Infant Asylum's trustees once again subsided into silence.[58]

Finally, in the spring of 1871, three years after the grand jury had pointed its accusing finger at them and six years after the disastrous winter in which the first New York Infant Asylum had closed its doors, the trustees took steps to reopen. They drafted, published, and circulated two documents. One was titled "Appeal in Behalf of the New York Infant Asylum, Chartered by the State of New York, and Organized Under the Management of Representatives from the Protestant Denominations of the City"; the other was called "A Statement in Behalf of the New York Infant Asylum." These were probably composed by Stephen Smith. The "Statement" was signed by eleven prominent physicians, including Smith. By Christmas of that year, the texts of the "Appeal" and the "Statement" had found their way to the office of *Harper's Weekly,* which used them as source material for a cover story, complete with an illustration of a policeman lifting a foundling from a doorstep in a windy rainstorm.[59] In April 1871, the New York Infant Asylum held a public meeting at Association Hall (which belonged to the Young Men's Christian Association), where they stated their renewed goals and called for funds and support.[60] This meeting was a

A police officer lifts a foundling from a doorstep
in a cover illustration from *Harper's Weekly* for
a story about the New York Infant Asylum soon
after it reopened. Sol Eytinge. *Harper's Weekly,*
December 23, 1871. Collection of the New-York
Historical Society, 77825d.

success, and in November the New York Infant Asylum reopened, this
time at 24 Clinton Place on Manhattan's Lower East Side.[61]

There were a number of reasons why the New York Infant Asylum
came back to life when it did. One was continuing alarm about the
growing number of foundlings in the city; the "Statement" asserted that
there were nearly three thousand babies abandoned in New York in
1870 and claimed that this was the same as the number of illegitimate

births in the city that year. Not only was the figure of three thousand improbably high, but the assertions that all foundlings were illegitimate and that all illegitimates were abandoned were also not in keeping with the facts.

Stephen Smith, the probable author of the "Statement" and a member of the Metropolitan Board of Health, had access to city statistics through his colleague Elisha Harris, the board's registrar of vital statistics. Harris was also a trustee of the New York Infant Asylum and a signer of the "Statement." Yet despite Harris's expertise, Smith's figure for the number of illegitimate babies and foundlings were no better than guesses. There was no truly accurate way that Smith and Harris could have determined how many illegitimate babies had been born in the city, since New York, in common with most other places in the United States, did not gather statistics on illegitimate births at that time.[62]

But the evidence they saw with their own eyes was perhaps sufficient to alarm Smith and the ten other physicians who signed the "Statement." Like Thomas Coram, who was horrified when he saw "young Children exposed, sometimes alive, sometimes dead, and sometimes dying" on his walks through early eighteenth-century London, the physicians who signed the "Statement" reported that the number of foundlings on the streets of New York was so great that they "literally crowd our daily walks." It seems likely that these physicians would have seen more babies abandoned on streets and doorsteps than other citizens were likely to see, as they walked around the city visiting patients at odd hours. It was probably this visceral evidence, rather than a set of frightening statistics cooked up to shock the deep-pocketed audience at Association Hall, that helped awaken their concern. At least one of the infant asylum doctors later came face to face with a foundling on his own doorstep: in 1875, a month-old baby was left outside the home of Joel Foster, a signer of the "Statement" and a member of the New York Infant Asylum's reconstituted board.[63]

Another factor that pushed the trustees of the New York Infant Asylum back into action was the success of the Sisters of Charity. The Sisters' New York Foundling Asylum had opened in 1869, while the Protestant New York Infant Asylum was closed. In a city in which Catholic and Protestant charities were carrying on a heated competition for the souls of the poor, particularly poor children, the Sisters' success—measured by the steady flow of babies they received, many more than the Protestant Nursery and Child's Hospital, and by their positive notices in the press—created ambivalent feelings among the trustees of the New York Infant Asylum. They were glad to see that the needs of abandoned infants were being met, but they did not like the idea that Protestant children might be disappearing into a Catholic institution.

All three of the privately run foundling asylums advertised themselves as "ecumenical"—open to babies and mothers of all religions. Yet all three were also committed to winning souls for their own faiths. The *Herald* noted that the Sisters of Charity's foundling asylum "prescribes neither creed, nor class, nor color—and there was a goodly representation from every source." Their admissions book shows that during its first months it received "A little Jewess!" It also took in Protestant babies, black as well as white.[64] In 1871, a *Herald* reporter peered into a crib at the New York Foundling Asylum and reported that "something mysteriously dark is seen above the white sheets, and you find by further inspection that the little wrinkled black faces belong to Sambo and his twin sister." The appearance of these African-American babies upset one of the nursing mothers residing in the institution. The reporter described how "The little blackamoors came late at night, and the good Sister, who knows no difference between black and white, called one of the Irish nurses to attend to their wants. But Bridget had not arrived at the advanced spiritual state required for such an act of leveling, and she answered, 'I'd do anything that ye'd [t]old me 'cept put a nager to me breast.' However, in spite of Biddy's prejudices, the young Africans are doing well."[65]

The trustees and supporters of the New York Infant Asylum acknowledged the work of "the good sisters of the Roman Catholic Foundling Asylum" but asserted firmly that a foundling asylum was still required for the "Protestant portion of the community." With only the limited resources of the Nursery and Child's Hospital to rely on, they argued, Protestant mothers would bring their unwanted infants to the "Asylum of the Roman Catholic Sisters."[66]

There was yet another force compelling the New York Infant Asylum to reopen in 1871—this was the developing alarm over baby farming. Baby farmers, poor women who cared for groups of babies and young children in their homes, were often accused in this era of making unwanted children disappear through neglect, starvation, or outright murder. In some cases, baby farmers were known to have abandoned their charges on the street because of nonpayment of board by their parents; more often, baby farmers brought children directly to the almshouse when they were not paid. Sometimes, this occurred through a pre-arranged plan between baby farmers and parents in which abandonment was accomplished by proxy. After the Mary Cullough affair of 1859, the almshouse was so frightened by the damage baby farmers could do—both to the babies and to its own reputation—that it pulled all of its infants out of their hands and returned them to the almshouse.

Baby farming was a simmering concern in the New York of the 1850s, as the Mary Cullough scandal demonstrates. But it did not emerge as a full-blown scandal of international proportions until a particularly notorious case unfolded in London in 1870. This case led to an investigation by a select committee of the British House of Commons and ultimately to the passage of England's Infant Life Protection Act of 1872, which regulated private child care.[67] As always, concerned New Yorkers kept a close eye on social-welfare practice in England. The *New York Times* reported on the investigations carried out by the British Select Committee on Infant Life Protection, and soon the paper was reporting on similar cases in New York. "There is no disguising the fact," the *Times* warned, "that many children are sent out to 'nurse' with the distinct understanding that they are to be 'put out of the way' by means that shall elude the law and defy detection." Noting that many of the children who fell victim to baby farmers were illegitimate, since single mothers were the ones who had the greatest need for the services of baby farmers, the *Times* argued that "Foundling asylums afford the readiest means of escape from this threatened death."[68]

The trustees of the New York Infant Asylum and their supporters were attentive to the issue of baby farming and saw their institution as a weapon with which to combat it. The "Statement" and "Appeal" made reference to baby farmers, "a class of immoral women, who care little for the life of either mother or child." In the "private institutions" run by baby farmers, as well as among the abortionists and midwives with whom they were alleged to work in league, the "Statement" reported a "distinct understanding of all parties that they [the babies] would not long survive."[69]

While there were some differences between the newly reopened New York Infant Asylum and the Nursery and Child's Hospital, their essential goals were exactly the same. "Our aim," the New York Infant Asylum proclaimed in an early annual report, "is to thwart and prevent suicide, infanticide and murder, those demons that follow hard upon the track of the unfortunate, and to shield, save and restore them as well as to protect their innocent offspring. They may have been ever so pure, ever so young, ever so much respected, before the one terrible false step, yet what a fearful future seems in store for them, a future of despair and in most cases of crime. When all else seems forbidding and pitiless, our Institution receives them."[70] Like Mary Du Bois and her colleagues, then, the trustees of the New York Infant Asylum understood the abandoning mother as a previously pure woman ruined by seduction, so overwhelmed by shame that she was in danger of killing her infant and then herself. If she lived, they believed, prostitution was inevitable.

Once it reopened, the New York Infant Asylum also operated very much like the nursery. While the infant asylum's charter required it to accept babies left on its doorstep—which it began to do as soon as the Clinton Place building opened—it preferred taking in mothers and babies together, since the reform of fallen women was a central goal. Within a few months of its opening, the trustees of the Infant Asylum became unhappy about the prospect of women arriving at the asylum with the expectation that they could leave their babies but not remain themselves, and they voted to decide each case individually rather than to adopt a blanket regulation. While they considered it "highly inexpedient" for the infant asylum to "to take their children off their hands," they realized that occasionally this would be necessary.[71]

For the illegitimate mothers who agreed to be admitted, the New York Infant Asylum functioned as a model home in which they could learn to amend their ways. Inside they received copious doses of sewing and housework—necessary to maintain the house, but also to prepare its inmates for their futures as trained domestic servants. A "devotional committee" led them in "singing and various religious exercises" as they sewed and mended. They attended Bible classes and religious services and had lessons in reading and writing. "Idleness finds no place within the walls of the New York Infant Asylum," reported the asylum's lady managers in 1877. That year, the busy inmates turned out 1,402 garments.

Once the inmates' moral transformation was complete and their domestic training accomplished, they were placed as domestic servants.[72] This was perhaps unfortunate. By training its resident mothers as servants, the infant asylum, like the nursery, propelled them back out into the very occupation that had provided the conditions for their troubles in the first place. Domestic servants, who typically lived in the homes of their employers, were generally not allowed to keep their children with them. And as young, single women, they were vulnerable to the sexual threats and temptations offered by the men of the household, both employers and fellow servants.[73]

Like the Nursery and Child's Hospital and the New York Foundling Asylum, the rejuvenated New York Infant Asylum opened its doors downtown, near the homes of the poor. When overcrowding in the institution became acute, however, it moved to larger, less expensive quarters in a more sparsely settled area uptown. In November 1872, one year after opening, the New York Infant Asylum bought a house at Sixty-first Street and Tenth Avenue, just across town from the nursery, which was on Lexington Avenue and Fifty-first Street, and the New York Foundling Asylum, on Lexington and Sixty-eighth. Two years later, the New York Infant Asylum built an addition onto the Sixty-first Street building. The asylum retained the house on Clinton Place for a "reception house." Then, like the nursery, the New York Infant Asylum acquired a country house, which opened in June 1872 in Flushing, Queens, still an area of farmland and villages. In 1879, they bought a second country house in Mount Vernon, Westchester County, north of the city. And in 1877, the infant asylum added a maternity ward.[74] But despite these efforts to prevent overcrowding and provide the mothers and babies with the salutary benefits of fresh air, the New York Infant Asylum, like its sister institutions, had difficulty keeping foundlings alive. Dr. Job Lewis Smith, Stephen Smith's brother and the physician in charge of the Sixty-first Street house, found that the death rate for babies living at the Asylum without their mothers was 40 percent.[75]

When the New York Infant Asylum came back to life in 1871, it formed a board of "lady managers," in recognition of the central roles that women often played in private, religious charities in the United States. At a time when women were barred from government positions and were not even permitted to vote, boards of "lady managers" created in effect a system of assistance to the poor that promoted their religious values through the charitable organizations they founded and ran. Such women, despite the active roles outside the home that their charitable work required, for the most part did not affiliate themselves with the movement for women's rights that officially began at the first women's rights convention at Seneca Falls, New York, in 1848. While Elizabeth Cady Stanton's Declaration of Sentiments, read at the Seneca Falls convention, promoted an uncompromising view of equality between men and women, the women who volunteered their labor at religious chari-

Abigail Hopper Gibbons. Collection of the New-York
Historical Society, 79724d.

ties typically saw their work as an extension of maternal values into the
public sphere rather than as a challenge to the balance of power between men and women in society.[76] The Nursery and Child's Hospital,
with its "first directress" and board of "lady managers," falls squarely
within this tradition. The New York Infant Asylum, even though it was
founded by a woman, inhabits this model only partially, as its lady
managers raised funds and took care of daily operations, but its administration remained in the hands of men.[77]

A founding member of the New York Infant Asylum's board of lady
managers was Abigail Hopper Gibbons. Gibbons, a Quaker and the
daughter of prominent Quaker abolitionist and prison reformer Isaac
Hopper, was involved in several important reform efforts of her era.
Like her father, she was an abolitionist and a prison reformer. She spent

the Civil War (as did Stephen Smith, another leader of the New York Infant Asylum) at the front, in her case nursing wounded soldiers. After the war, she became involved in the movement to prevent the legalization of prostitution.[78] Yet despite her deep involvement in reform, Gibbons's feelings about women's rights, like those of many women involved in antebellum religious charity, were no better than ambivalent. In 1860, she served as the vice president of the women's rights convention held in New York City, one of the annual conventions held after the first one in Seneca Falls. But for the most part she deflected the advances of such women's rights leaders as Susan B. Anthony and Elizabeth Cady Stanton. When in 1868 Anthony used Gibbons's name in a women's rights petition without asking her permission, her daughter Julia convinced her to send a disclaimer to the *Tribune*. Her work for women lay, for the most part, in charity and reform rather than in politics.[79]

Gibbons began her involvement with the New York Infant Asylum as one of the original members of its "ladies' board." In 1871, she was the board's vice president. In 1873, Gibbons was appointed to the infant asylum's house committee, and by 1878 she was the house committee's chair.[80] As a member of the house committee, Gibbons kept a close eye on the well-being of the "family," as she called the women and children who lived at the infant asylum, and she documented her observations in a journal. She kept track of the women's sewing and laundry work and rejoiced at the occasional marriage that took place between inmates and their baby's fathers. She was also able to laugh at inevitable slip-ups, such as the events that caused a blanket, a pair of baby's shoes, and a slice of bread to appear mysteriously on the front lawn of the infant asylum's house at Sixty-first Street and Tenth Avenue. The shoes, it turned out, were old ones thrown away by a mother who had come to bring her child a new pair. "As regards the blanket," she remarked, "the disposition is, the wind seized it—but it was rescued—the slice of bread must be of very rare occurrence—as in all our goings to and fro, we never met with a like adventure."[81]

Gibbons could be lighthearted, but she also took her responsibilities as a straightener of twisted souls seriously. For instance, she was unhappy about the behavior of one of the infant asylum's inmates, a woman named Kate. Kate had given birth at the asylum in January 1877 and departed in May, leaving her baby behind. The baby died, "as children abandoned by their mothers generally do," Gibbons observed. Before the year was out, Kate was back, pregnant again. As at the nursery, repeat offenders were not ordinarily allowed to return—but the managers relented and let Kate in again. Gibbons protested: "the New York Infant Asylum should be protected against all such offences, which are in direct violation of our rules, and the spirit of our established laws."[82]

Gibbons was more enthusiastic about Dr. Anna Angell, who began working as the infant asylum's resident physician in 1877.[83] On a cool summer day in 1879, Gibbons went to visit the children at the infant asylum and observed some of Dr. Angell's daily routine. Up at five, Angell supplied the children with glasses of milk, then sent them "over the river" or "down on the Elevated for a trip on the Staten Island Boat" to take advantage of the healthful breezes. "She is a rare woman," Gibbons wrote her daughter the next day, "and only a woman with genuine sympathies would put her shoulder to the wheel as she does."[84] Abigail Hopper Gibbons valued the thirty-four-year-old Angell's motherly ministrations as much as, or perhaps even more than, she appreciated her medical expertise.

Gibbons was a leader in the Women's Prison Association, which ran the Isaac T. Hopper Home (named for her father, the founder of the Prison Association of New York), a residential halfway house for women released from prison. The Hopper Home was an important model for her work at the New York Infant Asylum. In both places, the inmates agreed to jettison their former ways of life in exchange for religious instruction and training in domestic skills. The female ex-offenders of the Hopper Home, like the unwed mothers of the Infant Asylum, were placed as domestic servants.

Like the inmates of the New York Infant Asylum, many and probably most of the residents of the Hopper Home were "fallen women." By the middle of the nineteenth century, as agitation about the "fallen woman" rose, increasing numbers of women went to prison for sexual crimes. In crowded cities such as New York, more and more women were arrested for prostitution, vagrancy that gave the appearance of soliciting, and unseemly public behavior. Convictions for abortions may also have contributed to the number of women in prisons, since it was just at this time—the mid 1840s—that New York State law made women criminally liable for abortion (a change from earlier laws that made abortionists alone liable).[85]

In 1845, Margaret Fuller, whose influential book on women's rights,

Woman in the Nineteenth Century, had just come out, published an appeal for the Hopper Home in the *New York Tribune.* She asked the paper's readers to support "those who have not been guarded either by social influence or inward strength from that first mistake which the opinion of the world makes irrevocable for women alone."[86] Had Fuller not died in 1850, she might have written the same thing twenty years later in support of the New York Infant Asylum. For Abigail Hopper Gibbons, the compromised women of the Hopper Home and their fallen sisters at the Infant Asylum must have seemed very much the same.

Just as Abigail Hopper Gibbons was acquainted with fallen women before she got to the infant asylum, so was she familiar with foundlings from her by then long-established habit of paying holiday visits to the city's young wards at Long Island Farms and, after 1848, to the nurseries and the Infant Hospital for foundlings on Randall's Island, often with friends.[87] In 1875, Louisa May Alcott, already the author of *Little Women,* accompanied Abigail and James Gibbons to Randall's Island. Traveling over on the boat with them were the mayor, a city commissioner, and a reporter from the *Tribune.* According to Alcott, Abby Gibbons besieged the "rotundities"—Alcott's witty appellation for city officials fattened on graft—with her suggestions for "what *ought* to be done for the poor things on the Island."[88] The officials gathered up their girths and fled from what must have seemed like annoying female interference, but the two women attracted the admiration of the young *Tribune* reporter. He stuck to them throughout their visit, gathering copy for his paper while helping Alcott and the Gibbonses distribute toys and candy to the children.[89]

Alcott noted that things were in good order on the island at what was doubtless a carefully prepared-for event, but she also saw much that disturbed her. At a ceremony in the chapel, Alcott saw "a flock of girls in blue gowns and white aprons" in the audience of neatly dressed children and observed "what a pretty group they made, with gay ribbons in their hair. . . . But among forty girls, I counted fifteen with defective eyes, nine deformed, and seven lame ones for the blight of poverty, neglect and bad birth, was on nearly all, if one examined closely."[90] Alcott also saw infant foundlings in the Infant Hospital on Randall's Island. Of these Alcott remarked: "Pauper women are nurses; and Mrs. G. says the babies die like sheep, many being deserted so young nothing can be hoped or done for them."[91]

Despite the sadness she felt at what she saw, Alcott enjoyed her visit to Randall's Island. "Next week we go to the Tombs," she wrote her family with somewhat incongruous enthusiasm, "and some day I am to visit the hospital with her, for I like this better than parties, etc." Alcott was so entranced by her visit to Randall's Island that she repeated these sentiments in her journal: "A memorable day. Make a story of it. Enjoy these things more than the parties and dinners." The story she wrote appeared in the *Youth's Companion* the following spring.[92]

Alcott observed that Gibbons also enjoyed her visit to Randall's Island, despite the sad sights. After their visit there together in 1875, Gibbons breathed to Alcott, "There now, I shall feel better for the next year!"[93] Gibbons's work at the New York Infant Asylum brought her the same kind of pleasure. In 1874, during a bout of illness that confined her to her room and the perhaps overscrupulous care of her daughter Julia, she wrote her daughter Sarah longingly: "I believe if I was allowed Infant Asylum delights it would renew life and action; but I name the lovely charity of which I am so fond, at my peril, in the presence of Julia." The doctor who cared for her during this illness was Stephen Smith; as the secretary of the New York Infant Asylum's board, he may have been more sympathetic to her longings than was Julia. After Abigail recovered, she wrote to a friend: "Now, however, I am well and on duty as usual. Plenty to do, and I enjoy the work; especially the mothers and babies of the Infant Asylum."[94]

But hands-on charity work at the Isaac Hopper Home, Randall's Island, and the Infant Asylum provided more than pleasure for Gibbons —it was also a necessary source of consolation. In 1832, when her three-year-old half-brother died, she wrote to friends: "We all loved him too much, and I have made up my mind never to allow myself to become so devotedly attached to any child." This resolution was tested when her year-old son James died in 1844; her five-and-a-half-year-old son Isaac in 1847; her son Willie, after an accident in 1855 while he was a student at Harvard; and much later, her fifty-three-year-old daughter Julia. In all she bore six children, and only her daughters Sarah and Lucy survived her. She suffered the most from Willie's death, and when for a while it threatened to drown her in grief, she found, as she had during previous crises, that charitable work was the thing that could carry her back to dry ground. "Is there not an angel of consolation in the activity of benevolence?" Catharine Sedgwick wrote her on the occasion of Isaac's death. "You are wise in yielding to its heavenly influence."[95]

All of the foundling asylums were driven by an engine of grief fueled by tears shed over the premature deaths of children. Visitors to the Sisters of Charity's New York Foundling Asylum noticed that the women of the Ladies' Society that supported the institution with chores and fundraising appeared to be consoled by their work. In 1871, a reporter for the *Herald* remarked that these lay women included "many a mother, pining for her lost children," soothing "her heartache by making pretty things for these abandoned ones." Missionary Helen Campbell made a similar observation twenty years later; she noted the presence of women volunteers at the Sisters' institution who donated "food, money, and bundles of little garments, often from the drawer where they had been laid with tears, as the bereaved mother folded them away in memory of the little one who had put on angel raiment."[96] Mary Du Bois, who lost a young son, may also have used her foundling asylum work to sublimate sorrow. In at least one instance she used the memory of that sorrow to gain assistance for the nursery. Twenty-two years after her son's death, Du Bois evoked his memory in a letter to one of his friends, by then a state legislator in a position to assist her with a petition before his colleagues.[97]

Foundling asylum work was a source of consolation for the women (as well as the men) who ran these institutions. But if these well-meaning members of the middle class were unable to keep their own children alive, they were even less able to save these sickly and unwanted children of the streets.

"A Great Depot for Wet Nurses": The Almshouse Infant Department

The Infant Hospital on Randall's Island, which Abigail Hopper Gibbons visited with Louisa May Alcott in 1875, had opened in August 1869, but its inauguration was preceded by several years of unhappy experimentation on the part of the Commissioners of Public Charities and Correction. In 1860 the commissioners moved the babies who had been removed from their nurses in the aftermath of the Mary Cullough scandal to the almshouse on Blackwell's Island. This move represented an effort at better care for almshouse babies (and possibly also an effort at obscuring any failures from the scrutiny of the press and public), but its result was death for over 80 percent of the babies. Summing up at the end of the year, the warden of the almshouse deflected blame: "A large number were, when admitted, suffering from incurable diseases (inherited in most cases from diseased parents); a number of them have since been relieved by death of a life that could not have failed to have been a burden to them." But at a later date the commissioners ruefully admitted that "the diet was found improper; adequate medical attendance was not provided; the nurses, infirm old women, inmates of the Alms House, were anxious to escape from their unpaid duties, and these duties terminated with the death of the infants committed to their care. It was not surprising that, under these circumstances, life was of short duration."[98]

Dr. Job Lewis Smith, who cared for foundlings in the almshouse during this period, later recounted the dire situation there. "These waifs," he recollected, "were intrusted to the pauper women in the almshouse. Each woman occupied a cot, under which were the dirty clothes and broken utensils brought from her shanty or tenement-house in the city. Foundlings were transported every day to the almshouse, and distributed by the superintendent, who informed me at my first visit that it would be an act of humanity if each foundling were given a fatal dose of opium on its arrival, since all of them died."[99]

"The steamboat every morning brought foundlings to the island," he added in another recollection, "and every afternoon removed an equal number for burial in Potter's field."[100]

On June 1, 1866, in a bid to ameliorate this situation, the commissioners established a separate department for infants in the almshouse on Blackwell's Island. "An Infant Department," they proudly reported, "has been created, where the foundling infants hitherto distributed among the wards of the Almshouse, and consigned to the mercies of reluctant attendants, have been gathered under the care of a matron and kind and attentive nurses."[101]

The new Infant Department kept babies up to the age of about two-and-a-half (later this was raised to three or four, and it was probably always somewhat flexible). Like all of the city's foundling asylums, the Infant Department accepted mothers as well as babies and pressed them into service as wet nurses for unaccompanied foundlings. The children fell into two categories: "nurse children"—foundlings and other solitary babies cared for by nurses rather than their own mothers—and "mother's children"—babies accompanied by their destitute mothers. Children old enough to toddle were called "walking children."[102]

THE FOUNDLING—SCENE IN THE FIRST WARD OF THE ALMS-HOUSE.—(See Page 25.)

Female inmates caring for foundlings in the almshouse on Blackwell's Island soon after the establishment of the Infant Department there. *Harper's Weekly,* January 12, 1867. Collection of the New-York Historical Society, 77824d.

A house physician was appointed, two physicians from the medical board of the city-run Charity Hospital began making regular visits, and diet, clothing, and "the whole regime" were subjected to "radical changes."[103]

The babies came to the Infant Department from the same sources that had always supplied the almshouse: streets, stoops, baby farmers cheated out of their pay by absconding parents, and the police. By this time, the police force was in the middle of a process of professionalization that had begun with the founding of the city's first professional police department in 1845; the retrieval of abandoned babies was added officially to its list of "incidental duties of the department."[104] The Infant Department also received foundlings from a new source: the Emigrant Hospital on Ward's Island. Women who arrived pregnant and unmarried in New York's port could give birth at the city's Emigrant Hospital, but the commissioners of emigration threw these women out as soon as they recovered and required them to find work immediately. This rule was an effort on the part of the commissioners of emigration to prevent vagrancy, since a poor, unemployed immigrant, they believed, would become a nuisance on the city's streets. Most of the women ejected from the Emigrant Hospital went to work in private homes as domestic servants. As domestic servants, they typically could not keep their babies with them and were consequently left with no choice but to leave them behind in the hospital. These babies were then delivered to the Infant Department. Like the conflicting rules of entry at the Nursery and Child's Hospital and the New York Foundling Asylum, this was yet another of the bureaucratic conundrums that buffeted poor, single mothers in the city.[105]

Despite the improved conditions at the new Infant Department, one of the visiting physicians there had to admit that the almshouse "is, and always must remain an unsuitable place for the rearing of Infants."[106] In 1867, after a year's experience with the new regime, the commissioners reported that although there was "some" improvement and the babies were now "treated with tenderness and care," the "mortality continued at the same frightful ratio." It ranged, they estimated, between 85 and 100 percent. In an effort to stem this flood of death, they imported about fifty women from the city's two general hospitals, Bellevue and the Charity Hospital on Blackwell's Island, to work as wet nurses, in addition to the mothers already in residence.[107]

In this period when hospitals provided more shelter than cure, public hospital patients were poor people, and hospital nurses were typically recovered patients who had no homes to return to and thus remained to live and work in the hospital.[108] Thus these newly imported wet nurses were poor, sick women who happened to be lactating and who probably had no other place to go, which would explain why they agreed to take their own infants and live in the almshouse's Infant Department to feed foundlings for a while. At the Infant Department, they were housed away from the general almshouse population and fed well in a separate dining room, receiving such "extra diet" as ale, eggs, and milk.

They were also released from manual labor and clothed in "distinctive dress," which probably represented a meaningful gift of new clothing to them.[109]

The work of the wet nurses at first appeared to lead to a "manifest and immediate" improvement. More babies survived, and more ward space had to be cleared to house them. In January 1868, in search of extra space and in an effort to improve the babies' hygienic surroundings, the department was moved out of the Blackwell's Island almshouse and up the East River to the newly completed but still unoccupied Inebriate Asylum on Ward's Island.[110] Despite these changes, however, the commissioners' optimism was stillborn. What had at first looked like a "manifest and immediate" improvement turned out only to be a pattern of fluctuation; the infants' mortality rate sometimes fell, but at other times rose "to nearly the old rate." Thus the commissioners had to concede that the "mortality was a scandal to the [medical] profession and the Department."[111] Like all the city's foundling asylums, which collected many children together in their wards, the Infant Department created excellent conditions for the spread of infection, which it did not have any means to combat; no doubt this was one reason for its failure to lower the death rate substantially.

Physician Stephen Rogers, a critic of the Infant Department, toured its new quarters in the Inebriate Asylum on Ward's Island in the summer of 1868. He found the babies hot, uncomfortable, and pestered by flies and mosquitoes. Their food, care, and surroundings were all, he judged, inadequate. Dr. Rogers also noticed that the number of wet nurses was insufficient, since the commissioners had difficulty convincing them to remain on the island.[112] This was a situation with which the commissioners struggled bitterly. The wet nurses, much as they may have enjoyed the special treatment they received in the Infant Department, were not as docile as the commissioners wished. As lactating women willing to work as wet nurses were in high demand among families in the city, representatives of domestic service agencies crossed the river to Ward's Island to lure away these poor women with their valuable breast milk. The agents' offers of well-paid jobs in private homes were evidently tempting to the wet nurses, who were living in an empty building on a lonely East River island, nursing sick and dying infants without pay.

The officials of the Infant Department did not see it that way. Like the Sisters of Charity and the lady managers of the Nursery and Child's

Hospital, they viewed these poor women's decision to maximize their earnings and seek greater comfort for themselves as a failure of their maternal instincts. According to a special committee of physicians organized by the commissioners to investigate the department's continuing high death rate, the newly formed Infant Department had become nothing but a "great depot for wet nurses," and the "desire to be free from all restraint—even that of an offspring—"was what motivated these women to board the Manhattan-bound ferry with the wet-nurse agents, leaving not only their infant charges but also their own babies behind.[113]

Despite the committee's pique, it is clear that working conditions for wet nurses in the Infant Department were difficult and even dangerous to the health of the women and their own babies. The volume of babies that passed through the Infant Department was overwhelming, and the death rate, particularly among the foundlings, was tragically high. As at all of New York's foundling asylums, wet nurses in the department were required to nurse two babies, their own and a motherless foundling, but the death rate was such that the women actually nursed a succession of sick and dying foundlings. Compared to this, the promise not only of earning a substantial salary, but also of nursing a single, healthy infant in a comfortable home, even if it meant boarding her own baby elsewhere as wet nurses often did, or leaving it on the island, must have been tempting.

A glance at some numbers the commissioners reported during the Infant Department years demonstrates just why they were alarmed over the state of infants there. Between June 1, 1866, when the Infant Department opened, and the last day of that year, the department received 466 solitary babies. These joined the 88 motherless babies already on hand. After 53 babies were taken away by their parents, adopted, or sent to the Randall's Island nursery, about 82 percent of the remaining motherless babies died. During the same June-to-December period, 258 babies entered the department with their own mothers, to join 89 already there. After 178 went home with their parents, about 40 percent of the "mother's children" remaining in the Infant Department died. Two years later the situation was worse. In 1868 the Infant Department admitted 994 unaccompanied babies. With 164 remaining from the previous year, the total was 1,158. After 137 of these were discharged or adopted, 87 percent of those remaining died. That year the Infant Department admitted 583 babies along with their mothers, to add to the 146 remaining from the previous year. Of these, 51 percent died.[114]

Infant Department officials were acutely aware of the difference between the death rates of motherless babies, particularly foundlings, and of babies accompanied by their mothers. A visiting physician put this phenomenon into perspective: "In accordance with the universal experience, it is among the first class, the Foundlings, that the death-rate is incomparably higher." Foundlings, he explained, suffered from the rigors of exposure, including extremes of weather and lack of food during the hours that passed before they were plucked off stoops or out of tenement entryways by the police or kindly strangers. In addition, he noted, their loss of access to sufficient breast milk made their survival unlikely. The department's difficulty at retaining wet nurses meant that some foundlings had to be bottle-fed. This was a dangerous procedure before cow's milk could be kept reliably free of bacteria (and in this period the role of bacteria in illness was not yet understood). Thus digestive illnesses, probably picked up from impure milk and water, accounted for "the immense majority of deaths" among foundlings.[115] The Infant Department's house physician noticed that after "an exclusive course of bottle-feeding," foundlings suffered a mortality of "practically 100 per centum." The death rate of foundlings, he concluded, was "fearful," and "it cannot be otherwise than with the most profound interest that the subject must be considered."[116]

The committee of physicians assembled to investigate the Infant Department's death rate did not feel hopeful that the situation could improve. The task of keeping abandoned infants alive, its members warned, "enlists all the best sympathies of our nature; it is one that would be unendurable if we were not to recognize the incontrovertible fact that an appalling mortality is inevitable."[117]

The following year, the committee, whose members were Stephen Smith, Job Lewis Smith, Abraham Jacobi, Austin Flint, Isaac E. Taylor, and George T. Elliot, was made into a permanent medical board for the Infant Department. All were prominent members of the city's medical establishment, and Abraham Jacobi and Job Lewis Smith were pioneers in the emerging field of pediatrics. It was Smith who had observed the shocking death rate of foundlings in the almshouse in the period between the Mary Cullough scandal and the establishment of the Infant Department. Jacobi, Elliot, and the Smiths were also on the medical staffs of the Nursery and Child's Hospital and the New York Infant Asylum. George T. Elliot had been the chair of the committee; he became the president of the Infant Department's new medical board.[118]

Dr. Elliot put his committee's bleak warning into a broader (though equally grim) context when he spoke at an 1868 meeting of the Medical Society of the County of New York:

> I have been condemned to feel, as a father and as a physician, that do what we may, we cannot lay the spectre of the inevitable mortality of childhood. This discussion cannot be conducted in the elevated spirit that should characterize it, until full confession is made of this inevitable mortality. You must not confine your view to one city, to one country, to one zone. Go through the whole world; take reports of exploring expeditions; examine the statistics of mortality in families placed under the most favorable hygienic conditions in the world; go among your own patients of the most favored classes—where is the family that has succeeded in raising all its children, even under the best conditions and with the best medical advice?[119]

This was the state of medical practice with children in 1868. But something new was surfacing in the anxious attention that the commissioners and the members of the Infant Department's medical board now chose to pay to foundlings. Their attention was, in itself, a departure from the fatalism, even revulsion, toward abandoned infants manifested by all of the city's charities for women and children before the Civil War. J. Bayley Done, one of the Infant Department's visiting physicians, commented on this turn in attitudes in the year the department was founded. "In former years," he wrote, "it has been generally the feeling, pervading all classes of the community, that, to these waifs of society, death is a happy result. It is gratifying now to observe that a view more creditable to humanity is being adopted."[120]

The Randall's Island Infant Hospital, 1869

That "more creditable" view was expressed by the commissioners of Public Charities and Correction in the foundling asylum they began building on Randall's Island, probably in early 1868.[121] On August 9, 1869, with the building still incomplete, the women, babies, and "walking children" of the Infant Department made the short trip from their temporary home in the inebriate asylum on Ward's Island to their new one on adjacent Randall's Island. The Infant Department's herd of

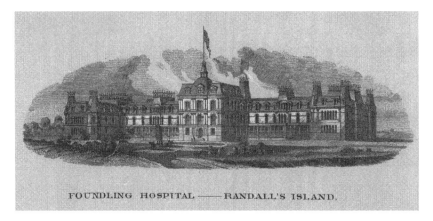

FOUNDLING HOSPITAL ——— RANDALL'S ISLAND.

The Randall's Island Infant Hospital, completed 1869. Collection of the New-York Historical Society, 79726d.

twelve cows did not accompany them. There was no room for them on Randall's Island, so they remained behind at the Ward's Island farm. The children lost the company of the cows but not their milk, for the farmer assured the commissioners that it would still be delivered morning and night.[122]

Randall's Island was already the site of the department's Nursery Department for destitute children ages four to sixteen. The placement of the Infant Hospital near the Nursery Department was logical, and it was also convenient, since babies from the Infant Hospital who beat the odds to survive past infancy and were neither adopted nor returned to their families were transferred to the Nursery Department when they reached approximately the age of four.[123]

Like the buildings of the Nursery Department, which had been constructed twenty years earlier, the Infant Hospital was a grand, hopeful gesture in masonry. Standing on the western (Manhattan) side of the island and facing the green hills of the Bronx (then part of Westchester County) to the north, the three-story brick and stone building consisted of a central pavilion with wings extended east and west. Festooned with porches, gables, and turrets, and with a jaunty American flag flying from the top of the central pavilion, the building was, according to one observer, "in the most approved style of modern hospital architecture."[124] The Infant Department's house physician, E. S. Dunster agreed, calling it a "noble building" and the best the department had erected so far, particularly "in the matter of light, ventilation and the capacity of the wards."[125] But Dunster also made serious criticisms. The building, despite its seeming grandness, was not large enough for all the babies, and he looked forward to the completion of an additional wing. Without more space, the smells created by hundreds of babies crowded together would only increase. According to the scientific knowledge available to Dr. Dunster, smell was equated with the "miasma" of deadly disease. It was not just unpleasant, then; it was dangerous.[126] Thus in 1871 Dr. Dunster, with his needs for space still unmet, complained about the "unpleasant and injurious odors that pervade the building, especially at night." "All my efforts," he insisted, "have been directed to economizing life, and this can only be done at expense of constant purity of air."[127]

Dr. Dunster also disapproved of the commissioners' habitual use of convicts and paupers as workers at their institutions. He objected especially to the use of convict and pauper nurses in the new Infant Hospital. To expect these women to give the infants good care was, he remarked bitterly, "simply chimerical."[128] He accused these women of "indifference, neglect, and sometimes almost criminal carelessness." "To rely on such assistance," he warned, "is not only an unwise and costly economy, but also the worst possible policy, in view of the degrading influences, and directly disastrous consequences to health and life that inevitably attend contact with such creatures."[129]

Dr. Dunster pled in vain. The commissioners were willing to provide some paid nurses for the department, but they would not relinquish their supply of unpaid captive labor. They were particularly unwilling—and in fact unable—to give up the valuable milk provided by those female inmates of the hospitals, almshouse, workhouse, and other public institutions who were able to supply it. Abraham Jacobi, who also deplored the commissioners' use of these "corrupt, lazy, whimsical or malicious women," realized that these were the only women whom the Infant Hospital could reliably get. Only the "sickly, the profligate, the very poor" would agree to work as wet nurses on Randall's Island, and "no married woman, as a rule . . . will ever consent to become a wet-nurse to any of our children," Jacobi reasoned.[130]

In its use of convict and pauper labor, the new Infant Hospital was following the practice established much earlier by the almshouse. All of the institutions run by the commissioners of the Department of Public Charities and Correction—the Almshouse Department's successor—used their inmates as their principal source of labor. Incarcerated men and boys did all the building and landscaping. Women and girls in the prison, almshouse, workhouse, nursery, hospitals, and insane asylum nursed their fellow inmates, washed, cleaned, mended, and produced endless streams of clothing and institutional linen. The twenty-thousand "new shirts and chemises" produced by female inmates in one year were, the commission's storekeeper estimated, "enough for an army," in this case a captive army of the poor.[131]

A wet nurse in the Infant Hospital would have lived in a building built by inmates of the Blackwell's Island Penitentiary, one made of stone quarried and dressed by inmates on the islands. The rooms she spent her days in were likely dusted and mopped by women from the workhouse, sent over as "help." She may have slept on sheets made by female inmates of the lunatic asylum, worn a dress made by a jailed prostitute, and had her apron mended by a little girl in the Randall's Island nurseries. Her laundry was among the 390,000 items that passed through the Randall's Island wash house yearly. Her breakfast probably included eggs and milk from the Ward's Island farm, rowed over to Randall's by a convict boatman. The cabbage she ate for dinner might have been grown on the grounds of the almshouse on Blackwell's Island. The seawalls that protected her from the river's rough currents had been built by prisoners and male inmates of the workhouse. These men had also graded the roads she walked on and planted the trees whose shade she enjoyed. When she wasn't tending to her own baby and the foundling assigned to her, she probably spent her time sweeping, sewing, and mending for her fellow inmates. And if she was unfortunate enough to die before she could leave the island, there was a shroud ready-made for her by the busy fingers of the insane, along with a grave in Potter's Field.[132]

Despite Dunster's accusation of "costly economy," the commissioners believed that they were operating efficiently and correctly. The wardens of all the institutions bragged about the vast amounts of food and clothing they produced, about the money they saved, and about the lessons in hard work absorbed by their charges, whom they considered naturally indolent, according to the era's tenets of charity. The production numbers they reported seem like efforts to quantify the increase in virtue among their inmates. The man who supervised work at the Ward's Island farm reported that in 1869 the farm yielded $3,941.26 worth of vegetables. "Every pound of vegetables raised may justly be considered as so much money saved," remarked the storekeeper who distributed this produce. The exact attention paid by these two functionaries to the cash value of each parsnip contrasts strangely with the loose accounting that characterized the city's financial transactions during this, the height of the pillaging Tweed era.[133]

Labor was also carefully measured. The warden of the penitentiary computed that, in one year, the men in his institution logged a total of 106,944 days of labor and the women, 25,054. The supervisor of the workhouse reported that his inmates "have been kept continually at work, breaking stone, grading and repairing sea wall, cultivating the grounds. Tailors, shoemakers, carpenters, blacksmiths, tinsmiths, horse shoers, painters, have been diligently kept at work, performing a large amount of work for the various institutions."[134] The use of inmate labor accomplished the goals intended, but an unintended consequence was the airless, hermetic feeling created by a closed system. The older children who lived on Randall's Island must certainly have felt it.

The location of many of the city's charitable and correctional institutions on islands added to their atmosphere of melancholy isolation. Dr. Stephen Rogers made note of this when he visited the Infant Department at the inebriate asylum on Ward's Island in 1868. In the time that it took foundlings to travel to the island, he complained, they could die of starvation. Infants, he reported, were "often delivered to the hospital almost moribund." Ward's Island's remoteness also made it difficult for visitors to get there. These visitors, he suggested, might have included charitable citizens willing to make donations, families wanting to adopt, and mothers ready to reclaim their abandoned babies. He angrily compared the remoteness of the commissioners' hideaway for their destitute and dying babies to the all-too-visible prominence of the Fifth Avenue home of the famous abortionist Madame Restell: "inasmuch as the finest street of our city counts among its palaces one which, to the disgrace of our people, is a gaudy monument to infanticide, placed where the crowds on their evening drives to our Park may gaze upon it, the asylum for those infants who escape this iniquitous institution should have an equally conspicuous and accessible place."[135]

The isolation of the city's public institutions for the poor had been a subject of comment for decades. As early as 1855, Isaac Townsend, then president of the Board of Governors of the almshouse, noted irritably that "the locations of our principal Institutions are such as to take them from the general examination and observation of similar Institutions elsewhere, and our citizens generally are in total ignorance of their extent or the service required to do justice to their organization or their inmates." The result, he complained, was neglect from city and state governments when it came time to allocate funds. Townsend's observations were backed up by an article in the *Tribune* from around the same time, which referred to the Randall's Island nurseries as "this almost unknown channel through which flows one of the City's noblest charities." As late as 1887, Infant Hospital officials were still complaining about how hard it was to get to Randall's Island, particularly in the winter when there was ice on the river. The commissioners begged city officials for a steam launch to replace the small, exposed rowboats they were forced to use.[136]

But the islands' isolation also served several positive purposes, according to public and official opinion. One author went so far as to call the East River islands "a sort of moral rampart to the great metropolis" erected to protect responsible citizens from contamination. At the same time, the wayward and the potentially wayward, such as the children on Randall's Island, were removed from urban temptations and learned to mend their ways, for in the self-sustaining ecosystem of the institutions of charity and correction, criminals, alcoholics, vagrants, pickpockets, fallen women, and destitute children learned to accustom themselves to hard work.[137]

Inmates were assisted in this process, most urban reformers believed, by exposure to the islands' rural beauty. At this time of bewilderingly rapid urbanization, many reformers believed that the countryside had the power to soothe and restore bodies and souls deformed by city life. Visitors to the institutions on the East River islands often commented on their beauty. The abolitionist and author Lydia Maria Child, on visiting the penitentiary on Blackwell's Island, described the island's "quiet loveliness of scenery, unsurpassed by anything I have ever witnessed. . . . [the island] abounds with charming nooks—open wells in shady places, screened by large weeping willows; gardens and arbours running down to the river's edge, to look at themselves in the waters; and pretty boats, like white-winged birds, chased by their shadows, and breaking the waves into gems." How "wise and kind," she concluded, "to place the erring and the diseased in the midst of such calm, bright influences."[138] Catharine Sedgwick described Randall's Island as "that lovely island in its rich natural beauty."[139]

A Visit to the "Children's Island"

The islands were beautiful, but they were beautiful prisons. Randall's, Blackwell's, Ward's, and the other islands were not easily accessible to the public and, of course, most of their residents were forbidden to leave. None of the sixteen ferry lines that busily worked the East River, illuminating the water at night with their colored lights, stopped at the islands.[140] Only the boats of the commissioners of Public Charities and Correction docked there.[141] Charles Dickens described the experience of being rowed to the islands in one of these boats by "a crew of prisoners, who were dressed in a striped uniform of black and buff, in which they looked like faded tigers."[142] For the children of Randall's Island, the city must have seemed worlds away—and the beautiful ferries a cruel temptation.

The East River islands were hard to get to, but the determinedly curious or charitable, people such as Alcott, Gibbons, Child, Sedgwick, and Dickens, were willing to make the effort. In 1874, William H. Rideing, author of a series of articles in *Appleton's Journal* about city life, visited the Infant Hospital on Randall's Island. Like many visitors to the East River islands, Rideing appreciated the beauty of the approach. The "children's island," as he called it, was tainted by "sin all in its area, to be sure," but at the same time it was "pretty and salubrious in its situation." "You must have seen it," he reminded the readers of *Appleton's Journal,* "and admired its undulating greenness in the summer-time." Ferry riders would be familiar with the Infants' Hospital building, since, with its turrets and outstretched wings, it was "a prominent object as the Harlem boat bears you swiftly down the river."

Once landed at Randall's Island, Rideing saw an inscription over the Infant Hospital's door: "I was sick, and ye came unto me." Walking in, he was assaulted by a "vociferous throng" of "twenty or thirty little scamps" who attacked their visitor with "violent demonstrations of friendship." These were the two- and three-year-old "walking children." Rideing was pleased with their appearance: "They are livelier and ruddier than most charity children," he found, "and are evidently better cared for and fed." Their dress was "common but neat." He was particularly impressed with the boldness of one little girl:

> One young lady marches coolly toward us, thrusts her companions aside, and, after reaching for our hands, strokes them fondly. This is but a prelude; for, having ingratiated herself with us, she dives her busy little fingers into our overcoat pockets, and brings out all they contain. As she finds only the morning newspaper and a handkerchief, and is not disappointed, we suppose her only motive is the inborn curiosity of her sex. Her sharp eyes detect our glasses dangling before us, and she holds them to her impudent little nose, archly turning her face upward and smiling at us angelically. Until now we do not perceive how sweet the siren is. Her hair is golden, her eyes are the darkest blue, and her skin is like a peach. "A foundling, aged two years and seven months." That's all the history of this frail, dear little blossom.

Rideing was less impressed with the babies he saw, "pulpy little creatures, ticketed in white cots." The doctor who accompanied him on his tour through the hospital showed off some of the healthier specimens, among them a baby found abandoned in a graveyard. "Came to the nursery almost a skeleton," the doctor explained tersely. "Been here ten months. Age sixteen months." But Rideing also noticed the occasional "wasted, pining, suffering child, tossing himself in pain and fever on his narrow bed." And, like everyone else who spent time at the Infant Hospital, he had something to say about the female convicts, paupers, and destitute, unmarried mothers who worked there as nurses. Some, he noted approvingly, had a "spruce" appearance and were careful in their work, and others were the babies' own mothers. But, he observed, "The most suitable women are not always available for the service, and many who are coarse and brutal foist themselves upon the hospital."

All in all, he concluded, it was better not to be brought up in the Infant Hospital: "Sick or well, the waifs have a sadness about them which is painful to the observer, though they may be unconscious of it themselves. The exuberance, the independence, and the frankness, that give to home-bred children their greatest charms, have only a very limited scope in the liliputian unfortunates of the almshouse."[143]

Lilliputian unfortunates or not, the children Alcott and Rideing encountered at the Infant Hospital and that they might have encountered at any of the four foundling asylums in New York City were more fortunate than their pre–Civil War counterparts, if only because they had been saved from death in the street. Many, however, died inside the new asylums. While this was a source of pain to the people who organized the asylums, it was not enough to discourage them from their work. By the second half of the nineteenth century, when all of the foundling asylums opened, that work, to rescue and reform fallen women and to uphold their separate standards in the battlefield of New York's religious conflicts, still looked as if it could be accomplished.

5

"Out-Heroding Herod"
The Foundlings and the Revolutionary

It took an outsider, in fact a revolutionary, to recognize that the new foundling asylums, with their troubling death rates, were misconceived. That revolutionary was the German-born physician Abraham Jacobi.

Jacobi, an attending physician at the Nursery and Child's Hospital and a member of the Randall's Island Infant Hospital's medical board, was a pioneer in the new field of pediatrics. He was a representative of a new laboratory-based medicine that was centered in Germany and France and brought to the United States by European physicians such as himself and by Americans who studied medicine in Europe.[1] Medicine based on scientific investigation gained authority as it became increasingly effective over the second half of the nineteenth century and particularly during the twentieth. As the medical and scientific ideas Jacobi represented gained power, the medical "quacks" that proliferated in the antebellum period gradually relinquished it.[2]

At the same time, the religious, charitable model for the care of the sick and erring poor, with its importance as an arena for flexing female power and its passivity in the face of a high infant death rate, increasingly came to seem obsolete, a relic of the years before the Civil War.[3] Jacobi's role as an emissary of an emerging scientific understanding of disease, which included a new understanding of the special nature of children's bodies and their diseases, made him unsympathetic to the religious and moral values of the Nursery and Child's Hospital. The result was a conflict with the nursery's "first directress," Mary Du Bois. This conflict set the terms of a broader debate that ultimately led to the downfall of the foundling asylums.

Abraham Jacobi and Mary Du Bois could not have come from more dissimilar worlds. Jacobi was born in a Prussian village in 1830 to a poor Jewish family.[4] Like his friend Carl Schurz, who flourished in the

Left, Mary Delafield Du Bois. Collection of the New-York Historical Society, 79751d. *Right,* Abraham Jacobi. Courtesy of the National Library of Medicine.

United States and ended his successful political career as secretary of the interior, Jacobi was a product of the German revolution of 1848. He had been a medical student at the University of Bonn when he joined the underground Cologne branch of the Communist League. In April 1851, he went to Berlin, where he immersed himself in the city's radical life. Soon after, he was arrested along with other members of the Cologne Communist League and spent more than a year in jail.[5] In May 1852, Jacobi escaped from jail and fled to England. After a brief and unsuccessful interval in England, where he camped first with Karl Marx and his family in London and then with Friedrich Engels in Manchester, Jacobi set sail for America. In November 1853, only months before Du Bois opened her Nursery for the Children of Poor Women, the twenty-three-year-old Jacobi arrived in New York.

Both Abraham Jacobi's political principles and his choice of a medical career resulted from his experiences as an ardent and involved young man at a time of dramatic revolutionary upheaval. Years later, referring to his own youthful experiences, he remarked that "among the revolutionary youth that died on the battlefields or pined in dungeons, not a few were students of medicine."[6] Like the scientist-statesman Rudolph Virchow, whose example he emulated, Jacobi believed that poverty and political oppression were the enemies of health. "Physicians," wrote Jacobi, quoting Virchow, "are the natural attorneys of the poor."[7] Thus it was not only as a physician interested in the diseases of children but also as an advocate of the poor that Jacobi was attracted to the problem of foundlings. He also believed that the republican United States, a place where so much was possible for the rootless individual, could be as receptive to the foundling as it was to the immigrant. The United States, he argued,

> with their uniform laws and institutions, their freedom from legal religious prejudices and ties, their immunities from petty or powerful individual sovereigns, their wealth and conservative magnanimity, their readiness to receive every stranger, rich or poor, amongst their citizens, their knowledge of the importance of every newcomer as an additional means of wealth and power, with the general principles of the Declaration of Independence pervading the communities of the country, are more than every other country of the globe entitled to the honor and duty of caring for the neglected and poor of every age and station. Thus no means have been spared, no attempts will remain untried, to save as many newborn and to raise them into healthy men and women and good citizens. Their salvation is the country's good.[8]

This passage, aflame with the ardor of the adopted citizen, suggests that Jacobi's equation of the isolated foundling with the rootless immigrant evolved at least partly out of his own experience as an exile who finally landed in the United States, where he found success and came to feel so much at home.

In New York, Jacobi maintained his radical connections. He settled at first in *Kleindeutschland,* "little Germany," the section of the Lower East Side that was home to the city's German immigrant population, and there he circulated in the world of radical German emigré physicians. In 1857 he helped found the New York Communist Club, and he maintained communication with Karl Marx and Friedrich Engels throughout the 1850s, even serving as their principal contact in the United States. At the same time, he rose rapidly in the medical profession. In 1860 he took the chair of pediatrics at the New York Medical College, the first in the field in the United States. (The college later burned down, taking Jacobi's papers with it. When a new Tammany Hall was built on the site, Jacobi quipped blackly: "Over the ashes of my property Tammany Hall was erected, which refuses to burn, at least in this world.")[9] In 1870 he joined the faculty of the College of Physicians and Surgeons, where he remained for the next thirty-two years. He was a cofounder of the *American Journal of Obstetrics and Diseases of Women and Children* and president of many medical organizations, among them the American Pediatric Society, the New York Academy of Medicine, and the American Medical Association. By the time of his death in 1919, he was a recognized pillar of the medical establishment, but one who continued to champion working people and the poor and to support advanced and often unpopular causes, including birth control.[10]

Jacobi accepted an appointment as an attending physician at the Nursery and Child's Hospital in 1863, and this affiliation came to an explosive end in 1870.[11] By then Jacobi was forty years old and had moved from *Kleindeutschland* to West Thirty-fourth Street, an address more in keeping with the requirements of the established, if still not entirely genteel, physician he had become. On January 15, 1870, Jacobi delivered a lecture at the clinic he had established at the nursery. There, with characteristic bluntness, he told the assembled medical students that the nursery's facilities were "the very worst refuge for infants, well or sick," and that this was a fact "well known to every one of your medical staff, to everybody, in fact, who visited it with anything like attention."[12]

To remedy this situation, Jacobi proposed that the nursery, along with the rest of New York's foundling asylums, all of which had only recently opened, close down and redistribute their foundlings to the homes of rural wet nurses. Jacobi's conclusions about the dangers of large institutions for infants and the healthful qualities of rural life were radical, but they appear not to have evolved out of his revolutionary thought, except to the extent that he deplored the degraded living conditions that industrialization had introduced into urban life.[13] Instead, Jacobi's recommendation arose out of his firsthand knowledge of conditions at both the nursery and the Randall's Island Infant Hospital. They also came from his observations of European foundling asylums, which he toured in 1869. Jacobi made this trip at the behest of the Commissioners of Public Charities and Correction just as they were opening their Infant Hospital on Randall's Island.[14] Jacobi published the results of his investigation in a report titled *The Raising and Education of Abandoned Children in Europe, With Statistics and General Remarks On That Subject.*[15]

The impressions Jacobi formed on his European visit were undoubtedly fresh in his mind when he gave his inflammatory lecture at the nursery only a few months after his return. One thing he learned was that the methods employed by New York's foundling asylums were out of date by European standards. By the time of his visit, European foundling asylums were in the process of closing down their turning wheels and transforming their institutions into depots where foundlings stayed only briefly before they were placed with wet nurses in rural areas.[16] These decisions were the response to the catastrophic death rates inside European foundling asylums during the eighteenth and nineteenth centuries.[17] The wicker basket that the New York Foundling Asylum left in its entryway for anonymous night deliveries was thus truly anachronistic from the moment the Sisters of Charity set it there in 1869, the very year of Jacobi's trip. For Jacobi, New York's construction of asylums where foundlings would be massed together was a maddening example of American obstinacy in the face of European scientific knowledge. He fumed: "The worst figures of the European foundling hells of former centuries are not more fearful than ours." Referring to the Roman ruler of Judea, infamous for having several of his sons killed, Jacobi continued: "Modern civilization, planning for the best, but mistaken about the means, has succeeded in out-heroding Herod."[18]

Jacobi subscribed to the contemporary belief that the countryside was healthier than the city and believed that rural placement was essential for foundlings. His vision of the urban landscape, as he articulated it after the turn of the century, was nightmarish. Envisioning the city as nothing more than a set of packed passageways in which the infectious jostled dangerously against the well, Jacobi wrote how the city, "with its intercommunication of roads and railroads, street and elevated and subways, cabs and taxicabs and stages, and sewers, is a network from which there is no escape." In his eyes, Manhattan's tenements, whose residents carry the diseases of the poor and "visit your help in your basement," were "airless, lightless, congested, and doomed."[19]

Crowded urban institutions whose conditions mimicked the city outside were, according to Jacobi, the cause behind the wholesale deaths of institutionalized foundlings. Even tenement households, he said, were healthier than large institutions. "The younger the children, and the larger the institution—the surer is death," he stated firmly. In rural homes, by contrast, foundlings would escape not only the dangers of congregate care, but also the "damaging influences of city life and city atmosphere."[20]

Jacobi realized that rural wet nurses were more difficult to come by in the United States than they were in Europe. The attending physician at the New York Foundling Asylum, Dr. Reynolds, had already found this out. "We can provide only a few wet nurses in the rural district, within any reasonable distance of our city;" he wrote, "for our small farmers have no necessity to tax their wives and families with the care of nurslings."[21] As a source for rural wet nurses, the American countryside, with its mobile, hopeful, well-fed population, could not compare with the perennially impoverished rural regions of France, Italy, and Russia, where the wet nursing of unwanted waifs was a cottage industry for generations of women.[22]

He also must have realized that his plan would meet resistance from the managers of the nursery; since their goal was reform, they needed to keep mothers and babies under their direct supervision. The lady managers of the nursery would have been bereft of what was to them a crucial spiritual task without inmates for whom to model appropriate female behavior. Of this task Mrs. Lemist, then the nursery's secretary, wrote in 1867: "We do not disguise the fact that *it is* laborious." But, she insisted, the opportunity to accomplish *"more* than the improving of bodily necessities," the chance to "snatch *one* from the grasp of sin," was a "richer reward."[23]

It was precisely this conception of the nursery's purpose, which made religious reform the paramount value, that Jacobi so deplored. In his report on European foundling asylums, Jacobi's harshest criticism was leveled at the London Foundling Hospital, which had been the model for the nursery's Infant's Home. Jacobi railed against the "cruelty and hypocrisy of a legislation like the English," whose Protestant morality closed English hearts to the plight of children produced outside of marriage.[24] He disdained the London Foundling Hospital's admission practices—the very same ones that Mary Du Bois so admired—which focused on the morality of the mother rather than on her material needs or those of her child. He also hated the use of the London Foundling Hospital as a center for music and art for people of fashion to visit—the very thing Isaac Townsend had admired and wanted to emulate in New York. "The philanthropic visitor," Jacobi wrote, "who goes on Sunday to see the institution, attend the service, and watch the public feeding, like the proceedings in a Zoological Garden, involuntarily comes to the conclusion that the children are retained there for nothing but the show of philanthropy, for no other education but Sunday choir singing and—withering."[25] The London Foundling Hospital, Jacobi sputtered, "is meant to exclude the infants, not to receive and raise them."[26] Russia and the Catholic countries of Europe, which accepted many more babies with many fewer questions asked, were ultimately more humane, Jacobi concluded.[27]

After his January 15 lecture—and a rather self-conscious repeat performance a week later, during which Du Bois and two other lady managers rustled into the lecture room and took seats in the gallery—Jacobi protested that his comments had been made purely in the spirit of science. "The remarks I made were not at all destined to be secret; they are scientific facts which students ought to learn and physicians to know, and managers to take into consideration. They were stated *sine ira et studio,* without shrinking and without my ever expecting them to give rise to any commotion."[28] But they were also rooted in an utter lack of sympathy with the nursery's evangelical intentions, and they were certainly impolitic. Looking back forty years later on the commotion his comments caused, he admitted: "Perhaps the revolutionary spirit of my youth and a warm temperament which boiled at a low temperature, made me overlook the slow pace at which reforms are established."[29]

Mary Du Bois responded swiftly to Jacobi's negative public comments about her institution. Less than one week after Du Bois attended his lecture, the nursery's board of managers informed Jacobi that it was the "unanimous desire of the ladies" that he be expelled. Jacobi, hackles up, resisted his ouster for nearly a year, during which he and the nursery's managers traded charges. Drawing on the language of his revolutionary experience, Jacobi compared the power that Mary Du Bois wielded at the nursery to "the curse of monarchy."[30] As the fracas proceeded, Dr. Delafield warned Jacobi that the "enmity of the ladies," including that of his niece Mary Du Bois, had become "uncontrollable."[31] The fact that Jacobi did not demonstrate any inhibitions based on what Du Bois would certainly have judged his social failings—he was a foreigner (he must have spoken with an accent), a Jew, an atheist, a political radical, and a former inhabitant of a German jail cell—must have been particularly irritating to this daughter of New York's mercantile elite.

The enmity between Jacobi and Du Bois was also rooted in an incident in which Jacobi became angry at the mother of a baby with diphtheria, or what Jacobi called "membranous croup," when she refused to allow him to perform a tracheotomy. The disease Jacobi described as "membranous croup," which was not clearly differentiated from diphtheria in this period, was a common and often fatal infectious disease of young children. It caused a membrane to form in the throat that made breathing difficult and could strangle the patient. As a result, croup was a particularly violent and frightening disease for children, as well as for the parents and physicians who had to watch its agonizing progress, knowing that there was not much they could do to stop it.[32]

French author Gustave Flaubert had witnessed a child suffocating from croup, and he used this memory in his novel *Sentimental Education,* which was published in 1869. Flaubert's fictional little boy "kept frowning and dilating his nostrils; his poor little face had grown paler than his sheets; and his breathing became shorter and shorter, dry and metallic, producing a whistling sound with every intake of breath. His coughing was like the barking noise made by the crude devices inside toy dogs. . . . Now and then the child would sit up all of a sudden. Convulsive movements shook his chest-muscles, and as he breathed in and out his stomach contracted as if he were choking for breath after a race."[33]

It was evidently the terror and desperation caused by a scene such as this that made Jacobi lose his temper with the unwilling mother. Disapproving observers of the encounter noted that Jacobi became so angry with this woman that he almost struck her—an observation that evolved into the accusation that he had struck her. Jacobi did not deny that he became excited during this incident. "You see doctor," he commented to a nearby colleague, "how easy it is to have children and how difficult to save one!"[34]

In an open letter he wrote to the secretary of the nursery in October 1870, Jacobi evoked the real horrors of croup to defend his outbreak of temper: "I ask the ladies, have they seen a child getting strangled with membranous croup, and can they understand the 'excitement' of a physician who is refused the only possibility of saving its life?"[35] This "only possibility" Jacobi referred to was a tracheotomy, an operation in which a physician or a surgeon made an incision in the throat in order to free the breathing passage. In 1870, it was the only known method with which to restore a croup patient's breathing.[36] As a pioneer in the diseases of children, Abraham Jacobi was especially interested in diphtheria, a particularly dangerous strain of which had emerged in the 1850s, just as he was beginning his medical career in the United States.[37] Thus Jacobi became an experienced practitioner of tracheotomy. By the 1880s, when the procedure had become widely accepted among physicians, Jacobi, by then acknowledged as an expert on diphtheria, was responsible for approximately half of all the tracheotomies performed in the United States.[38]

Despite Jacobi's expertise, the success rate for tracheotomy was in fact low. Physicians in Britain and France in this period reported recovery rates after tracheotomy of around 25 to 30 percent. Recovery was further complicated by the fact that even if a tracheotomy saved the patient in the short term from strangling, death might still result from the disease already present in the patient's blood.[39] But in the excitement of the moment, Jacobi blamed the anxious mother for daring to oppose her soft, maternal obscurantism to his hard, scientific knowledge.[40] The fact that the procedure did not succeed in most cases did not hinder his conviction, bolstered by both his training and his gender, that his authority was greater.

On the whole, Jacobi had no use for the values that dominated the nursery—neither the evangelical Protestantism of the lady managers nor their acceptance of "irregular" medicine. Jacobi commented bitterly, for instance, about the fact that the managers of the nursery were followers of homeopathy. Homeopathy, whose tiny, essentially harmless doses of medicine were a relief to Americans weakened by such "heroic" medical tactics as bleeding with leeches and dosing with large quantities of calomel (mercury), was an important medical sect in the United States starting in the mid-1820s. It had its own training schools, hospitals, and practitioners, all outside the realm of and in competition with the "regular" medical establishment to which Jacobi belonged.[41]

Most of all, Jacobi resented the fact that women with no medical training were in charge of making decisions at the nursery. (The editors of the *Medical Record* were also appalled at the power women wielded at the nursery, and they chided the members of the nursery's medical board for allowing the lady managers to dictate Jacobi's ouster.)[42] Jacobi, like other regular physicians of his era, established himself as the enemy not only of quackery, but of all the medical services that had traditionally been provided by women. These included nursing, midwifery, abortion, the dispensing of herbal remedies, and the circulation of medical information and advice among women. His "Rules for the Management of Infants During the Summer Months," published by the city in 1868 for distribution in the tenements, advised mothers: "When you see the doctor, trust in him and not in the women. They do not know better than you do yourself."[43] Much later, at eighty-seven and at the top of his profession, he triumphantly dismissed "old ladies" who "believe in the efficacy of hot chamomile tea" and remarked proudly: "I have survived them."[44]

Jacobi castigated the managers of the nursery who failed to follow his medical advice and dared to follow their own experience and common sense instead. His nemeses at the nursery, he asserted, were the same women "to whom I had occasion to repeatedly speak of the impropriety of distributing crackers and candies in wards crowded with babies and children, sick and well, at improper times, and without direction or advice." They would have done better, he sputtered, to heed his advice and that of his colleagues on the medical board who were "so far as pathology and therapeutics go, in all probability the superiors of some of the Lady Managers who collect ten-dollar contributions, attend a few monthly meetings, and sell ball tickets once a year."[45]

Despite the anti-woman sentiments that Jacobi spurted during this incident, he cannot be classified simply as a misogynist. His emotion was the byproduct of his passionate advocacy of science and professionalism in medicine in the face of competition from healing practices such as herbalism and midwifery, which traditionally had been practiced by women, and from such irregular medical practices as the homeopathy advocated by the ladies of the nursery.[46] In fact, Jacobi was a supporter of medical education for women. His clinic at the nursery was open to medical students, in his deliberate words, "both male and female."[47] Significantly, he was married to physician and women's rights advocate Mary Putnam Jacobi.[48] Jacobi objected not to women as medical practitioners, but to the nonscientific medical practices that he associated with quacks and with traditional female healers.

Despite Jacobi's European medical training and his great confidence in his methods, he actually had very little to offer the city's foundlings in terms of real medical therapy. His central proposal, that foundlings should be farmed out to wet nurses in the countryside, was a sanitary rather than a medical measure.[49] So his insistence on deference from the women of the nursery was at least as much a product of the medical politics of his day as it was the result of true professional efficacy. It would be decades before physicians understood how to combat the infectious diseases that took the lives of so many foundlings.

Some of Jacobi's rage over his encounter with the mother who resisted tracheotomy for her dying baby was surely the product of his personal experiences. His first two wives died, along with five children; Mary Putnam was Jacobi's third wife, and two of their three children died in childhood. Of these, seven-year-old Ernst died of diphtheria in 1883. For a physician specializing in the diseases of children, this parade of his own children into the grave must have been a proof of professional impotence that was as demoralizing as it was heartbreaking.

In all, Jacobi fathered eight children, of whom only one lived to adulthood.[50] He was widowed for the third time when Mary Putnam Jacobi died in 1906. Like Abigail Hopper Gibbons and many of the women who worked in New York's foundling asylums, Jacobi carried a burden of grief that he learned to lighten by devoting his working life to ill and needy young children. Unlike the women, however, his professional training, rather than his emotional experience, was all the justification he needed to offer to explain his choice of work.

Jacobi's departure from the Nursery and Child's Hospital—which came in November 1870, when the medical board, acting on Mary Du Bois's behalf, finally succeeded in ousting him—only enhanced his standing in the eyes of his medical colleagues.[51] Honors accrued to him that were based in part on his open criticism of medical conditions at the nursery and his championship of foundlings. In 1871, for instance, the Medical Society of the State of New York appointed him chairman of its Committee on Foundlings and Foundling Institutions, a group of physicians assembled to investigate the high mortality of foundlings. The report that this committee completed a year later restated the points that Jacobi had made in *The Raising and Education of Abandoned Children in Europe,* including parts critical of the nursery.[52] When Jacobi became the president of the New York County Medical Society in 1872, he used his inaugural speech to restate his criticisms of the nursery, this time in front of a roomful of physicians.[53]

Jacobi's appointment to leadership positions by his medical colleagues even as he was being booted out of the nursery demonstrates just how little Mary Du Bois's opinion mattered to New York's community of regular physicians, despite her blood connections to it. As medicine accrued knowledge and gained authority after the Civil War, the evangelical, voluntaristic, woman-headed model of charity for the sick poor declined in power. Mary Du Bois may have succeeded in expelling Abraham Jacobi from her institution, but she could not counter the trend he represented.

"The Best of All Asylums": Rural Homes

Jacobi's view that the countryside was best for infants was based on his own observations and the observations of others, which suggested strongly that filthy, overcrowded cities had a deleterious effect on the health of the poor, particularly poor children. His view also owed something to ideas about the virtues of the countryside and country people that in the United States dated back to Thomas Jefferson. Yet there was significant truth to Jacobi's inference that infants placed with wet nurses in rural homes were more likely to stay alive than infants housed en masse in city institutions. Recent studies have shown that infants living in large cities in the nineteenth century did have higher rates of mortality than those who lived in rural places. Crowded conditions, which led to the spread of infectious diseases, and the bacterial contamination of water, which led to the intestinal conditions that contributed to the annual summer spike in infant deaths, were among the reasons.[54]

Jacobi argued, based on what he had learned on his European trip, that the death rates of all city children were higher than those of their rural counterparts. For institutionalized infants, who were more likely to be exposed to infection, lacked individual care, and may not have had a regular source of breast milk, the danger was even greater. At the Nursery and Child's Hospital, Jacobi argued, babies who entered in good health sickened in the institution and died there at a rate of 66.25 percent. "I mean to prove the absolute impossibility of raising infants in a large institution, a fact that has been ever so many times proved in Europe," he wrote.[55]

The belief that the noxious environments of crowded, industrial cities contributed to the ill health of the poor, particularly for young children, was also a central tenet of the sanitary-reform and child-welfare movements of the mid- to late nineteenth century. Alarm over the miserable squalor of big cities similarly stimulated political thinkers such as Jacobi's revolutionary colleague, Friedrich Engels. Like the physicians and social and religious reformers who investigated the teeming poor districts of big cities in the industrial age, Engels took a tour through Manchester and was shocked at the unsanitary conditions endured there by the poor. The Old Town of Manchester gave Engels an appalling impression of "filth, ruin, and uninhabitableness, the defiance of all considerations of cleanliness, ventilation, and health which characterize the construction of this single district, containing at least twenty to thirty thousand inhabitants. And such a district exists in the heart of the second city of England, the first manufacturing city of the world. If anyone wishes to see in how little space a human being can move, how little air —and such air!—he can breathe, how little of civilization he may share and yet live, it is only necessary to travel hither."[56]

Twenty years later, New York's Metropolitan Board of Health echoed Engels, complaining of New York's "bad air, impure water, insufficient food, and ill-ventilated dwellings." The members of the Metropolitan Board of Health saw that infants and young children died at higher rates in cities than they did in the countryside, and they believed that it was the miasma-producing filth of cities that endangered "these delicate beings."[57]

Among poor children, foundlings were the most vulnerable to the dangers of city life. In 1872 the *Medical Record,* a New York medical journal that editorialized in favor of Jacobi's placing-out plan, alleged that "the mortality of Foundlings in cities is actually three times that in rural districts." The causes of this carnage, as the editors of the *Medical Record* understood them, were overcrowded and dirty streets and dwellings; impure supplies of milk, water, and food; the "vitiated" air thought to carry the seeds of miasmatic disease; and weak constitutions passed on to infants by their morally profligate, immigrant parents.[58]

Jacobi sought to remove foundlings from the well-documented dangers of city life, but he did not take into account the difficulties and dangers associated with placing children in the country. He argued that "the poorest country woman who takes charge of a society's child, under the superintendence of the proper authority, under the eyes of her neighbors, and with motherly feelings developed in the poorest one bound in marriage and family ties, will succeed in saving a nursling from certain death."[59] But such situations had not always worked out that way. In the eighteenth century, New York's almshouse had had mixed experiences with rural placements for infants and older children. And, as Jacobi knew, rural wet nurses were hard to find. Even when available, they were not always competent. The New York Foundling

Asylum's attempt to place foundlings with nurses on rural Long Island was a failure. "Not an infant have we been able to raise in the rural districts of Long Island," the foundling asylum's physician, James Reynolds, complained.[60] Dr. Joel Foster, a trustee of the New York Infant Asylum and a dissenting member of the state medical society's Committee on Foundlings and Foundling Institutions (which Jacobi chaired), further punctured Jacobi's expectations of the countryside when he argued that "it is well known to all physicians who have practised in the country, that very little attention is paid to sanitary science, and that the most absurd ideas prevail among the greater portion of the common people."[61]

Another factor that made establishing a rural wet-nursing program difficult was the reality that the United States lacked a national or regional system of social welfare that would have linked cities to rural areas, such as those found in many European countries. While these systems tended to breed corruption and to mark their charges permanently with the stigma of being foundlings, they appealed to Jacobi because they seemed efficient when compared to New York's fragmented and precariously funded methods of foundling care. So Jacobi proposed establishing such a centralized, state-run program in New York. He envisioned a system in which a state "department of the foundlings," with officials appointed by the governor, supervised the distribution of unwanted babies to rural nurses at taxpayer expense.[62] He argued that New York's foundlings were a state responsibility and that there was nothing "unrepublican" about such a centralized foundling system. To him, assigning the state responsibility for foundlings through a statewide system would constitute the "performance of a duty of the commonwealth toward the feeble and dependent young."[63]

Yet such a system would have been particularly hard to establish in the United States in the early 1870s, when the climate of political corruption was particularly intense. These were the years in which corruption—in the Grant administration in Washington, in the newly reconstructed governments of the South, and in the city government of New York, where the excesses of the Tweed Ring were exposed daily by the press—made many Americans skeptical of government bureaucracies. Indeed, New York Infant Asylum trustee Joel Foster argued that a government-run foundling system would quickly devolve into a vehicle for corruption. A placing-out system, Foster claimed, would "create numerous foundling bureaus in every large town in the state, with paid superintendents, agents, and clerks, with a central distributing reservoir, and would soon become a political engine—an asylum for worn-out politicians, instead of a refuge for the unfortunate and despairing mother and her helpless infant."[64] Corruption had played a part in the almshouse's system for placing out foundlings before the Civil War, as the career of Mary Cullough demonstrated, so Foster's fears were not far-fetched.

Like Thomas Jefferson, and like the officials of the antebellum almshouse, Abraham Jacobi subscribed to an at least partly idealized vision of the countryside. One reason for this may have been the fact that many urban reformers had come to the city from farms or small towns and villages. They shared this characteristic with many urban residents; in the nineteenth century, most Americans were country-born, and the city's population was made up largely of migrants from other places, primarily rural.

The chief advocate of rural life for poor city children, Charles Loring Brace, was born in 1826 in Litchfield, Connecticut. Litchfield, where the young Mary Delafield went to school, was an important Connecticut town, but it was not a city on the scale of New York.[65] Samuel Halliday was born on a farm in New Jersey, and it was Halliday, baffled by the behavior of the urban poor, who wondered: "Why do the needy thus crowd together in our over-populated towns?"[66] The physician brothers Stephen and Job Lewis Smith were born on a farm in upstate New York; Stephen, an important urban sanitary reformer, gave partial credit for his longevity to the rigorous farm work he did in his youth (he lived to be almost one hundred years old).[67] Arabella Mott of the Nursery and Child's Hospital and Elisha Harris of the New York Infant Asylum and the Metropolitan Board of Health hailed from Vermont. Harris would later champion what he called "child-planting in the west" as a means to help delinquent, neglected, and abandoned children.[68] Abraham Jacobi himself had left the rural village of his childhood, where he lived in a smoky cottage and suffered from rickets, for the exciting metropolitan attractions of Berlin.[69] To the eyes of these transplanted country or small-town people, the noise, physical and moral risks, and frightening complexity of big-city life seemed most dangerous, especially when compared to the remembered arcadia of their youths. The fact that they had once turned their backs on that arcadia may have contributed to their later nostalgia.

During the era of the foundling asylums, the tactic of replanting poor city children in the countryside was most actively promoted by Charles Loring Brace, founder of the Children's Aid Society. The Children's Aid Society's first orphan train left New York in 1853, the year the society was founded. Headed for Michigan, it carried forty-six children, aged seven to fifteen, accompanied by an agent. By 1890, the year Brace died, the Children's Aid Society had swept approximately 90,000 children off the streets of New York and sent them to rural homes in New York, New Jersey, the New England states, the South, and the Midwest.[70]

Like Police Chief Matsell, Brace worried that the city's "embryo courtezans and felons" were more than a nuisance—to him, they also carried the threat of future civic disorder on a disastrous scale. If they remained unreached by "the civilizing influences of American life," Brace warned, "we should see an explosion from this class which might leave this city in ashes and blood."[71] Brace wanted to rid the city of these young saplings of social disorder, but he also wanted to give urban street children the particularly American opportunity to remake themselves on the western frontier. Brace opposed the use of institutions for poor, parentless children such as foundlings and argued instead that "the best of all Asylums for the outcast child, is the *farmer's home*."[72]

Brace's orphan trains provided a solution for some of New York's foundling asylums, which had to cope with the problem of what to do with their parentless children as the children grew older. The New York Infant Asylum and the Nursery and Child's Hospital sent some of their grown foundlings west on the orphan trains of the Children's Aid Society.[73] Brace considered the alliance between the nursery and the Children's Aid Society a success. "It is astonishing," Brace wrote Mary Du Bois, "when you consider the parentage of these children, how well they have done."[74]

The experience of a boy named Willie, who left the nursery for the west in 1900, exemplified Brace's ideal. "I am getting along well," this former unwanted waif of the urban streets wrote the nursery. "I go to school, I do chores and husk corn. I go after the cows horseback and ride a horse to Sunday School, two and a half miles from here." The nursery's annual report, in which this letter is printed, commented that Willie was "an enterprising little chap" who planned to "buy a watch by his own earnings."[75]

The New York Foundling Asylum did not consign its older children to the Children's Aid Society, since Brace's organization was explicitly Protestant and the Sisters of Charity wanted to be sure that their foundlings went to Catholic homes. But the Sisters emulated Brace's methods, sending their three- to five-year-olds to Catholic homes in western states. By 1890, the New York Foundling Asylum had placed more than six thousand children in western homes.[76] According to Homer Folks, a turn-of-the-century leader in child welfare reform, the New York Foundling Asylum could "justly be regarded as one of the largest placing-out agencies in the country."[77]

The almshouse, too, placed children in homes in the countryside, and it had been doing so long before Brace invented the orphan train.[78] Since at least the end of the eighteenth century, almshouse placements had been divided between the city and surrounding rural areas, but by the middle of the nineteenth century, as the density and squalor of the city began to increase, almshouse officials began voicing a wistful preference for a rural future for their children. In 1853, George Kellock, the Superintendent of Outdoor Poor, expressed his view that "it has always been most desirable to place these children as far from the City as practicable, and a majority of them have been so disposed to respectable farmers and mechanics, in the country towns of this and adjoining states."[79]

By at least the mid-fifties, the almshouse was sending its children to Charles C. Townsend's Orphans Home of Industry in Iowa City, where, according to Kellock, the "Western Country presents opportunities of providing comfortable homes for this class."[80] Townsend sent glowing reports of the forty-six children sent to him from the New York almshouse. Some were placed in the homes of "the good families of the country," where they were "contented and happy." [81] The children in Iowa, Kellock reported in 1858, were doing so well that "no one of them would wish to return."[82] A few years later, however, a visitor to Townsend's institution gave a very different report of conditions there. This was George W. Du Bois, a relative (possibly a brother-in-law) of Mary Du Bois. The Du Boises were interested in the Iowa Home because the nursery also placed children there. Du Bois reported back to Mary Du Bois that conditions in Iowa institution were "most unfavorable" and the children were in a "pitiful and destitute condition."[83] Once again, the countryside, even the supposedly bracingly wholesome American west, did not always live up to expectations.

The Asylums Respond

Jacobi's January 1870 attack was aimed at the Nursery and Child's Hospital, but it came at a particularly bad time for the New York Infant Asylum, which began preparing to reopen in the spring of 1871 and opened the following fall. This unfortunate timing meant that the struggling infant asylum faced the scorn of Jacobi and his followers just as it was attempting to raise funds and gather support. The editors of the *Medical Record* castigated the New York Infant Asylum's trustees for their "persistent stupidity in refusing to learn from the experiences of others." The *New York Times* concurred: "Let these ladies," the *Times* editorialized (presuming inaccurately that the board of the New York Infant Asylum was made up of women), "instead of crowding the little helpless creatures in one building, contrive a machinery similar to that of the 'Children's Aid Society' of this City, for placing these infants with kind hearted respectable nurses in the country." Charles Loring Brace weighed in on the question, his anti-Catholic prejudice at the forefront: "Why will our benevolent ladies and gentlemen keep up the old monastic ideas of the necessity of herding these unfortunate children in one building? . . . Let us not found in New York that most doubtful institution—a Foundling Asylum—but use the advantages we have in the ten thousand natural asylums of the country." Jacobi himself tore apart the infant asylum's "Appeal in Behalf of the New York Infant Asylum" piece by piece at a meeting of the Medical Society of the County of New York at which he presided.[84]

The New York Infant Asylum's determination to stick to its methods in the face of this criticism is a testament to just how strongly its trustees valued their role as reformers of fallen women over their role as saviors of infant lives. To use their building simply as a depot for infants en route to wet nurses in the country, as Jacobi suggested, did not fit with their plan to create a model home for unwed mothers and their babies. The nursery had resisted Jacobi's suggestion for the same reason.

Even though the nursery and the infant asylum resisted placing out, they agreed with Jacobi's assertion that the countryside was healthier than the city. Mary Du Bois believed that "in regard to a proper location of a building for a Nursery or Home for Mothers and Children, of course a place in the country is best, where pure air, good water, and well drained ground can be obtained. Such places are not, however,

appreciated by the poor, who really enjoy the crowded rooms of tenement houses more than the benefits of salubrious surroundings. They
complain of being lonely when there are no liquor shops to welcome
them, and where a fight now and then is more exciting than the rules of
a well-ordered Institution."[85]

The "country home" that the nursery operated on Staten Island, and
the New York Infant Asylum's similar institution in Flushing, and later
in Mount Vernon, were evidence of their concurrence that rural life
was good for babies.[86] But Jacobi was bitterly opposed to the nursery's
Staten Island branch. He believed that the branch, a "petted plan of
Mrs. Du Bois," starved the main institution of funds to the detriment of
the children there, and that conditions on Staten Island were such that it
was nothing but a "cheap burying ground for babies." Mary Du Bois
opened the Staten Island branch in July 1870, during the furor over Jacobi's denunciation of the nursery. It appears to have been a concession
to his suggestion about the virtues of rural life. But Jacobi did not see it
that way. He was infuriated that Du Bois had tried to convince him to
state, against his own judgment, that it was his "positive opinion that
the selection of that place in Staten Island was preferable, at the time, to
the erection of a quarantine in addition to the city building."[87] That
judgment, however, was poisoned by his conflict with Mrs. Du Bois.

James Reynolds, the physician at the New York Foundling Asylum,
was also reluctant to accept Jacobi's suggestion. His institution's experience of rural placement for foundlings made him skeptical of Jacobi's
touting of the virtues of the countryside. Even when rural wet nurses
could be found there was no guarantee that they would be able to provide the kind of wholesome country life dreamed up by urban reformers. "The poorer class of people in the country who will take them,"
Reynolds argued in response to Jacobi's report, "are more careless than
the same class in the city tenement houses."[88] Reynolds acknowledged
that "hospital air" could be dangerous for infants, but he concluded
that in spite of that "the chances of rearing infants in a well regulated
institution, with large, sunny, well-ventilated walls, are fully as good as
in the outside nursing or boarding."[89]

The only foundling asylum that agreed to try a placing-out program
specifically in response to Jacobi's suggestion was the Randall's Island
Infant Hospital, on whose medical board he served and at whose behest
he had carried out his study of European foundling asylums in 1869. In
1871 the Infant Hospital placed fifty foundlings with lactating women

in private homes in Westchester County as an experiment.[90] The following year, the hospital adopted the placing-out program as a regular policy, and it continued, fitfully, until 1891. Foundlings from the Infant Hospital were placed with Westchester County farm wives, and a local doctor was appointed to oversee them.[91]

One child who benefited from the Westchester program was Annie Martin, a two-week-old girl rescued from a stoop on St. Mark's Place on a cold January evening in 1883. When Annie was found, she was wrapped up in a shawl; a bundle left with her contained two changes of clothing. Nestled into the shawl with her was a bottle of milk; a rubber tube connected the bottle to her lips. Annie's mother was probably a German immigrant, as she had chosen to leave her daughter at a house whose sign indicated, in German, that a midwifery school was inside. The man who lived in the house, a Mr. Krumm, commented: "I've often said that we should find a deserted baby on our stoop some night, because people might think this was a hospital or an asylum." The matron of the police department's nursery, Mrs. Webb, who was practiced in such matters, believed that Annie was a German baby because of her clothing: "Tell me that wasn't a German bab[y]. There is no mistake about it," Mrs. Webb told a reporter. "See these jackets [and] this shirt. No woman with any understanding [would] make things with ruffles on 'em like that. De[ar] [D]ear! Look at that sleeve. Do you suppose that [a bab]y could get her arm through there?"

The reactions of those who found and helped Annie reveal the ubiquity of infant abandonment in the post–Civil War city. Mr. Krumm was not especially surprised to find a baby on his doorstep, and Matron Webb was experienced in the care of foundlings. So was Jacob Wiebe, the police officer who conveyed Annie to the police station. Officer Wiebe, a father of six, made a specialty of retrieving foundlings. The *Herald* reporter took down his words, complete with German accent: "So many children I haf handled since I was on dis post!" Wiebe said. "De cap'en and sergeants all send for me to look out for dose young ones."

The *Herald*'s story describes how Annie was conveyed smoothly through the city's foundling system, passed from one practiced hand to the next. After the facts of her discovery were recorded in the police station's blotter, Officer Wiebe carried her to Matron Webb's nursery at the police department's central office on Mulberry Street. There Matron Webb fed her, changed her, and put her to bed for the night. She confiscated the baby's bundle of clothing to redistribute among other foundlings who had come less well provided for. In the morning, Mrs. Webb sent the baby to the Department of Public Charities and Correction at Third Avenue and Eleventh Street. There she joined three other foundlings. The baby's only name up until that point was "8," the number assigned by the clerk at the Department of Public Charities and Correction when she arrived. The Superintendent of Outdoor Poor gave all four babies new names in preparation for their next phase of life and wrote them on cards, which were tied around their necks with string. "Annie Martin" was the reporter's suggestion.

From the Department of Public Charities and Correction building, all four foundlings were taken in a horse-drawn van to the Bellevue Hospital dock on the East River at Twenty-Sixth Street. Annie made the trip in the arms of a woman who was going to visit an inmate of the insane asylum on Blackwell's Island. A nurse, probably one of the poor women who lived on Randall's Island and nursed babies in the Infant Hospital, met the four foundlings on the ferry. After stops at Blackwell's and Ward's Islands, the boat arrived at Randall's, where the Infant Hospital was their destination. Annie was bathed and examined by the house physician, and Dr. James Healy, the medical superintendent of the Infant Hospital, recorded her arrival.

At this point, Annie's fate diverged from those of her companions. A woman arrived at the door of the Infant Hospital with a note from Dr. Archibald Campbell of Mount Vernon, the physician who supervised the foundlings in Westchester, authorizing her to take a child to her Westchester home to nurse. The appropriate forms were completed, and Dr. Healy handed Annie over to her new foster mother. The *Herald* editorialized on the good luck that this change in Annie's fate represented, but it feared for the future of the babies left behind: Annie's "little sisters in misery, left in the pauper hospital, have small prospect of future happiness. It may be better for them that they soon find a grave in the Potter's Field, as we read is the case with a great proportion of the infants left in the city's care."[92]

The Infant Hospital's Dr. Healy also believed that the Westchester program gave the foundlings a better chance. He judged the placing-out program a success, as foundlings lodged with families in Westchester had a better rate of survival than those who remained in the Infant Hospital (although their death rate was still higher than that of the infants who lived at the hospital with their own mothers). Between 1872, the

AN INVOICE OF BABIES.

Two foundlings on the way from the Twenty-sixth Street dock to the Infant Department of the almshouse on Blackwell's Island. In 1883, Annie Martin left the same dock for the Infant Hospital on Randall's Island. W. H. Davenport. *Harper's New Monthly Magazine*, December 1867. Collection of the New-York Historical Society, 79758d.

official first year of the program, and 1888, Dr. Healy estimated that infants nursed by their own mothers in the Infant Hospital died at a rate of 15 percent; motherless babies in the Infant Hospital died at a rate of 52 percent, and the death rate of foundlings sent to Westchester was 25 percent.[93] The Westchester program also had the side benefit of freeing up space in the crowded Randall's Island building, and Healy believed that the death rate in the building had been lowered as a result.[94]

Dr. Campbell, the Mount Vernon medical supervisor, was also an enthusiastic supporter of the program. "To my mind," he wrote to an inquirer, "any moral family, however humble their circumstances, will afford a better home for these children, than found within the palatial walls of our city asylums." He hoped that the Westchester foundlings could remain in the country in permanent adoptive homes. Some did, but Campbell believed that the Commissioners of Public Charities and Correction were not doing enough to make this happen: "It has seemed to me that if especial efforts were made nearly all of these children could be placed in homes, relieving the State of the burden of their support & themselves of the odium of pauperism. I would venture the statement that there are today one hundred homes in Westchester County who desire to adopt a child but do not know where to go to look for one. I do not know what your ideal home for these waifs may be, mine is that afforded by the artisan or the farmer, where they will of necessity be taught to work & thereby become useful citizens."

Like just about everyone who entered the nearly hopeless lives of foundlings, Dr. Campbell derived pleasure and satisfaction from his work. "Pardon my rambling & rather lengthy reply to your question," he apologized to his correspondent, "but you touched upon my hobby."[95]

Despite the Westchester program's success, in November 1883, the Infant Hospital cancelled it and returned all the infants then living in Westchester to Randall's Island. This was only ten months after Annie Martin was delivered to Westchester; if she was still alive, she would have been among the group returned to the Infant Hospital. One possible reason for this abrupt decision was cost. In 1882, it cost forty-two cents per day to maintain an infant in Westchester, and only twenty-nine cents to keep one on Randall's Island. An unspecified "question of its legality" was also a factor. The Infant Hospital's medical superintendent, James Healy, was dismayed. He recommended a "speedy return to the farmed out system." It was costly, he admitted, but it saved lives.[96]

Dr. Healy got his wish in 1885, when the Infant Hospital began placing foundlings in Westchester again.[97] In 1887, Healy reported triumphantly that "To praise the Farmed-out System would be quite superfluous, as the accompanying Tables amply show the many benefits still accruing from its continuance."[98] In acknowledgment of this success, the Infant Hospital placed more children in Westchester, and the Commissioners of Public Charities and Correction granted it an additional ten thousand dollars for the purpose.[99]

The program continued until 1891 and then was abruptly stopped again.[100] The reason again appears to have been cost; politics may also have been a factor. On December 31, 1892, the last day of his administration, Tammany mayor Hugh Grant was presented with a report from the city's accounting department charging that the Department of Public Charities and Correction was "extremely lax and inefficient; so bad, in fact, that large loss to the City was caused thereby." Mayor Thomas F. Gilroy, another Tammany figure, took over in 1893. In a report to the new mayor, the Commissioners of Public Charities and Correction fumed about the accounting department's accusations. The fact that the accusations were made at such short notice only proved, the commissioners reasoned angrily, "that they were brought with some other object than the good of the City. Whatever the object, the only legitimate effect could be to embarrass your administration at the start."[101] Nevertheless, Mayor Gilroy, who took cost-cutting seriously, instituted changes at the Infant Hospital.[102] In this environment of acrimony and parsimony, the costly but life-saving Westchester program was doomed, this time for good.

Abraham Jacobi realized that big cities were dangerous to the health of infants, but his battle with Mary Du Bois and the lady managers of the nursery took place at a time, right after the Civil War, when doctors still lacked the tools and knowledge necessary to save the lives of infants, particularly of vulnerable foundlings. As Jacobi's tragic personal experience demonstrates, doctors could not save even their own children.[103] As the century went on, however, medical and sanitary knowledge increased, and Jacobi moved to the front of his field. His early collision with the nursery had the effect of enhancing, not harming his reputation in the eyes of his colleagues, as his appointment to the presidency of one medical society after another demonstrates. The foundling asylums, however, would go on to struggle through a series of blows that would ultimately finish them off.

6

The End of the
Foundling Asylums

Abraham Jacobi's attack on the nursery's foundling asylum in 1870 was just one in a series of misfortunes that all the foundling asylums endured within their very first decade. Another was the collapse of the Tweed Ring in 1871. A significant byproduct of the exposure of that generous but unprincipled group of politicians was an enhanced mistrust on the part of the state legislature toward private religious charities that survived on public funds, as New York charities traditionally did. An element of ethnic struggle came into the debate as well, as after the Civil War, most recipients of charity in New York were Catholic in a city and state still largely controlled by Protestant elites. As a result, public funding for the foundling asylums became precarious and remained so for as long as they existed.

The decade in which all of the foundling asylums opened was made tumultuous by the exposure of William M. Tweed, Richard Connolly, and their cohort in 1871. This cleansing catastrophe most directly affected the New York Foundling Asylum, which had relied on the Democratic machine for significant financial support. The Tweed collapse, which took place just as Abraham Jacobi was attacking foundling asylums as dangerous to the health of their inmates, ushered in an era that would conclude with the end of all of the foundling asylums—except, ironically, the New York Foundling Asylum.

At the height of the Tweed Ring's power, journalist James D. McCabe recorded, its members "gave sumptuous entertainments, they flaunted their diamonds and jewels in the eyes of a dumbfounded public, they made ostentatious gifts to the poor, and munificent subscriptions to cathedrals and churches, *all with money stolen from the city.*"[1] The New York Foundling Asylum had been among the recipients of this money. As comptroller of the city, Richard Connolly oversaw the system of phony vouchers and padded bills that kept the pockets of the ring's members flush with cash. As a member of the New York Foundling Asylum's Ladies' Society, Mary Connolly was able through the influence of her husband to pour the stolen dollars of the Tweed Ring into the foundling asylum's treasury.

Mary Connolly's ability to help this favorite charity lasted only a short time. In November 1871, Comptroller Connolly, after first betraying his colleagues on the Tweed Ring, was arrested himself. (Abraham Jacobi, who was working on his report for the State Medical Society's Committee on Foundlings and Foundling Institutions as the downfall of the ring unfolded, drew an analogy between the corruption of the ring and the complex bureaucracies of foundling asylums. With their many managers, Jacobi wrote, foundling asylums are "meddlesome, fidgety, inconsistent, incongruous"; neither, he added, "is the transaction of business by a ring, if we are well informed, cheap or expedient.")[2] Connolly's bail was set at one million dollars, but on New Year's Day in 1872, he forfeited it and fled to Europe. His wife fled with him.[3]

Novelist Edith Wharton offers some insight into why Mary Connolly so abruptly left behind her home and her work at the Foundling Asylum and the other charities she supported. "In *their* day," Wharton has some elderly ladies reminisce in *The Age of Innocence,* "the wife of a man who had done anything disgraceful in business had only one idea: to efface herself, to disappear with him."[4] But Mary Connolly was more than simply a loyal wife—she was culpable herself. A bitter critic of Richard Connolly's conceded that the "cold, crafty, and cowardly" Connolly had one redeeming trait: his "strong affection for his wife and children."[5] Mary Connolly's reciprocal affection provided her husband with critical support as his world began to collapse around him, and as Connolly's enemies closed in, Mary Connolly scurried to hide several conspicuously bulky lumps of money. The largest of these was a half-million dollars that she transferred to Joel Fithian, husband of her daughter Fanny and holder of several lucrative city titles, including assistant receiver of taxes. Reporting on Mrs. Connolly's last-minute financial maneuvers, the *Times* sneered: "It must be so consoling to the tax-payers to learn of the continued prosperity of their masters."[6] The Connollys went first to join the Fithians, who, loot in hand, had settled in Vevey, Switzerland. After a sad period of wandering in Europe, Mary Connolly died in Vevey in 1879. Her husband died in Marseilles a year later. Neither of them set foot in their city again; they returned to New York only in their coffins.[7]

For those who had known Mary Connolly as a generous benefactress, including the Sisters of Charity, none of this was enough to make them withhold their public expressions of sorrow at her death. Her funeral at the Fourth Universalist Church in New York was a festival of forgiveness, as friends, family, and representatives of the charities she supported chose to remember her "kindness, charity, and constant goodness" and to forget her Tammany connections and the choices such connections caused her to make. Her casket was overwhelmed with masses of flowers sent by admirers, a wild Victorian mélange of tree ferns, palms, violets, ivy, evergreens, roses, lilies, and calla lilies. Representatives of Mary Connolly's three principal charities, the Chapin Home, Hahneman and Women's Hospital (a homeopathic institution—as at the nursery, the irregular medical practice of homeopathy had a foothold at the New York Foundling Asylum), and the New York Foundling Asylum, served as pallbearers. The foundling asylum sent a "beautifully engraved copy of verses addressed 'To the Memory of Mrs. Connolly.'" The book was mounted in a walnut frame and placed in a prominent position near the casket. Even the vengeful *Times*—which had been a central player in the pursuit and destruction of Tweed and his followers—reported on the event respectfully, describing Mrs. Connolly's son-in-law Robert C. Hutchings, another deposed Tammany appointee, as "ex-Surrogate" without comment and forbore from mentioning Richard Connolly at all.[8]

The collapse of the Tweed Ring deprived the New York Foundling Asylum of one of its most energetic fundraisers and of her generous circle of friends. But the exposures of corruption in city government had wider ramifications for every foundling asylum, as it did for all of the city's private, religious charities that had benefited from the ring's generosity. The Tweed Ring's support of parochial schools, charities, and job-generating public works earned Boss Tweed the title of "champion of the immigrant" at a time when the majority of immigrants in the city were Catholic.[9] As a Protestant in a city brimming with Catholic immigrants from Ireland and Germany, Tweed understood where the majority of votes were to be found. Even though Tweed's munificence was not limited to the Catholic poor, the city's Protestant elite identified the issue of public funding for private charities as an outrage perpetrated by or on behalf of Catholics. In 1872, the *New York Times,* which associated Protestant faith with upper-class status, reported that "considerable interest is felt by the intelligent part of the community—those of Protestant faith" about the "sectarian and Romish influence" that led to the spending of public money "to help to support a religion and a class of teaching foreign to the mass of our people in every respect." To fund private charities with public funds was, according to the *Times,* to "allow the disbursement to fall into Roman Catholic, or which is the same thing, Ring hands."[10]

The *Times*'s bias is clear, but Catholic institutions, since they served the largest group of immigrant poor, did absorb the largest share of public funds granted to private charities. This was as true of the foundling asylums as it was of the city's other religious charities. All of the foundling asylums, Protestant as well as Catholic, benefited from a state law passed in 1866 that directed the city to grant a per-capita allowance to inmates of private charitable institutions. The per-capita allowance became, according to one historian, "the lifeblood of children's institutions."[11] Mary Du Bois, whose Protestant nursery was the first of the foundling asylums to receive the per-capita funding, was grateful for the passage of this law to which, she believed, her institution owed whatever financial security it had.[12] The New York Foundling Asylum, which had a larger population than either of the two Protestant foundling asylums and therefore received more in per-capita funds, had even more reason to be grateful.

Reform forces, fueled by Protestant resentment over public money disappearing into the coffers of Catholic charities, mounted periodic attacks on New York's system of distributing public money to private, religious institutions, a system that had evolved earlier in the century, when most of the city's religious charities had been Protestant. One of these attacks was mounted at the New York State constitutional convention of 1867, at which an amendment was proposed prohibiting the use of state funds for private charities. Mary Du Bois, with the rather paradoxical assistance of nativist Erastus Brooks, who was chair of the convention's committee on charities, protested the amendment. Her position was that private charities such as the Nursery and Child's Hospital performed services that public ones could not. The almshouse, Du Bois claimed, was adequate for poor women shameless enough to declare the names of the fathers of their babies to public authorities in order to receive publicly mandated benefits, but not good enough for the properly penitent women who came to her institution. Du Bois ended her petition to the state legislators with the eerie image of an "immense number of children now left at our doors, and in our docks, sewers, and open lots, [who] call piteously for legislative action."[13]

The 1867 amendment failed, sparing the nursery's funding, but in 1873 the issue came up again. In the aftermath of the Tweed Ring's downfall, reformist forces in the state legislature proposed limiting the public funding given to private, religious charities. The vehicle this time was a new city charter. The reform city charter passed in 1873 contained a clause forbidding the expenditure of city funds on religious charities.[14] Since the New York Foundling Asylum, which had opened in 1869, benefited the most from public funds, it suffered the most when these funds were threatened. The *Herald* sprang to the Sisters' defense, urging that "some sure provision will be made for this institution, and that the famous anti-sectarian clause may be so amended as to avert the possibility of closing up or suspending so noble a work."[15]

The Sisters' work had faced another threat in 1872. That year, the city reduced its per-capita allowance to the foundling asylums to match the rate paid to its own Infant Hospital on Randall's Island. The reasons for the cut were multiple and somewhat obscure, but one appears to have been competition for funds between the public foundling asylum and the private ones, since it was at the behest of the Commissioners of Public Charities and Correction that the cut was made. The precipitating reason for the cut appears to have been the revival and rechartering of the New York Infant Asylum. Looking back on the episode years later, Stephen Smith recalled that the cut was made because the Commissioners of Public Charities and Correction opposed the rechartering of the New York Infant Asylum and sought to limit the public funds it could receive.[16]

Even though the cut in per-capita funding was partly a response to the reopening of the beleaguered New York Infant Asylum, it was the New York Foundling Asylum, with its greater reliance on public funds, that again suffered the most.[17] The Sisters were forced to bring their reception crib inside so as to limit the number of foundlings left at their door. The result, they claimed, was death for "the unfortunates who were refused, for cases of infanticide were again frequently reported."[18] The *Herald* rushed to support the Sisters, arguing that the cut "tends to increase greatly the heavy burden under which the institution is at present laboring, and makes the duties of the good ladies in charge more wearing and wearying on them."[19]

The situation was alleviated in 1874 when Governor John A. Dix, after visiting Sister Irene at the foundling asylum, agreed to sign a bill restoring the asylum's lost funding.[20] Despite this deliverance, the 1870s continued to be stressful for the foundling asylums. In 1873, the United States suffered an economic crash that was followed by a depression of several years. In 1875, the New York Infant Asylum recorded that the depression had undermined its ability to attract funding from its supporters.[21] In the midst of all this, the ones who were the least to blame but suffered the most were the foundlings.

Children's Institutions, Placing Out, and the Children's Law of 1875

Funding and political problems were not all that the foundling asylums had to contend with. During the last third of the nineteenth century, Abraham Jacobi's stand against institutionalization for poor children without homes or with inadequate homes gradually became the dominant position among the public and private social-welfare organizations that were founded during this period. By the early twentieth century, placing out, or foster care, as it eventually came to be known, became the preferred mode of care for these children. This was the case not only in New York, but nationally. In New York, however, alarm over institutionalization was the result, in part, of the unintended consequences of New York's Children's Law, passed in 1875.

Almshouses had long had a reputation for squalor, as nineteenth-century observers such as Ezra Stiles Ely reported. In almshouses, children mingled indiscriminately with other, often unsavory, inmates. In 1875, William Pryor Letchworth, a commissioner of the New York State Board of Charities and, by the end of the century, an important voice in national child-welfare reform, proposed a bill recommending that children be removed from the state's almshouses. In that same year the state complied, passing its "Children's Law" that forbade the placement of healthy children between the ages of three and sixteen in almshouses.

Letchworth hoped that children removed from almshouses as a result of the Children's Law would be placed with families or, as the law phrased it, in "fitting asylums."[22] As it turned out, the children were placed not in families, but in private, religious institutions. This was because of the so-called "religious clause" of the Children's Law, which designated that children removed from the almshouses be placed in institutions run by people of the same faith as their parents. The religious clause was an effort to avoid stirring up the religious rivalries that had long existed between New York's Catholic and Protestant charities. Its unintended result was the ballooning of the size and number of private, religious institutions for children in New York State, as children released from almshouses and those who came later were redistributed among them, and public money for the children's upkeep followed.[23]

The Children's Law did not benefit foundling asylums as much as it did orphanages, because it only applied to children over the age of three (though in 1878 the law was amended and the age was lowered to two). But it did affect the city's foundlings in two important ways. The first was the effect the law had on Randall's Island, the "Children's Island." At the end of 1875, in compliance with the Children's Law, the city nurseries located there since 1848 were closed. Left behind on Randall's Island were all of the children not covered by the law: the inmates of the Idiot Asylum and Hospital, the juvenile delinquents of the House of Refuge (which was a private institution), and the foundlings of the Infant Hospital. Now that only the ill, the mentally disabled, and the abandoned remained, Randall's Island, only a few decades after its hopeful beginnings, became a site of unmitigated bleakness.[24]

The Children's Law also had the effect of setting back the movement in favor of placing out, and here, too, it affected foundlings. But this setback was only temporary, as the rise in the number of institutionalized children in the state caused by the Children's Law created a backlash against institutionalization. Members of the state's social-service agencies, including Letchworth and others who had originally supported the Children's Law, watched with alarm as the number of institutionalized children grew. The public also took alarm. Letchworth noted that the massive increase in institutionalization meant that asylums for children began losing their "hold upon popular favor."[25]

This rise in the number of institutionalized children in New York State after the passage of the Children's Law was enormous.[26] In 1875, there were 9,363 children being cared for in public and private institutions in the city. In 1894, the number had risen to 17,076 in the religious institutions alone. Statewide, there were 33,558 children living in institutions in 1894, more than half of whom were in New York City.[27] The State Charities Aid Association of New York, a private group established in 1872 to inspect conditions in the state's public institutions, commented that this growth was much faster than "the growth of population or industrial conditions would warrant."[28] As a result of their concern over the rising numbers of institutionalized children in the state, social-welfare organizations such as the State Charities Aid Association and the New York State Board of Charities, a public body founded in 1867 to oversee the operation of charities in the state, committed themselves to the principle that dependent children ought to be placed in homes. By the early twentieth century, most social-welfare workers—not only in New York State but nationwide—had come to believe that home placement was best and that institutionalization ought to become a thing of the past.[29]

At least some of the alarm expressed by the mainly Protestant members of the new social-welfare organizations had to do with the fact that most of the children's institutions funded by the Children's Law were Catholic.[30] The State Charities Aid Association carefully charted the comparative population statistics of Catholic, Protestant, and Jewish children's institutions after the passage of the Children's Law. Every year, Catholic institutions captured the bulk of the funding, a trend that continued into the first decade of the twentieth century.[31]

Josephine Shaw Lowell, who was active in the State Charities Aid Association and a commissioner of the State Board of Charities, had roots in Boston's Protestant elite and believed that Catholic and Jewish charities had rushed to take advantage of the religious clause of the Children's Law. There is no doubt, she wrote, "that these institutions were established in consequence of the passage of that act, and to take advantage of the facilities granted for the education at public cost of large numbers of children in the Roman Catholic and Hebrew faiths."[32] Her inclusion of Jews is unfair, since Jewish children were institutionalized in the smallest numbers. Also unbalanced is her condemnation of what she felt was Catholic alacrity to take advantage of public funds. The greater number of Catholic institutions for poor children was a reflection, more than anything else, of the poverty of the state's immigrant Catholic population, which by the turn of the century had expanded to include Italians as well as Irish and Germans.

In any case, the anti-institutional feeling created by the Children's Law resulted in greater scrutiny of conditions in children's institutions, including the foundling asylums. The State Charities Aid Association's method was to send visiting committees to inspect each of the state's public charities, county by county. In 1888, the State Charities Aid Association's New York County Visiting Committee was dismayed by conditions at the Randall's Island Infant Hospital. Everything, the visitors observed, was going wrong there: "The plumbing is undergoing renovation, and the hospital is in great disorder; rats still abound. Winter cloaks for the babies were not furnished till March. The mothers are often untidy; being kept till their babies are two years old, there seems no reason why they should not be required to do a moderate amount of work in return for their livelihood. The Committee believes the whole system to be wrong—a premium upon idleness and vice."

Worst of all, they found that not one child admitted during the eighteen months prior to their visit had managed to survive to the age of one.[33] Medical superintendent Healy admitted to the "defective state of our plumbing," but he denied the visiting committee's worst charge. "Our records show eleven who have attained and passed that age [of one year]," he reported indignantly. The committee, he suggested, had simply missed seeing them, since they had been adopted and were thus out of the institution. "There is every reason to believe," he added with the lack of specificity typical of the bureaucracies that ran New York's complex of public institutions in the nineteenth century, that they "are now alive and well." On rats, cloakless infants, and idle, sloppy mothers, Healy remained silent.[34]

The State Charities Aid Association expressed concern about conditions at the Randall's Island Infant Hospital through the 1880s and 1890s. Between 1895 and 1897, the organization discovered, foundling death rates there ranged between 99 and 100 percent—just what they had been at midcentury. The *New York Tribune,* reporting on this finding in its Sunday edition, noted that "this frightful state of affairs appealed to the public imagination as few things could."[35] In 1898, the State Charities Aid Association decided to step in and effect a change. With funds provided by a private benefactor, the association and an older charity organization, the New York Association for Improving the Condition of the Poor, formed the Joint Committee on the Care of Motherless Infants. In January, the joint committee approached the Commissioner of Public Charities for Manhattan and the Bronx and offered to remove a group of foundlings from the Infant Hospital and place them in the homes of foster mothers in the surrounding countryside, women who had their own infants or who had recently lost their

This baby was found by a police officer under a bush in Central Park in July 1901. The Joint Committee on the Care of Motherless Infants placed him with a family in Westchester County; he was subsequently adopted by another family. SCAA/AICP Joint Committee on the Care of Motherless Infants, Annual Report, 1902. Courtesy of the New York State Library, Manuscripts and Special Collections.

infants.[36] Their proposal was nothing more than what Abraham Jacobi had suggested in 1870 and what the Infant Hospital had attempted with its intermittent Westchester program between 1871 and 1892.

The program began in April 1898 with a group of twenty-five foundlings, and it quickly expanded.[37] By the fall of 1900, the Commissioner of Public Charities had agreed to hand over to the Joint Committee on the Care of Motherless Infants all Protestant foundlings retrieved from the streets of Manhattan and the Bronx. In December, reflecting the integration of the five boroughs into Greater New York, the committee began including foundlings from Brooklyn and Queens.[38] Because the joint committee accepted only Protestant foundlings, a group called the Guild of the Infant Savior was organized to place Catholic foundlings. In early 1901, the Commissioner of Public Charities began delivering Catholic foundlings to the Guild of the Infant Savior for placement in Catholic foster homes.[39]

This separate treatment of Protestant and Catholic foundlings was an attempt by the public authorities to step carefully around the ever-present tension between Catholic and Protestant charities in the city. Catholics had long been alarmed at the efforts of Protestant-run placing-out agencies, such as Charles Loring Brace's Children's Aid Society, to place city waifs, many of whom were Catholic, with Protestant farm families. Yet when it came to placing infant foundlings, the situation was more complex than it was with older children. Some foundlings were left with religious medals, notes, or other indicators of their religion, but many were not. Thus it was not always possible to tell the religious heritage of an abandoned baby. By the 1890s, the Commissioner of Public Charities had worked out a solution for this problem: foundlings were baptized alternately by a Catholic priest or a Protestant minister, regardless of their actual, usually unknown origins.[40] After these ad hoc religious assignments had occurred, a representative of the Department of Public Charities named the babies in a similarly random manner. By the early twentieth century, these ceremonies were performed at Bellevue Hospital, and those doing the naming relied on two large books, one containing names for boys, the other, names for girls. Irish, Anglo-Saxon, and Jewish names (even though no children were religiously designated as Jews) were mixed together, and all were spread randomly throughout both books. As each foundling arrived, it was assigned the next available name, regardless of perceived heritage. In 1909, a reporter for the *Herald*'s Sunday magazine regaled his readers with the peculiar results of what he called this "haphazard, helter-skelter method." Jewish names, he wrote, usually fell "to the lot of some fair haired, blue eyed child. Infants with the dark, oily skin of the Orient are placed among the Catholics, while snub faced, red haired boys and girls fall to the Protestants."[41]

The city's effort to be evenhanded in the assignment of religion inevitably created problems. In 1901, for instance, a furor erupted when a six-week-old girl abandoned in a Third Avenue hallway with Catholic religious medals around her neck was given by city authorities to the Protestant Joint Committee on the Care of Motherless Infants with her medals missing. The medals had been removed, apparently, at the police station. The result, the *Herald* reported, was "a serious religious controversy."[42]

Also problematic was the failure of the alternate baptizing scheme to designate any foundlings as Jews (which the Department of Public Charities might have done for boys with the traditional Jewish *bris*, or circumcision ritual), even though some foundlings were given Jewish names. The number of Jewish foundlings was small during the nineteenth century; during the first half of the century this was reflective, in part, of the small size of the city's Jewish community. But even after the city's Jewish population rose as a result of waves of immigration from Eastern Europe during the late nineteenth and early twentieth centuries, there were still few Jewish foundlings. In 1901, the *New York Tribune* noted that "occasionally a baby is found with a request pinned on its clothes that it should be brought up as a Hebrew, and this desire is, of course, respected; but these cases are extremely rare."[43] The fact that Jews tended to come to the United States in family groups probably protected young, unmarried Jewish women from becoming unexpectedly pregnant. Their experience in that regard was very different from that of the many young, unmarried Irish women who came to the United States on their own.[44] Also, Jewish women did not work as live-in servants in any significant numbers, and servants, mostly American born at the start of the century and then mostly Irish after the mid-century famine migration, dominated the ranks of abandoning mothers. The rarity of Jewish foundlings, however, only explained in part why Jews were overlooked at the city's alternating baptizing ceremonies. The practice of alternate baptism was a response to a specific, bitter, entrenched, longtime rivalry between Catholics and Protestants that simply did not take Jews (or for that matter, members of any other religious or national group) into account.[45] Only the bestowal of Jewish names (albeit to children designated as Catholics and Protestants) seems to represent an effort, if an awkward one, to address Jewish feelings.

One result of the work of the Joint Committee on the Care of Motherless Infants and the Guild of the Infant Savior was that the number of foundlings delivered to the Infant Hospital began to lessen significantly as these two groups siphoned them off. Another was that the mortality rate of the placed-out foundlings, once removed from the infectious environment of the Infant Hospital and provided with individual attention, dropped rapidly. In 1899, after one year of operation, the joint committee reported that the mortality rate of its foundlings was 55.9 percent; a year later it was 31.1 percent, and in 1901, after four years of operation, the committee was able to report that the mortality rate of the foundlings it had placed with foster mothers was only 18.9 percent. This rate, they remarked proudly, was "not greatly in excess of the estimated mortality among all children of corresponding age in New York City."[46]

The city's arrangements with the Joint Committee on the Care of Motherless Infants and the Guild of the Infant Savior came to an end in 1907. During the nine years of its operation, the joint committee took charge of a thousand foundlings. It placed 407 of these in permanent, adoptive homes.[47]

The end of this system came at least in part as a result of bribe-taking in the office of the city comptroller. Hermann Metz, the comptroller, and Daniel C. Potter, chief of the comptroller's Bureau of Charitable Institutions, carried on a campaign against the placing-out program starting in 1905. Metz was offended at what he saw as a Protestant effort to convert Catholic babies. The rhetoric of these two officials was edged with real animosity toward reform, a symptom of the ongoing conflict between reform forces and those of machine politics in the city. According to Comptroller Metz, the work of the joint committee was no more than "professional philanthropy in its boldest, most heartless and most reckless form," and Virginia Walker, the joint committee's agent, was nothing but "a hired female clerk, with a basket in her arm, peddling a live baby around the city."

Metz and Potter's accusations against the placing-out program were rather vague. In 1905 Potter charged that since the Joint Committee on the Care of Motherless Infants was only an unchartered experiment, the work it was carrying out was illegal. When this charge did not take hold, Potter accused the joint committee of placing babies in "unfit homes and with drunken guardians." This accusation was denied by Homer Folks, the reform leader and vocal supporter of placing out who had been the Commissioner of Public Charities from 1902 to 1903, while the joint committee was in operation. Metz insisted that the children should be cared for only by institutions "possessing buildings and equipment for the actual physical care of children," even though, as the beleaguered joint committee pointed out, the institutionalization of foundlings was well known by this time to result in death. In 1910, a subsequent city comptroller discovered that Potter had received a five-hundred-dollar bribe from a group of Catholic institutions. They had benefited from the per-capita rates paid out of public coffers and were therefore threatened by placing-out programs that took children out of their hands, along with the funding that came with them. Once again, the fate of the city's foundlings was determined by conflict between rival groups.[48]

Despite this serious setback, by the first decade of the twentieth century, placing out was widely accepted among the new social-work professionals of the Progressive era as the best method for caring for all children lacking viable homes, including abandoned infants. In 1908, a new city department, the Bureau of Child Hygiene, took over the care of foundlings. Its head, physician and Progressive reformer Sara Josephine Baker, believed as Jacobi had, almost four decades earlier, that placing out, even with poor women in the tenement districts, was preferable to keeping foundlings in institutions.[49] The following year, a widely influential White House Conference on the Care of Dependent Children supported Dr. Baker's view, judging that home life was preferable to institutional life for dependent children and noting that, when the child's biological family was unavailable, a foster or adoptive home was best. This idea was adopted by professional social workers and local welfare officials nationwide and remained in force throughout the twentieth century.[50]

Ultimately, even the New York Infant Asylum and the Nursery and Child's Hospital succumbed to the new thinking on placing out. In 1902, the New York Infant Asylum formed a boarding-out department that placed some of its foundlings. By 1915, the boarding-out department of the Nursery and Child's Hospital and the New York Infant Asylum—which in 1910 merged to form one institution, the New York Nursery and Child's Hospital—was no longer housing babies in its building; all were placed in the homes of wet nurses or foster mothers.[51]

The New York Nursery and Child's Hospital justified this radical shift in policy by allying itself with the authorities of the day, including the 1909 White House Conference.[52] "Today the most advanced social worker endeavors to make the healthy foundling one of a family group. . . . that it [boarding-out] is the surest way to help our little foundlings and waifs to better health, there seems little doubt," the institution claimed in 1915.[53]

Mothers and babies at the Nursery and Child's Hospital, 1904; a baby is being weighed at center. Courtesy of New York Weill Cornell Medical Center Archives.

Boarding out, as the New York Nursery and Child's Hospital practiced it in the early twentieth century, was invested with the administrative efficiency that was the hallmark of the era. Gone was the "old system of 'baby farming,' under which almost any indigent female who wished to turn an honest or dishonest penny could get children to board for the asking"; the difference, according to the New York Nursery and Child's Hospital, was skilled oversight.[54] The boarding-out department and local health boards investigated the homes of potential nurses before placing out children, and the children were visited by trained nurses once or twice a week and sometimes even more frequently. When medical care was necessary, the children returned to the institution's children's hospital. The New York Nursery and Child's Hospital tried to place most of its children outside the city, and in middle-class rather than poor homes, with working fathers present and no other young children to distract the foster mother. One home in Jersey City was described by the boarding-out department in 1916 as ideal. It was "an old-fashioned, two-family house with a yard where the children play together. The children sleep in big, sunny rooms, each in a crib or cradle; each one has a tooth-brush, comb and towel. The children's physical condition proves that the food is abundant and wholesome, and the little fellows' happiness and their evident fondness for the home and family are gratifying proof of a normal, happy life."[55]

In order to maintain oversight over the boarded-out children, the New York Nursery and Child's Hospital had to keep them relatively close. Thus children were placed within a radius of no more than twenty miles from New York City, on Long Island, in New Jersey, and in the city's five boroughs.[56] This represented a retreat from the pastoral romanticism of Charles Loring Brace and Abraham Jacobi, but by this time, the dangers of placing children alone in faraway rural homes were increasingly recognized, particularly by the western states that had been left with the responsibility of caring for cases that went wrong. The orphan train program of the Children's Aid Society also came to an end in this era.[57]

Also not in keeping with Brace's or Mary Du Bois's nineteenth-century vision for foundlings and other poor city children was the New York Nursery and Child's Hospital's reliance on Italian immigrant women as wet nurses. While the institution did idealize the middle-class, suburban home as the best for its babies, it had very good success with immigrant Italian women living with their families in East Harlem and Little Italy. The New York Nursery and Child's Hospital placed its youngest babies, including some premature ones, with Italian wet nurses and marveled at the success they had, even with the most fragile babies. According to the groups that used these nurses, the intense, loving attention that these poor, immigrant women paid to their charges bolstered their chances for survival.

The joint committee and the Guild of the Infant Savior had also relied on Italian wet nurses to care for some of their foundlings, and all who saw them remarked on the warmth of these Italian mothers and their ability to help otherwise unwanted infants thrive. "The natural love of the Italian wet-nurses for babies is great," the New York Nursery and Child's Hospital observed. The Joint Committee on the Care of Motherless Infants noted similarly that "there is a physical vigor and warmth of nature in the Italian mother which makes her a most desirable nurse."[58] The press enjoyed watching the Italian wet nurses at work; in 1904 the *Herald*'s Sunday magazine described how "the babies boarded out in Little Italy soon become, for the time being, virtually Italian babies, and it is rather ludicrous to see one of the little mites in its Latin environment. Perhaps the baby presents every race characteristic of its Irish or German or Scandinavian parentage, and sometimes, but not often, the little face bears the unmistakable trace of Hebrew ancestry. But whatever its race or nationality may be, it seems to imbibe with its milk all the cunning ways of the real Italian child."[59]

Despite the success of the Italian wet nurses, the gap in culture between them and the representatives of the organizations that employed them created problems. Miss Entwhistle, the agent for the Guild of the Infant Savior, complained that the Italian nurses' "very virtues become their greatest fault. They will insist upon spoiling the children with over-attention, and in their motherly pride of them they are prone to break all the rules of health and hygiene." These included feeding babies macaroni and dressing them in "gorgeous robes of lace and embroidery" that they made and paid for themselves. "It is a common sight," Miss Entwhistle reported, "to walk into an Italian's house and find the foundling baby literally bowed down with its wealth of beads and amulets, all precious keepsakes of its foster family."[60]

The New York Nursery and Child's Hospital and the Joint Committee on the Care of Motherless Infants also had reservations about the Italian wet nurses. They appreciated the maternal magic the nurses worked with their foundlings but did not consider these immigrant Italian households suitable as adoptive homes. For Miss Entwhistle of the Guild of the Infant Savior, cultural differences and lack of education, particularly in the new sanitary ideals, were the problem. For the Protestant New York Nursery and Child's Hospital and the Joint Committee on the Care of Motherless Infants, religion was also an issue. Yet when the time came to separate the foundlings from their Italian foster mothers, many tears were shed. "The foster mother learns to love the little 'bambino' for whom she cares with a strength she does not appreciate until the parting," the joint committee reported, "and it is very difficult to resist the pleadings that must be refused, when a desirable home for adoption has been found for the baby." The New York Nursery and Child's Hospital agreed that these moments were "very sad."[61]

Overall, the New York Nursery and Child's Hospital judged its placing-out program a success and chose to forget how bitterly its predecessor organizations had resisted it. The New York Nursery and Child's Hospital even claimed, erroneously, to be among the first in New York to board out babies.[62] By the Progressive era, placing out had become so accepted a trend among social-welfare professionals that it was very hard to resist.

The End of an Era: The Randall's Island Infant Hospital Closes, 1905

The success of placing out as the newly reigning paradigm meant the end of the foundling asylums as residential institutions for infants. The first of the foundling asylums to close was the Randall's Island Infant Hospital in 1905. By the 1880s, the public, in accord with the observations of the State Charities Aid Association, had come to think of the Infant Hospital as a place where babies went to die. In 1884, a *Herald* reporter asked a baby farmer if the respectable-looking man and woman who had left a three-month-old girl with her had come back to take the baby away or pay for its care. "Indeed they have not," the baby farmer replied indignantly, "and I am real sorry for it, for if I am compelled to send the baby to the Commissioners of Charities and Correction it will be dead within three days."[63] Three years later, a poor father discovered that the baby farmer's assessment of the possibility of survival at the Infant Hospital was correct. When his wife died in childbirth, this man brought his healthy, newborn twins to Randall's Island when he was unable to care for them on his own. Only a few weeks later, they were delivered back to him near death; they quickly died. The doctor who examined them claimed that "the poor little things had been either starved or beaten to death." He refused to grant death certificates and referred the grieving father to the coroner.[64] In truth, death rates among almshouse infants had always been high. By this time, however, the scrutiny of such oversight organizations as the State Charities Aid Association, and an increasingly vigilant child-saving movement, helped to make high infant death rates less tolerable than they had ever been before.[65] By 1903, the Commissioner of Public Charities justified his decision to rename the Randall's Island institutions the "New York City Children's Hospitals and Schools" on the grounds that it was "free from some objections which have come to attach to the words 'Randall's Island.' "[66]

Even in the last decades of the nineteenth century, however, not all reports of conditions on Randall's Island were negative; some outside visitors made positive assessments of conditions there. These reflect efforts to bring the Infant Hospital up to then-current standards of hygiene. In 1880, for instance, a reporter for the *New York Tribune* went to the island to investigate accusations of dirt and "impure air." Escorted by two physicians from the island's institutions, the reporter found the Infant Hospital a model of everything that contemporary sanitary wisdom prescribed. Sunshine streamed into a ward and "lit up the pale faces of three little children who were playing on the floor. There were windows on both sides of this room, with flowers and creepers prettily arranged in the alcoves, the walls and the floor were perfectly clean. The beds were neatly made, the sheets and coverlets without stain, and the blankets thick and comfortable. There was no offensive odor, and the light and ventilation were perfect."[67] In 1896, a *Herald* reporter observed that Randall's Island was a "paradise" compared to the "stifling tenements" and noted approvingly that the Infant Hospital was a place where "science holds sway."[68]

These mixed opinions on conditions at Randall's Island reflect two sides of a complex reality. Sanitary conditions at the Infant Hospital during the last decades of the nineteenth century were a clear improvement over those at the almshouse during previous decades. Yet despite the improved conditions, death rates for motherless babies at the Infant Hospital remained high. During the 1880s, the Infant Hospital admitted an average of 439 motherless babies yearly. Including those remaining from previous years, the Infant Hospital cared for an average of 526 motherless babies each year. (This was many more than it had cared for during the first half of the century.) Of this total number, an average of 316 died each year.

Virginia M. Walker, the agent for the Joint Committee on the Care of Motherless Infants (the same woman Comptroller Metz had accused of peddling live babies around the city) was attuned to this paradox in a way that the reporters from the *Herald* and the *Tribune* were not. Everything, she reported, appeared to be in good order at the Infant Hospital when she saw it in 1898. The equipment, nurses, and "rows of little white beds" were up to the standards of a "properly conducted institution." Yet, she recognized, the seeming order masked the fact that the death rate at the Infant Hospital was still unacceptably high. Walker identified the cause as "mothersickness," or the absence of individual maternal care.[69]

TABLE 6.1
*Motherless Infants at the New York City Department of
Public Charities and Correction's Infant Hospital on
Randall's Island, 1880–89*

	On hand, start of year	Received during year	Total	Died
1880	72	406	478	291
1881	87	375	462	294
1882	80	415	495	324
1883	88	460	548	339
1884	107	489	596	396
1885	123	447	570	329
1886	84	391	475	267
1887	53	435	488	263
1888	92	467	559	321
1889	77	508	585	333

Note: All figures in this table come from the columns referring to "orphans," the term the Infant Hospital used to refer to motherless infants, in Table A, Census Report of Infant Hospital, Randall's Island, in the annual reports of the PCC. In 1880–83, the babies the Infant Hospital sent to Westchester were not included in the count of orphans received; in 1885–89 they were (in 1884 the Westchester program was temporarily suspended). The number recorded for deaths refers just to deaths of motherless babies in the Infant Hospital. Table A shows that those who survived were discharged, adopted, or transferred to other institutions. Some were described as having "eloped." Since they could not have run away on their own, this must mean that they were removed in some unofficial manner. The Infant Hospital identified the babies it sent to Westchester specifically as foundlings.

Dr. S. Josephine Baker, as head of the city's Bureau of Child Hygiene, came to the same conclusion. "There were the wretched little foundlings dying wholesale under fine hygienic conditions" but flourishing when placed with foster mothers in the tenements, where they received "personal care from a maternally minded woman." That, she added, "was why I became and still am a firm believer in mothering for babies: old-fashioned, sentimental mothering, the kind that psychologists decry. It should not be carried to excess and it should not be continued too long, but there is little doubt in my mind that many a baby has died for lack of it."[70]

The accumulated weight of a poor reputation based on its persistent failure to keep motherless babies alive and new thinking about the care of young children ultimately doomed the Infant Hospital. In September 1905, after thirty-six years of operation, the Infant Hospital discharged its last foundling, and the building was turned into a general-purpose hospital for the children remaining on Randall's Island.[71]

The End of the New York Infant Asylum and the Nursery and Child's Hospital, 1934

The New York Infant Asylum and the Nursery and Child's Hospital were the next to go, though the 1910 merger kept them from going under entirely for several decades. At the nursery, an era came to an end with the death of Mary Du Bois in 1888. Her successor, Mary Mildred Sullivan, brought a more relaxed set of values to the role of first directress. Sullivan, wife of Algernon Sidney Sullivan, a prominent lawyer in New York, was involved with the nursery as early as 1857, at first through its annual fundraising ball.[72]

Sullivan adapted comfortably to the Progressive era's more pragmatic perspective on unmarried mothers and the poor. In 1917, when she was eighty-one years old, Sullivan observed that attitudes toward unmarried mothers had softened in the previous twenty years. Her own views had relaxed even earlier. "I can look back," she reminisced, "to a time when I was called very wicked for telling the unmarried girl mothers in our hospital that I hoped their babies would bring them comfort, incentive, and happiness." "In those days," she continued, "the mistaken idea prevailed that sympathy encouraged people to be bad and that punishment and ostracism were good for their souls. It was hard to get funds even for the help of the poor little babies." "I was regarded as a violent radical," she added.[73]

By the early twentieth century, neither the nursery nor the New York Infant Asylum made the moral reform of fallen women a central goal any longer. At the nursery, the tolerant personality of Mary Sullivan probably had something to do with this; yet even before this time, all of the foundling asylums realized they had simply failed at this aspect of their work. In 1891, the chair of the New York Infant Asylum's ladies' committee admitted woefully that the "moral evils" that produced illegitimate babies were "as illimitable and unchanging as the flowing of a mighty river," a powerful and persistent natural force against which, she admitted, her institution was able to have little effect. "We stand at the mouth [of the river]" she wrote, evoking an image of profound helplessness, "appalled at its remorseless currents, and reach out our hands to such as are driven by its onrushing, to succor and save."[74]

Both institutions were also battered by the increase in the city's population, caused by the late-century waves of immigration from southern and eastern Europe. These waves were reflected in their own rising population figures. The New York Infant Asylum saw its yearly number of inmates rise from 661 in 1880 to 1,517 in 1900.[75] In 1888, the year of Mary Du Bois's death, the nursery cared for nearly two thousand women and children.[76] And complaints about overcrowding appeared regularly in the annual reports of the New York Infant Asylum during these years. "Our beds are always full," the report's authors noted in 1886. In 1893, they reported, not for the first time, that the house was so full that "we have been compelled to turn many applicants away."[77]

Their aging buildings could not cope with the onslaught. In 1893, the nursery complained that its old buildings required constant, expensive repairs.[78] The New York Infant Asylum similarly reported that its "present buildings are very old, and in such a condition that they can only last a few years more."[79] Their treasuries also felt the strain. Both institutions relied on the per-capita funding they received from the city, additional city money from the board of education, and private money that they raised on their own, as well as dividends from investments. The public money the foundling asylums relied on was uncertain, reflecting the public's discomfort about spending public money on private, religious institutions. While this hostility was directed chiefly by Protestants at Catholic charitable institutions, Protestant institutions, as the foundling crises of the 1860s and 1870s demonstrate, could be caught in the same antisectarian net.

In 1910, giving into sharp financial pressure, including a 1900 cut in the per-capita allowance, the Nursery and Child's Hospital and the New York Infant Asylum merged, renaming the consolidated institution the New York Nursery and Child's Hospital.[80] "Consolidation is the order of the day," remarked the board of managers of the New York Infant Asylum bravely, placing themselves in the company of the business monopolies and metropolitan consolidations of the late nineteenth century. But the real reason, which they did not conceal, was lack of funds.[81]

The unpredictable ups and downs of public funding meant that all three of the private foundling asylums relied on fundraising events such as fairs, concerts, art exhibitions, theatrical events, and balls.[82] In 1872, the New York Infant Asylum held an evening of "*tableaux vivants*" at the Union League Club's theater. Tableaux vivants were "living pictures" in which attractive, young society women dressed in costumes and posed as the subjects of mythical or historical scenes or famous paintings. Edith Wharton set a scene in her novel *The House of Mirth* at a party at which these were the central entertainment. Wharton's fictional partygivers understood that *"tableaux vivants* and expensive music were the two baits most likely to attract the desired prey."[83] The foundling asylums also knew that events such as these were an effective way to squeeze funds out of the pockets of their society supporters. This was particularly true of the two Protestant institutions, which had greater access to the private wealth of the city than either the public almshouse or the Catholic New York Foundling Asylum did.

The nursery relied on an annual fundraising ball that, as an annual rite of New York's high society, became more popular than the nursery itself. Its first ball was held at the Academy of Music in 1856. Mary Sullivan remembered it as a "gorgeous spectacle" attended by "beautifully gowned ladies. . . . And all were the best people."[84] Yet by the early twentieth century, the ball had developed a reputation as a relic of "old New York."[85]

The ball was a successful magnet for funds.[86] The acerbic observer George Templeton Strong was so impressed by the ball's success that he considered suggesting one to support his own charitable interests: "the Nursery makes about $6,000 net by its ball," he commented in his diary in 1858. "Why not open St. Luke's Hospital with a ball (St. Vitus quadrille, tetanus polka, and so on)."[87] In 1870, the nursery's secretary reported that the "brilliant success always attendant on the Ball" allowed the nursery to pay its debts and replenish its bank account.[88] Ironically, and despite the funds it took in, the ball sparkled even as the nursery itself struggled and then declined. In the end, the ball outlasted the nursery, spinning off on its own, devoting its earnings to new causes, and holding its centennial in 1956.[89]

During the twenty-four years that the New York Nursery and Child's Hospital survived into the twentieth century (and in the ten years prior, in which it was two separate institutions), it gradually let go of the characteristics that had defined it in the nineteenth and took on ones more in keeping with the new century. The institution reconstituted itself during these years as a modern medical and social-welfare agency for women and children.

Like all of New York's foundling asylums, the two institutions that folded into it—the Nursery and Child's Hospital and the New York Infant Asylum—had always had medical functions. Both had maternity wards, and the nursery ran a children's hospital and a dispensary. Despite these medical functions, however, the nineteenth-century nursery and New York Infant Asylum did not see themselves as strictly medical institutions. Instead, they participated in a tradition that defined inpatient hospital care as a charitable service for the poor. In an era in which hospitals were not able to provide much in the way of cures, they were essentially custodial institutions, often with a strong reform dimension, since many were run by religious groups. New York's nineteenth-century foundling asylums, with their residential populations of infants who died more often than they were helped, fall neatly within this model. Their maternity wards, too, were guided by moral goals. In an era in which most women gave birth at home, lying-in hospitals typically served poor women, including the widowed, abandoned, homeless, and unmarried. Lying-in hospitals that accepted unmarried women could be tainted, as foundling asylums were, by accusations that they provided support services to those who had violated society's sexual rules. When the New York Infant Asylum opened its maternity hospital in 1877, it had to combat the idea "that such an asylum increases crime."[90]

During the second half of the century, hospitals began to attract a more prosperous clientele, as medicine was becoming safer and more effective and cities were filling with people far from the support that family had traditionally provided at times of illness. By the first decades of the twentieth century, hospitals had changed their functions radically. They were no longer institutions for the sick poor where moral reform was as important a part of the treatment as medical care. Instead, they became institutions to which people of all classes went to get well. Patients paid more often for the services they received and did not expect to receive lectures on their moral behavior as a part of their treatment.[91] The New York Nursery and Child's Hospital adapted to these new norms. During the first decades of the twentieth century, it increased and refined its medical functions, adding a laboratory for children's diseases and offering a formal training program for nurses in conjunction with several city hospitals.[92]

One result of the medicalization of institutions such as foundling asylums was that the women who ran them, particularly the all-woman nursery, suffered a precipitous loss in authority as the moralistic model of medical charity in which their institutions were rooted faded into obsolescence. When there wasn't much that medicine could do to help sickly foundlings, they were consigned to the moral and maternal care of female volunteers. Once physicians learned how to battle effectively with disease and death, they took over these institutions themselves. Abraham Jacobi had been a member of the advance guard of this trend, and within a few decades of his ouster from Du Bois's institution, the balance of power at charitable foundling asylums had shifted drastically. Gone were the days when a board of lady managers with no medical training was able to throw a trained medical doctor out of their institution.

The New York Nursery and Child Hospital's continuing work with unmarried mothers also took on the Progressive era's commitment to professional standards. By 1910, the year of the merger, the new institution had adopted the language of Progressivism to describe the services it provided to its inmates. Unmarried mothers in the institution were said to learn about the "different branches of home work" not only from the labor they carried out there, but "under efficient teachers." The reformative value of hard labor and the moral example of virtuous middle-class women was no longer enough.[93]

Even though the new institution altered its values to adjust to the times, and despite the 1910 merger, the New York Nursery and Child Hospital continued to experience problems with funding.[94] During the twenties, the institution's finances revived as a result of the country's overall prosperity, but it could not weather the stock market crash of 1929. In 1934, rather than having to close down entirely for lack of funds, the New York Nursery and Child's Hospital was absorbed into New York Hospital.

The Exception: The New York Foundling Hospital

After 1934, only one of the four nineteenth-century foundling asylums was left standing: the Sisters of Charity's New York Foundling Asylum. Of the four, the New York Foundling Asylum had always enjoyed the best reputation with the public and the press. This was due to its more generous entrance policies; to the charm and charisma of its first head, Sister Irene Fitzgibbon; and to the fact that it appears to have been run more efficiently than the other foundling asylums in the city. The New York Foundling Asylum, or "the Foundling," as it was familiarly called, benefited from the full-time devotion of its resident sisters, some of whom began as novitiates in training and then established long relationships with the institution. After Sister Irene died in 1896, her place was taken by a series of administrators, many of whom had already spent years there. This was an advantage that the two Protestant foundling asylums could not match, with their changing groups of volunteers; nor could the public Infant Hospital enjoy such continuity, with its barely tolerated convict and pauper laborers and shifting casts of often-corrupt political administrators.

As a result of its popularity, the New York Foundling Asylum was better able than the others to attract supporters and funds as these became more scarce. In the twentieth century, the foundling asylum established productive relationships with the New York City Fire Department, the Knights of Columbus, and even a popular television show, *Ted Mack's Amateur Hour*.[95] The foundling asylum also attracted the special interest of Cardinal Francis Spellman, who donated the royalties from his novel, *The Foundling,* to the institution.[96]

The foundling asylum also continued to survive because it adapted successfully to changing times. It changed its name to the New York Foundling *Hospital* to reflect the medicalization that was appropriate for a twentieth-century institution for the physically vulnerable. Its administrators devoted funds to the professional training of its staff in developing fields such as social work and psychology, as such training became a requirement in these fields.[97] By 1958, its new building on Seventh Avenue at Thirteenth Street, near St. Vincent's Hospital and only a few blocks from its original site on East Twelfth Street, was staffed with professional social workers, psychiatrists, psychologists, and physicians. Still active in the early twenty-first century, the New York Foundling Hospital provides such social services as child-abuse prevention, assistance for teen mothers, foster care and adoption, medical care, mental-health care, and other programs in keeping with the needs of a new era. The only thing missing from the Seventh Avenue building is the wicker basket that sheltered so many foundlings in the nineteenth century.[98]

7

Conclusion
The Foundling Disappears—Almost

In the first decades of the twentieth century, three out of
New York's four foundling asylums closed their doors. According to
their own goals, they had failed. They had been unable to effect any
change in the moral complexion of their society, and they could cope
neither with the massive immigration that overburdened their resources
nor with the political and ethnic strife in which they became entangled.
Worst of all, they had not been able to stem the persistent, tragic death
rate of the infants they took in. But despite their failures, and as a result
of no efforts of theirs, infant abandonment as a mass phenomenon receded dramatically in the twentieth century.

The inadequacy of government record-keeping on foundlings makes
it difficult to provide exact figures, and it is also hard to know which
groups of twentieth- and twenty-first-century children are the precise
counterparts of nineteenth-century foundlings. Can the children who
were never born as a result of the greater availability and efficacy of birth
control and abortion in the twentieth- and twenty-first centuries be considered the equivalents of babies who were born and abandoned in the
nineteenth? Are "boarder babies"—newborn babies afflicted by poverty,
drug use, and AIDS who were left behind by their parents in hospitals
in epidemic numbers in the late twentieth century—equivalent to the
foundlings of the nineteenth century, the products of poverty and illegitimacy?[1] But if we look simply at the numbers of babies picked up in the
streets, abandoned at foundling asylums, or born in foundling asylums,
the available figures create a very striking picture of change.

Between 1880 and 1885, a period for which figures from all four asylums are largely complete and roughly comparable, the four institutions
together received an average of approximately 2,041 babies each year
(including both babies born inside the institutions and those brought
in from outside). In the twentieth and twenty-first centuries, New York

TABLE 7.1

Children Born in and Received at New York City's
Foundling Asylums, 1880–85

	Infant Hospital, Randall's Island[a]			NY Foundling Asylum[b]			NY Infant Asylum[c]			Nursery and Child's Hospital[d]		
	Rec'd.	Born	Total	Rec'd.	Born	Total	Rec'd.	Born	Total	Rec'd.	Born	Total
1880	406	—	406	[752]	[29]	[781]	—	—	160	149	155	304
1881	375	—	375	893	85	978	—	—	244	162	181	343
1882	415	—	415	878	128	1006	—	—	247	223	232	455
1883	460	—	460	928	133	1061	—	—	242	275	219	494
1884	489	—	489	811	128	939	—	—	286	196	212	408
1885	447	—	447	904	144	1048	—	—	295	136	229	365

[a] From Table A, Census Report of Infant Hospital, in PCC, annual reports, 1880–85. These are the children identified by the Infant Hospital during these years as "orphans," or motherless babies. No babies were born in the Infant Hospital since it did not have childbirth facilities. See the table 6.1 note for additional information.

[b] NYFA, biennial report, 1879–81, 22–23; annual reports, 1881, 16; 1882, 14; 1883, 13; 1884, 45; 1885, 49. The admissions figures in the 1879–81 biennial report are for October 1, 1879 to January 1, 1881. The figures presented here in the 1880 row of this table are my estimates for a twelve-month period based on the fifteen-month period presented in the report. In 1881 the NYFA began issuing annual reports starting January 1.

[c] NYIA, annual report, 1887, 14–15. These figures represent children born in the Asylum as well as those left at it. The table from which these figures come does not break it down. NYIA medical reports which do make the distinction are insufficiently clear or complete.

[d] NCH, annual reports, 1879–80, 25; 1880–81, 19; 1881–82, 19; 1882–83, 19; 1883–84, 21; 1884–85, 19. In this period the Nursery's reporting year began in March, thus the figure I list for 1880, for instance, is really 1879–80.

City statistics on foundlings have become scattershot. There are no longer four foundling asylums with resident populations to count, and neither city, state, or federal governments maintain a count of foundlings.[2] Still, it is possible to assemble a few figures. In December 2000, for instance, the Brooklyn district attorney's office estimated that during the preceding *decade* a total of forty-seven newborns had been abandoned in Brooklyn.[3] For the two-and-a-half-year period ending in June 2003, the city's Department of Children's Services reported that a total of thirteen babies under five months were abandoned in all five boroughs. Of these, just two were picked up in Manhattan—an enormous change from the era when a foundling was named for nearly every downtown corner.[4] Resorting to press reports for its source material, the United States Department of Health and Human Services concluded that in 1991, in all of the United States, sixty-five babies were abandoned in public places. In 1998, the number rose to 105. In 2006, just six abandoned newborns were collected in New York City.[5] By the opening of the twenty-first century, the foundling problem, according to one Illinois public official, was "hardly a national epidemic."[6]

The Foundling Disappears: Domestic Service, the Progressives, and Deinstitutionalization

At the start of the twentieth century, an assortment of economic, political, demographic, and cultural trends began to make infant abandonment a thing of the past. One of these was the decline of domestic service as the principal occupation for working women in the urban north.[7] The mothers of many nineteenth-century foundlings, in New York and elsewhere, had been live-in servants. But by the 1920s, significant economic and demographic shifts had transformed domestic service. White women chose to take the new occupations opening up for them in factories, offices, stores, and public schools. At the same time, the great migration of African Americans from the rural south to northern cities brought a new population to take their places, but mostly as day laborers, not as live-in servants.[8] The African-American maids who replaced the Irish, live-in domestic servants of the nineteenth century faced difficulties of their own. But the end of live-in domestic service as an occupation that absorbed large numbers of poor, single, women meant the end of the conditions that had forced so many of these women to choose between their jobs and their children.

Another factor was a fundamental change in government policy. In the early twentieth century, the federal government began for the first time to focus on problems of social welfare. Poor, single women with children had been affected disproportionately by the uncontrolled poverty of the nineteenth century. In the early twentieth century, Progressives in state and federal government and particularly at the Federal Children's Bureau began to pay special attention to mothers and children. Some of their initiatives made a difference in the lives of foundlings and their mothers and may have enabled some women to keep their babies.

The Progressives' record in regard to foundlings is mixed. They did not take any special interest in foundlings and at times they discriminated against unwed mothers, but their intense focus on the welfare of mothers and children did result in improved conditions for poor women who in an earlier era might have felt they had no choice but to abandon their babies. With the creation of the Federal Children's Bureau in 1912, the Progressives established the principle that child welfare was a responsibility of the federal government.[9] This precedent and others established by the Progressives extended into the New Deal Era with the passage of the Social Security Act of 1935.

The very first project the Federal Children's Bureau took on was the reduction of infant mortality. Their studies showed that illegitimate babies died at up to twice the rate of babies born to married parents—something that nineteenth-century foundling asylum administrators had known all too well.[10] Yet despite their awareness of the special vulnerability of illegitimate babies, programs that the Federal Children's Bureau ran or supported often excluded never-married mothers and favored widows.[11] This was the case with the mothers' pensions that forty states had passed by 1920 and that the Federal Children's Bureau endorsed.[12]

The purpose of the mothers' pensions was to support families that had lost their male breadwinners and to reward women's unpaid labor as mothers, just as the contributions of soldiers were recognized by the federal government with military pensions. The mothers' pension laws, which were supported by a wide range of women's organizations—conservative ones such as the Women's Christian Temperance Union as well as progressive ones such as the Consumer's League—were meant not as charity but as pensions, even wages, for a job performed—child-rearing—that benefited the state. Despite this generous approach, states typically gave their aid only to poor widows; single mothers who could not prove they had been married were usually excluded. New York, which passed its mothers' pension law in 1915, was among the states that offered aid only to widows, excluding not only never-married mothers but also deserted wives.[13] Just like the religious charities of the nineteenth century, the administrators of New York's mothers' pension suspected deserted wives of culpability at best, immorality at worst.

By the twenties, the broad view of mothers' pensions as wages for mothering had unraveled. Mothers' pensions, or Aid to Dependent Children (known by the acronym ADC and the ancestor of Aid to Families with Dependent Children, or AFDC), as these state programs came to be known, had devolved into charity. In 1935 ADC was incorporated into the newly formed Social Security Administration, but it was placed in a "lower tier" of Social Security programs that treated their recipients as undeserving in a manner reminiscent of the rules of the antebellum charities that had excluded the "unworthy."[14]

The most significant contribution the Progressives made to the welfare of foundlings was to drive the final nail into the coffin of institutionalization. The White House Conference of 1909 was where this contribution was made manifest. By championing family preservation and foster care over institutionalization, the 1909 conference changed the paradigm for the care of dependent children nationwide. This new model, which had been gestating for decades, had two strong advocates in New York. One was Homer Folks, the longtime leader of the State Charities Aid Association, former Commissioner of Public Charities, and opponent of the foundling asylums.[15] The other was Dr. S. Josephine Baker, the head of New York City's Bureau of Child Hygiene, the city department, founded in 1908, that took over the care of foundlings after the Randall's Island Infant Hospital closed in 1905. Dr. Baker, who had ties to the national Progressive movement, strongly supported home placement for foundlings. According to Baker, infants that diminished into "poor little potential ghosts" in foundling asylums flourished when they were placed in tenement homes with "maternally minded" women.[16]

The deinstitutionalization advocated by the White House Conference, and long advocated in New York, brought the city more closely into line with the practices of European cities. As early as 1869, Abraham Jacobi observed that European foundling asylums were closing down their wheels and using their great urban institutions as nothing more than transit stations for babies on their way to rural wet nurses.[17] In New York, as in Europe, the deinstitutionalization of foundlings may also have removed one of the causes of abandonment. Historians have asserted that there is a link between the availability of foundling asylums and the frequency of infant abandonment.[18] Something like this was probably operative in New York, particularly by the second half of the nineteenth century, when there were four foundling asylums in the city.

Homer Folks certainly thought this was so. In 1912, as head of the State Charities Aid Association, Folks attacked the record of New York's foundling asylums. He argued that the very existence of foundling asylums in New York and other cities had magnified the incidences of abandonment. "So far as the evidence goes," he told colleagues at a meeting in Washington, "it would seem to indicate that, in those cities in which infants are most freely received from their parents, and in the largest numbers, there, also, the largest number of other infants are actually abandoned upon the streets and other places."[19] Folks's words bring to mind the experience of Mary Anderson, the woman who ninety years earlier had looked for a "gentleman's door" at which to leave her baby. Understanding how New York's almshouse system worked, she believed that if she laid the baby at someone's door, it would be picked up and brought to the almshouse, where not only would it be "taken care of," but the baby's father would be made to pay.[20] The irony, of course, is that the people who opened New York's four foundling asylums, intending to reform fallen women and thereby lessen the number of foundlings, may actually have made the problem worse.

Adoption

When twentieth-century social workers and the unmarried mothers they served turned away from institutionalization, they turned toward adoption. By then, the imperfect methods for binding a child to a family, such as the informal, sometimes precarious adoptions negotiated by the New York almshouse, the indenture agreements that were so inappropriate for infants, and the poorly defined forms of "placement" practiced by the Children's Aid Society and the foundling asylums, were replaced by adoption laws. New York passed its adoption law in 1873.[21] By the twenties and even more so by the postwar era, many illegitimate babies who might have been left in the streets a century earlier were legally and permanently absorbed into adoptive families.[22]

More than the creation of a legal structure for adoption was necessary to make it the popular alternative it became for so many unmarried mothers and childless families in the twentieth century. While infant abandonment was one result of the shock produced by the rapid urbanization that characterized New York City, adoption was the product, in part, of a society that was adjusting to urbanization. Over the nineteenth and twentieth centuries, American cities grew in both size and number; the federal census of 1930 showed that the urban population of the country had overtaken the rural.[23] The rise in infant adoption was assisted by this transformation of the United States from a largely agricultural society to an increasingly urban one. In the nineteenth century, infants had been of little use to farmers, who took older children from the orphan trains primarily for their labor. Twentieth-century American families, who lived in cities, towns, and suburbs, had no use for farm laborers. Their need was a sentimental one: for children to join their families as full members. For their requirements, infants were best.

By the mid-twentieth century, adoption was facilitated by a culture that still did not tolerate out-of-wedlock births, even as its illegitimacy rate boomed. Between 1940 and 1957, the number of babies born out-side of marriage in the United States tripled.[24] During the Cold War years, young, white women who became pregnant outside of marriage were urged by their families and social workers to give their babies up to the waiting adoption market. The situation was somewhat different for black women, as their families did not shun unmarried mothers and their children to the same extent that white families did. As a result, un-married black mothers were far less likely to give their children up for adoption.[25] The experience of black children born to unmarried moth-ers in the twentieth century and absorbed into their own communities faintly echoes that of some black foundlings—children such as Letitia Finder, Elizabeth Houston, and Lawrence Black—in nineteenth-century New York who were abandoned on black doorsteps, retrieved by black neighbors, and nursed by black women in a system facilitated by the almshouse.

Many postwar maternity homes for unwed mothers were run by na-tional organizations such as the Salvation Army and the Florence Crit-tenton Association, which were motivated by the same religious goals as the foundling asylums and, like them, were founded in the second half of the nineteenth century. These homes undertook to perform the same transformative magic that the foundling asylums had sought to per-form. Women (that is, white women, as many of these homes barred en-try to black women) could disappear into them before their pregnancies became apparent, give birth, and then depart, leaving their babies and their secrets behind. In the nineteenth century, the foundling asylums conspired to wipe clean the slates of fallen women because they believed that the only alternative path for them led to prostitution or even sui-cide. In the twentieth century, the future projected for women and girls who had sex before marriage was not nearly so dire, but the stigma of unmarried motherhood remained strong enough to support the prolifer-ation of maternity homes for unwed mothers.[26]

"Names Must be Short and Sane": The End of Fatalism

A factor that did not contribute directly to the drop in the rate of in-fant abandonment but that nonetheless transformed the experience of foundlings and their caretakers in the twentieth century was the dissipa-tion of the traditional fatalism about infants and young children. It was this fatalism that had allowed the leaders of the foundling asylums to put moral reform above the evidently hopeless task of saving the lives of their infant inmates, as well as to see their institutions as no better than hospices for doomed infants.

It is hard to overestimate the degree to which this fatalism about infant life permeated American society in the era before scientific medicine. An obstetrics textbook published by a respected doctor in 1849 contained this observation: "A child that is born does not surely belong to its parents until it has obtained its sixth year; it seems to me that such a child is a loan."[27] The author might as well have been quoting the New England poet Anne Bradstreet, who in 1678 referred to her granddaughter as a "fair flower that for a space was lent."[28] As late as 1883, when the New York Foundling Asylum had been in operation for almost fourteen years, Sister Irene Fitzgibbon admitted frankly that the death rate in her institution was "appalling" and that an early death was the fate "hanging over all foundlings."[29] The best that could be accomplished for abandoned infants, the administrators of New York's three privately run foundling asylums believed, was to salvage their souls and retrieve their mothers from sin.

Abraham Jacobi was among the first to challenge this fatalism about infant death, but not until the first decades of the twentieth century was his optimism justified. Starting in the mid-1890s, the infant death rate in the United States began a remarkable plunge downward. The discovery of the tubercle bacillus in the early 1880s, the development of diphtheria antitoxin in the 1890s, improvements in surgical technique, and other medical developments that helped to prevent or halt disease certainly played a role. Probably even more important were improvements in sanitation, such as the provision of clean water and the pasteurization and regulation of milk, which helped reduce the bacterial illnesses that caused the deaths of so many infants each hot New York summer.[30]

The steep drop in infant mortality continued through the twentieth century. In 1915, the infant mortality rate in the United States was 99.9. (The infant mortality rate is calculated as the number of deaths of children under age one per thousand live births, so in 1915 just under one in ten children died before reaching the age of one.) In 1934, the year the New York Nursery and Child's Hospital was absorbed into New York Hospital, the rate was 64.6. In 2002, it was 7.[31] Figures for New York City also show a drop; in 1866, New York's Metropolitan Board of Health speculated that one-third of all infants in American cities died

234 | Conclusion

before their first birthdays. In 1950, less than a century later, the rate of infant mortality in New York City was 25. In 2001, it was 6.1.[32]

In the early decades of the twentieth century, foundlings and illegitimate babies still died at a higher rate than those raised in the homes of married parents, but it was no longer possible to assume that nothing could be done to save their lives.[33] Since the officials in charge of assigning them names knew that foundlings might live to adulthood, they were more careful, and perhaps were spurred on by the continuing interest of the press. "How many children," the *New York Times* needled, "burdened with names suggestive of variety farce have been sent out in the world to earn their living?" When at the turn of the century the Commissioner of Public Charities learned that his department had been bestowing names such as Virginia Broiler (found under a Virginia creeper on a hot day), Daisy Labor (found on Labor Day), and Rebecca Wet (which needs no explanation), he was, the *Times* reported, aroused to action. He may also have been sensitive to the outrage of people whose names were plucked out of the city directories and given to foundlings.[34]

In 1909, a *Herald* reporter watched city officials naming foundlings at Bellevue Hospital and described the city's new, more humane naming policy: "names must be short and sane and easily pronounced. No one has the right to saddle a poor little waif with a ponderous or awkward name." By the twenties, foundlings were given names that seemed appropriate for their assigned religion, their gender, and also their race, but these names—such as Alfred Stevens for a white boy and Florence Jackson for a black girl—were determinedly plain, scrupulously hiding the fact that their bearers were foundlings.[35]

Disappearing along with the careless naming practices was the idea that foundlings were permanently stained by their mothers' sin.[36] By the end of the nineteenth century, the idea that young children were intrinsically innocent had been very largely absorbed into the popular imagination. As a result, the public came to believe that there was no reason why those foundlings lucky enough to live past infancy and be adopted could not go on to lead successful lives. Illegitimacy, however, still carried a stigma, which meant that keeping the facts of the foundling's birth a secret was key. The New York Foundling Asylum kept the foundlings they sent to western homes ignorant about their origins, and their adoptive families kept the secret. The New York Nursery and Child's Hospital emphasized that "every effort is made to so care for the children that they shall find homes in which they may receive religious and intellectual instruction, and where they shall not be reminded of the place of their birth." The Department of Charities (the product of an 1895 split of the Department of Public Charities and Correction and the latest incarnation of the old almshouse) also believed it should mislead its former charges about their origins. When adults who had been foundlings appeared at the department's offices in the early twentieth century to ask about their parents, they were deflected gently by officials who replied to their questions with "a greater or less elasticity as to the recorded facts" and let the adult foundling go away "without any loss of self respect and in ignorance of the true circumstances which combined to make him the city's adopted child."[37]

When the early histories of adult foundlings were incompletely erased or angrily revealed at moments of tension in adoptive families, they could cause serious problems. Money was often at the root of the trouble. In 1893, a woman named Marcella Edwards sued the estate of her estranged (and most likely adoptive) mother, Sclenda M. Guthrie, in order to receive a share of Mrs. Guthrie's property. Mother and daughter had disagreed over the daughter's choice of husband, and Mrs. Guthrie told her lawyer that she had no children, even though there existed "a woman whom she had allowed to pass as her daughter." Relatives of the dead woman testified that they had always believed that Marcella, who was supposedly born in 1845, was her daughter, but one nephew revealed that Mrs. Guthrie had told him: "She is not my daughter. Her name is Lizzie O'Neal. I got her from Bellevue Hospital in New York." Whatever the truth behind this imbroglio, the informality of adoption arrangements in the pre–Civil War years left foundlings vulnerable when disagreements frayed their ties to their adoptive families.[38]

An even more dramatic case involved a man who had been left as an infant on the steps of the New York Foundling Asylum in 1871, then raised by a Maryland farmer. The man, named Henry J. King, became obsessed with the idea that he was heir to an inheritance left him by wealthy parents and that the Sisters of Charity were keeping his riches from him. He insisted, even though he was only a day old when left on the steps of their foundling asylum, that he remembered a tall young woman dressed in black who had carried him in a basket. Now a man in his early thirties, he took a room near the foundling asylum and pestered the Sisters, pleading with them to tell him whatever they knew about his origins. One day in 1902, King rushed into the asylum with a gun and shot two of the Sisters and then himself, none fatally. As four policemen dragged him into a patrol wagon, he ranted: "This thing has preyed on my mind night and day. . . . All that I wish to do is to gain my rights. The law would not help me, and I had to take the law into my own hands. No matter who my mother was, I have a right to know it."[39]

Despite these sensational stories, and despite the fact that there was still a stigma attached to illegitimacy, New Yorkers of the late nineteenth and early twentieth centuries had been converted to a belief in the innocence of childhood that their antebellum ancestors had only started to awaken to, and thus they thought that illegitimate birth and abandonment could be submerged and forgotten. The British author Oscar Wilde's Lady Bracknell is scandalized when she learns that her daughter's suitor was once an infant found in a handbag in London's Victoria Station. "You can hardly imagine that I and Lord Bracknell would dream of allowing our only daughter—a girl brought up with the utmost care—to marry into a cloakroom, and form an alliance with a parcel?" she exclaims.[40] A real baby discovered in a "common oil-cloth satchel" in New York's Grand Central Station in 1889 was lucky to have been found in a city whose citizens, many of whom were immigrants, were more tolerant of irregular beginnings.[41]

"Millionaire Baby": Foundling Tales in the Gilded Age

Henry J. King's dream of wealth was a stock element in the repertoire of foundling tales long resident in New Yorkers' collective imagination. The press reported King's story eagerly and did not hesitate to use the language of fairy tale to speculate about the histories and destinies of other babies picked up in the street. In the Gilded Age, when fortunes were made and lost with breathtaking rapidity, these rags-to-riches or riches-to-rags stories seemed timely.

Disturbed former foundlings and sensation-seeking reporters were not the only ones to nurture fantasies about the unexpected origins of foundlings. Hard-headed medical professionals could harbor such fantasies, too. In 1889, two policemen found a baby girl abandoned in the cellar of a wrecked building. They brought her to New York Hospital, where Irene Sutliffe, the superintendent of the hospital's nursing school, took the baby under her wing. Laura York, as the baby was called, lived

Foundling Laura York (*center*) in the arms of
Irene Sutliffe. New York Hospital nursing school,
class portrait, 1891. Lillian Wald is on Laura's
right. Courtesy of New York Weill Cornell
Medical Center Archives.

in the hospital with nurses for foster mothers until she was nearly three,
when she died. She appears at the center of the nursing school's 1891
class portrait in the arms of Miss Sutliffe. Lillian Wald, who graduated
in that class and who would later found the Visiting Nurse Service and
become a leader in the settlement-house movement, is standing beside
her. These trained nurses, none of whom could have been very naive
about where abandoned babies came from, when commenting about
Laura were "united in the opinion that she was of no common origin."[42]

The reverse story, that a baby found in the trash might rise from her
humble origins and find an adoptive home on Fifth Avenue, also appealed to readers of New York newspapers. In 1909, the *Herald*'s Sunday magazine printed the story of a baby wrapped in an old blanket,
placed in a dirty basket, and left on top of an ash barrel. "Another kid
shoved out in the cold," the policeman who found her remarked matter-
of-factly. "Too bad, baby, too bad." But her fortunes soon improved.

When a wealthy couple adopted her, she became a "millionaire baby," a "dainty young lady who is already beginning to attract attention for her beauty and who rules a certain Fifth avenue mansion with a high hand." "This isn't a fairy story," the *Herald* advised its readers, "though it reads like one."[43] Even the New York Infant Asylum was capable of evoking fairy tales about the futures of its adopted foundlings: "It would read like a romance, were we to describe the transition of many of our children, into homes of wealth and culture," its president reported dreamily in 1887.[44]

The sight of foundlings often gave rise to musings about birth and opportunity. Much of the imaginative literature about foundlings has to do with how well or badly the individual fares when untethered from inherited limitations (such as illegitimate birth) or advantages (such as royal or magical birth). Foundling literature also asks, as with the story of Oedipus, whether it is possible to escape one's fate. Melville dealt in these issues in "Billy Budd," his story about a foundling who grows up to be a sailor. Discovered in a "pretty silk-lined basket," Billy Budd excites the admiration and jealousy of all who recognize his evident natural superiority. Of his heritage Melville writes: "Yes, Billy Budd was a foundling, a presumable by-blow, and, evidently, no ignoble one. Noble descent was as evident in him as in a blood horse."[45] Melville wrote this story near the end of his life and left it unpublished at his death in 1891. A meditation on virtue and vulnerability, Billy Budd's story is no less a product of its age than the stories of his real-life contemporaries, New York's foundlings.

"Very Poor. My Parents Will Kill Me": Foundlings in the Twentieth Century and Today

Even though epidemic infant abandonment is gone, foundlings have never completely disappeared. And the methods people used to abandon babies in the twentieth century remained the same as those used in the nineteenth, although the new century provided new venues and contexts for old practices. Subway stations, phone booths, parking lots, Dumpsters, and apartment-house garbage chutes were added to the townhouse stoops, tenement entryways, and ash barrels of the nineteenth century.[46] In an East Harlem incident that took place in 1927, a woman asked a stranger to hold her baby while she went to get help after a car accident. The helpful stranger waited on the corner of Lexington Avenue and 122nd Street for several hours. When she finally gave up and brought the eighteen-month-old girl to the police, she learned that there had been no accident and that she had been the victim of a deception.[47] It is hard to know whether this ruse so commonly practiced in the nineteenth century was preserved in urban folk memory or whether it was simply what would logically occur to someone who wanted to rid themselves of a baby without submitting the child directly to the dangers of the street.

Poverty and the shame of unmarried motherhood, the causes behind most infant abandonment in the nineteenth century, still lead some women and girls to abandon their babies today. In 1996, a thirteen-year-old girl wrapped her newborn in a blanket and left her in the entry of an apartment building in Brooklyn. The note she left with the baby explained in Spanish that she was "Very poor. My parents will kill me. Please take care of my baby."[48] Her note echoes so many written by young women, many of them also immigrants, in the nineteenth-century city. But despite these continuities, there has been a very significant change: the practice of infant abandonment has subsided from the mass phenomenon it was in the nineteenth century to something that occurs no more than occasionally today.

During the first half of the twentieth century, several factors combined to erode the conditions that had earlier led to epidemic infant abandonment. These include the rise of adoption as a legal and accepted practice, the decline in domestic service as a mass employer of single women, and the spread of a social safety net by the federal government. Significantly, after World War II and particularly after the Civil Rights and Women's Liberation movements of the mid-twentieth century, life changed very dramatically for women in the United States. One unintended byproduct of the transformative changes produced by these movements was that infant abandonment receded into history to become a largely forgotten Victorian relic. Educational and employment opportunities for women expanded unprecedentedly, liberating many (although certainly not all) single women from poverty. The availability of legal, safe, and effective birth control and abortion, particularly after the introduction of the Pill in 1960 and the outcome of *Roe v. Wade* in 1973, means that women have more control over their reproduction than they ever had before.[49]

A final factor is the recent destigmatization of illegitimacy. While birth outside of marriage remains controversial and single women with children still suffer financial insecurity, the period of extreme moral anxiety about out-of-wedlock birth that began early in the nineteenth century and started to crumble in the 1960s, appears now to be over.[50] New York's foundlings and foundling asylums were products of that period, and both have disappeared along with it.

The foundlings that populated nineteenth-century New York in such tragically high numbers were produced by the economic realities and social values of their time. Today, those conditions have gone the way of their century, and infant abandonment as a commonplace reality has receded. For the most part, foundlings have retreated off the streets and back into the pages of imaginative literature, where they have dwelled since antiquity.

Not only have foundlings largely disappeared from New York's streets, but many twenty-first century Americans have forgotten that they ever existed, imagining that the foundlings of novels and movies are figments of the imagination only. According to this author's very informal survey, most people cannot even define the word *foundling,* nor are very many familiar with its association with illegitimacy. This could never have been said of the nineteenth-century New Yorkers who encountered unwanted babies in the streets, on their doorsteps, and in the daily papers. That foundlings have been forgotten is remarkable considering how regular a sight they once were on the city's nighttime streets, and how worrisomely significant they seemed to a generation of urban public officials and reformers. For them, the foundling, no matter how tiny, vulnerable, and voiceless, served as a symbol for a group of unacceptable female behaviors: sex outside of marriage, prostitution, abortion, baby farming, and infanticide. To urban leaders, particularly those rooted in religious reform, these behaviors signified uncontrolled sexuality, a rejection of domestic and maternal values, and the transformation of the country's largest city into a frightening and unrecognizable "city of strangers."

Attention paid to foundlings in the middle of the nineteenth century signified a transformation in sensibility that began to make the child the center of the home, and the home the antithesis of the street. Foundlings, along with child workers such as newsboys and bootblacks, were literally on the street; their helpless infancy only made the street more incongruous a place for them. That foundlings are no longer remembered today is a marker of just how far that sensibility regarding children has progressed. People who discover foundlings today often react with shock and disbelief.[51] They do not know that as recently as the nineteenth century foundlings were familiar denizens of the urban landscape. Unlike their antebellum counterparts, people like Philip Hone and his dinner companions, contemporary New Yorkers do not feel that infant abandonment is normal. Instead, they recognize it as out of step with the values of their society.

In 2004, the *New York Times* reported the story of a young man who returned home to Brooklyn one evening to find a shopping bag in the entry of his apartment building. Drawn to the bag by a noise that he thought sounded like the mewing of a cat, he looked inside and saw a baby girl. The man dialed 911 for help and rearranged the baby's blanket so she could breathe more easily, but he did not attempt to take the baby out of the bag. "I didn't unwrap the baby or take it out of the bag, because I don't know how to hold a baby," the young man explained to a reporter. "It was crying," he continued. "I was pretty nervous for the child."[52]

Neither he nor the reporter thought to use the word *foundling*, a word that for a historian conjures up so many similar nineteenth-century scenes. In fact, the word rarely appears in press reports of abandoned babies today. Those who do use it probably do not even realize that it was once synonymous with illegitimacy. The word *foundling*, with its freight of sin and shame so meaningful to nineteenth-century New Yorkers, has been forgotten, and the whole structure of institutions and understandings erected to cope with the tragedy of thousands of discarded babies has collapsed.

Notes

NOTES TO THE INTRODUCTION

1. Oliver Twist, AFV, no. 184, May 19, 1841; Charles Dickens, *American Notes for General Circulation* (London: Penguin, 1972), 127–44. *Oliver Twist* was first published in *Bentley's Miscellany* in 1837.

2. That J. K. Rowling's Harry Potter, an orphaned, legitimate baby, is left on a doorstep, and that Harry's legitimacy is taken for granted throughout the series, demonstrates how thoroughly the association between illegitimacy and infant abandonment has been forgotten in the twenty-first century.

3. Charles Smith Pugsley, AFV, no. 65, February 15, 1839.

4. For abandonments resulting in death, see Howard [pseud.], "Domestic Economy," *National Advocate,* June 6, 1820. When a woman named Omey Kirk was turned away from the almshouse and gave birth in a nearby yard, her infant was found, alive, by a group of children as pigs approached the baby, who "but for the accidental discovery of the children, would infallibly have been devoured." *A Faithful Report of the Trial of the Cause of Philip I. Arcularius . . .* (New York: Bernard Dornin, 1807), 4. I am grateful to Margaret Hofer of the New-York Historical Society for bringing this case to my attention.

5. This attitude gradually changed during the nineteenth century. Nancy Schrom Dye and Daniel Blake Smith, "Mother Love and Infant Death, 1750–1920," *Journal of American History* 73 (September 1986): 329–53; Philip Greven, *The Protestant Temperament: Patterns of Child-Rearing, Religious Experience, and the Self in Early America* (Chicago: University of Chicago Press, 1977); Steven Mintz, *Huck's Raft: A History of American Childhood* (Cambridge, MA: Harvard University Press, 2004).

6. Gert Brieger, "Stephen Smith: Surgeon and Reformer" (Ph.D. diss., Johns Hopkins University, 1971), 196.

7. For New York's development in the nineteenth century as a center of both poverty and wealth, see Robert Albion, *The Rise of New York Port, 1815–1860* (New York: Scribner's, 1839); Edwin G. Burrows and Mike Wallace, *Gotham: A History of New York City to 1898* (New York: Oxford University Press, 1999); Thomas Kessner, *Capital City: New York City and the Men behind America's Rise to Economic Dominance, 1860–1900* (New York: Simon and

Schuster, 2003); Raymond Mohl, *Poverty in New York, 1783–1825* (New York: Oxford University Press, 1970); Edward K. Spann, *The New Metropolis: New York City, 1840–1857* (New York: Columbia University Press, 1981).

8. For more on St. Mary's Asylum for Widows, Foundlings, and Infants, incorporated in Buffalo, New York, by the Sisters of Charity, see William Pryor Letchworth, "History of Child-Saving Work in the State of New York," in *History of Child Saving in the United States: Twentieth National Conference of Charities and Correction, Chicago, June 1893* (Boston: Geo. H. Ellis, 1893), 165.

9. The Temporary Home for foundlings opened in Boston around 1864, and the Massachusetts Infant Asylum for foundlings and other "deserted and destitute infant children" was chartered in 1867 and opened in 1868; see Massachusetts Infant Asylum, annual reports, 1868, 5, 16–17; 1869, 8, 34. The Chicago Foundlings Home opened in 1871; see George E. Shipman, *God's Dealings with the Chicago Foundlings Home* (Chicago: George E. Shipman, M.D., 1888). The San Francisco Foundling Asylum opened around 1869; see Bruce Come, "Asylum or Adoption: The Foundling in Progressive San Francisco" (MA thesis, California State University, Hayward, 1992). The Washington Hospital for Foundlings was incorporated by Congress for the District of Columbia in 1870 and opened in 1887; see *Report of the President of the Washington Hospital for Foundlings to the Secretary of the Interior* (Washington, DC: U.S. Government Printing Office, 1902), p. 5; "An Act for Incorporating a Hospital for Foundlings in the City of Washington," 41st Congress, 2d Session, chap. 61.

10. Based on a survey, the Massachusetts Infant Asylum concluded, "The city of New York has done the most in this direction, as is natural where the number of such infants is the largest" Massachusetts Infant Asylum, *Annual Report, 1868,* 30. For a later comparison between New York and Chicago, Boston, Baltimore, and Buffalo, see Homer Folks, "The Foundling," in *International Congress on Hygiene and Demography 15, Transactions* (Washington, DC, 1912), 87. Between 1895 and 1904 the Washington Hospital for Foundlings reported collecting an average of fifty-two foundlings each year; see Washington Hospital for Foundlings, annual reports, 1895–1904. In 1880 at the Chicago Foundlings Home the average number of infants was fifty-five; see Chicago Foundlings Home, annual report, 1881, 2. During the first half of the 1880s New York's four foundling asylums collectively gathered an annual average of 2,041 babies; see table 7.1.

11. Works that deal with American foundlings, either tangentially or directly, include Come, "Asylum or Adoption"; Peter C. English, "Pediatrics and the Unwanted Child in History: Foundling Homes, Disease, and the Origins of Foster Care in New York City, 1860–1920," *Pediatrics* 73 (1984): 699–711; Maureen Fitzgerald, "The Perils of 'Passion and Poverty': Women Religious and the Care of Single Women in New York City, 1845–1890," *United States Cath-*

olic Historian 10 (1991): 45–58; Paul Gilje, "Infant Abandonment in Early Nineteenth-Century New York City: Three Cases," *Signs* 8 (Spring 1983): 586–87; Linda Gordon, *The Great Arizona Orphan Abduction* (Cambridge, MA: Harvard University Press, 1999); Virginia Metaxas Quiroga, "Female Lay Managers and Scientific Pediatrics at the Nursery and Child's Hospital, 1854–1910," *Bulletin of the History of Medicine* 60 (1986): 194–208; Quiroga, *Poor Mothers and Babies: A Social History of Childbirth and Child Care Hospitals in Nineteenth Century New York City* (New York: Garland, 1989); Peter Romanofsky, "Saving the Lives of the City's Foundlings: The Joint Committee and New York City Child Care Methods, 1860–1907," *New York Historical Society Quarterly* 61 (1977): 49–68. Some histories of New York City contain fleeting references to foundlings. They include Tyler Anbinder, *Five Points: The Nineteenth-Century New York City Neighborhood that Invented Tap Dance, Stole Elections, and Became the World's Most Notorious Slum* (New York: Penguin, 2001), 224–25; Burrows and Wallace, *Gotham*; Christine Stansell, *City of Women: Sex and Class in New York, 1789–1860* (Urbana: University of Illinois Press, 1987). Works on wet nursing in the United States also mention foundlings; see Janet Golden, *A Social History of Wet Nursing in America: From Breast to Bottle* (Cambridge: Cambridge University Press, 1996); Jacqueline H. Wolf, " 'Mercenary Hirelings' or 'A Great Blessing'?: Doctors' and Mothers' Conflicted Perceptions of Wet Nurses and the Ramifications for Infant Feeding in Chicago, 1871–1961," *Journal of Social History* 33 (1999): 97–120.

12. The most daring, wide-ranging, and controversial of the historians of European foundlings was John Boswell, who proposed that in the ancient and medieval world infant abandonment was essentially a functional system for the redistribution of unwanted children; John Boswell, *The Kindness of Strangers: The Abandonment of Children in Western Europe from Late Antiquity to the Renaissance* (New York: Vintage Books, 1988). For a critique of Boswell's thesis, see Louise A. Tilly, Rachel Fuchs, David I. Kertzer, and David L. Ransel, "Child Abandonment in European History: A Symposium," *Journal of Family History* 17 (1992): 1–23. Other histories of European foundlings published in English include Françoise Barret-Ducrocq, *Love in the Time of Victoria: Sexuality, Class and Gender in Nineteenth-Century London,* trans. John Howe (London: Verso, 1991); Claude Delasselle, "Abandoned Children in Eighteenth-Century Paris," in *Deviants and the Abandoned in French Society, Selections from the* Annales, Économies, Sociétés, Civilisations, ed. Robert Forster and Orest Ranum (Baltimore: Johns Hopkins University Press, 1978); Rachel Fuchs, *Abandoned Children: Foundlings and Child Welfare in Nineteenth-Century France* (Albany: State University of New York Press, 1984); Philip Gavitt, *Charity and Children in Renaissance Florence: The Ospedale degli Innocenti, 1410–1536* (Ann Arbor: University of Michigan Press, 1990); Volcker Hunecke, "The Abandonment of Legitimate Children in Nineteenth-Century Milan and the

European Context," in *Poor Women and Children in the European Past,* ed. John Henderson and Richard Wall (London: Routledge, 1994); David Kertzer, *Sacrificed for Honor: Infant Abandonment and the Politics of Reproductive Control* (Boston: Beacon Press, 1993); Ruth McClure, *Coram's Children: The London Foundling Hospital in the Eighteenth Century* (New Haven, CT: Yale University Press, 1981); Brian Pullan, *Orphans and Foundlings in Early Modern Europe* (Berkshire, UK: University of Reading, 1989); David Ransel, *Mothers of Misery: Child Abandonment in Russia* (Princeton, NJ: Princeton University Press, 1988); Joseph Robins, *The Lost Children: A Study of Charity Children in Ireland, 1700–1900* (Dublin: Institute of Public Administration, 1980); Joan Sherwood, *Poverty in Eighteenth-Century Spain: The Women and Children of the Inclusa* (Toronto: University of Toronto Press, 1988), 51–91; Richard Trexler, "The Foundlings of Florence, 1395–1455," *History of Childhood Quarterly* 1 (1973): 259–84; Otto Ulbricht, "The Debate about Foundling Hospitals in Enlightenment Germany: Infanticide, Illegitimacy, and Infant Mortality Rates," *Central European History* 18 (September/December 1985): 211–56. There is much more to say about infant abandonment in India, China, and many other places around the world. Since nineteenth-century New Yorkers followed British and Continental models, I am limiting myself to that historiography here and throughout this book.

13. For comparisons between the slums of New York and those of London, see Dickens's description of the Five Points in *American Notes,* 136–40.

14. For a comparison of the Catholic and Protestant systems, see Hunecke "Abandonment of Legitimate Children," 123; McClure, *Coram's Children,* 96–97; Pullan, *Orphans and Foundlings,* 20–21.

15. Job Lewis Smith, "Hindrances to the Successful Treatment of the Diseases of Infancy and Childhood," *Transactions of the New York State Medical Association* 13 (1896), 95.

16. PCC, annual report, 1867, 24.

17. Metropolitan Board of Health, annual report, 1866, 10.

18. New York City Municipal Archives, Almshouse Children's Records, vol. 0161, Henry Foundling, December 24, 1819; William Unknown, February 4, 1820; vol. 081, Phineas T. Barnum, July 8, 1863.

19. Carroll Smith-Rosenberg, *Religion and the Rise of the American City: The New York Mission Movement, 1812–1870* (Ithaca, NY: Cornell University Press, 1971).

20. For the transformation of Western attitudes toward children, see Philippe Ariès, *Centuries of Childhood: A Social History of Family Life* (New York: Vintage Books, 1962); Hugh Cunningham, *Children and Childhood in Western Society since 1500* (London: Longman, 1995); Cunningham, "Histories of Childhood," *American Historical Review* 103 (October 1998), 1195–1208; Mintz, *Huck's Raft;* Steven Ozment, *Ancestors: The Loving Family in Old Europe*

(Cambridge, MA: Harvard University Press, 2001); Linda Pollock, *Forgotten Children: Parent-Child Relations from 1500 to 1900* (Cambridge: Cambridge University Press, 1983); Viviana Zelizer, *Pricing the Priceless Child: The Changing Social Value of Children* (New York: Basic Books, 1981).

21. George W. Matsell, *Semi Annual Report of the Chief of Police from May 1–October 31, 1849* (New York: Board of Aldermen, 1849), 58.

22. Charles Loring Brace, "What Shall Be Done with Foundlings?" in *The Dangerous Classes and Twenty Years' Work among Them* (New York: Wynkoop and Hallenbeck, 1872).

23. Ibid.; Miriam Z. Langsam, *Children West: A History of the Placing-Out System of the New York Children's Aid Society, 1853–1890* (Madison: State Historical Society of Wisconsin for the University of Wisconsin, 1964); Stephen O'Connor, *Orphan Trains: The Story of Charles Loring Brace and the Children He Saved and Failed* (Chicago: University of Chicago Press, 2004).

24. See, for instance, Nancy Cott, "Passionlessness: An Interpretation of Victorian Sexual Ideology, 1790–1850," *Signs* 4 (1978): 219–36; Dye and Smith, "Mother Love"; Barbara Welter, "The Cult of True Womanhood: 1820–1860," *American Quarterly* 18, no. 1 (Summer 1966): 150–74.

25. An example of the former would be Florence's Ospedale degli Innocenti, which opened in 1445 and still operates in modified form today; see Kertzer, *Sacrificed for Honor,* 9.

26. "Babies Born to Singles Are at Record: Nearly 4 in 10," *New York Times,* November 22, 2006.

NOTES TO CHAPTER I

1. Philip Hone, *The Diary of Philip Hone, 1828–1851,* ed. Allan Nevins (New York: Dodd, Mead, 1927), 369–72; AFV, no. 55, December 8, 1838. The structure of Hone's sentence makes it sound as though Alfred's taunters, rather than Alfred, are illegitimate, but I think his meaning is clear.

2. The AFV begins on May 1, 1838, and records foundling no. 81 on May 2, 1839. For the other two foundlings left on Great Jones Street, where Hone lived in 1838, see AFV, nos. 8 and 40. By way of contrast, in 1998 (the last year for which the U.S. government has supplied a figure) 105 babies were abandoned in public places in the whole United States; see Administration for Children and Family Services, Department of Health and Human Services, *ACF News, Statistics,* http://www.acf.hhs.gov/news/stats/abandon.htm (accessed February 8, 2007).

3. For the entrenchment of infant abandonment in European societies, see Volcker Hunecke, "The Abandonment of Legitimate Children in Nineteenth-Century Milan and the European Context," in *Poor Women and Children in the European Past,* ed. John Henderson and Richard Wall (London: Routledge,

1994), 123; Brian Pullan, *Orphans and Foundlings in Early Modern Europe* (Reading, UK: University of Reading, 1989), 10. For the possible biological bases of infant abandonment, see Sarah Blaffer Hrdy, *Mother Nature: A History of Mothers, Infants, and Natural Selection* (New York: Pantheon, 1999).

4. John Boswell, *The Kindness of Strangers: The Abandonment of Children in Western Europe from Late Antiquity to the Renaissance* (New York: Vintage, 1990), 51–137, especially 58–59, 65, 67.

5. Boswell, *Kindness of Strangers*, 415–17; David Kertzer, *Sacrificed for Honor: Italian Infant Abandonment and the Politics of Reproductive Control* (Boston: Beacon Press, 1993), 9–10.

6. Boswell, *Kindness of Strangers*, 15–16, 20.

7. Abigail Adams to Elizabeth Smith Shaw, Auteuil, January 11, 1785, in Richard Alan Ryerson, ed., *Adams Family Correspondence* (Cambridge, MA: Harvard University Press, 1993), vol. 6, pp. 57–58; Ruth McClure, *Coram's Children: The London Foundling Hospital in the Eighteenth Century* (New Haven, CT: Yale University Press, 1981), 19.

8. McClure, *Coram's Children*, 86; Abraham Jacobi, *The Raising and Education of Abandoned Children in Europe, with Statistics and General Remarks on that Subject* (New York: Bellevue Hospital Printing Office, 1870), 23.

9. Abigail Adams to Elizabeth Smith Shaw, Auteuil, January 11, 1785, in Ryerson, *Adams Family Correspondence,* vol. 6, pp. 55–59.

10. *New-York Packet,* April 25, 1788.

11. New York Almshouse and Bridewell Commissioners, Minutes, May 2, 1796, New York Public Library, Manuscripts Division.

12. Kertzer, *Sacrificed for Honor,* 13; Jacobi, *The Raising and Education of Abandoned Children in Europe.*

13. Rachel Fuchs, *Abandoned Children: Foundlings and Child Welfare in Nineteenth-Century France* (Albany: State University of New York Press, 1984), 70; Peter Laslett et al., eds., *Bastardy and Its Comparative History: Studies in the History of Illegitimacy and Marital Nonconformism in Britain, France, Germany, Sweden, North America, Jamaica, and Japan* (Cambridge, MA: Harvard University Press, 1980), 26–27.

14. William Shakespeare, *The Winter's Tale* (Cambridge: Cambridge University Press, 1950), 3.3.70–74; Henry Fielding, *The History of Tom Jones, a Foundling* (New York: Modern Library, 1950), 7.

15. For the debate surrounding the causes of the rise in illegitimacy, see Cissie Fairchilds, "Female Sexual Attitudes and the Rise of Illegitimacy: A Case Study," *Journal of Interdisciplinary History* 8 (1978): 627–77; Laslett et al., *Bastardy*; Edward Shorter, *The Making of the Modern Family* (New York: Basic Books, 1975); Louise A. Tilly, Joan W. Scott, and Miriam Cohen, "Women's Work and European Fertility Patterns," *Journal of Interdisciplinary History* 6 (1976), 447–76. Laslett argues that illegitimacy rates rose all over Europe, even

when and where industrialization and urbanization were not factors; see *Bastardy*, 26–27.

16. On migration and accidental pregnancy, see Rachel Fuchs and Leslie Page Moch, "Pregnant, Single, and Far from Home: Migrant Women in Nineteenth Century Paris," *American Historical Review* 95 (October 1990): 1007 31. On wages and working conditions for women in this period, see Faye E. Dudden, *Serving Women: Household Service in Nineteenth-Century America* (Middletown, CT: Wesleyan University Press, 1983); Alice Kessler-Harris, *Out to Work: A History of Wage-Earning Women in the United States* (New York: Oxford University Press, 1982); Christine Stansell, *City of Women: Sex and Class in New York, 1789–1860* (Urbana: University of Illinois Press, 1987).

17. On the migration of Irish women to New York and their work as servants, see Hasia Diner, *Erin's Daughters in America: Irish Immigrant Women in the Nineteenth Century* (Baltimore: Johns Hopkins University Press, 1983). For the sexual vulnerability of servants, and servants as mothers of foundlings, see Françoise Barret-Ducrocq, *Love in the Time of Victoria: Sexuality, Class and Gender in Nineteenth-Century London,* trans. John Howe (London: Verso, 1991); John R. Gillis, "Servants, Sexual Relations and the Risks of Illegitimacy in London, 1901–1900," *Feminist Studies* 5, no. 1 (1979): 142–69; McClure, *Coram's Children,* 85–86. For domestic servants' inability to keep their children, see Dudden, *Serving Women,* 205–7; Golden, *A Social History of Wet Nursing in America,* 46; McClure, *Coram's Children,* 85.

18. Kertzer, *Sacrificed for Honor,* 144–53.

19. For the rise in illegitimacy in eighteenth-century America, see Daniel Scott Smith and Michael Hindus, "Premarital Pregnancy in America, 1640–1966," *Journal of Interdisciplinary History* 6 (1975): 537. For the claustrophobic quality of life in colonial America, see Helena Wall, *Fierce Communion: Family and Community in Early America* (Cambridge, MA: Harvard University Press, 1990). For an example of enforced marriage in a small New England town, see Laurel Thatcher Ulrich, *A Midwife's Tale: The Life of Martha Ballard, Based on Her Diary, 1785–1812* (New York: Knopf, 1990), 147–60. For infanticide, see Ulrich, *Good Wives: Image and Reality in the Lives of Women in Northern New England, 1650–1750* (New York: Vintage Books, 1982), 198–201; Peter C. Hoffer and N. E. H. Hull, *Murdering Mothers: Infanticide in England and New England, 1558–1803* (New York: New York University Press, 1982).

20. Isaac Townsend, Washington Smith, and Anthony Dugro, *Report of the Select Committee, Appointed March 17, 1857, by the Board of Governors of the Almshouse, New-York, Deputed to Investigate the Claims of the City to the Institution, and Erection of a Foundling Hospital* (New York, 1858) (hereafter cited as Almshouse Foundling Report), xxxviii–xl. For an example of how a young woman could carry on a secret love life under cover of the bustling urban

complexity of nineteenth-century New York, see Amy Gillman Srebnick, *The Mysterious Death of Mary Rogers: Sex and Culture in Nineteenth Century New York City* (New York: Oxford University Press, 1994).

21. New York City Department of Records, Municipal Archives, AH records, Children's Records, vol. 214, microfilm reel 30, p. 280, continued in vol. 0123, p. 11. See also a case of a baby found by a physician under the stoop of the Northern Dispensary, a clinic for the poor on Waverly Place. A notation in the almshouse records reveals that the mother, Betsy Myers of Greenwich Street, was known to a Mrs. Bloomer, who supplied her identity to the almshouse; AFV, no. 20, July 14, 1838. The AFV contains more such cases.

22. For the turning wheel, see John Boswell, *The Kindness of Strangers: The Abandonment of Children in Western Europe from Late Antiquity to the Renaissance* (New York: Vintage Books, 1988), 433; for its demise, see Fuchs, *Abandoned Children,* 21–22; Kertzer, *Sacrificed for Honor,* 155.

23. Hunecke, "Abandonment of Legitimate Children," 118, 123, 125; Kertzer, *Sacrificed for Honor,* 78–79.

24. Fuchs, *Abandoned Children,* 12–13. Infant abandonment was further systematized after the Revolution, when foundlings were redefined as assets of the state; Fuchs, *Abandoned Children,* 16–27.

25. Jean-Jacques Rousseau, *The Confessions,* trans. J. M. Cohen (London: Penguin, 1953), 322; 332–33.

26. Ibid., 515–16.

27. Ibid., 333.

28. Pullan, *Orphans and Foundlings,* 10.

29. Jane Austen's brother Francis went on his first sea voyage at fourteen after attending naval school. See Claire Tomalin, *Jane Austen: A Life* (New York: Knopf, 1997), 61.

30. Ariès, *Centuries of Childhood,* 365; John Demos, *A Little Commonwealth: Family Life in Plymouth Colony* (London: Oxford University Press, 1970), 71–75; Peter Laslett, *The World We Have Lost* (London: Methuen, 1965), 12; Wall, *Fierce Communion,* chap. 4. For the indenture of poor children in the late nineteenth century, see Joan Jacobs Brumberg, *Kansas Charley: The Story of a Nineteenth-Century Boy Murderer* (New York: Viking, 2003), 19.

31. Peter Kolchin, *American Slavery, 1619–1877* (New York: Hill and Wang, 1993), 125–26.

32. For baby-farming, see Margaret L. Arnott, "Infant Death, Child Care and the State: The Baby-Farming Scandal and the First Infant Life Protection Legislation of 1872," *Continuity and Change* 9 (1994): 271–311; Sheri Broder, "Child Care or Child Neglect? Baby Farming in Late-Nineteenth-Century Philadelphia," *Gender and Society* 2 (1988): 128–48.

33. For nurses or baby farmers who brought babies to the almshouse after

they failed to receive payment, see AFV, nos. 7, 15, 31, 37, 45, 47, 94, 109, 126, 129, 133, 134, 137–39, 141, 148, 151, 157, and 161.

34. Cited in McClure, *Coram's Children,* 173.

35. Fuchs, *Abandoned Children,* 18.

36. Hector Malot, *Nobody's Boy,* trans. Florence Crew-Jones (New York: Cupples and Leon, 1916), 120.

37. James Stirling, *Letters from the Slave States* (London: J. W. Parker and Son, 1857), 253.

38. Ibid., 19. For the stigma attached to being a foundling, see Nancy Fitch, "'*Les Petits Parisiens en Province*': The Silent Revolution in the Allier," *Journal of Family History* 11 (1986): 132; McClure, *Coram's Children,* 9–12; Pullan, *Orphans and Foundlings,* 5–6. For the methods used to identify foundlings, see Fuchs, *Abandoned Children,* 122–24; Kertzer, *Sacrificed for Honor,* 100, 115; McClure, *Coram's Children,* 194–95; Joseph Robins, *The Lost Children: A Study of Charity Children in Ireland, 1700–1900* (Dublin: Institute of Public Administration, 1980), 16, 25, 57; David Ransel, *Mothers of Misery: Child Abandonment in Russia* (Princeton, NJ: Princeton University Press, 1988), 177. For physical disfigurement as a punishment for criminals in England, see David M. Schneider, *The History of Public Welfare in New York State, 1609–1866* (Chicago: University of Chicago Press, 1938), vol. 1, p. 45. For the branding of slaves, see Kolchin, *American Slavery,* 10, 57–58. For the branding of adulterers in Puritan New England, see Cornelia Hughes Dayton, *Women before the Bar: Gender, Law, and Society in Connecticut, 1639–1789* (Chapel Hill: University of North Carolina Press, 1995), 164, 170.

39. Wendy Sigle, David Kertzer, and Michael J. White argue that in nineteenth-century Bologna foundlings may have maintained positive relationships with their foster families; see "Abandoned Children and Their Transitions to Adulthood in Nineteenth-Century Italy," *Journal of Family History* 25 (July 2000): 326–40.

40. Quoted in Pullan, *Orphans and Foundlings,* 14. For the unmarriageability of foundlings, see George Sand, *The Country Waif* (Lincoln: University of Nebraska Press), 102.

41. On grown foundlings as social marginals, see Fitch, "*Les Petits Parisiens,*" 132; Fuchs, *Abandoned Children,* 263; Kertzer, *Sacrificed for Honor,* 152–53. On grown foundlings as prostitutes in Ireland, see Robins, *Lost Children,* 58. For grown foundlings as creators of a self-reproducing caste in France and Russia, see Ransel, *Mothers of Misery,* 72.

42. John Adams to John Taylor, April 15, 1814, in John Adams, *The Works of John Adams, Second President of the United States* (Freeport, NY: Books for Libraries Press, 1969), vol. 6, p. 452.

43. William Dimond, *The Foundling of the Forest: A Play in Three Acts* (Philadelphia: Thomas H. Palmer, 1824).

44. Ibid., 10, 35.

45. Arthur Hornblow, *A History of the Theatre in America from Its Beginnings to the Present Time* (Philadelphia: J. B. Lippincott, 1919), vol. 1, p. 310; Joseph N. Ireland, *Records of the New York Stage from 1750–1860* (New York: Benjamin Blom, 1966), vol. 2, pp. 266, 394, 493–94; George C. Odell, *Annals of the New York Stage* (New York: Columbia University Press, 1927), vol. 2, pp. 334, 349, 380, 389, 404, 416, 428, 457, 468, 554.

46. "Hamlet," review of *The Foundling of the Forest,* by William Dimond, *The Columbian* (New York), September 22, 1810.

47. For these and other foundlings in Greek and Roman mythology, see Robert Graves, *The Greek Myths* (Baltimore: Penguin, 1955).

48. Stith Thompson, *Motif-Index of Folk-Literature* (Bloomington: Indiana University Press, 1966). On foundling tricksters, see also Robert Darnton, "Peasants Tell Tales: The Meaning of Mother Goose," in *The Great Cat-Massacre and Other Episodes in French Cultural History* (New York, 1984), 55.

49. See, notably, Natalie Zemon Davis, *Fiction in the Archives: Pardon Tales and Their Tellers in Sixteenth Century France* (Stanford, CA: Stanford University Press, 1987); see also Daniel A. Cohen, *Pillars of Salt, Monuments of Grace: New England Crime Literature and the Origins of American Popular Culture, 1674–1860* (New York: Oxford University Press, 1993).

50. On the connection between hunger and fairy stories, see Darnton, "Peasants Tell Tales"; see also Boswell, *Kindness of Strangers,* 75–100; Marina Warner, *From the Beast to the Blonde: On Fairy Tales and Their Tellers* (New York: Farrar, Straus and Giroux, 1994). On the factual basis of foundling stories in the Bible, see Meir Malul, "Adoption of Foundlings in the Bible and Mesopotamian Documents: A Study of Some Legal Metaphors in Ezekiel 1.1–7," *Journal for the Study of the Old Testament* 46 (1990): 97–126. My thanks to Molly Karp and Rebecca Jacobs for the biblical references.

51. Bridget Waters, AFV, no. 130, May 15, 1840; Hannah Gilmore/Emeline Toby, AFV, no. 14, June 14, 1838. For a later period, see "Waif Left in a Parlor. Somebody Went into Mrs. Manson's Flat and Went Away, Leaving a Pretty Baby," *New York Herald,* August 2, 1894.

52. Fielding, *Tom Jones,* 6.

53. *Subterranean,* November 4, 1843. For advertisements and commentary, see *Subterranean,* November 11 and 20, 1843; *New York Herald,* January 22, 1844. On Sue and his *Mysteries,* see Michael Denning, *Mechanic Accents: Dime Novels and Working-Class Culture in America* (London: Verso, 1987); Peter G. Buckley, "Culture, Class, and Place in Antebellum New York," in *Power, Culture, and Place: Essays on New York City,* ed. John Hull Mollenkopf (New York: Russell Sage Foundation, 1988), 42.

54. "A Young Subterranean," *Subterranean,* July 22, 1843; "The Young Subterranean," *Subterranean,* August 12, 1843. On the popularity of the *Mys-*

teries in New York, see, e.g., "Cheap Literature," *New York Herald,* November 17, 1843; advertisements such as *New York Tribune,* November 1, 1843; and commentary on a dramatization, *New York Herald,* November 24, 1843.

55. *New York Tribune,* February 17, 1859.

56. Hone, *Diary,* 371.

57. The note is pasted into the back of the AFV and copied into the volume where the case (no. 55, December 8, 1838) is recorded. Hone also transcribed part of it into his diary; Hone, *Diary,* 371–72.

58. For the *Pulaski,* see *A Minute and Circumstantial Narrative of the Loss of the Steam-Packet Pulaski, Which Burst Her Boiler, and Sunk on the Coast of North-Carolina, June 14, 1838, with Many Affecting Incidents Connected with that Disastrous Event, by which Nearly One Hundred Persons Lost Their Lives!* (Providence: H. H. Brown, 1839); *New York Post,* June 22, 23, 25, and 26, 1838. Lists of passengers in these sources do not mention anyone named Douglas. Commentary on the dangers of steamboat travel is in *New York Post,* June 26, 1838, and in *Minute and Circumstantial Narrative,* unpaged.

59. John Green, AFV, no. 122, March 28, 1840. The note, which is addressed to "Mr. John Green in car [*sic*] of his father," is pasted in the back of the volume. I have added punctuation.

60. Edward K. Spann, *The New Metropolis: New York City, 1840–1857* (New York: Columbia University Press, 1981), 103.

61. Fanny Burney, *Evelina* (New York: Macmillan, [1903]), 18; Cynthia Kierner, *Scandal at Bizarre: Rumor and Reputation in Jefferson's America* (New York: Palgrave Macmillan, 2004), 21; Patricia Cline Cohen, *The Murder of Helen Jewett: The Life and Death of a Prostitute in Nineteenth-Century New York* (New York: Vintage Books, 1998), 266.

62. Linda Kerber, *Women of the Republic: Intellect and Ideology in Revolutionary America* (Chapel Hill: University of North Carolina Press, 1980), 193.

63. Cathy Davidson, *Revolution and the Word: The Rise of the Novel in America* (New York: Oxford University Press, 1986); Davidson, introduction to Susanna Haswell Rowson, *Charlotte Temple* (New York: Oxford University Press, 1986); Kerber, *Women of the Republic,* 233–64.

64. Frank Luther Mott, *American Journalism: A History, 1690–1960* (New York: Macmillan, 1962).

65. For infants left on stoops, see AFV, nos. 12, 27, 28, 38, 39, 49, 100, 102, 113, 150, 163, 169, 180, 181; AH Children's Records, vol. 214, Martha Washington, 1807, p. 71; Clarinda Friday, 1808, p. 118. For babies left in baskets, see "A Foundling," *New York Evening Post,* January 25, 1816; AFV, nos. 34, 49, 63, 106, 162. The examples listed here and in the notes below are not meant to be comprehensive, and there is plenty of overlap between categories.

66. For abandoners who rang doorbells or slammed doors, see AFV, nos. 49 and 55 (Alfred Godfrey Douglas), 60, 61; "An Infant Starved to Death," *New*

York Tribune, February 22, 1854. For a later use of this method, see "One of the Waifs," *New York Herald,* January 24, 1883.

67. George Church, AH Children's Records, vol. 214, p. 142; Sarah White, AFV, no. 63, February 14, 1839. For "unmarketable freight," see "Foundling Babies, How They Are Cared For," *New York Times,* February 14, 1859. For infants left at or near houses, see "A Foundling," *New York Evening Post,* January 25, 1816; Jane Palmer, 1835, AH Children's Records vol. 0149, p. 44; AFV, nos. 4, 14, 34, 40, 50, 58, 106, 174, 175, 178.

68. For infants left in alleys, see Mary Sweezy, 1808, AH Children's Records, vol. 214, p. 207; AFV, nos. 89, 101, 131. For infants left in entries, see AH Children's Records, vol. 214, Caroline Monday, 1807, p. 92; Melissa Frances Whittey, 1809, p. 269; Benjamin Martin, 1809, p. 319; AFV, nos. 3, 10, 36, 68, 96, 173, 179, 182, 184; "An Infant Starved to Death," *New York Tribune,* February 22, 1854. For infants left in a vacant lot, see AFV, no. 112. A privy, AFV, no. 136. For infants left near railroad tracks, see AFV, no. 147. For infants left near the East River, see AFV, no. 183. For infants left in other remote or dangerous areas and/or inadequately dressed, see Biddy Doyl, 1808, AH Children's Records, vol. 214, p. 187; AFV, nos. 46, 62, 104, 152, 177.

69. For infants left with caretakers—sometimes described simply as "a woman," sometimes with greater information as to their roles as nurses—see AH Children's Records, vol. 214, John Ball, 1807, p. 6; Julian Longman, 1809, p. 301; George Dougherty, 1809, p. 351; vol. 0123, Stephen Simonson, 1815, p. 63; AFV, nos. 7, 15, 25, 31, 37, 42, 45, 47, 94, 109, 126, 129, 133, 134, 137–39, 141, 148, 151, 157, 161, 172. See also Broder, "Child Care or Child Neglect?," 139–41.

70. Hone, *Diary,* 370–71; Alfred G. Douglas, AFV, no. 55, December 8, 1838.

71. Paul Gilje, "Infant Abandonment in Early Nineteenth-Century New York City: Three Cases," *Signs* 8 (Spring 1983), 589–90.

72. Ibid., 586–87. See also Edwin G. Burrows and Mike Wallace, *Gotham: A History of New York City to 1898* (New York: Oxford University Press, 1999), 503.

73. See Oliver L. Barbour, *The Magistrate's Criminal Law* (Albany: Gould and Company, 1841), 77. The law reads: "If the father or mother of any child under the age of six years, or any other person to whom it shall have been confided, shall expose such child in any highway, street, field, house, or out house, with the intent wholly to abandon it, he or she may be imprisoned in a state prison, not exceeding seven years, or in a county jail not more than one year." The law was revised in 1881, 1892, 1903, 1909, and 1965. See Section 260, "Abandonment of a Child," in McKinney's *Consolidated Laws of New York,* book 39, *Penal Code* (Stamford, CT: West Group, 2000), 22–23.

74. Thomas Glover, AFV, nos. 3 and 28; Hugh Maxwell, lawyer, AFV, no. 12; George Bell, grocer, AFV, no. 38; William Bakewell, "Sailduck," AFV, no. 39; John Van Nostrand, grocer, AFV, no. 46; Thomas Fitzpatrick, milkman, AFV, no. 52; Robert Munn, attorney, AFV, no. 82. See *Longworth's American Almanac, New-York Register, and City Directory*, 1837–38 and 1839–40 (New York: Thomas Longworth, 1837, 1839).

75. For Maxwell's role in the Jewett case, see Cohen, *Murder of Helen Jewett*, 333. For the economic status of Maxwell's address, see Spann, *New Metropolis*, 432.

76. Hannah Frost, AH Children's Records, vol. 214, p. 284.

77. The *New York Herald* commented frequently and in detail on the dress of foundlings; see "Abandoned Her Babe," April 10, 1878; "The Woman in Black, A Richly Clad Child Abandoned by the Mother, Who Is Believed to Have Drowned Herself," May 15, 1878; "Twin Babes Were at Her Door," September 12, 1891; "Three Little Waifs," November 30, 1880; "Mystery of a Pretty Baby," May 21, 1892; "Gave Her Child to Two Boys," September 1, 1894; "Foundling in Fifth Avenue," April 5, 1895; "Found a Waif on Christmas Eve," December 25, 1895; "Refined Woman Deserts a Babe," *New York Herald,* May 31, 1896; "Pretty Baby in Silks Deserted by Mother in Department Store," March 29, 1907.

78. "Baby Finds a Mother, Mrs. Newkirk, of Jersey City, Adopts the Waif in Bellevue Named Annie Wilson," *New York Herald,* March 18, 1896.

79. "Tiny Waifs Found," *New York Herald,* April 15, 1897.

80. "Abandoned to the City's Care," *New York Herald,* January 14, 1895. For Blake as "godfather," see "Seen in Waifland, Life of the City's Doorstep, Wards Who Live on Randall's Island," *New York Herald,* October 25, 1896.

81. "A Pauper Two Weeks Old," *New York Herald,* January 23, 1883.

82. "Left at a Minister's Door," *New York Herald,* September 17, 1888.

83. Jacob Riis, *How the Other Half Lives* (New York: Dover, 1971), 145.

84. "Left the Baby a Public Charge," *New York Herald,* October 11, 1896. For the baby's discovery, see "Richly Dressed Foundling," *New York Herald,* October 10, 1896.

85. " 'Blue Silk Baby' Unclaimed," *New York Herald,* October 13, 1896; " 'Blue Silk Baby' Is Gone," *New York Herald,* October 16, 1896.

86. "Seen in Waifland, Life of the City's Doorstep." This tactic was used again a decade later; see "Pretty Baby in Silks Deserted by Mother in Department Store," *New York Herald,* March 29, 1907.

87. "Blue Silk Baby' Unclaimed," *New York Herald,* October 13, 1896.

88. John Luke, AH Children's Records, vol. 214, p. 172.

89. Lawrence Black, AFV, no. 10, May 31, 1838. This record indicates that the infant was found at the house where "John Luke (B)" lives. There is no John

Luke in the city directory for this year. That this was an uncommon name leads me to believe that the John Luke of Laurens Street in 1838 was the same one abandoned as an infant in 1808. His address comes from the AFV. "B" in the AFV appears to have been used to mean "black." The three nurses were Julia Ann Smith, 35 Laurens Street, AFV, no. 174; Elizabeth Fuller, 45 Laurens Street, AFV, no. 179; Louisa Butler, 49 Laurens Street, AFV, no. 180. For Public School no. 2, see David T. Valentine, *Manual of the Corporation of the City of New York* (New York, 1842–54), 81). John Luke denied "any knowledge of the child." For the end of slavery in New York, see Graham Hodges, *Root and Branch: African Americans in New York and East Jersey, 1613–1863* (Chapel Hill: University of North Carolina Press, 1999).

90. Alexander Clements, AFV, no. 25, August 11, 1838. See also Stansell, *City of Women*, 246 n. 56.

91. Mary Ann Davis, AFV, no. 121, March 24, 1840. For foundling fraud, see Stansell, *City of Women*, 57; for the oath, see ibid., 246 n.56. For a case in which there is explicit mention of such an oath, see Mary Williams, AFV, no. 80, April 21, 1839.

92. Ann McGann, AFV, no. 117, February 26, 1840. For babies left with strangers, see AFV, nos. 6, 8, 44 (in a thread and needle store), 73, 142, 170. See also Stansell, *City of Women*, 55–56.

93. John Knox, AFV, no. 73, April 11, 1839. See also "Gave Her Child to Two Boys. Directed Them to Take It to the Foundling Asylum and Then Disappeared," *New York Herald*, September 1, 1894.

94. Mary Mitchell, AFV, no. 142, July 17, 1840; Emily Charlton, no. 164, (William E. Johnson), November 12, 1840.

95. Mary Mitchell (Catherine Reed), AFV, no. 142, July 17, 1840; Laura Miranda Bowerhorn, no. 170, February 11, 1841.

96. Matilda Campbell, AFV, no. 104, December 2, 1839; Maria Moulton, no. 179, April 18, 1841.

97. Martin Pringle, AFV, no. 13, June 13, 1838; John J. Astor, no. 112, January 3, 1840; Maria West, no. 183, May 13, 1841.

98. William Frost, AFV, no. 50, November 25, 1838; George Davis, AFV, no. 52, November 28, 1838; James Spring, AFV, no. 58, January 15, 1839.

99. Howard [pseud.], "Domestic Economy," *National Advocate*, June 6, 1820. For infanticide cases reported in the *National Advocate* in 1820, see May 4, 24, and 27 (floating in the slip); June 1 (Essex-street), 5 (pond at corner of Chapel and Canal), 16; July 4; August 1, 9, and 20. See also *Commercial Advertiser*, June 7 and 14. For other unambiguous cases of infanticide, see, e.g., the case of a baby girl who was beaten and thrown into the East River, reported in the *New York Evening Post*, July 28, 1804. The AFV contains a case (no. 136, June 21, 1840) in which a baby was thrown in a privy. Dr. A. B. Mott described

additional cases of babies thrown in privies in his testimony before the Special Committee of the Board of Councilmen on the Projected Foundling Hospital in 1858, "The Projected Foundling Hospital," *New York Times,* June 9, 1858. The New York Foundling Asylum, founded by the Sisters of Charity in 1869, equated infant abandonment with infanticide, describing "the innocent offspring of passion or poverty, for whom the door-step, the street, the sink, the river, the string, and the knife present each a means of riddance." NYFA, annual report, 1872, [5].

100. Woman with Tuscan hat, AFV, no. 18, June 28, 1838; William Bleecker, AFV, no. 43, October 9, 1838; Morgan Dascey, AFV, no. 62, February 14, 1839. For contemporary speculations on similar cases, see K. Drescher-Burke, J. Krall, and A. Penick, *Discarded Infants and Neonaticide: A Review of the Literature* (Berkeley: National Abandoned Infants Assistance Resource Center, University of California at Berkeley, 2004). For the phenomenon of infanticide, see Hoffer and Hull, *Murdering Mothers.*

101. Hone, *Diary,* February 18, 1837, 243.

102. AFV, no. 71, April 3, 1839 (no name given).

103. The letters quoted in this chapter and throughout the book come from the following sources: almshouse records, newspapers, and a collection of volumes containing letters held by the New York Foundling Hospital Archives.

104. Josephine Park, AFV, no. 51, November 25, 1838.

105. John Rome, AFV, no. 6, May 15, 1838.

106. Catherine Rogers, AFV, no. 154, October 1, 1840.

107. Eliza Smith, AFV, no. 74, April 16, 1839.

108. Charles Mortimer Reeder, AFV, no. 79, April 20, 1839.

109. William Haviland, AFV, no. 66, March 2, 1839.

110. Robert McClinchia, AFV, no. 21, July 17, 1838.

111. Ellen Lynch, AFV, no. 158, October 24, 1840. Other cases where fathers abandon babies because the mother is dead include Joanna Harrigan, AFV, no. 98, October 23, 1839; Catherine Dermady, AFV, no. 108, January 6, 1840; Michael Harrigan, AFV, no. 157, October 16, 1840.

112. These figures are calculated from 143 of the 184 foundling cases recorded in the AFV. Because of the ambiguity of some of these cases, these figures should be regarded as approximate. I am defining "newborns" as babies specifically described as newborns and those listed as up to one day old.

113. Smaller, more stable American communities tended to assist poor and single parents through community pressure and law; see Dayton, *Women before the Bar*; Ulrich, *A Midwife's Tale*; and Wall, *Fierce Communion.*

114. R. W. B. Lewis, *Edith Wharton: A Biography* (New York: Harper and Row, 1975), 13.

115. Hone, *Diary,* 372.

NOTES TO CHAPTER 2

1. Homer Folks, *Care of Destitute, Neglected, and Delinquent Children* (New York: Macmillan, 1902; reprint, New York: Johnson Reprint Co., 1970), 55; William Pryor Letchworth, "History of Child-Saving Work in the State of New York," in *History of Child Saving in the United States: Twentieth National Conference of Charities and Correction, Chicago, June 1893* (Boston: Geo. H. Ellis, 1893); Raymond Mohl, *Poverty in New York, 1783–1825* (New York: Oxford University Press, 1970), 145.

2. For orphanages and other childcare institutions, see David Rothman, *The Discovery of the Asylum: Social Order and Disorder in the New Republic* (Boston: Little Brown, 1971), 207. New York's first such institution was the New York Orphan Asylum, founded in 1806. It was followed by the Association for the Benefit of Colored Orphans; Hebrew Benevolent and Orphan Society; Leake and Watts Orphan House; Orphan's Home and Asylum of the Protestant Episcopal Church; Protestant Half-Orphan Asylum; Roman Catholic Orphan Asylum; St. Joseph's Orphan Asylum; and the Society for the Relief of Half-Orphans and Destitute Children. David T. Valentine, *Manual of the Corporation of the City of New York for 1860* (New York, 1860), 335–55 (hereafter cited as *Valentine's Manual*); Moses King, *King's Handbook of New York City* (Boston: Moses King, 1892), 394, 396; Edwin G. Burrows and Mike Wallace, *Gotham: A History of New York City to 1898* (New York: Oxford University Press, 1999), 811.

3. NYFA, "Souvenir of 1889," in NYFA, biennial report, 1888–90, [16].

4. Joan Jacobs Brumberg, *Kansas Charley: The Story of a Nineteenth-Century Boy Murderer* (New York: Viking, 2003), 16.

5. NCH, annual report, 1859, 8. Children's institutions that did not accept infants included Leake and Watts Orphan House, organized in 1831 for full orphans ages three to twelve; Orphan's Home and Asylum of the Protestant Episcopal Church, founded 1851 for orphans and half-orphans ages three to eight; and the Society for the Relief of Half-Orphans and Destitute Children, founded in 1835 for Protestant children ages four to ten. King, *King's Handbook,* 393–96. The Colored Orphan Asylum did not take children under two; see PCC, annual report, 1882, 164; 1884, 182.

6. Amy Gillman, "From Widowhood to Wickedness: The Politics of Class and Gender in New York City Private Charity, 1799–1860," *History of Education Quarterly* 24 (1984): 62–63; Mohl, *Poverty in New York,* 149, 167; Christine Stansell, *City of Women: Sex and Class in New York, 1789–1860* (Urbana: University of Illinois Press, 1987), 70–71.

7. NCH, annual report, 1866, 7.

8. Laurel Thatcher Ulrich, *A Midwife's Tale: The Life of Martha Ballard, Based on Her Diary, 1785–1812* (New York: Knopf, 1990), 157–58; Susanna

Haswell Rowson, *Charlotte Temple,* ed. Cathy Davidson (New York: Oxford University Press, 1986), xi–xiv.

9. Peter C. Hoffer and N. E. H. Hull, *Murdering Mothers: Infanticide in England and New England, 1558–1803* (New York: New York University Press, 1982); Mohl, *Poverty in New York,* 38–39, 55. Relevant laws include "An act for the relief of cities and towns from such charges as may arise from bastard children born within the same," passed February 7, 1788, *Laws of the State of New York Passed at the Sessions of the Legislature Held in the Years 1785, 1786, 1787 and 1788, inclusive* (Albany, 1886), 618–20. This law requires "parents" to pay, but the almshouse records only show fathers posting bastardy bonds. A New York City statute of 1853 authorized the mayor and recorder or any two aldermen or special justices to commit abandoned children to the almshouse; *The Charter of the City of New York* (New York, 1854), 296. The records of the almshouse reveal the presence of many mother-infant pairs; see AH, annual reports 1852, 3; 1859, 7. As for fathers found through local informants, see William Lambert, AH Children's Records, vol. 0123, p. 11; and Elsie Park, AFV, no. 24, August 7, 1838, in which a woman called at the almshouse to say "the child belongs to Thos. Barry."

10. William Henry Niblo, AH Children's Records, New York City Department of Records, Municipal Archives, vol. 0123, p. 312, and vol. 0161, February 18, 1820. On William Niblo and Niblo's Gardens, see Burrows and Wallace, *Gotham,* 585; George C. Odell, *Annals of the New York Stage* (New York: Columbia University Press, 1927), vol. 2, pp. 490, 546, 605, and vol. 3, pp. 372, 540–41. Niblo was in New York by 1816; see the listing for him at 45 Pine Street in *Longworth's American Almanac, New York Register and City Directory* (New York: David Longworth, 1816). For "Miss Hanna," see Odell, *Annals of the New York Stage,* vol. 3, p. 295.

11. William Lambert, New York City Department of Records, Municipal Archives, AH Children's Records, vol. 214, p. 280, and vol. 0123, p. 11. For many references to bonds put up by fathers to "indemnify the public with respect to a bastard child" and to resulting legal cases, see the New York City Almshouse and Bridewell Minutes, 1791–1799, Manuscript Division, New York Public Library and AH Children's Records, vols. 0123 and 0149. See also AH, annual report, 1849,194.

12. For unmarried mothers who nursed their own babies with help from the almshouse, see AH Children's Records, vols. 0123 and 0149.

13. Ann Louisa Harned, AH Children's Records, vol. 0123, p.141.

14. Elizabeth Levy, AH Children's Records, vol. 0149, p.19. For a similar case, see Susan Wheeler and Isaac Seixas, 1809, AH Children's Records, vol. 214, pp. 265, 302. For the Levy and Seixas families, see Arthur Hertzberg, *The Jews in America: Four Centuries of an Uneasy Encounter: A History* (New York: Simon and Schuster, 1989), 28–31, 64, 141.

15. Burrows and Wallace, *Gotham,* 45, 156. New York's nineteenth-century almshouse was not unlike Paris's Hôpital Général; see Michel Foucault, *Madness and Civilization: A History of Insanity in the Age of Reason* (New York: Random House, 1965), 39; Rachel Fuchs, *Abandoned Children: Foundlings and Child Welfare in Nineteenth-Century France* (Albany: State University of New York Press, 1984), 8.

16. For the components of the almshouse department on the eve of the Civil War, see PCC, annual report, 1860. For Bellevue as the largest structure in the city, see Mohl, *Poverty in New York,* 85.

17. For the fate of the almshouse buildings, see I. N. Phelps Stokes, *Iconography of Manhattan Island, 1498–1909* (New York: Robert H. Dodd, 1928; reprint, New York: Arno Press, 1967), March 23, 1829; March 24, 1831; August 5, 1848. For Vanderlyn and the Rotunda, see Burroughs and Wallace, *Gotham,* 468; Stokes, *Iconography,* April 12, 1818; May 26, 1820; May 26, 1823; July 18, 1825; March 23, 1829. On crowds and ventilation, see AH, annual reports, 1851, 129, and 1857, 294.

18. AH, annual report, 1847, 38–39 (emphasis in original).

19. AH, annual report, 1848, 41.

20. Mohl, *Poverty in New York,* 55.

21. AH, annual report, 1856, xl–xli (emphasis in original). Draper was an auctioneer and Whig leader; see Amy Bridges, *A City in the Republic: Antebellum New York and the Origins of Machine Politics* (New York: Cambridge University Press, 1984), 130; Eric Homburger, *Scenes from the Life of a City: Corruption and Conscience in Old New York* (New Haven, CT: Yale University Press, 1994), 141–42.

22. For another rendition of this image, used on the cover of the 1862 annual report, see Julie Miller, "The Murder of the Innocents: Foundlings in Nineteenth-Century New York City," *Prospects* 30 (2005): 264.

23. AH, annual reports, 1847, 6 (emphasis in original). See also AH, annual report, 1855, xix; Mohl, *Poverty in New York,* 65.

24. Michael Grossberg, *Governing the Hearth: Law and the Family in Nineteenth Century America* (Chapel Hill: University of North Carolina Press, 1985), 268–80; the phrase "absurd and repulsive" appears on p. 272.

25. John Ferguson, AFV, no. 126, April 21, 1840, and nurse section, Sarah McClennan, April 22, 1840. Wooldridge adopted John Ferguson on December 4, 1841.

26. Martha Clarissa Night, AH Children's Records, vol. 214, p. 100.

27. Hannah Gilmore/Emeline Toby, AFV, no. 14, June 14, 1838. Thomas McConnell, AH Children's Records, vol. 214, p. 282. For more foundlings returned to parents, see AFV, nos. 7, 17, 20, 24, 89, 133. See also Table 2.1.

28. For insightful discussions of naming practices used for European foundlings, see Guy Brunet, "La Dénomination des Enfants Recueillis par la Charité

de Bourg en Bresse au Debut du XIX Siècle" (unpublished MS); Carlo Corsini, "Prénom et Classe Sociale: Les Enfants Trouvés à Sienne, 1766–1768," in *Le Prénom, Mode et Histoire,* ed. Jacques Dupâquier, Alain Bideau, and Marie-Elisabeth Ducreux (Paris: École des Hautes Études en Sciences Sociales, 1984); David Kertzer, *Sacrificed for Honor: Infant Abandonment and the Politics of Reproductive Control* (Boston: Beacon Press, 1993), 119–22.

29. Foundling Babies. How They Are Cared For," *New York Times,* February 14, 1859.

30. Charles Dickens, *Oliver Twist* (New York: Oxford University Press, 1982), 6.

31. Oliver Twist, AFV, no. 184, May 19, 1841.

32. AH Children's Records, vol. 081, Vanderbilt, December 8, 1860; Barnum, July 8, 1863. For a similarly grandiose name, Reine (Queen) Marquis, see Guy Brunet, "Dénomination," [5].

33. Alexander Burr, AH Children's Records, vol. 214, p. 8.

34. Martha Washington, AH Children's Records, vol. 214, March 14, 1807; Childs, AH Children's Records, vol. 081, September 24, 1860; Davis, AH Children's Records, vol. 081, April 24, 1860; Lincoln, AH Children's Records, vol. 081, August 25, 1860 and November 7, 1860; George Washington, AH Children's Records, vol. 081, April 14, 1861.

35. William Unknown, AH Children's Records, vol. 0161, February 4 and April 14, 1820. Babies surnamed "Foundling" appear in AH Children's Records, vols. 0160 and 0161. For Henry Foundling, see December 24, 1819 to May 5, 1826 in those volumes.

36. Brunet, "Dénomination," [5]; Kertzer, *Sacrificed for Honor,* 120.

37. William Frost, AFV, no. 50, November 25, 1838. Martha Clarissa Night, AH Children's Records, vol. 214, p. 100.

38. Juliana Saturday, AH Children's Records, vol. 214, 1807, p. 80; Caroline Monday, AH Children's Records, vol. 214, 1807, p. 92; Clarinda Friday, AH Children's Records, vol. 214, 1807, p. 118. Leonora Monday, AH Children's Records, vol. 0161, December 21, 1821. Mary Monday, AH Children's Records, vols. 0160 and 0161, December 20, 1822–December 31, 1824. Ezra Stiles Ely, *Visits of Mercy* (Philadelphia: Samuel F. Bradford, 1829), 80.

39. For foundlings named after streets in France, see Fuchs, *Abandoned Children,* 110; in Ireland, see Joseph Robins, *The Lost Children: A Study of Charity Children in Ireland, 1700–1900* (Dublin: Institute of Public Administration, 1980), 7. For Henrietta Garden, see "Future of Foundlings, Infants No Longer Named for Choice Localities," *New York Times,* June 28, 1903.

40. Secondstreet, AH Children's Records, vol. 0161, April 27–June 8, 1821; Bleecker, AFV, no. 43, October 9, 1838; Bowery, AH Children's Records, vol. 081, September 26, 1860; Dey, AFV, no. 102, November 11, 1839 and AH Admissions Book 102, November 16, 1839; Charlton, AFV no. 164, November

12, 1840. Jane Broadway, AH Children's Records, vol. 082, June 21, 1863. There are many more of these; see, e.g., AH Children's Records, vol. 081, early 1860s, and AFV, 1838–1841, which include children with the surnames Barclay, Beekman, Bond, Centre, Clinton, Cortlandt, Delancey, Eldridge, Forsyth, Fulton, Greenwich, Jones (for Great Jones Street), Laight, Mott, Mulberry, Spring, Varick, and Vesey, all of which are street names in lower Manhattan.

41. Mary Park, AFV, no. 1, May 1, 1838; Elsie Park, AFV, no. 24, August 7, 1838; Josephine Park, AFV, no. 51, November 25, 1838; Henry Park, AFV, no. 67, March 2, 1838; Ann and Perry Alley, AH Children's Records, vol. 0163, December 21, 1832.

42. Brunet, "Dénomination," [3].

43. Mary Parker, AFV, no. 162, November 10, 1840; Maria Parker, AFV, no. 165, November 14, 1840; Palmer, AH Children's Records, vol. 0149, p. 44. For Draper and Tiemann, see "Foundling Babies. How They Are Cared For," *New York Times,* February 14, 1859.

44. William Frost, AFV, no. 50, November 25, 1838; Martha Clarissa Night, AH Children's Records, vol. 214, p. 100; Melissa Frances Whittey, AH Children's Records, vol. 214, p. 269.

45. Pringle, AFV, no. 13, June 13, 1838; Maxwell, AFV, no. 12, June 7, 1838; Waters, AFV, no. 130, May 1, 1840.

46. On the naming of slaves, see Ira Berlin, "From Creole to African: Atlantic Creoles and the Origins of African-American Society in Mainland North America," *William and Mary Quarterly,* 3d ser., 53 (1996): 251–88; Cheryl Ann Cody, "Naming, Kinship, and Estate Dispersal: Notes on Slave Family Life on a South Carolina Plantation, 1786–1833," *William and Mary Quarterly,* 3d ser., 39 (January 1982): 192–211; Herbert Gutman, *The Black Family in Slavery and Freedom, 1750–1925* (New York: Pantheon, 1976); Peter Kolchin, *American Slavery, 1619–1877* (New York: Hill and Wang, 1993), 45. For foundling names, see John Boswell, *The Kindness of Strangers: The Abandonment of Children in Western Europe from Late Antiquity to the Renaissance* (New York: Vintage Books, 1988), 120, 432; Fuchs, *Abandoned Children,* 120–22; Kertzer, *Sacrificed for Honor,* 119–22.

47. The World Wide Web reveals a few people surnamed Foundling in the Midwest.

48. Mary Jane Furman, AFV, no. 39, September 21, 1838.

49. Almshouse and Bridewell minutes, January 9, 1792. On almshouse wet nursing, see Janet Golden, *A Social History of Wet Nursing in America: From Breast to Bottle* (Cambridge: Cambridge University Press, 1996), 77.

50. Mary Lyons, AFV, no. 42, October 6, 1838.

51. Ely, *Visits of Mercy,* 33–34, 88–89.

52. Ibid., 73.

53. Ibid., 88–89.

54. AH, annual report, 1853, 6.

55. *By-laws and Ordinances of the Mayor, Aldermen and Commonalty of the City of New York* (New York, 1839), 102.

56. "The Foundlings of the City," *Tribune*, February 14, 1859. Data about wet nurses' own children for 1838–41 is in the AFV, nurse section. In its use of poor, urban women as wet nurses for foundlings, nineteenth-century New York was like eighteenth-century Madrid. See Joan Sherwood, *Poverty in Eighteenth-Century Spain: The Women and Children of the Inclusa* (Toronto: University of Toronto Press, 1988), 51–91.

57. [Frances] McCarty, AFV, nurse section, May 10, 1838. Janet Golden notes that "only the most desperate mothers turned to wet nursing immediately after giving birth"; Golden, *Social History of Wet Nursing*, 28.

58. For the intake process for foundlings and the payment of their nurses, see AH, annual report, 1848, 42–43. The nursing paybooks are at the New York City Department of Records, Municipal Archives; see AH Children's vols. 0161 (1819–1824), 0160 (1824–1829), and 0163 (1829–1835). On page 1 of vol. 0161, of the twenty-six nurses who received payments, nineteen signed with marks.

59. For the closing of the "literacy gap" between men and women between 1780 and 1850, see Linda Kerber, *Women of the Republic: Intellect and Ideology in Revolutionary America* (Chapel Hill: University of North Carolina Press, 1980), 193.

60. AH annual report, 1848, 42–43.

61. On the worthy widow, see Gillman, "From Widowhood to Wickedness."

62. The nurse section of the AFV consists of the applications and work records of 199 women (with some repetitions) who applied to the almshouse department to work as independent wet nurses between April 18, 1838, and July 8, 1840.

63. For the occupations of the nurses' husbands, see AFV, nurse section.

64. [Frances] McCarty, AFV, nurse section, May 10, 1838. Mary Surtzer, July 30, 1838, had a "sickly" husband and a "large family." Elsie Brower, May 4, 1838, was another widow. Women whose husbands were on board ship included sailors' wives Elizabeth Hutchings, May 4, 1838; Mary Keely, August 1, 1838; and Mary Falconi, September 6, 1838, a native New Yorker whose husband was an "Italian mate of Ship Anson of Charleston." Jane Maria Martin, December 4, 1838, said her husband was a ship's carpenter at sea; Bridget Taylor, September 7, 1838, was married to a soldier. Women with husbands who were simply "away" include Mary Ann Hill, August 1, 1838; and Eliza Peters, September 28, 1838. Sarah Lawrence, September 21, 1938, stated that her husband abandoned her. This is not an exhaustive list.

65. Elizabeth Hutchings, AFV, nurse section, May 4, 1838; [Frances] McCarty, AFV, nurse section, May 10, 1838; Cath Conley, AFV, nurse section,

June 7, 1838; Sarah Jusley, AFV, nurse section, July 23, 1838. Bracketed material is mine.

66. Mary Ann Bunce, AFV, nurse section, July 24, 1838.

67. Letitia Finder, AFV, no. 123, April 27, 1840; Elizabeth Houston, AFV, no. 174, March 9, 1841. Other examples of black babies matched with black nurses in the AFV are no. 72, William Shotwell, April 6, 1839; no. 179, Maria Moulton, April 18, 1841; no. 180, Margaret Ann Butler, April 19, 1841. There is a concentration of addresses (35, 45, and 49, cases 10, 174, 179, and 180) on Laurens Street (today, West Broadway north of Canal Street). In 1838–41 this was an African-American neighborhood. Janet Golden finds city authorities attempting to match black babies and nurses in eighteenth-century Philadelphia; see Golden, *Social History of Wet Nursing,* 30. For cross-race wet nursing in the South, see Elizabeth Fox-Genovese, *Within the Plantation Household: Black and White Women of the Old South* (Chapel Hill: University of North Carolina Press, 1988), 151–52, 315.

The end of slavery in New York might have, but did not, lead to a surfeit of black foundlings in the first decade of the nineteenth century. New York's Emancipation Act of 1799 specified that babies born to enslaved women after July 4, 1799, were officially free, but were required to serve the masters of their mothers until age twenty-five, if they were girls, or twenty-eight for boys. In an effort to pacify slave holders who protested that the cost of raising these children would not cover the amount of labor they would provide, the act included a clause that allowed masters to abandon them to the local overseers of the poor (in New York City the commissioners of the almshouse) once they reached the age of one. The state agreed to pay $3.50 per month to the almshouse to care for these children, and when they were old enough the almshouse was to bind them out, as they would any pauper children. What appears to have actually happened is that slave owners abandoned these babies only in name, appropriating the $3.50 per month for themselves. According to Arthur Zilversmit, the clause was in reality a "disguised scheme for compensated abolition." The abandonment clause proved expensive to the state and was repealed in 1804. See Chap. 62, "An Act for the Gradual Abolition of Slavery," Passed March 29, 1799, *Laws of the State of New York,* vol. 6 (Albany, 1887); Graham Hodges, *Root and Branch: African Americans in New York and East Jersey, 1613–1863* (Chapel Hill: University of North Carolina Press, 1999), 170; Arthur Zilversmit, *The First Emancipation: The Abolition of Slavery in the North* (Chicago: University of Chicago Press, 1967), 180–84.

68. For dry nurses, see Caroline Sherriden, AFV, nurse section, no. 1, April 18, 1838; Sarah Jusley, AFV, nurse section, no. 32, July 23, 1838; Mary Surtzer, AFV, nurse section, no. 35, July 30, 1838; Susan McGovern, AFV, nurse section, no. 91, April 8, 1839. For an elderly nurse, see "The Murder of the Innocents," *New York Tribune,* February 9, 1859.

69. For Croton Water, see Burrows and Wallace, *Gotham,* 625–28. For adulterated milk and water, cholera infantum, and dry nursing, see John Duffy, *A History of Public Health in New York City, 1866–1966* (New York: Russell Sage Foundation, 1968); E. Melanie Du Puis, *Nature's Perfect Food: How Milk Became America's Drink* (New York: New York University Press, 2002); Golden, *Social History of Wet Nursing,* 17; Richard A. Meckel, *Save the Babies: American Public Health Reform and the Prevention of Infant Mortality, 1850–1929* (Baltimore: Johns Hopkins University Press, 1990); Julie Miller, "To Stop the Slaughter of the Babies: Nathan Straus and the Drive for Pasteurized Milk, 1893–1920," *New York History* 74 (April 1993): 159–84; George D. Sussman, *Selling Mothers' Milk: The Wet Nursing Business in France, 1715–1914* (Urbana: University of Illinois Press, 1982), 10–11, 84–85. On infant formula, see Harvey Levenstein, " 'Best for Babies' or 'Preventable Infanticide'? The Controversy over Artificial Feeding of Infants in America, 1880–1920," *Journal of American History* 70 (June 1983): 77. On Smith, see NYIA, annual report, 1875, 27.

70. For age at weaning, see Almshouse and Bridewell minutes, December 28, 1795; May 2, 1796; AH, annual report, 1846, 387; 1848, 42–43.

71. Martha Skaats and the children she cared for, Henry Foundling, Lewis Bunill/Burrell, and Margaret Watters, appear in AH Children's Records, vols. 0161 and 0160. Martha's name is variously spelled Skates and Skatts, while Henry appears sometimes as Henry Fondling or Henry Bondling. Henry and Martha appear first on December 24, 1819. Martha may have had Henry before that date, but previous volumes are not available. On May 5, 1826, there is a note indicating that Henry was taken into the almshouse. On December 28, 1827, Martha was caring for Marg[aret] Watters. On December 19, 1819, she was also nursing Lewis Bunill; on April 9, 1824 she had Lewis Burrell (I am guessing these are the same child).

72. Of the fifty-one babies placed with nurses by the almshouse commissioners in 1839 (as recorded in the AFV), twenty-eight (55 percent) died. Of the sixty placed in 1840, twenty-two (36.6 percent) died. The women who were given babies by the almshouse commissioners between April 1838 and July 1840, as recorded in the AFV, each cared for between one and five infants during this time.

73. For cases of neglect, see nurse Ann McCullock, AFV, nurse section, June 29, 1838; and AFV, nurse section, no. 50, baby William Frost, November 25, 1838.

74. For Johanna Hill, see AFV, nurse section, April 20, 1838. For Mary Park see children's section, no. 1, May 1, 1838. For Charles Smith Pugsley's history see Charles Smith Pugsley, AFV, no. 65, February 15, 1839, and nurse section, nurses Eliza Reed, February 19, 1839; Cath Dougherty, March 9, 1839; Caroline Williams, March 22, 1839; Eliza Gallon, March 23, 1839; Johanna Hill, March 11, 1839.

75. See David Kertzer, "Syphilis, Foundlings, and Wet Nurses in Nineteenth Century Italy," *Journal of Social History* 32 (Spring 1999): 589–602; David Ransel, *Mothers of Misery: Child Abandonment in Russia* (Princeton, NJ: Princeton University Press, 1988), 278–90. For smallpox at the Nursery and Child's Hospital before the Civil War, see Mary Du Bois, "Thirty Years' Experience in Hospital Work," in *Infant Asylums and Children's Hospitals, Medical Dilemmas and Developments, 1850–1920,* ed. Janet Golden (New York: Garland, 1989), 18.

76. For the unsavory reputations of "baby farmers," see Margaret L. Arnott, "Infant Death, Child Care and the State: The Baby-Farming Scandal and the First Infant Life Protection Legislation of 1872," *Continuity and Change* 9 (1994): 271–311; Golden, *Social History of Wet Nursing,* 101.

77. "The Murder of the Innocents," *New York Tribune,* February 9, 1859

78. Elliot, "Inauguration of the Nursery and Child's Hospital" [1858], 12, Records of the New York Nursery and Child's Hospital, New-York Historical Society.

79. Augusta Alexander, AFV, nurse section, February 18, 1839; Sarah White, AFV, nurse section, no. 63, February 14, 1839. Alexander returned the baby on March 7, 1839, after less than a month.

80. For children returned to the almshouse, see Juliana Saturday, AH Children's Records, vol. 214, August 1, 1809; William Lambert, December 31, 1813, vol. 0123, 11; Henry Foundling, vol. 0160, May 5, 1826.

81. For early references to the almshouse school, see Almshouse and Bridewell minutes, September 24, 1792; February 29, March 21, June 6, 1796.

82. For admissions of children to the almshouse 1826–41, see Almshouse Admissions Books, vols. 102 and 146. Richard Shannon, vol. 146, February 1, 1827. For children born in the almshouse, see reference to the almshouse midwife, Almshouse and Bridewell minutes, March 12, 1792; November 17, December 1, 1794. Ely describes a family of children born in the almshouse; quoted in Seth Rockman, *Welfare Reform in the Early Republic: A Brief History with Documents* (Boston: Bedford/St. Martin's, 2003), 81–82. For a blind, parentless boy and a crippled boy in the almshouse, see Ely, *Visits of Mercy,* 68, 79.

83. AH, annual report, 1849, 194–95.

84. According to Homer Folks, the city bought Long Island Farms, then three farms, around 1831, at the same time it bought Blackwell's Island. Folks, *Care of Destitute, Neglected, and Delinquent Children,* 15. On the construction of the building for children there, see AH, annual report, 1837, 238. It appears that children were living at Long Island Farms even before this building went up, along with the adult paupers who worked the farm. For the location of Long Island Farms, see *Valentine's Manual,* 1842–43, 79, which describes Long Island Farms as "opposite Blackwell's Island." By 1837 Long Island Farms was

being used for children. AH, annual report, 1837, 216–39. Long Island Farms closed in 1847. For the removal of the children in 1847, see AH, annual report, 1847, 16.

85. AH, annual report, 1837, 216, 238, 250–51. For the appropriation of funds for the nursery building on Long Island Farms, see Municipal Archives, City Clerk, Filed Papers, Committee on Charity and Alms House, 1836.

86. Lydia Maria Child, who visited Long Island Farms in 1842, and James Gibbons, who visited in 1846, both reported that there were six hundred children there. See Lydia Maria Child, "Letters from New York, Number 29," in *A Lydia Maria Child Reader*, ed. Carolyn L. Karcher (Durham, NC: Duke University Press, 1997), 325; and James Gibbons diary excerpt in Sarah Hopper Emerson, *Life of Abby Hopper Gibbons, Told Chiefly through Her Correspondence* (New York: G. P. Putnam's Sons, 1897), 135. According to the almshouse there were 463 children at Long Island Farms in 1836 (AH, annual report, 1837, table following page 251) and 698 in 1840 (New York City Department of Records, Municipal Archives, City Clerk, Filed Papers, Committee on Charity and Almshouse, 1839). *Valentine's Manual* reports 475 there in 1845; *Valentine's Manual*, 1845–46, 190.

87. For personnel at Long Island Farms, see *Valentine's Manual*, 1845–46, 39. For the exclusion of black children, see AH, annual report, 1837, 226–27. For references to the school there, see AH, annual report, 1837, 219; and *Valentine's Manual*, 1842–43, 79; 1844–45, 198. For conditions for African Americans at Bellevue, see AH, annual report, 1837, 238.

88. Two of the most famous antebellum visitors of American institutions were Alexis de Tocqueville, who came to see prisons in the United States, and Charles Dickens, who describes these visits in his 1842 *American Notes for General Circulation*. For visitors to children's institutions, see Rothman, *Discovery of the Asylum*, 223–24.

89. Child, "Letters from New York, Number 29," in Karcher, *Lydia Maria Child Reader*, 325–26.

90. John Griscom, *The Sanitary Condition of the Laboring Population of New York* (New York: Harper and Bros., 1845), 3.

91. Quoted in Emerson, *Life of Abby Hopper Gibbons*, vol. 1, p. 135. For the Gibbons's holiday practice of visiting almshouse children, see Mary E. Dewey, ed., *The Life and Letters of Catharine M. Sedgwick* (New York: Harper and Bros., 1871), 421.

92. AH, annual report, 1846, [376].

93. Emerson, *Life of Abby Hopper Gibbons*, vol. 1, p. 134.

94. AH, annual report, 1847, 16–19.

95. John Duffy, "Social Impact of Disease in the Late Nineteenth Century," in *Sickness and Health in America: Readings in the History of Medicine and Public Health*, ed. Judith Walzer Leavitt and Ronald L. Numbers (Madison:

University of Wisconsin Press, 1985), 416; Charles Rosenberg, *The Cholera Years: The United States in 1832, 1849, and 1866* (Chicago: University of Chicago Press, 1987), 203.

96. For Randall's Island Nursery, see AH, annual reports, 1847, 9; 1848, 17–27. For the breakup of Bellevue, see AH, annual reports, 1847, 11–12, and 1856, 23–24; King, *King's Handbook,* 421–22, 456–60; Mohl, *Poverty in New York,* 86; Edward Spann, *The New Metropolis: New York City, 1840–1857* (New York: Columbia University Press, 1981), 76–79.

97. AH, annual report, 1847, 8.

98. Ibid., 24.

99. J. F. Richmond, *New York and Its Institutions, 1609–1871* (New York: E. B. Treat, 1871), 568–71; Raymond Mohl, "Humanitarianism in the Preindustrial City: The New York Society for the Prevention of Pauperism, 1817–1823," *Journal of American History* 57 (December 1970): 594–95.

100. AH, annual report, 1848, 17. Except where otherwise noted, my description of the Randall's Island Nursery is based on the extensive description in AH, annual report, 1848, 17–27.

101. For bath houses and the benefits of bathing, see AH, annual reports, 1850, 158; 1851, 138.

102. For "ornamental trees," see AH, annual report, 1848, 22; for playhouses, see 1848, 23; for gymnasium equipment, see 1856, 211; for the farm, see 1846, 383.

103. "Habits of Industry," AH, annual report, 1855, 126. For the farm and the tailor, see AH, annual reports, 1855, 126; 1856, 211–12. For items made by children see AH, annual reports, 1855, 128; 1856, 212.

104. For "ennobling mission," see AH, annual report, 1848, 22.

105. For overcrowding at the Randall's Island school, see AH, annual reports, 1856, 214; 1857, 211. For epidemics, see AH, annual reports, 1851, 140; 1855, 107–8.

106. AH, annual report, 1848, 24–25.

107. AH, annual report, 1854, 141. For complaints by almshouse officials about convict and pauper labor at Randall's Island, see AH, annual reports, 1869, 122; 1870, 268; 1871, 202–3, 206; 1877, vii–viii; 1893, 138. As late as 1902 men from the penitentiary on Blackwell's Island were at work making roads at Randall's Island; PCC, annual report, 1902, 180.

108. "Visit of the New-York Legislature Elect to Randall's and Blackwell's Islands," *New York Tribune,* December 15, 1853.

109. "Flag Presentation to the Randall's Island Boys," *New York Times,* December 12, 1864.

110. Abigail Hopper Gibbons, "Sketch of Miss Sedgwick's Connection with the Women's Prison Association of New York," in Dewey, *Catharine M. Sedgwick,* 421.

111. For age at apprenticeship, see AH, annual report, 1837, 218. For an almshouse boy apprenticed to a factory in 1811, see Ely, *Visits of Mercy*, 60.

112. Almshouse and Bridewell minutes, 1791–99.

113. Folks, *Care of Destitute, Neglected, and Delinquent Children*, 8.

114. John McGrath, AH, annual reports, 1846, 455 (Chapman), 456 (Petit), 458 (Dey); 1847, 98 (Chapman). Peter Dey, AFV, no. 102, November 11, 1839, and AH Admissions Book 102, November 16, 1839.

115. McGrath, Report, in AH, annual report, 1847, 87 (Thomas B. Mathers), 104 (Margaret McGowen).

116. McGrath, Report, in AH, annual report, 1847, 91 (John Chandler, Joseph Kelly), 95 (Catherine Fauzer, Elizabeth Smith), 96 (Margaret Bell), 100 (Ellen McCluskey, Ellis Rushton, Jane Wright), 103 (Henrietta Valentine). The three boys who ran away from one master are Charles Williams, Patrick Cunnion, and Owen Ward; ibid., 88.

117. Almshouse and Bridewell Minutes, December 3, 1792. For references to infants placed with nurses in areas north of the city, see July 7, 1791 (Sing Sing in Westchester), and AFV, nurse section, May 4, 1840, for nurse Sarah Jewell of Nyack in Rockland County.

118. AH, annual report, 1856, 211.

119. AH, annual reports, 1853, 102; 1856, 281. For more on rural placements, see AH annual reports, 1854, 214; 1855, 191, 193.

120. For Charles C. Townsend, see AH, annual reports, 1858, 281–84; 1859, 295–97.

121. Virginia Penny, *The Employments of Women: A Cyclopaedia of Women's Work* (Boston: Walker, Wise and Co), 1863, 425.

122. "Institution Life. I. Foundling Asylum," *Illustrated American*, May 17, 1890, 308.

123. Samuel B. Halliday, *The Lost and Found; or, Life among the Poor* (New York: Blakeman and Mason, 1859), 247.

124. Horatio Alger, *Ragged Dick and Struggling Upward* (New York: Penguin, 1985), 7–8.

NOTES TO CHAPTER 3

1. Isaac Townsend, Washington Smith, and Anthony Dugro, *Report of the Select Committee, Appointed March 17, 1857, by the Board of Governors of the Almshouse, New-York, Deputed to Investigate the Claims of the City to the Institution, and Erection of a Foundling Hospital* (New York, 1858) (hereafter cited as Almshouse Foundling Report); Samuel Galpin, John C. Frazer, and George Ross, *Report of the Select Committee on Foundling Hospital*, Document no. 17, *Documents of the New York City Board of Councilmen*, vol. 5 (New York, 1858) (hereafter cited as Councilmen's Foundling Report). The council-

men formed their committee on July 6, 1857; *Proceedings of the Board of Councilmen of the City of New York,* vol. 67 (New York, 1858), 8. "The Infants' Home. Laying of the Corner Stone—Address by Rev. H. E. Montgomery," *New York Times,* December 29, 1859.

2. Howard [pseud.], "Domestic Economy," *National Advocate,* June 6, 1820. See Paul Gilje, "Infant Abandonment in Nineteenth-Century New York City: Three Cases," *Signs* 8 (Spring 1983): 583.

3. Oliver L. Barbour, *The Magistrate's Criminal Law* (Albany: Gould and Company, 1841), 77.

4. "Foundlings: The Hospital for Foundlings in East Twelfth Street," *New York Herald,* November 22, 1869.

5. For the transformation of the family and changes in attitudes toward women, children, and motherhood, see, e.g., Philippe Ariès, *Centuries of Childhood: A Social History of Family Life* (New York: Vintage Books, 1962); Nancy Schrom Dye and Daniel Blake Smith, "Mother Love and Infant Death, 1750–1920," *Journal of American History* 73 (September 1986): 329–53; Carole Shammas, *A History of Household Government in America* (Charlottesville: University of Virginia Press, 2002); Edward Shorter, *The Making of the Modern Family* (New York: Basic Books, 1975); Lawrence Stone, *The Family, Sex, and Marriage in England, 1500–1800* (London: Weidenfeld and Nicolson, 1977); Barbara Welter, "The Cult of True Womanhood: 1820–1860," *American Quarterly* 18 (Summer 1966): 150–74.

6. See Otto Ulbricht, "The Debate about Foundling Hospitals in Enlightenment Germany: Infanticide, Illegitimacy, and Infant Mortality Rates," *Central European History* 18 (September/December 1985): 247.

7. For the correlation between urban growth and a high rate of infant mortality in the nineteenth century, see Richard A. Meckel, *Save the Babies: American Public Health Reform and the Prevention of Infant Mortality, 1850–1929* (Baltimore: Johns Hopkins University Press, 1990). For contemporary commentary, see David Meredith Reese, *Report on Infant Mortality in Large Cities: The Sources of Its Increase, and Means for Its Diminution* (Philadelphia: American Medical Association, 1857). For urban conditions, see Citizens' Association of New York, *Report of the Council of Hygiene of the Citizens' Association of New York upon the Sanitary Condition of the City* (New York: Appleton, 1865); Jacob Riis, *How the Other Half Lives* (New York: Charles Scribner's Sons, 1890; reprint, New York: Dover Books, 1971). For the city's water supply, see Gerard Koeppel, *Water for Gotham: A History* (Princeton, NJ: Princeton University Press, 2000).

8. For Smith's life, see Gert Brieger, "Stephen Smith: Surgeon and Reformer" (Ph.D. diss., Johns Hopkins University, 1971); for Smith and the New York Infant Asylum (hereafter cited as NYIA), see "Address of Dr. Stephen Smith of the State Board of Charities," in NYIA, annual report, 1900. For Elisha Harris and

the Nursery and Child's Hospital, see NCH, annual report, 1886, 34. For their role in founding the Metropolitan Board of Health, see Eric Homburger, *Scenes from the Life of a City: Corruption and Conscience in Old New York* (New Haven, CT: Yale University Press, 1994), 67–85.

9. Metropolitan Board of Health, annual report, 1866, 10. For infant mortality as a public issue, see also Meckel, *Save the Babies*, 5.

10. "The Slaughter of the Innocents," *New York Times,* February 17, 1859.

11. Councilmen's Foundling Report, 5.

12. Elliot, "Inauguration of the Nursery and Child's Hospital," 10–13, in New York Nursery and Child's Hospital Records, New-York Historical Society; Mott, NCH, annual report, 1859, 5–6; Du Bois, NCH, annual report, 1882, 8.

13. David T. Valentine, *Manual of the Corporation of the City of New York for 1860* (New York, 1860), 432. Hereafter cited as *Valentine's Manual.*

14. Almshouse and Bridewell Minutes, May 2, 1796, Manuscript Division, New York Public Library; 1809: *Minutes of the Common Council of the City of New York, 1784–1831* (New York: City of New York, 1917), vol. 5, p. 548. For the embargo, see Edwin G. Burrows and Mike Wallace, *Gotham: A History of New York City to 1898* (New York: Oxford University Press, 1999), 409–13.

15. Homer Folks, *Care of Destitute, Neglected, and Delinquent Children* (1823; New York: Johnson Reprint Co., 1970), 8. For the city's population, see *Valentine's Manual,* 1857, 347.

16. New York City Municipal Archives, City Clerk, Filed Papers, Committee on Charity and Almshouse, Annual Report of the Superintendent of the Almshouse, May 1, 1840–May 1, 1841.

17. AH, annual report, 1849, 193. Charles Rosenberg, *The Cholera Years: The United States in 1832, 1849, and 1866* (Chicago: University of Chicago Press, 1987).

18. Even the word "infant" is suspect, since in the nineteenth century it was often used to refer to young children, not just babies. In the almshouse reports, however, I am looking at lists of "infants at nurse," meaning babies placed with wet nurses.

19. AH, annual report, 1848, 42. Leonard refers to the 160 to 200 infants his department cared for yearly as "foundlings and otherwise abandoned infants." As always, these numbers should not be regarded as strictly accurate. In 1850, for instance, the almshouse reported receiving ninety babies who were "foundlings or abandoned," a lower number than what Leonard reports, and possibly an indication that Leonard's estimate was inflated. AH, annual report, 1850, 120.

20. AH, annual report, 1851, 128.

21. For the "panic" of 1857, see Burrows and Wallace, *Gotham,* 842–51.

22. See Table 2.1. See also Rachel Fuchs, *Abandoned Children: Foundlings*

and Child Welfare in Nineteenth-Century France (Albany: State University of New York Press, 1984), 68. In 1801 the Hôpital des Enfants Trouvés became the Hospice des Enfants Trouvés. See Fuchs, *Abandoned Children*, 18.

23. For the flour riots, see Burrows and Wallace, *Gotham*, 609–11; Philip Hone, *The Diary of Philip Hone, 1828–1851*, ed. Allan Nevins (New York: Dodd, Mead, 1927), 241–42. For the election day riots, see Tyler Anbinder, *Five Points* (New York: Penguin, 2002), 27–32, 141–44. For race riots, see Anbinder, *Five Points*, 7–13. For the Astor Place riot, see Edward K. Spann, *The New Metropolis: New York City, 1840–1857* (New York: Columbia University Press, 1981), 234–41. For the draft riots, see George Templeton Strong, *Diary of George Templeton Strong*, ed. Allan Nevins and Milton Halsey Thomas (New York: Octagon Books, 1974), vol. 3, pp. 334–43. On the "decade of disorder," see Spann, *New Metropolis*, 253–54, 390–91. On crime in New York, see Kenneth Stampp, *America in 1857: A Nation on the Brink* (New York: Oxford University Press, 1990).

24. George Washington Matsell, *Semi-Annual Report of the Chief of Police from May 1 to October 31, 1849* (New York, 1849). AH, annual report, 1858, 161.

25. Charles Loring Brace, *The Dangerous Classes and Twenty Years' Work among Them* (New York: Wynkoop and Hallenbeck, 1872).

26. Brace, *Dangerous Classes*, 406.

27. NCH, annual report, 1879, 9.

28. "Death of Mr. Isaac Townsend," *New York Evening Post*, April 2, 1860, 2; "New York as Murderer," *Harper's Weekly*, March 5, 1859; AH, annual report, 1858, xv; PCC, 1875, 15 (list of almshouse governors); Du Bois: NCH, annual report, 1879, 9.

29. Almshouse Foundling Report, lix. I do not have direct evidence that Townsend went to London, although his descriptions, seemingly based on direct observations, strongly suggest that he did. The almshouse department did send officials on investigative trips. A decade later they sent Dr. Abraham Jacobi to Europe to study foundling asylum management. See Abraham Jacobi, *The Raising and Education of Abandoned Children in Europe, with Statistics and General Remarks on That Subject* (New York: Bellevue Hospital Printing Office, 1870). On art and music in London, see Ruth McClure, *Coram's Children: The London Foundling Hospital in the Eighteenth Century* (New Haven, CT: Yale University Press, 1981), 66–72; Benedict Nicholson, *Treasures of the Foundling Hospital* (London: Oxford University Press, 1972); Jenny Uglow, *Hogarth: A Life and a World* (New York: Farrar, Straus and Giroux, 1997), 322–38; 429–38.

30. Almshouse Foundling Report, lviii.

31. Ibid.

32. Sidney Smith, review of Seybert, *Annals of the United States, Edinburgh Review* (January 1820), 79–80.

33. Thomas Bender, *New York Intellect: A History of Intellectual Life in New York City, from 1750 to the Beginnings of Our Own Time* (New York: Knopf, 1987); Neil Harris, *The Artist in American Society, The Formative Years, 1790–1860* (New York: George Braziller, 1966).

34. Almshouse Foundling Report, lviii.

35. Ibid., lvii.

36. Burrows and Wallace, *Gotham,* 468; I. N. Phelps Stokes, *Iconography of Manhattan Island, 1498–1909* (1928; reprint, New York: Arno Press, 1967), vol. 5, p. 1591.

37. Frances Trollope, *Domestic Manners of the Americans* (London: Penguin, 1997), 267.

38. Almshouse Foundling Report, liv.

39. Ibid., lvii.

40. Ibid., xxxviii, lv.

41. NCH, annual report, 1870, 8.

42. Mary Du Bois had an uncertain recollection of the date of Mott and Halliday's survey, noting in one place that it occurred in 1853–54 and in another in 1856–57. See Du Bois, "Thirty Years Experience in Hospital Work," in *Infant Asylums and Children's Hospitals: Medical Dilemmas and Developments, 1850–1920: An Anthology of Sources,* ed. Janet Golden (New York: Garland, 1989), 14; NCH, annual reports, 1876, 10; 1879, 8. Halliday wrote that the survey occurred "some two years since," or around 1857, in his book, *The Lost and Found; or Life among the Poor* (New York: Blakeman and Mason, 1859). I think early 1857 or the winter of 1856–57 is correct. Halliday's description of his slum tour is in "Report Made to the Governors Two Years Ago," in "The Murder of the Innocents," *New York Tribune,* February 9, 1859; Samuel B. Halliday, *The Little Street Sweeper; or, Life among the Poor* (New York: Phinney, Blakeman, and Mason, 1861), 147–66; Councilmen's Foundling Report, 5–6.

43. Halliday, *Little Street Sweeper,* 149, 153.

44. Carroll Smith-Rosenberg, *Religion and the Rise of the American City: The New York Mission Movement, 1812–1870* (Ithaca, NY: Cornell University Press, 1971).

45. For the urban investigation in New York, see Homburger, *Scenes from the Life of a City,* 10–85; in Britain, see Oz Frankel, "Scenes of Commission: Royal Commissions of Inquiry and the Culture of Social Investigation in Early Victorian Britain," *European Legacy* 4 (1999): 20–41.

46. "Death of an Old Citizen—William F. Mott," *New York Times,* May 4, 1867.

47. On Halliday, see "Rev. S. B. Halliday Dead," *New York Times,* July 10, 1897; Tyler Anbinder, *Five Points* (New York: Penguin, 2002), 236–40; Denise Bethel, "Mr. Halliday's Picture Album," *Seaport* 28 (Fall 1994): 16–21; Homburger, *Scenes from the Life of a City,* 3–6; Smith Rosenberg, *Religion and the Rise of the American City,* 207. "Presentation at the Workingwomen's Home," *New York Times,* September 30, 1868, finds Halliday as the superintendent of the Workingwomen's Home.

48. The AFV shows nurses moving frequently. On May 1 as moving day in New York, see Trollope, *Domestic Manners,* 349.

49. For housing conditions in New York slums in the nineteenth century, see Anbinder, *Five Points,* 72–110; Riis, *How the Other Half Lives,* 5–11.

50. "Report Made to the Governors Two Years Ago," in "The Murder of the Innocents," *New York Tribune,* February 9, 1859.

51. Halliday, *Little Street Sweeper,* 152.

52. Halliday, *Lost and Found,* 222–23; John Griscom, *The Sanitary Condition of the Laboring Population of New York* (New York: Harper and Bros., 1845), 23.

53. Halliday, *Little Street Sweeper,* 155.

54. Councilmen's Foundling Report, 5–6.

55. Ibid., 3.

56. Storer's antiabortion effort began in May 1857; see James C. Mohr, *Abortion in America: The Origins and Evolution of National Policy, 1800–1900* (New York: Oxford University Press, 1978), 152, 154. For abortion as a threat to the family, see Carroll Smith Rosenberg, "The Abortion Movement and the AMA, 1850–1880," in Smith-Rosenberg, *Disorderly Conduct: Visions of Gender in Victorian America* (New York: Oxford University Press, 1985). For further threats to the authority of the nineteenth-century household head, see Shammas, *A History of Household Government.*

57. Janet Farrell Brodie, *Contraception and Abortion in Nineteenth-Century America* (Ithaca, NY: Cornell University Press, 1994); Michael Grossberg, *Governing the Hearth: Law and the Family in Nineteenth Century America* (Chapel Hill: University of North Carolina Press, 1985); Mohr, *Abortion in America*; Smith-Rosenberg, "The Abortion Movement and the AMA."

58. For descriptions of these "cures" as experienced by two well-known sufferers, see Janet Browne, *Charles Darwin: The Power of Place* (New York: Knopf, 2002); Joan Hedrick, *Harriet Beecher Stowe: A Life* (New York: Oxford University Press, 1994).

59. Robert P. Hudson, "Abraham Flexner in Perspective: American Medical Education, 1865–1910," in *Sickness and Health in America: Readings in the History of Medicine and Public Health,* ed. Judith Walzer Leavitt and Ronald L. Numbers (Madison: University of Wisconsin Press, 1985), 153.

60. Daniel Scott Smith, "Family Limitation, Sexual Control, and Domestic Feminism in Victorian America," in *Clio's Consciousness Raised: New Perspectives on the History of Women,* ed. Mary Hartman and Lois W. Banner (New York: Harper and Row, 1974), 123.

61. Brodie, *Contraception;* Andrea Tone, *Devices and Desires: A History of Contraceptives in America* (New York: Hill and Wang), 2001. Nineteenth-century women also practiced a form of the rhythm method, but since doctors did not yet understand how the reproductive cycle worked, they mistook the fertility period, making this method ineffective; see Brodie, *Contraception,* 28–30. The degree to which poor women had access to birth control is hard to determine; see Tone, *Devices,* 79–87.

62. For examples of poor, single women who used abortion, see Clifford Browder, *The Wickedest Woman in New York: Madame Restell, the Abortionist* (Hamden, CT: Archon Books, 1988).

63. Brodie, *Contraception,* 225.

64. Browder, *The Wickedest Woman in New York;* for the use of a whalebone, see p. 48.

65. James L. Crouthamel, *Bennett's New York Herald and the Rise of the Popular Press* (Syracuse, NY: Syracuse University Press, 1989), 53. For women as readers, see Linda Kerber, *Women of the Republic: Intellect and Ideology in Revolutionary America* (Chapel Hill: University of North Carolina Press, 1980), 193.

66. Burrows and Wallace, *Gotham,* 810.

67. "Alexander B. Mott. Dead," *New York Herald,* August 13, 1889. For Arabella Mott as nursery founder, see Golden, *Infant Asylums,* 31; as secretary, see NCH, annual reports, 1857–1863.

68. "The Projected Foundling Hospital," *New York Times,* June 9, 1858 (emphasis in the original); Councilmen's Foundling Report, 3; Almshouse Foundling Report, xxxvii.

69. David Meredith Reese, *Humbugs of New York: Being a Remonstrance against Popular Delusion; Whether in Science, Philosophy, or Religion* (New York: John S. Taylor; Boston: Weeks, Jordan, Co., 1838), 125.

70. Reese, *Report on Infant Mortality.*

71. Ibid., 6, 11.

72. Reese's association of stillbirth with abortion was backed by Dr. James Wynne, who also testified to the councilmen; see "Proposition for a Foundling Hospital in New York. Interesting Statement of Dr. James Wynne—Remarkable Statistics," *New York Herald,* December 12, 1857.

73. Reese, *Report on Infant Mortality,* 9, 10.

74. Ibid., 14.

75. Ibid., 17.

76. Ibid., 9.

77. "The Projected Foundling Hospital," *New York Times,* June 9, 1858; Councilmen's Foundling Report, 2.

78. Almshouse Foundling Report, xxxiv, lxx.

79. Ibid., xxxvi.

80. For the "fallen woman," see Estelle Freedman, *Their Sisters' Keepers: Women's Prison Reform in America, 1830–1930* (Ann Arbor: University of Michigan Press, 1981), 14–15. While the notion of ruin existed before, it reached a hysterical height in the nineteenth century; see Cornelia Hughes Dayton, *Women before the Bar: Gender, Law, and Society in Connecticut, 1639–1789* (Chapel Hill: University of North Carolina Press, 1995), 204.

81. Brace, *Dangerous Classes,* 115, 116.

82. Almshouse Foundling Report, lxviii.

83. Timothy Gilfoyle, *City of Eros: New York City, Prostitution, and the Commercialization of Sex, 1790–1920* (New York: W. W. Norton, 1992), 117–78.

84. Ibid., 29–54, especially 33, map 5.

85. Councilmen's Foundling Report, 2.

86. William Sanger, *The History of Prostitution: Its Extent, Causes, and Effects throughout the World, Being an Official Report to the Board of the Alms-House Governors of the City of New York* (New York: Harper and Bros., 1858), 29.

87. [George G. Foster], *New York in Slices: By an Experienced Carver: Being the Original Slices Published in the New York Tribune* (New York: William H. Graham, 1848), 5. In the mid-nineteenth century prostitutes could earn several dollars per night, while seamstresses earned only pennies per day. For prostitutes, see Gilfoyle, *City of Eros,* 59–60, 68–69; Matsell, *Semi-Annual Report, 1849,* 63–64 (on earnings of child prostitutes). For the earnings of women workers, see Virginia Penny, *The Employments of Women: A Cyclopaedia of Women's Work* (Boston: Walker, Wise and Co., 1863).

88. Of the 2,000 prostitutes in Sanger's study, 525 gave destitution as the reason they turned to prostitution. A little less than half that number, 258, cited that they were "seduced and abandoned." Another 24 reported that they had been seduced on board immigrant ships or in boarding houses catering to immigrants. Twenty-seven said they had been "violated" (raped). Others gave reasons such as drink, bad company, idleness, or the persuasion of other prostitutes. Abuse by families or husbands was cited by 164 of the women. Sanger found it hard to explain the 513 who reported that they turned to prostitution out of "inclination." Sanger, *History of Prostitution,* 488.

89. Ibid., 525.

90. Ibid., 492.

91. For Townsend's influence on Sanger, see ibid., 27–28. For Sanger's influence on Townsend, see Almshouse Foundling Report, xcii, and compare Town-

send's Belgian and Russian statistics (lxxxiii, lxxxv), with Sanger's (*History of Prostitution,* 187, 275).

92. Sanger, *History of Prostitution,* 167, 371; Almshouse Foundling Report, xci–xcii.

93. Councilmen's Foundling Report, 1–2. Sanger stated that at least some of the children at the Randall's Island nurseries were the offspring of prostitutes; see Sanger, *History of Prostitution,* 484.

94. Almshouse Foundling Report, xlix. For abandoned children as prostitutes in Rome, see John Boswell, *The Kindness of Strangers: The Abandonment of Children in Western Europe from Late Antiquity to the Renaissance* (New York: Vintage Books, 1988), 112–13. Robins states that from one-third to one-quarter of the inmates of the Magdalen Asylum in Dublin had been raised in the city's foundling asylum or the charter schools, and girls from the foundling asylum in Cork often became prostitutes; Joseph Robins, *The Lost Children: A Study of Charity Children in Ireland, 1700–1900* (Dublin: Institute of Public Administration, 1980), 51, 58.

95. "Proposition for a Foundling Hospital in New York," *New York Herald,* December 12, 1857. Councilmen's Foundling Report, 3, 4. Almshouse Foundling Report, lxxx–lxxxii.

96. Councilmen's Foundling Report, 2; Almshouse Foundling Report, xxxii.

97. Almshouse Foundling Report, lvi.

98. For Mary Delafield and her family, see John Ross Delafield, *Delafield: The Family History* (privately printed, 1945), vol. 1, pp. 250–53; Virginia A. Metaxas Quiroga, *Poor Mothers and Babies: A Social History of Childbirth and Child Care Hospitals in Nineteenth-Century New York City* (New York: Garland, 1989), 59–60; see also the obituary of Cornelius Du Bois in the *New York Times,* May 6, 1882. On Edward Delafield, see the obituary in the *New York Times,* February 15, 1875; Howard Kelly and Walter Burrage, *Dictionary of American Medical Biography* (New York: Appleton, 1928). For Delafield's association with the nursery, see NCH, annual reports, 1875, 25; 1886, 32. For his association with the NYIA, see NYIA, minutes, March 27, 1865.

99. For the Litchfield Female Academy, known also as Miss Pierce's School, see Kerber, *Women of the Republic,* chap. 7; Kathryn Kish Sklar, *Catharine Beecher: A Study in American Domesticity* (New York: W.W. Norton, 1976), 15–19.

100. Charter, Nursery for the Children of Poor Women, 1854, [3].

101. Du Bois, "Thirty Years," 15. Du Bois does not name the physician, but he was probably George T. Elliot, with whom she consulted as she planned the nursery, and who later worked there with her. Elliot wrote that the Nursery and Child's Hospital "originated in a conversation in my office with Mrs. Du Bois." *Medical Record* 3, 1868, 427.

102. For the affiliation of Anna Emmet (and also the wife of Dr. George T.

Elliot—her own name is not listed) with the Lying-In Asylum, see Barbara Berg, *The Remembered Gate: The Origins of American Feminism; The Woman and the City, 1800–1860* (New York: Oxford University Press, 198), 235–36; *Valentine's Manual,* 1857, 277; James J. Walsh, *History of Medicine in New York: Three Centuries of Medical Progress* (New York: National Americana Society), 1919, 825–26. *Valentine's Manual* for 1857 lists other organizations that adhere to this pattern, including the Association for the Relief of Respectable Aged and Indigent Females, 276; Association for the Benefit of Colored Orphans, 282–82; Colored Home, 282; and the Magdalen Female Benevolent Asylum, 287–88.

103. For "coverture," the English common law imported to America that subsumed a married woman's civil identity beneath that of her husband, see Kerber, *Women of the Republic,* 139–55. For married women's property acts, see Marylynn Salmon, *Women and the Law of Property in Early America* (Chapel Hill: University of North Carolina Press, 1986). For the persistence of legal inequities in marriage into the twentieth century, see Nancy Cott, *The Grounding of Modern Feminism* (New Haven, CT: Yale University Press, 1987), 186. These acts were, in fact, part of a broader liberalization of family law in the nineteenth century; see Grossberg, *Governing the Hearth.*

104. I primarily owe this interpretation of the empowering role of charities on the women who ran them to Kathleen D. McCarthy; see "Women, Politics, Philanthropy: Some Historical Origins of the Welfare State" in *The Liberal Persuasion: Arthur Schlesinger, Jr., and the Challenge of the American Past,* ed. John Patrick Diggins (Princeton, NJ: Princeton University Press, 1997. See also Mary Ryan, *Cradle of the Middle Class: The Family in Oneida County, New York, 1790–1865* (Cambridge: Cambridge University Press, 1981). For New York's willingness to fund private charities, including religious ones, see Folks, *Care of Destitute, Neglected, and Delinquent Children,* chap. 7.

105. For the move to the new Lexington Avenue buildings, see NCH, annual report, 1858, 2.

106. For the wet nurses' placement service, see "Rules in Relation to Wet Nurses Employed by the Nursery," NCH, annual report, 1854, 13–16. For the dispensary and servants' school, see NCH, annual report, 1859, 3.

107. On the nursery's initial refusal to admit illegitimates and Du Bois's change of heart, see Du Bois, "Thirty Years," 20; "Petition of the First Directress of the Nursery and Child's Hospital," NCH, annual report, 1868, [20].

108. NCH, annual report, 1879, 7.

109. For the councilmen's field trip to the nursery, see Councilmen's Foundling Report, 4.

110. For the London Foundling Hospital's reception process, see Françoise Barret-Ducrocq, *Love in the Time of Victoria: Sexuality, Class and Gender in Nineteenth-Century London,* trans. John Howe (London: Verso, 1991); John R.

Gillis, "Servants, Sexual Relations and the Risks of Illegitimacy in London, 1901–1900," *Feminist Studies* 5, no. 1 (1979): 142–69; McClure, *Coram's Children,* 76–78, 139–44; R. B. Outhwaite, " 'Objects of Charity': Petitions to the London Foundling Hospital," *Eighteenth-Century Studies* 32 (1999): 497–510; Bernd Weisbrod "How to Become a Good Foundling in Early Victorian London," *Social History* 10 (May 1985): 198–203. Weisbrod describes this entrance process as a kind of symbolic "commitment ceremony." For another look at the role of ritual in reintegrating fallen women, see Joan Jacobs Brumberg, " 'Ruined' Girls: Changing Community Responses to Illegitimacy in Upstate New York, 1890–1920," *Journal of Social History* 18 (Winter 1984): 246–72.

111. NCH, annual report, 1880, 7. See also "Petition," NCH, annual report, 1868, 22–23.

112. Alice Barlow, NCH, annual report, 1866, 6; Mary Du Bois, "Petition," NCH, annual report, 1868, 23.

113. Councilmen's Foundling Report, 4–5.

114. For Halliday's testimony, see ibid., 6; for Reese's, see ibid., 4.

115. Ibid., 7–8.

116. Mary Cullough's name sometimes appears as "Carlock," which is probably how it was pronounced. I am presuming that her name was Cullough.

117. "Murder of the Innocents," *New York Tribune,* February 5, 1859.

118. "How the Alms-House Children Are Reared," *Harper's Weekly,* February 19, 1859, 117.

119. "The Murder of the Innocents. Defense of the Governors," *New York Tribune,* February 9, 1859. The doctor's name is given as Bibbins, Bevins, and Beviss. I chose Bevins as the most likely possibility.

120. "The Murder of the Innocents," *New York Tribune,* February 9, 1859. For Halliday's account of his and Mott's delivery of their report, see Halliday, *Little Street Sweeper,* 156.

121. "The Murder of the Innocents," *New York Tribune,* February 9, 1859. The "Hall" referred to here is city hall.

122. "The Slaughter of the Innocents," *New York Times,* February 17, 1859. On city patronage jobs in New York in the 1840s and 1850s, see Spann, *New Metropolis,* 350–51. Cullough was subsequently tried and convicted; see "New York as Murderer," *Harper's Weekly,* March 5, 1859.

123. "Foundling Babies. How They Are Cared For," *New York Times,* February 14, 1859.

124. Ibid.; "The Foundlings of the City. Munificent Charity of New-York," *New York Tribune,* February 14, 1859.

125. "The Murder of the Innocents," *New York Tribune,* February 9, 1859. The *Tribune* printed the epithet as "the d–d black b–h."

126. Ibid.

127. Ibid.

128. "How the Alms-House Children Are Reared," *Harper's Weekly,* February 19, 1859, 117. Thomas Nast, who worked for *Harper's,* drew many simian-ized Irishmen, but he joined the magazine in 1860, so this drawing, which is un-signed, is probably not by him. For a longer treatment of this theme, see L. Perry Curtis, Jr., *Apes and Angels: The Irishman in Victorian Caricature* (Washington, DC: Smithsonian Institution Press, 1971), especially 94–108. For the "gorilla craze" of the 1860s see Curtis, *Apes and Angels,* 99; Browne, *Charles Darwin,* 156–60.

129. "The Foundlings of the City," *New York Tribune,* February 14, 1859; "The Slaughter of the Innocents," *New York Times,*" February 17, 1859; "New York as a Nursing Mother," *Harper's Weekly,* February 26, 1859, 130.

130. "The Infants' Home. Laying of the Corner Stone—Address by Rev. H. E. Montgomery," *New York Times,* December 29, 1859.

131. On the reorganization of the almshouse department, see *Sub-Agency History Record,* Human Resources Administration, Municipal Reference and Research Library. On the foundlings' move into the almshouse, see PCC, annual report, 1860, 6; Folks, *Care of Destitute, Neglected, and Delinquent Children,* 22. Folks guesses that the babies were returned to the almshouse between 1863 and 1866, but the new department's first annual reports pin the date down clearly as the second half of 1860. For Isaac Townsend's death, see "Death of Mr. Isaac Townsend," *New York Evening Post,* April 2, 1860. For Mary Du Bois's recollection of him, see NCH, annual report, 1879, 9.

132. On Du Bois's retirement, see NCH, annual reports, 1861, 9–10 (the text of her "farewell letter"); 1865, 7.

133. Strong, *Diary,* vol. 2, pp. 263–64.

134. Abraham Jacobi, "In Re the Nursery and Child's Hospital," in Golden, ed., *Infant Asylums,* 166.

135. The complaints of Du Bois's accusers and her own reply are in Du Bois's handwriting in a document titled "Mrs. Van Buren charge 1855." New York Nursery and Child's Hospital Records, New-York Historical Society.

136. On neurasthenia, see Barbara Sicherman, "The Uses of a Diagnosis: Doctors, Patients and Neurasthenia," in Leavitt and Numbers, eds., *Sickness and Health*; Carroll Smith-Rosenberg, "The Hysterical Woman: Sex Roles and Role Conflict in Nineteenth-Century America," in Smith-Rosenberg, *Disorderly Conduct*; Jean Strouse, *Alice James: A Biography* (Boston: Houghton Mifflin, 1980), 103–6.

137. Strong, *Diary,* vol.2, 264; NCH, annual report, 1861, 6.

138. PCC, annual report, 1863, viii; NCH, annual reports, 1863, 7; 1865, 3, 4.

139. George Fitzhugh, "Our Athenian Friend," *Debow's Agricultural, Commercial, Industrial Progress and Resources* 29, no. 1 (July 1860): 88.

140. [H. F. James], *Abolitionism Unvailed!* (New York: T. V. Paterson,

1850), advertised in "Editor's Department, New Books," *De Bow's Review* 8 (April, 1850): 406.

141. Du Bois, "Thirty Years," 20.

NOTES TO CHAPTER 4

1. NCH, annual report, 1876, 8–9. For Du Bois's return to the nursery, see NCH, annual report, 1865.

2. NCH, annual report, 1866, 5–6.

3. NCH, annual report, 1876, 9.

4. NCH, annual report, 1866, 12.

5. NCH, annual reports, 1875, "Rules for the Lying-in Wards," 41–42; 1880, 6; 1885, 10; "Rules of Admission." On pay rates for domestic servants, see Virginia Penny, *The Employments of Women: A Cyclopaedia of Women's Work* (Boston: Walker, Wise and Co., 1863), 424–26.

6. NCH, annual reports, 1869, 7; 1876, 10.

7. NCH, annual report, 1879, 7; NYFA, biennial report, 1869–71, [1].

8. NYIA, annual report, 1872, 11; Moses King, *King's Handbook of New York City* (Boston: Moses King, 1892), 402; David T. Valentine, *Manual of the Corporation of the City of New York for 1860* (New York, 1860), 342 (hereafter cited as *Valentine's Manual*); James J. Walsh, *History of Medicine in New York: Three Centuries of Medical Progress* (New York: National Americana Society, 1919), 827.

9. For Smith, see Gert Brieger, "Stephen Smith: Surgeon and Reformer" (Ph.D. diss., Johns Hopkins University, 1971); Eric Homburger, *Scenes from the Life of a City: Corruption and Conscience in Old New York* (New Haven, CT: Yale University Press, 1994), 67–85.

10. For Hoffman and Keyser, see NYIA, minutes, May 12, June 27, 1865; Feb 28, 1870; May 12, 1871; for Tweed, see May 12, 1865. Hoffman resigned from the board on June 27, 1865. Keyser was still serving on May 12, 1871. For more on the Tammany members, see "A Foundling Asylum for New-York —The Project of the Grand Jury," *New York Times*, March 7, 1868. For Keyser as "plumbing tycoon," see Alexander B. Callow, *The Tweed Ring* (New York: Oxford University Press, 1966), 194.

11. The Tweed Ring, named for William Magear Tweed (1823–1878), its central figure, is the synonym for political corruption in nineteenth-century New York City. Centered on Tammany Hall, a political club affiliated with the Democratic Party, the Tweed Ring gathered votes through bribery and violence and its members lined their pockets with money obtained through graft. Members of the Tweed Ring were first active in the 1850s, and held a variety of public offices in New York city and state government. Tweed himself was briefly a U.S. Congressman. In 1871 the Tweed Ring, pursued by a group of reformers known

as the Committee of Seventy, was exposed in the pages of the *New York Times* and brought down. Its members were arrested or fled the country; Tweed himself died in jail.

The Tweed Ring derailed democracy and stole millions from the city. Still, because of its relationship with ordinary working men, on whom it relied for votes and to whom it provided jobs, members of the Tweed Ring were generally more responsive to the needs of working people and the poor than reform leaders were, as their relationship with the city's foundling asylums demonstrates. See Callow, *Tweed Ring*; Homburger, *Scenes from the Life of a City*, 141–211; James D. McCabe, Jr., *Lights and Shadows of New York Life; or, the Sights and Sensations of the Great City* (Philadelphia: National Publishing Co., 1872; reprint, New York: Farrar, Straus and Giroux, 1970), 75–117.

12. Woodlawn is variously described as being on 104th Street and 105th Street. It appears to have previously been the Strawberry Hill Hotel; see print from *Valentine's Manual*, 1856, in the collection of the Museum of the City of New York. I am grateful to Andrew Dolkart for his help finding out about Woodlawn. For death statistics, see NYIA, minutes, December 15, 1865. Coments of Elisha Harris are in "Medical Society of the County of New York, Adjourned Meeting, Oct. 12, 1868," *Medical Record* 3, November 16, 1868, 426. For Smith's recollections, see "Address by Dr. Stephen Smith of the State Board of Charities," in NYIA, annual report, 1900.

13. NYIA, annual report, 1872, 11. Minutes, May 12, December 15, 1865; January 16, May 18, 1866. "Foundling Hospitals," letter to the editor from "One of the Trustees" of the New York Infant Asylum, *New York Times*, March 22, 1868, 5:5.

14. NYFA, "Souvenir of 1889," in NYFA, biennial report, 1888–90, 17.

15. "End of a Noble Nun. Sister Mary Irene Dies Here at an Advanced Age," unattributed newspaper clipping, Sisters of Charity Archives, Mount St. Vincent College, Bronx, NY; "Sister Irene Passes Away," *New York Tribune*, August 15, 1896; "Sister Mary Irene Dead," *New York Times*, August 15, 1896; NYFA, "Souvenir of 1889," 16–17. Letters addressed to Sister Irene by women—and others—abandoning babies are at the Archives of the New York Foundling Hospital.

16. For Catholic institutions, see Edwin G. Burrows and Mike Wallace, *Gotham: A History of New York City to 1898* (New York: Oxford University Press, 1999), 748–52; Jay Dolan, *The Immigrant Church: New York's Irish and German Catholics, 1815–1865* (Baltimore: Johns Hopkins University Press, 1975); Maureen Fitzgerald, *Habits of Compassion: Irish Catholic Nuns and the Origins of New York's Welfare System, 1830–1920* (Urbana: University of Illinois Press, 2006); Fitzgerald, 'The Perils of 'Passion and Poverty': Women Religious and the Care of Single Women in New York City, 1845–1890," *United*

States Catholic Historian 10 (1991): 45–58. One of the most important Catholic charitable institutions, the Roman Catholic Orphan Asylum, was founded in 1817, thus predating the wave.

17. For religious competition, see, e.g., Diane Ravitch, *The Great School Wars: New York City, 1805–1973; A History of the Public Schools as a Battlefield of Social Change* (New York: Basic Books, 1974).

18. Two unsigned letters in the handwriting of Mary Du Bois, one headed "To the Editor of the New York Freeman's Journal," 1856, and an unsigned draft ms. headed "Mrs. Du Bois's hand." NYNCH Records, New-York Historical Society. Duplication of "which" is in the original.

19. Diary, Sister Teresa Vincent McCrystal, 1869, Sisters of Charity Archives, Mount St. Vincent College. The Sisters of St. Joseph, another American Catholic order, while it did not open any foundling asylums, also admitted infants and abandoned babies to its orphanages. See Carol Coburn and Martha Smith, *Spirited Lives: How Nuns Shaped Catholic Culture and American Life, 1836–1920* (Chapel Hill: University of North Carolina Press, 1999), 207, 208, 211, 214.

20. For antebellum religious charity, see Mary Ryan, *Cradle of the Middle Class: The Family in Oneida County, New York, 1790–1865* (Cambridge: Cambridge University Press, 1981); for the involvement of the federal government by the twentieth century, see Theda Skocpol, *Protecting Soldiers and Mothers: The Political Origins of Social Policy in the United States* (Cambridge, MA: Harvard University Press, 1992).

21. See SCAA, annual report, 1904, 10–11.

22. NCH, annual report, 1879, 9.

23. For the NYFA's reception cradle, see "The Foundling Asylum: One of New York's Most Noble Charities," *New York Herald,* March 4, 1871; "The Little Waifs: The Opening of the New Foundling Asylum," *New York Herald,* October 22, 1873; "History of a Cradle: A Visit to the Foundling Asylum of New York City," *Moline (Illinois) Dispatch and Chimes,* February 8, 1889.

24. Helen Campbell, *Darkness and Daylight: or, Lights and Shadows of New York Life: A Woman's Narrative of Mission and Rescue Work in Tough Places . . . The Whole Portraying Life in Darkest New York by Day and by Night* (Hartford, CT: A. D. Worthington and Co., 1891), 382–83.

25. Admissions Book, 1869–92, NYFH Archives; NYFA biennial report, 1869–71, 10–11. For the 1875 figure, see "Foundling Asylum, Yesterday's Musical Matinee," *New York Herald,* November 11, 1875.

26. NYFA, biennial report, 1869–71, 8. In 1871 the Sisters reported about one hundred children in the asylum and seven hundred more nursing out; see "The Foundling Asylum: What It Has Been Doing," *New York Herald,* November 11, 1871.

27. For the NYFA's founding and early years, see NYFA, "Souvenir of 1889," in NYFA, biennial report, 1888–90.

28. NYFA, biennial report, 1869–71, 4.

29. For an interpretation of the London Foundling Hospital's admissions rules, see Bernd Weisbrod, "How to Become a Good Foundling in Early Victorian London," *Social History* 10 (May 1985): 193–209.

30. NYFA, biennial report, 1871–72, 7; see also 1879–81, 14.

31. See Janet Golden, *A Social History of Wet Nursing in America: From Breast to Bottle* (Cambridge: Cambridge University Press, 1996). Wet nursing was never as widely used in the United States as it was, for instance, in France; see George D. Sussman, *Selling Mothers' Milk: The Wet-Nursing Business in France, 1715–1914* (Urbana: University of Illinois Press, 1982).

32. NCH, annual report, 1859, 7.

33. NYFA, biennial report, 1879–81, 18. For widowers and angry fathers, see the volumes of letters left with babies, NYFH archives.

34. See the volumes of letters left with babies, NYFH Archives, some of which are from fathers and married parents, particularly abandoned wives, and widows.

35. NYFA, biennial report, 1869–71, 8, 9.

36. Jacob Riis, *How the Other Half Lives* (New York: Charles Scribner's Sons, 1890; reprint, New York: Dover Books, 1971), 146.

37. NYFA, "Souvenir of 1889," 23; biennial report, 1888–90, 9.

38. *Daily Graphic,* March 14, 1873, 3–4; May 25, 1885; see also "Poor Little Waifs!" *New York Herald,* January 16, 1872.

39. NYFA, biennial report, 1869–71, 9, 13.

40. For the Ladies' Society, see NYFA, biennial report, 1869–71, 17–18, 20; "The Hospital for Foundlings," *Frank Leslie's Illustrated Weekly,* December 25, 1869, 219; "The Foundling Asylum, One of New York's Most Noble Charities," *New York Herald,* March 4, 1871; "The Foundling Asylum, First Monthly Meeting of the Board of Managers," *New York Herald,* October 11, 1876; "The New York Foundling Asylum," *New York Herald,* October 17, 1877.

41. Obituary, Richard Barrett Connolly, *New York Herald,* June 1, 1880; Homburger, *Scenes from the Life of a City,* 141–211; McCabe, *Lights and Shadows,* 105–6.

42. "Obituary. Richard Barrett Connolly," *New York Herald,* June 1, 1880; Homburger, *Scenes from the Life,* 150.

43. Homburger, *Scenes from the Life of a City,* 151, 185; Edith Wharton, *The Age of Innocence* (New York: Simon and Schuster, 1996), 33.

44. Mrs. R. B. Connolly to Sister Irene, December 8, 1869, 1870, NYFH Records, Sisters of Charity Archives; "The Asylum for Foundlings, Munificent Subscription to the Fund—A Lady's Work in the Cause," *New York Herald,*

December 5, 1869. The "lady" referred to in the title of the article was the wife of John Fox, a minor Tweed Ring figure; see Callow, *Tweed Ring,* 23.

45. Alexander Bond, AFV, no. 106, December 6, 1859. For Ely Jr.'s gift, see "The Asylum for Foundlings. Munificent Subscription to the Fund—A Lady's Work in the Cause," *New York Herald,* December 5, 1869. Smith Ely was mayor of New York 1877–79.

46. Mrs. R. B. Connolly to Sister Irene, February 8, 1870.

47. NYFA, biennial report, 1869–71, 28; NYFA, "Souvenir of 1889," 21; "The Foundling Asylum, Returns for the Institution from the Late Fair," *New York Herald,* February 12, 1871, 3:2; Fitzgerald, "Passion and Poverty," 52.

48. Mary Du Bois, "Thirty Years Experience in Hospital Work," in *Infant Asylums and Children's Hospitals: Medical Dilemmas and Developments, 1850–1920: An Anthology of Sources,* ed. Janet Golden (New York: Garland, 1989), 21; J. B. Wald, Mayor's Office to Erastus Brooks, June 9, 1865, NYNCH Records, New-York Historical Society.

49. *Dictionary of American Biography,* s.v. "Erastus Brooks (Jan.31, 1815–Nov.25,1886)"; "Erastus Brooks Dead," *New York Herald,* November 26, 1886; "A Veteran Editor Gone," *New York Times,* November 26, 1886. Brooks was also the co-editor, with his brother James, of the *New York Express,* 1843–77. For his assistance to the nursery with state funds, see "Petition of the First Directress of the Nursery and Child's Hospital, in behalf of the Board of Managers, praying that the State Convention, in regulating the charities of the State, will consider the claims for a Foundling Hospital," 1868, NCH, annual report, 1868, and in NYNCH Records, New-York Historical Society, where the document is identified as no. 37. Concerning an earlier petition, see Erastus Brooks to Mrs. Du Bois, April 19, 1856. For his roles at other NCH events, see "Address of the Hon. Erastus Brooks at the Laying of the Cornerstone of the Nursery and Child's Hospital, in the City of New-York, June 22, 1957" and "Inauguration of the Nursery and Child's Hospital, Address of Erastus Brooks," in NYNCH Records, New-York Historical Society; "The Infant's Home. Laying of the Corner Stone," *New York Times,* December 29, 1859. For his role as an advisor, see NCH, annual report, list of officers, n.p.

50. For "Rat Brooks," see George Templeton Strong, *Diary of George Templeton Strong,* ed. Allan Nevins and Milton Halsey Thomas (New York: Octagon Books, 1974), vol. 3, p. 256; On Du Bois's party, see vol. 2, pp. 302–3.

51. James L. Crouthamel, *Bennett's New York Herald and the Rise of the Popular Press* (Syracuse, NY: Syracuse University Press, 1989), 151.

52. "Foundlings. The Hospital for Foundlings in East Twelfth Street—How It Was Established by the Sisters of Charity and How It Is Succeeding—The Innocent Little 'Anonymas' of the Great Metropolis—A Work for the Charitable," *New York Herald,* November 22, 1869.

53. "Poor Little Waifs! The Foundling Asylum," *New York Herald*, January 16, 1872.

54. "The Foundling Asylum, One of New York's Most Noble Charities," *New York Herald*, March 4, 1871.

55. "New York Foundlings: How the Little Ones are Cared For in the Asylum—Kindly Treatment, Good Nursing and Elementary Instruction," *New York Herald*, May 22, 1881. For more from the *Herald* on the foundling asylum, see "A Haven for the Innocent Waifs," November 13, 1869; "Foundlings: The Hospital for Foundlings," November 22, 1869; "The Asylum for Foundlings," December 5, 1869; "The Foundling Asylum," February 12, 1871; "The New York Foundling Asylum: Its Good Work," December 21, 1871; "The New Foundling Asylum of the Sisters of Charity," October 19, 1873; "The Foundling Asylum," October 16, 1874; "The Foundlings: A Field Day among Humanity's Waifs," December 3, 1874; "The Foundling Asylum," October 11, 1876; "The New York Foundling Asylum," October 17, 1877; "Foundling Asylum Reception," May 12, 1878; "The Foundlings' Home," April 1, 1883; "Religion for the Waifs: The New Chapel for the Foundling Asylum Dedicated," October 21, 1884; "Children of the State: Little Inmates of the Foundling Asylum Who Grow Up to Be Citizens," October 30, 1887. This is just a selection. The *Herald* was not the only publication that reported admiringly on the Foundling Asylum; see, e.g., "The Hospital for Foundlings," *Frank Leslie's Illustrated Newspaper*, December 25, 1869; Herbert W. Burdett, "Institution Life. I. Foundling Asylum," *Illustrated American*, May 17, 1890, 308–10.

56. "The Foundling Asylum: A Glimpse into Its Workings," *New York Tribune*, June 10, 1883. For the new maternity hospital and projected children's hospital, see NYFA, biennial report, 1881–82, 7–8.

57. "A Foundling Hospital for New York—The Project of the Grand Jury," *New York Times*, March 7, 1868; "Foundling Hospitals," letter to the editor from "One of the Trustees," *New York Times*, March 22, 1868. For more on the grand jury and the Infant Asylum's responsibilities, see Stephen Rogers, "Neglected Causes of Infant Mortality in New York," *Medical Record*, September 14, 1868, 345.

58. NYIA, minutes, February 28, 1870.

59. "The Foundlings," *Harper's Weekly*, December 23, 1871. The "Appeal" and "Statement" are bound together with the NYIA, annual report, 1872, at the New York Weill Cornell Medical Center Archives. Both the "Appeal" and "Statement" are undated. The "Appeal" is unsigned; the "Statement" is signed by physicians E. R. Peaslee, Isaac E. Taylor, B. Fordyce Barker, James Anderson, Joel Foster, Alfred Underhill, H. D. Bulkeley, Stephen Smith, S. T. Hubbard, Job Lewis Smith, and Elisha Harris. On Smith's probable authorship, see minutes of the NYIA's board for April 18, 1871, which report that Smith read a paper on foundling hospitals that was approved by the board and ordered to be signed by

physicians, printed, and sent with circulars calling the public to the meeting to be held at Association Hall on April 27.

60. "Aid for Helpless Infants: Meeting at Association Hall to Organize an Infant Asylum and Foundling Institute," *New York Herald,* April 28, 1871; "The New York Infant Asylum: The Reorganization," [April 28, 1871], unattributed clipping at Sisters of Charity Archives, Mount St. Vincent College.

61. NYIA, annual report, 1872, 12.

62. PCC, 1870, 267. In the nineteenth century the United States lacked the kind of centralized systems for gathering vital statistics that were common in Europe. New York City law had required the registration of marriages and births since 1847, but, as the Metropolitan Board of Health complained in 1866, reporting was irregular. The birth certificate form used by the city had no space in which to record illegitimacy; see Metropolitan Board of Health, annual report, 1866, appendix C, p. 8. In 1860 the City Inspector complained that all birth records were inaccurate "owing to the neglect of physicians, clergymen, and others, to report"; *Valentine's Manual,* 1860, 245. As late as 1920 New York City still did not require registration of information about illegitimate births; see Emma O. Lundberg and Katherine F. Lenroot, *Illegitimacy as a Child Welfare Problem* (Washington, DC: United States Department of Labor, Children's Bureau, 1920), 19.

63. Ruth McClure, *Coram's Children: The London Foundling Hospital in the Eighteenth Century* (New Haven, CT: Yale University Press, 1981), 19; "Statement," 6. "Foundling Left at Dr. Foster's Door," NYIA, Admissions Book, Children, 1871–77, volume 87c, entry no. 496, May 7, 1875.

64. "The Foundlings: A Field Day among Humanity's Waifs," *New York Herald,* December 3, 1874. For black babies at the New York Foundling Asylum, see also Daniel Connolly, "New-York Foundlings," *Appleton's Journal,* August 17, 1872, 184. Connolly estimated that approximately two-thirds of the children admitted were "of non-Catholic parentage." The "little Jewess" is in the NYFA's first admissions book, no. 13, November 3, 1869, NYFH Archives.

65. "The Foundling Asylum: One of New York's Most Noble Charities," *New York Herald,* March 4, 1871.

66. "Aid for Helpless Infants," *New York Herald,* April 28, 1871; "Appeal," 2, 5.

67. Margaret L. Arnott, "Infant Death, Child Care and the State: The Baby-Farming Scandal and the First Infant Life Protection Legislation of 1872," *Continuity and Change* 9 (1994): 271–311; Lionel Rose, *Massacre of the Innocents: Infanticide in Great Britain, 1800–1939* (London: Routledge and Kegan Paul, 1986), 93–114. For a similar French statute, the Roussel law of 1873, which regulated wet nursing, see Alisa Klaus, *Every Child a Lion: The Origins of Maternal and Infant Health Policy in the United States and France* (Ithaca, NY: Cornell University Press, 1993), 56–57.

68. "Slaughter of the Innocents, Baby Farming in England—A Description of the Business—Some Startling Statements," *New York Times,* August 20, 1871; "Slaughter of the Innocents," *New York Times,* August 6, 1874.

69. "Statement," 4, 5; see also "Appeal," 2; Homburger, *Scenes from the Life of a City,* 105–8.

70. NYIA, annual report, 1873, 11.

71. "An Act to Incorporate the New York Infant Asylum," March 11, 1865, amended April 18, 1872. For babies at the door, see NYIA, annual report, 1873, [15]. For "children off their hands," see NYIA, minutes, February 20, 1872.

72. NYIA, annual reports, 1873, 16; 1875, [13]; 1877, 13.

73. For domestic servants' inability to keep their children, see Faye E. Dudden, *Serving Women: Household Service in Nineteenth-Century America* (Middletown, CT: Wesleyan University Press, 1983), 205–7. For the sexual vulnerability of servants, see John R. Gillis, "Servants, Sexual Relations and the Risks of Illegitimacy in London, 1901–1900," *Feminist Studies* 5, no. 1 (1979): 142–69. For a contemporary alternative vision of the kind of work women could do, see Penny, *Employments of Women.*

74. NYIA, minutes, November 19, 1872 (purchase of the 61st Street house). NYIA, annual reports, 1873, 15–16; 1875, 10–11; 1878, 9–13; 1880, 29–30.

75. NYIA, annual report, 1875, 27.

76. For the network of social services created by women in antebellum America, see Lori Ginzberg, *Women and the Work of Benevolence: Morality, Politics, and Class in the Nineteenth-Century United States* (New Haven, CT: Yale University Press, 1990); Nancy Hewitt, *Women's Activism and Social Change: Rochester, New York, 1822–1872* (Ithaca, NY: Cornell University Press, 1984); Mary Ryan, *Cradle of the Middle Class: The Family in Oneida County, New York, 1790–1865* (Cambridge: Cambridge University Press, 1981).

77. For the lady managers and their role, see NYIA, minutes, May 18, 1866 (when the board of lady managers was first proposed); March 8, 1871; June 8, 1871; November 28, 1871.

78. Margaret Hope Bacon, *Abby Hopper Gibbons: Prison Reformer and Social Activist* (Albany: State University of New York Press, 2000); Lydia Maria Child, *Isaac T. Hopper: A True Life* (Boston: John P. Jewett), 1853; Sarah Hopper Emerson, *Life of Abby Hopper Gibbons, Told Chiefly through Her Correspondence* (New York: G. P. Putnam's Sons, 1897); Lori Ginzberg, " 'Moral Suasion Is Moral Balderdash': Women, Politics, and Social Activism," *Journal of American History* 73 (December 1986): 601–22; Estelle Freedman, *Their Sisters' Keepers: Women's Prison Reform in America, 1830–1930* (Ann Arbor: University of Michigan Press, 1981), 24–30; 35; Timothy Gilfoyle, *City of Eros: New York City, Prostitution, and the Commercialization of Sex, 1790–1920* (New York: W. W. Norton, 1992), 185.

79. Bacon, *Abby Hopper Gibbons,* xi; Emerson, *Life of Abby Hopper Gibbons,* vol. 1, pp. 151–52, 252; Freedman, *Sisters' Keepers,* 35.

80. On Gibbons' vice-presidency of the ladies' board, see NYIA, minutes, June 8, 1871. Her appointment to the house committee on May 30, 1873, is recorded in a note in the back of her New York Infant Asylum journal, Manuscripts Division, New York Public Library.

81. Gibbons journal, February 14, 1878.

82. Ibid.

83. For Anna Angell, see Regina Markell Morantz-Sanchez, *Sympathy and Science: Women Physicians in American Medicine* (New York: Oxford University Press, 1985), 146. For Angell's career at the New York Infant Asylum, see NYIA, annual reports, lists of personnel, 1877 and 1878.

84. Emerson, *Life of Abby Hopper Gibbons,* vol. 1, pp. 202–3.

85. Freedman, *Sisters' Keepers,* 7, 11–13, 14; Michael Grossberg, *Governing the Hearth: Law and the Family in Nineteenth Century America* (Chapel Hill: University of North Carolina Press, 1985), 173. For overzealous, wrongful arrests of women as prostitutes, see Marilynn Wood Hill, *Their Sisters' Keepers: Prostitution in New York City, 1830–1870* (Berkeley: University of California Press, 1993), 117–18.

86. *New York Tribune,* June 19, 1845. This article is unsigned, but Estelle Freedman identifies it as Fuller's; see Freedman, *Sister's Keepers,* 31.

87. For the Gibbons's visits to Long Island Farms and Randall's Island, see Emerson, *Life of Abby Hopper Gibbons,* vol. 1, pp. 134–35, 187–88, 244; Mary E. Dewey, *The Life and Letters of Catharine M. Sedgwick* (New York: Harper and Bros., 1871), 420–21. See also AH, annual report, 1855, 108; PCC, annual reports, 1876, 121; 1881, 71.

88. Louisa May Alcott, *Selected Letters of Louisa May Alcott,* ed. Joel Myerson and Daniel Shealy (Athens: University of Georgia Press, 1987), 210.

89. The *Tribune* reporter's observations are in "The Christian Festival, Christmas Cheer in New-York," *New York Tribune,* December 27, 1875, 5.

90. Louisa May Alcott, "A New Way to Spend Christmas," *Youth's Companion,* March 9, 1876, 76.

91. Alcott, *Selected Letters,* 212.

92. Ibid; Louisa May Alcott, *The Journals of Louisa May Alcott,* ed. Joel Myerson and Daniel Shealy (Athens: University of Georgia Press, 1989), 197. For more impressions of this day, see Madeleine B. Stern, *Louisa May Alcott* (Norman: University of Oklahoma Press, 1950), 253–55; Emerson, *Life of Abby Hopper Gibbons,* vol. 1, p. 187.

93. Alcott, *Selected Letters,* 212; Alcott, *Journals,* 197.

94. Emerson, *Abby Hopper Gibbons,* vol. 1, pp. 180–82.

95. Bacon, *Abby Hopper Gibbons,* 25, 50, 74–79, 166; Emerson, *Life of Abby Hopper Gibbons,* vol. 1, pp. 139, 248.

96. "The Foundling Asylum: One of New York's Most Noble Charities," *New York Herald,* March 4, 1871; Campbell, *Darkness and Daylight,* 384.

97. Mary Du Bois to J. H. Anthon, [November or January] 16, [1856], NYNCH Records, New-York Historical Society.

98. PCC, annual reports, 1860, 6, 238; 1866, xvii–xviii.

99. Job Lewis Smith, "Hindrances to the Successful Treatment of the Diseases of Infancy and Childhood," *Transactions of the New York State Medical Association* 13 (1896): 95.

100. Harold K. Faber, "Job Lewis Smith, Forgotten Pioneer," *Journal of Pediatrics* 63 (1963): 797. Over the course of his career Smith, who became prominent in the emerging field of pediatrics, was affiliated with three out of New York's four foundling asylums: New York Infant Asylum, Nursery and Child's Hospital, and Randall's Island Infant Hospital.

101. PCC, annual report, 1866, viii.

102. For the categories of babies, see PCC, annual reports, 1866, 98; 1867, 385. For "walking children," see PCC, annual report, 1868, 334.

103. PCC, annual report, 1866, xviii.

104. Metropolitan Police, annual report, 1860–61, 102. In 1860–61 the police picked up 104 foundlings. In 1869 they reported that between 48 and 176 foundlings had been picked up annually from 1864 to 1869; see Metropolitan Police, annual report, 1869, 65. In 1887 the department's annual report estimated that no more than 30 percent of foundlings passed through the hands of the police. Police Department, annual report, 1887, 46.

105. On the Emigrant Hospital, see PCC, annual report, 1866, "Report of Arbitrators," 410–23; 1868, 311–12, 346.

106. PCC, annual report, 1866, 102.

107. PCC, annual report, 1867, 24–25.

108. Susan M. Reverby, *Ordered to Care: The Dilemma of American Nursing, 1850–1945* (Cambridge: Cambridge University Press, 1987).

109. PCC, annual report, 1867, 391–92; 1868, 308. On hospital patients, see Charles Rosenberg, *The Care of Strangers: The Rise of America's Hospital System* (New York: Basic Books, 1987).

110. PCC, annual report, 1868, [307], 340.

111. PCC, annual report, 1867, 24; 1868, 23. The commissioners reported that of the 1,535 babies that passed through the Infant Department in 1867 (191 remaining from the previous year and 1,344 admitted in 1867), 1,237 (81 percent) died. Of the 1,535, 928 were specifically identified as "nurse children." Children who entered on their own were designated "nurse children" and included as foundlings. PCC, annual report, 1867, 302, 385.

112. Rogers, "Neglected Causes," 342.

113. PCC, annual report, 1868, 308, 346.

114. PCC, annual report, 1866, 200–201; 1868, 314. Appendix C of the

1866 report lists a different set of figures. Since the author of this appendix, Dr. J. Bayley Done, remarks that his information is "imperfect" and the records he was working with incomplete, I have chosen to use the figures presented by warden James Owens on p. 201. All figures from city departments in this period of great corruption in city government must be viewed skeptically.

115. PCC, annual report, 1866, 103.

116. PCC, annual report, 1868, 328–29.

117. Ibid., 348–49.

118. PCC, annual reports, 1868, 339; 1869, [115].

119. *Medical Record,* November 16, 1868, 427.

120. PCC, annual report, 1866, 100.

121. In 1869 the commissioners reported that the Infant Hospital had been under construction for the previous two years and was "partially completed"; PCC, annual report, 1869, 13.

122. For the move, see PCC, annual report, 1869, 117. For the cows, see page 493.

123. For the ages of the nurseries' children, see PCC, annual report, 1868, 24; J. F. Richmond, *New York and Its Institutions, 1609–1871* (New York: E. B. Treat, 1871), 563.

124. Richmond, *New York and Its Institutions,* 564.

125. PCC, annual report, 1869, 122–23.

126. On miasma and disease, see John Duffy, *From Humors to Medical Science: A History of American Medicine* (Urbana: University of Illinois Press, 1993), 169–70; Richard A. Meckel, *Save the Babies: American Public Health Reform and the Prevention of Infant Mortality, 1850–1929* (Baltimore: Johns Hopkins University Press, 1990), 15–16; Charles Rosenberg, *The Cholera Years: The United States in 1832, 1849, and 1866* (Chicago: University of Chicago Press), 1987, 199–200; Rosenberg, *Care of Strangers,* 160.

127. PCC, annual report, 1871, 203–4.

128. PCC, annual report, 1869, 268.

129. PCC, annual report, 1870, 202.

130. Abraham Jacobi, *The Raising and Education of Abandoned Children in Europe, with Statistics and General Remarks on that Subject* (New York: Bellevue Hospital Printing Office, 1870), 40–41.

131. PCC, annual report, 1875, xx.

132. For the city's use of pauper labor, see McCabe, *Lights and Shadows,* 631–47; for cabbages growing in the almshouse garden on Blackwell's Island, see illustration, p. 637. For inmates at work, see, e.g., PCC, annual reports, 1869, 261, 313–15, 436–37, 454–56, 491–92, 495; 1875, xii.

133. PCC annual reports, 1869, 495 (Ward's Island farm); 1875, xxii (storekeeper).

134. PCC annual report, 1869, 436 (workhouse), 456 (penitentiary).

135. Rogers, "Neglected Causes." Dr. Rogers's criticisms touched off a volley of indignant responses from doctors associated with the Infant Department, including Abraham Jacobi, George T. Elliott, and Elisha Harris. See *Medical Record* 3 (1868): 404, 426, 464, 466, 499, 580. See also Russell Viner, "Healthy Children for a New World: Abraham Jacobi and the Making of American Pediatrics" (Ph.D. diss., Cambridge University, 1997), 237–40.

136. AH, annual report, 1855, x; "Presentation of a Flag to the Randall's Island Boys," *New York Tribune,* January 17, 1854; PCC, annual report, 1887, v–vi.

137. Richmond, *New York and Its Institutions,* 562.

138. Letters from New York, no. 29, Lydia Maria Child, *A Lydia Maria Child Reader,* ed. Carolyn L. Karcher (Durham, NC: Duke University Press, 1997), 319.

139. Dewey, *Catharine M. Sedgwick,* 421.

140. McCabe, *Lights and Shadows,* 299.

141. Ibid., 631.

142. Charles Dickens, *American Notes for General Circulation* (London: Penguin, 1972), 142. Dickens confuses Blackwell's Island with Long Island in this passage.

143. W. H. Rideing, "The Children's Island," *Appleton's Journal* 2 (January 10, 1874): 46–47.

NOTES TO CHAPTER 5

1. Russell Viner, "Healthy Children for a New World: Abraham Jacobi and the Making of American Pediatrics" (Ph.D. diss., Cambridge University, 1997).

2. Charles Rosenberg, "The Therapeutic Revolution: Medicine, Meaning, and Social Change in 19th-Century America"; Ronald L. Numbers and John Harley Warner, "The Maturation of American Medical Science," in *Sickness and Health in America: Readings in the History of Medicine and Public Health,* ed. Judith Walzer Leavitt and Ronald L. Numbers (Madison: University of Wisconsin Press, 1985).

3. For the antebellum web of social welfare institutions created by women, see Lori Ginzberg, *Women and the Work of Benevolence: Morality, Politics, and Class in the Nineteenth-Century United States* (New Haven, CT: Yale University Press, 1990); Mary Ryan, *Cradle of the Middle Class: The Family in Oneida County, New York, 1790–1865* (Cambridge: Cambridge University Press, 1981).

4. Unless otherwise noted, information on Jacobi comes chiefly from the work of Russell Viner: "Abraham Jacobi and German Medical Radicalism in Antebellum New York," *Bulletin of the History of Medicine* 3 (Fall 1998): 434–63; "Healthy Children for a New World"; "Early Social Medicine in New York

City: Abraham Jacobi and the German Community," *The Malloch Room Newsletter* (New York Academy of Medicine) 15 (Winter 1996); "Politics, Power, and Pediatrics," *Lancet* 355 (January 16, 1999): 232–34; talk at the New York Academy of Medicine, November 6, 1996. See also F. H. Garrison, "Dr. Abraham Jacobi," *Science,* August 1, 1919, 102–4; Abraham Jacobi, "Author's Preface," in Abraham Jacobi, *Collectanea Jacobi,* ed. William J. Robinson (New York: Critic and Guide Co., 1909).

5. Karl Marx and Friedrich Engels, *The Cologne Communist Trial,* trans. Rodney Livingstone (London: Lawrence and Wishart, 1971).

6. Abraham Jacobi, "Virchow as Citizen," *The Medical News,* October 19, 1901, 264.

7. Ibid.

8. Abraham Jacobi, *The Raising and Education of Abandoned Children in Europe, with Statistics and General Remarks on That Subject* (New York: Bellevue Hospital Printing Office, 1870), 26.

9. Jacobi, "Author's Preface," *Collectanea Jacobi,* vol. 1, p. 9.

10. For just a few examples of Jacobi's continuing social activism, see "Dr. Jacobi, in Visit to Court, Helps Woman Ill about to Be Evicted," *New York Herald,* June 3, 1902; Jacobi, "The Physical Cost of Women's Work," originally published 1907, in *Collectanea Jacobi,* vol. 8, pp. 415–26; Jacobi's introduction to William J. Robinson, *Fewer and Better Babies; or, The Limitation of Offspring by the Prevention of Conception* (New York: Critic and Guide Co., 1916).

11. NCH, annual report, 1886, 32.

12. Abraham Jacobi, "In Re the Nursery and Child's Hospital," in *Infant Asylums and Children's Hospitals: Medical Dilemmas and Developments, 1850–1920: An Anthology of Sources,* ed. Janet Golden (New York: Garland, 1989), 140.

13. For Jacobi's views on the effects of "soulless industrialism" on working women, and on the virtues of "good country air," see Abraham Jacobi, "The Physical Cost of Women's Work," in *Collectanea Jacobi,* vol. 8, pp. 415, 418–19. As a young man Jacobi read the work of such utopian socialists as Charles Fourier, who advocated the reorganization of work and social life in self-sufficient rural communes. But by the time of his involvement in the German revolution of 1848 Jacobi had rejected the utopian socialists and fallen in, instead, with Marx, who advocated a far more thorough reorganization of society. See Viner, *Healthy Children,* 28, 58; Charles Fourier, *The Utopian Vision of Charles Fourier,* ed. Jonathan Beecher and Richard Bienvenu (Boston: Beacon Press, 1971). The Fourierist vision was realized in the United States at Brook Farm in Massachusetts; see Henry W. Sams, ed., *Autobiography of Brook Farm* (Englewood Cliffs, NJ: Prentice-Hall, 1958).

14. For Jacobi's trip, see PCC, annual report, 1871, ix–x; Viner, "Healthy

Children," 240; Jacobi, *Raising and Education*; Jacobi, "In Re the Nursery and Child's Hospital," 158.

15. Jacobi, *Raising and Education.*

16. For the closing of the wheels, see Rachel Fuchs, *Abandoned Children: Foundlings and Child Welfare in Nineteenth-Century France* (Albany: State University of New York Press, 1984), 111; David Kertzer, *Sacrificed for Honor: Infant Abandonment and the Politics of Reproductive Control* (Boston: Beacon Press, 1993), 81, 154–61; R. Burr Litchfield and David Gordon, "Closing the Tour: A Close Look at the Marriage Market, Unwed Mothers, and Abandoned Children in Mid-Nineteenth Century Amiens," *Journal of Social History* 13 (Spring 1980): 458–73. For the transformation of European foundling hospitals into depots, see Jacobi, *Raising and Education,* 10–11, 41.

17. Jacobi found that death rates ranged from a low of 50 percent in St. Petersburg in 1830–33 to a high of 100 percent in Irkutsk (no date). The rates in Paris, Vienna, Madrid, Dublin, Brussels, Belgium as a whole, and Moscow ranged from 54 percent (Belgium, 1823–33) to 89 percent (Dublin, 1791–98); see Jacobi, *Raising and Education,* 32.

18. Ibid., 37.

19. Abraham Jacobi, "The Interdependence of the Upper and Lower Strata of Society in Fighting Disease," in *Collectanea Jacobi,* vol. 8, pp. 453, 454. Originally delivered as a speech in 1908.

20. Jacobi, *Raising and Education,* 37, 38, 41.

21. NYFA, biennial report, 1869–71, 9.

22. For France, see Nancy Fitch, "'*Les Petits Parisiens en Province*': The Silent Revolution in the Allier," *Journal of Family History* 11 (1986): 131–55.

23. NCH, annual report, 1867, 8.

24. Jacobi, *Raising and Education,* 23.

25. Ibid.

26. Ibid.

27. Ibid., 18.

28. Jacobi, "In Re the Nursery and Child's Hospital," 140–41, 143–44.

29. Jacobi, "Author's Preface," *Collectanea Jacobi,* vol. 1, p. 11.

30. Jacobi, "In Re the Nursery and Child's Hospital," 144, 153.

31. Ibid., 144.

32. Anne Hardy, "Tracheotomy versus Intubation: Surgical Intervention in Diphtheria in Europe and the United States," *Bulletin of the History of Medicine* 66 (1992): 536–59. In 1859 one physician referred to the disease as "croupal diphtheria"; ibid., 543.

33. Gustave Flaubert, *Sentimental Education,* trans. Robert Baldick (Harmondsworth, UK: Penguin, 1964), 279.

34. Jacobi, "In Re the Nursery and Child's Hospital," 147. See also Rhoda Truax, *The Doctors Jacobi* (Boston: Little, Brown, 1952), 140–44; Virginia

Metaxas Quiroga, *Poor Mothers and Babies: A Social History of Childbirth and Child Care Hospitals in Nineteenth Century New York City* (New York: Garland, 1989), 76–78.

35. Jacobi, "In Re the Nursery and Child's Hospital,"148.

36. Jacobi would subsequently champion intubation, a less invasive method that was introduced in 1885 by Dr. Joseph O'Dwyer at the New York Foundling Asylum. In 1894 the city's health board inoculated all the children at the New York Infant Asylum with their newly developed diphtheria antitoxin. The foundling asylums, with their pools of parentless infants, were attractive to physicians experimenting in the treatment of childhood diseases. See Hardy, "Tracheotomy"; Elizabeth Fee and Evelynn M. Hammonds, "Science, Politics, and the Art of Persuasion: Promoting the New Scientific Medicine in New York City," in *Hives of Sickness: Public Health and Epidemics in New York City*, ed. David Rosner (New Brunswick, NJ: Rutgers University Press for the Museum of the City of New York, 1995), 173.

37. Hardy, "Tracheotomy," 540.

38. Ibid., 546.

39. Ibid., 537, 541, 542–43, 545.

40. Ibid., 540–44.

41. On homeopathy, see Ronald L. Numbers, "The Fall and Rise of the American Medical Profession," in Leavitt and Numbers, *Sickness and Health*, 187. For Jacobi's comments on homeopathy at the nursery, see Jacobi, "In Re the Nursery and Child's Hospital," 140.

42. "Nursery and Child's Hospital, and the Expulsion of a Physician by the Staff!" *Medical Record,* January 2, 1871, 494–95.

43. Cited in Viner, "Healthy Children," 236.

44. Garrison, "Dr. Abraham Jacobi," [3].

45. Jacobi, "In Re the Nursery and Child's Hospital," 139.

46. On female nursing and midwifery in early America, see Laurel Thatcher Ulrich, *A Midwife's Tale: The Life of Martha Ballard, Based on her Diary, 1785–1812* (New York: Knopf, 1990).

47. Jacobi, "In Re the Nursery and Child's Hospital," 138.

48. For Mary Putnam Jacobi, see Carla Bittel, "The Science of Women's Rights: The Medical and Political Worlds of Mary Putnam Jacobi" (Ph.D. diss., Cornell University, 2003).

49. This insight is the product of a conversation with Gerald Markowitz, for which I thank him.

50. For Jacobi's first two wives and the births and deaths of his children, see Truax, *Doctors Jacobi,* 160, 178, 184, 189–90, 197–99.

51. NCH Medical Board, minutes, November 10, 1870.

52. Abraham Jacobi, "Foundlings and Foundling Institutions," in Golden, *Infant Asylums,* 33–136.

53. Viner, "Healthy Children," 244; *Medical Record,* December 1, 1870, 449–52; "Infant Asylums: Dr. Jacobi's Views," *New York Times,* January 19, 1872.

54. See, notably, Samuel Preston and Michael Haines, *The Fatal Years: Child Mortality in Late Nineteenth Century America* (Princeton, NJ: Princeton University Press, 1991), 36–37.

55. "Infant Asylums," *New York Times,* January 19, 1872.

56. Friedrich Engels, *Condition of the Working Class in England* (New York: Oxford University Press, 1993), 65.

57. Metropolitan Board of Health, annual report, 1866, 10, 11.

58. "The Farming-Out System for Foundlings," *Medical Record,* November 15, 1872, 513.

59. "Infant Asylums," *New York Times,* January 19, 1872.

60. NYFA, annual report, 1872, 12.

61. Joel Foster, "A Minority Report on Foundlings and Foundling Institutions," *Medical Record* 8 (1873), 424.

62. "Infant Asylums," *New York Times,* January 19, 1872; see also Jacobi, "Foundlings and Foundling Institutions," 135–36.

63. Jacobi, "Foundlings and Foundling Institutions," 136.

64. Foster, "Minority Report," 424.

65. In 1880 three-quarters of Americans lived in rural areas or small villages; see Arthur Schlesinger, *The Rise of the City, 1878–1898* (New York: Macmillan, 1933), 1. For Litchfield, see Kathryn Kish Sklar, *Catharine Beecher: A Study in American Domesticity* (New York: W. W. Norton, 1976), 15–16.

66. Samuel Byram Halliday, *The Lost and Found; or, Life among the Poor* (New York: Blakeman and Mason, 1859), 247.

67. "Dr. Stephen Smith Dies in 100th Year," *New York Times,* August 27, 1922.

68. Elisha Harris, *The Educational and Correctional Treatment of Juvenile Delinquents, and of Depraved, Neglected, Abandoned, and Other Children in Danger of Falling into a Criminal Career* (New York: National Prison Association, 1877), 5.

69. Truax, *Doctors Jacobi,* 147–49.

70. "The Children's Aid Society of New York, Its History, Plans and Results, Compiled from the Writings and Reports of the Late Charles Loring Brace," in *History of Child Saving in the United States: Twentieth National Conference of Charities and Correction, Chicago, June 1893* (Boston: Geo. H. Ellis, 1893; reprint, Montclair, NJ: Patterson Smith, 1971), 30.

71. Charles Loring Brace, *The Dangerous Classes and Twenty Years' Work among Them* (New York: Wynkoop and Hallenbeck, 1872), 29.

72. Brace, *Dangerous Classes,* 225.

73. For the nursery's dealings with the Children's Aid Society, see NCH, annual reports, 1880, 6; 1885, 8; 1884, 9; 1895, 10–11; 1903, 9. See also an undated letter from Mary Du Bois to "Dear Sir," New York Nursery and Child's Hospital, New-York Historical Society. For the New York Infant Asylum's experience with the Children's Aid Society, see NYIA, annual report, 1886, 23, 45.

74. Undated letter by Charles Loring Brace to Mary Du Bois, reprinted in NCH, annual report, 1903, 9–10.

75. NCH, annual report, 1900, 21.

76. NYFA, biennial report, 1888–90, 10. Linda Gordon states that by around 1904 about one-third of the thirty-five thousand children who had passed through the Foundling Asylum had been sent west; Linda Gordon, *The Great Arizona Orphan Abduction* (Cambridge, MA: Harvard University Press, 1999), 3.

77. Homer Folks, *Care of Destitute, Neglected, and Delinquent Children* (New York: Johnson Reprint Co., 1970), 124. In the 1890s Folks was the executive secretary of the State Charities Aid Association; in 1902 he became New York's Commissioner of Public Charities.

78. For children placed in the country in the 1840s, see the report of the almshouse visitor John McGrath, in AH, annual report, 1847, 88–91. For placements with farmers in New Jersey, see AH, annual report, 1851, 128.

79. AH, annual report, 1853, 102.

80. AH, annual report, 1858, 281. Townsend's letters to Kellock are in AH annual reports, 1858, 281–84; 1859, 295–97.

81. AH, annual report, 1858, 283.

82. Ibid., 281.

83. George W. Du Bois to Mrs. Cornelius Du Bois, Dubuque, September 22, 1865, and "Caution to the Charitable Public," NYNCH, Records, NYHS.

84. "The Care of Our Foundlings," *Medical Record*, February 1, 1872, 541; "Foundling Asylum," *New York Times*, December 26, 1871; Brace, *Dangerous Classes*, 415–16; "Infant Asylums," *New York Times*, January 19, 1872.

85. Mary Du Bois, "Thirty Years Experience in Hospital Work," in Golden, ed. *Infant Asylums*, 23–24.

86. For Flushing, see NYIA, minutes, December 14, 1871; May 21, 1872; annual report, 1873, [9], [15]–16. For Mount Vernon, see NYIA, annual report, 1880, 29–30.

87. Jacobi, "In Re the Nursery and Child's Hospital," 164–65.

88. NYFA, annual report, 1872, 12.

89. NYFA, biennial report, 1869–71, 9.

90. PCC, annual report, 1871, ix–x. Although foundlings were not always distinguished from "nurse children" in the Infant Hospital's reports, the Westchester program was explicitly for foundlings; see PCC, 1883, 42. During the

program's first eight years, starting in 1872, the Infant Hospital regularly maintained an average of fifty-five to eighty foundlings in Westchester; PCC, annual reports, 1877, xxi; 1878, 82; 1883, 42.

91. For the Westchester placing-out program, see PCC, annual reports, 1877, xxi, 123; 1878, 82; 1879, 67; 1883, 42–43.

92. For Annie Martin, see *New York Herald*: "A Pauper Two Weeks Old," January 23, 1883; "The Foundling Farmed Out," January 24, 1883; "The City's Infant Wards," January 24, 1883.

93. PCC, annual report, 1888, 106.

94. PCC, annual report, 1886, 62.

95. Arch. M. Campbell to Charles W. Woolsey, committee chairman, Westchester County Temporary Home for Protestant Children, August 9, 1880, Isaiah Williams Papers, Manuscript Division, NYPL. I would like to thank Iris Towers for discovering this letter and bringing it to my attention.

96. PCC, annual reports, 1883, 42–43; 1884, 64–65. See also Peter Romanofsky, "Saving the Lives of the City's Foundlings: The Joint Committee and New York City Child Care Methods, 1860–1907," *New York Historical Society Quarterly* 61 (1977): 58.

97. PCC, annual report, 1885, 69.

98. PCC, annual report, 1887, 53. One of these tables shows that in 1887 at the Infant Hospital 19 percent of the babies accompanied by their mothers died; 62 percent of the babies without mothers died; and of the children farmed out to Westchester, all of whom were foundlings, 35 percent died; see AH, annual report, 1887, 55, Table A. For more praise of the Westchester program, see PCC, annual reports, 1886, 62; 1887, 53; 1889, 59.

99. PCC, annual report, 1888, 106.

100. According to Romanofsky the Westchester program stopped in 1891; see "Saving the Lives," 58. The PCC reports show that it lasted until February 1891; see references to "farmed-out children" in PCC, annual report, 1891, 98, 100. This category has disappeared in PCC annual report, 1892, 79–85.

101. PCC, annual report, 1893, 9–10.

102. PCC, annual report, 1893, 137–38. For Gilroy as a cost-cutter, see the entry on Gilroy in Kenneth Jackson, ed., *Encyclopedia of New York City* (New Haven, CT: Yale University Press; New York: New-York Historical Society), 1995.

103. Preston and Haines note that as late as the 1890s medical knowledge was still so limited that the mortality rate of the children of physicians was only 6 percent below the national average; *Fatal Years*, 209.

NOTES TO CHAPTER 6

1. James D. McCabe, *Lights and Shadows of New York Life; or, The Sights and Sensations of the Great City* (Philadelphia: National Publishing Co., 1872), 87.

2. Abraham Jacobi, "Foundlings and Foundling Institutions," in *Infant Asylums and Children's Hospitals: Medical Dilemmas and Developments, 1850–1920: An Anthology of Sources,* ed. Janet Golden (New York: Garland, 1989), 127. Jacobi became chair of the Committee on Foundlings and Foundling Institutions in February 1871; the exposure of the Tweed Ring first appeared in the press in the summer of 1870 and the story continued for the next few years; see Edwin G. Burrows and Mike Wallace, *Gotham: A History of New York City to 1898* (New York: Oxford University Press, 1999), 1008–12.

3. Burrows and Wallace, *Gotham,* 1008–12; Eric Homburger, *Scenes from the Life of a City: Corruption and Conscience in Old New York* (New Haven, CT: Yale University Press, 1994), 206–7.

4. Edith Wharton, *The Age of Innocence* (New York: Appleton and Co., 1920; reprint, New York: Simon and Schuster, 1996), 290.

5. Charles F. Wingate, "An Episode in Municipal Government," *North American Review* 119, no. 245 (October 1874): 377.

6. Homburger, *Scenes from the Life,* 200; *New York Times,* September 11 and 14, 1871.

7. Homburger, *Scenes from the Life,* 207–10; Obituary, "Richard Barrett Connolly," *New York Herald,* June 1, 1880; "Mrs. R. B. Connolly's Funeral," *New York Times,* April 13, 1879; "Mrs. Connolly's Funeral," *New York Herald,* April 13, 1879.

8. "Mrs. Connolly's Funeral," *New York Herald,* April 13, 1870; "Mrs. R. B. Connolly's Funeral," *New York Times,* April 13, 1879. For Hutchings's appointment as Surrogate, see Homburger, *Scenes from the Life,* 177. For Hahnemann Hospital, see Moses King, *King's Handbook of New York City* (Boston: Moses King, 1892), 435.

9. Leo Hershkowitz, *Tweed's New York* (Garden City, NY: Anchor Press, 1977), 141.

10. "The Charities of New York," *New York Times,* February 17, 1872.

11. Peter C. English, "Pediatrics and the Unwanted Child in History: Foundling Homes, Disease, and the Origins of Foster Care, 1860–1920," 701. The law is Chapter 774, "An Act Making Appropriations for Certain Public and Charitable Institutions," April 24, 1866, in *Laws of the State of New York Passed at the Eighty-Ninth Session of the Legislature,* vol. 2, January 2–April 20, 1866 (Albany, NY: William Gould, 1866), 1674–78.

12. Mary Du Bois, "Thirty Years Experience in Hospital Work," in Golden, *Infant Asylums,* 25.

13. Du Bois, "Petition," in NCH, annual report, 1868, 23–24, and in Records of the NYNCH, NYHS. On the 1867 amendment, see Homer Folks, *Care of Destitute, Neglected, and Delinquent Children* (New York: Johnson Reprint Co., 1970), 116–17.

14. "An Act to Reorganize the Local Government of the City of New York," passed April 30, 1873, Chapter 757, section 10, Appendix I. See also *New York Times*, January 8, 9, 12, 31 and February 17, 19, 20, 22, 22, 25, 1873; Burrows and Wallace, *Gotham*, 1028–29.

15. "The Charter and the Charity," *New York Herald*, March 2, 1873.

16. "Address by Dr. Stephen Smith of the State Board of Charities," in NYIA, annual report, 1895, 4. The New York Infant Asylum's revised charter was issued in April 1872.

17. NYFA, "Souvenir of 1889," in NYFA, annual report, 1889, 21–22; Marie de Lourdes Walsh, *The Sisters of Charity of New York, 1809–1959* (New York: Fordham University Press, 1960), 76–78; "Address by Dr. Stephen Smith," 4–5.

18. NYFA, "Souvenir of 1889," 22; Maureen Fitzgerald, "The Perils of 'Passion and Poverty': Women Religious and the Care of Single Women in New York City, 1845–1890," *United States Catholic Historian* 10 (1991): 52–53.

19. "The Charter and the Charity," *New York Herald*, March 2, 1873.

20. "An Act to Amend the Charter of the Foundling Asylum of the Sisters of Charity, in the City of New York," passed June 23, 1874, *Laws of New York*, chap. 644; NYFA, "Souvenir of 1889," 21–22; Walsh, *Sisters of Charity*, 76–78; "Sister Mary Irene Dead," *New York Times*, August 15, 1896; "A True Sister of Charity, Sister Irene Gone to Her Eternal Reward" [1896], unattributed clipping at Sisters of Charity Archives; Elisha Harris, letter to Governor John A. Dix, May 7, 1874, New York Foundling Asylum Records, Sisters of Charity Archives.

21. NYFA, annual report, 1875, 11. For the "panic" of 1873, see Robert H. Wiebe, *The Search for Order, 1877–1920* (New York: Hill and Wang, 1867); Burrows and Wallace, *Gotham*, 1020–38.

22. William Pryor Letchworth, "What Shall Be Done with Pauper Children?" in *Children and Youth in America: A Documentary History*, ed. Robert M. Bremner (Cambridge, MA: Harvard University Press, 1971), 252.

23. Letchworth, "Pauper Children" and "An Act to Provide for the Better Care of Pauper and Destitute Children" (both 1875), in Bremner, *Children and Youth in America*, 252–54; William Pryor Letchworth, "History of Child-Saving Work in the State of New York" in *History of Child Saving in the United States: Twentieth National Conference of Charities and Correction, Chicago, June 1893* (Boston: Geo. H. Ellis, 1893), 181–83. See also Folks, *Care of Destitute, Neglected, and Delinquent Children*, 75–77; Reena Sigman Friedman, " 'These Are Our Children': Jewish Orphanages in the United States, 1880–

1925," (Ph.D. diss., Columbia University, 1991), 7–9. The law was amended in 1878 to lower the age to two; see Folks, *Care of Destitute, Neglected, and Delinquent Children,* 77.

24. On closure of the nurseries, see PCC, annual report, 1875, vi, 271; 1876, xv. For the transformation of antebellum asylums founded in idealism and hope into desolate warehouses for society's outcasts, see David Rothman, *The Discovery of the Asylum: Social Order and Disorder in the New Republic* (Boston: Little, Brown, 1971), 237–64.

25. Letchworth, "History of Child Saving," 182.

26. Folks, *Care of Destitute, Neglected, and Delinquent Children,* 120–24; Letchworth, "History of Child Saving," 181–82.

27. Josephine Shaw Lowell, New York State Board of Charities, annual report, 1889, in Bremner, *Children and Youth,* 281; SCAA, annual report, 1904, 10.

28. SCAA, annual report, 1904, 9. For the founding of the SCAA, see Michael Katz, *In the Shadow of the Poorhouse: A Social History of Welfare in America* (New York: Basic Books, 1996), 36.

29. Peter Romanofsky, "Saving the Lives of the City's Foundlings: The Joint Committee and New York City Child Care Methods, 1860–1907," *New York Historical Society Quarterly* 61 (1977): 50–52.

30. Folks, *Care of Destitute, Neglected, and Delinquent Children,* 123–24.

31. SCAA, annual report, 1904, 10–11.

32. Josephine Shaw Lowell, "The Subsidy System in New York," in Bremner, *Children and Youth,* 281.

33. SCAA, annual report, 1888, 40–41.

34. PCC, annual report, 1888, 106–7.

35. SCAA, annual report, 1898, 27–28; "Saving the Foundlings," *New York Tribune,* April 28, 1901; Romanofsky, "Saving the Lives," 59.

36. "Saving the Foundlings," *New York Tribune,* April 28, 1901.

37. For this placing-out effort, see SCAA, annual report, 1898, 27–32; SCAA/AICP Joint Committee, annual report, 1901, 5–21; Romanofsky, "Saving the Lives"; Virginia M. Walker, "How to Save the Babies of the Tenements," *Charities,* August 5, 1905, 975–80; "Saving the Foundlings," *New York Tribune,* April 28, 1901; "Will Look After New York Foundlings, Guild of Infant Saviour Incorporated," *New York Herald,* June 10, 1901; "Care of City's Foundlings," *New York Herald,* June 3, 1902.

38. SCAA/AICP Joint Committee, annual report, 1900–1901,13; PCC, annual reports, 1902, 59–60; 1903, 97–98.

39. For the Guild of the Infant Savior, see "Saving the Foundlings," *New York Tribune,* April 28, 1901; "Will Look After Foundlings" *New York Herald,* June 10, 1901.

40. For alternate baptism, see "Abandoned to the City's Care," *New York*

Herald, January 14, 1895; "Catholic Waif in Protestant Hands," *New York Herald,* August 22, 1901; *New York Herald,* Sunday magazine, March 27, 1904; "Ashcan Baby Finds a Home in Fifth Avenue," *New York Herald,* Sunday magazine, December 26, 1909; "What's My Name?" *New York Tribune,* April 18, 1948. Alternate baptizing, or religious assignment, which eventually did include Jews, lasted until the 1960s; see Nina Bernstein, *The Lost Children of Wilder: The Epic Struggle to Change Foster Care* (New York: Pantheon, 2001), 58.

41. "Ashcan Baby Finds a Home in Fifth Avenue," *New York Herald,* Sunday magazine, December 26, 1909. By 1896 foundlings were taken first to Bellevue, and then to Randall's Island. See "Seen in Waifland," *New York Herald,* October 25, 1896, sec. 6.

42. "Catholic Waif in Protestant Hands," *New York Herald,* August 22, 1901.

43. "Saving the Foundlings," *Tribune,* April 28, 1901.

44. Hasia Diner, *Erin's Daughters in America: Irish Immigrant Women in the Nineteenth Century* (Baltimore: Johns Hopkins University Press, 1983).

45. There are references in the press and in almshouse and asylum records to Jewish foundlings. Mrs. Webb, the matron of the police department nursery, noted the occasional presence of a Jewish foundling; see "One of the Waifs," *Herald,* June 24, 1883. The New York Foundling Asylum recorded the admission of Jewish foundlings; see NYFA's first admissions book, no. 13, November 3, 1869. Mary Du Bois reported that the nursery welcomed unmarried Jewish women and their babies; see NCH, annual report, 1892, 8, in which the case of a Jewish woman who converted to Christianity at the nursery is recorded. For Jewish foundlings in the homes of Italian wet nurses, see "Some Foundlings Who Have Landed in the Homes of the Well-to-Do," *New York Herald,* March 27, 1904. The Hebrew Infant Asylum, founded in New York in 1896, specifically excluded illegitimate children; Hebrew Infant Asylum, annual report, 1896, 35. For Jewish women and Jewish immigration see Charlotte Baum, Paula Hyman, and Sonya Michel, *The Jewish Woman in America* (New York: New American Library, 1976); Hasia Diner, *A Time for Gathering: The Second Migration, 1820–1880* (Baltimore: Johns Hopkins University Press, 1992).

46. SCAA/AICP Joint Committee, annual report, 1901, 7; "Saving the Foundlings," *New York Tribune,* April 28, 1901. The death rate of children under five in the United States in 1900 was 18 percent; see Michael Preston and Samuel Haines, *The Fatal Years: Child Mortality in Late Nineteenth Century America* (Princeton, NJ: Princeton University Press, 1991), 208.

47. PC, annual report, 1907, 311–12; SCAA, annual report, 1907, 34–35.

48. Romanofsky, "Saving the Lives," 65–68; SCAA, annual report, 1907, 32–41; "Wants City Aid Cut Off, Two Children's Societies Accused of Improper Care of Charges," *New York Times,* January 23, 1907.

49. S. Josephine Baker, *Fighting for Life* (New York: Arno Press, 1974),

118–22; Charles-Edward A. Winslow, *The Life of Hermann M. Biggs: Physician and Statesman of the Public Health* (Philadelphia: Lea and Febiger, 1929), 214–15.

50. Kriste Lindenmeyer, *"A Right to Childhood": The U.S. Children's Bureau and Child Welfare, 1912–46* (Urbana: University of Illinois Press, 1997), 18–22.

51. See reports of the boarding-out department in NYNCH, annual reports, 1914–15, 20–21; 1915–16, 19–23; 1921–22, 48–49.

52. NYNCH, annual report, 1915–16, 19.

53. NYNCH, annual report, 1914–15, 21.

54. NYNCH, annual report, 1915–16, 20.

55. NYNCH, annual reports, 1914–15, 23; 1915–16, 21, 23.

56. NYNCH, annual report, 1915–16, 21, 23.

57. The orphan trains stopped in 1929. Miriam Z. Langsam, *Children West: A History of the Placing-Out System of the New York Children's Aid Society, 1853–1890* (Madison: State Historical Society of Wisconsin for the University of Wisconsin, 1964). For an orphan train boy who went bad, see Joan Jacobs Brumberg, *Kansas Charley: The Story of a 19th-Century Boy Murderer* (New York: Viking, 2003).

58. NYNCH, annual report, 1915–16, 21–22; SCAA/AICP Joint Committee, annual report, 1903, 21.

59. "Some Foundlings Who Have Landed in the Homes of the Well-to-Do," *New York Herald,* March 27, 1904.

60. Ibid.

61. SCAA/AICP Joint Committee, annual report, 1903, 21; NYNCH, annual report, 1915–16, 22.

62. NYNCH, annual report, 1915–16, 20.

63. "Who Owns the Baby?" *New York Herald,* August 7, 1884.

64. "Slaughter of the Innocents," *New York Herald,* May 25, 1887.

65. For child-saving, see Richard A. Meckel, *Save the Babies: American Public Health Reform and the Prevention of Infant Mortality, 1850–1929* (Baltimore: Johns Hopkins University Press, 1990); Steven Mintz, *Huck's Raft: A History of American Childhood* (Cambridge, MA: Belknap Press, 2004), 154–84. For declining tolerance of infant death in private families, see Nancy Schrom Dye and Daniel Blake Smith, "Mother Love and Infant Death, 1750–1920," *Journal of American History* 73 (September 1986): 329–53.

66. PC, annual report, 1903, 21.

67. "New-York's Charities. Management at Randall's Island," *New York Tribune,* February 5, 1880.

68. "Seen in Waifland . . . Science Is Their Guide," *New York Herald,* October 25, 1896, sec. 6, 5:4.

69. Walker, "How to Save the Babies of the Tenements," 975, 976.

70. Baker, *Fighting for Life,* 121. Baker is reporting on an experiment, funded by the Russell Sage Foundation, in which she removed foundlings from one of the city's foundling asylums and placed them with tenement nurses. She does not identify the foundling asylum or when the experiment occurred, but her conclusions are essentially the same as those Walker came to in 1905.

71. PC, annual report, 1905, 25.

72. Anne Middleton Holmes, *Mary Mildred Sullivan: A Biography* (Concord, NH: Rumford Press, 1924); "Address of Mrs. George Gordon Battle," in *In Memoriam, Mary Mildred Sullivan, 1836–1933* (New York: The Mary Mildred Sullivan Chapter, United Daughters of the Confederacy).

73. "In Fifty Years City Learns to Smile When It Gives," *Evening Mail,* February 26, 1917.

74. NYIA, annual report, 1891, 32.

75. Table of Inmates, NYIA, annual report, 1905–7, n.p.

76. NCH, annual report, 1889, 8.

77. NYIA, annual reports, 1886, 40; 1893, 28. For overcrowding at the NYIA, see also NYIA annual reports, 1885, 39; 1887, 32; 1891, 36.

78. NCH, annual report, 1893, 9.

79. NYIA, biennial report, 1899–1900, 12.

80. For financial pressures, see NCH, annual report, 1900, 7; NYIA, annual report, 1900–1901, 10. For the merger, see NYNCH, annual report, 1911, 10–11.

81. NYIA, biennial report, 1905–7, 9.

82. For a viewing of Albert Bierstadt's painting *A Storm in the Rocky Mountains* at the nursery, see NCH, annual report, 1866, 9. For fundraisers at the NYFA, see *New York Herald*: "The Foundling Asylum, Returns for the Institution from the Late Fair," February 12, 1871; "The Feeble Foundlings," April 27, 1873; "The Foundling Asylum," October 16, 1874; "Foundling Asylum Reception," May 12, 1878.

83. Edith Wharton, *The House of Mirth* (New York: New American Library, 1964), 138; NYIA, annual report, 1873, 26.

84. "Mrs. Sullivan Tells of Charity Balls of Fifty Years Ago," *Globe and Commercial Advertiser,* January 21, 1913.

85. Train of Memories in Wake of Annual Charity Ball," *New York Times,* January 31, 1915.

86. The first ball took in $7,200.60. In 1910, the year the nursery and the New York Infant Asylum merged, it collected $14,886.53. See treasurers' reports in NCH and NYNCH annual reports, 1857–58, 1910.

87. George Templeton Strong, *Diary of George Templeton Strong,* ed. Allan Nevins and Milton Halsey Thomas (New York: Octagon Books, 1974), vol. 2, p. 263.

88. NCH, annual report, 1870, 8.

89. "Support Is Wide for Charity Ball," *New York Times,* March 18, 1956; "When Charity Ball Was Younger," *New York Times,* April 11, 1956.

90. NYIA, annual report, 1878, 12.

91. Charles Rosenberg, *The Care of Strangers: The Rise of America's Hospital System* (New York: Basic Books, 1987); David Rosner, *A Once Charitable Enterprise: Hospitals and Health Care in Brooklyn and New York, 1885–1915* (Princeton, NJ: Princeton University Press, 1982); Morris J. Vogel, *The Invention of the Modern Hospital, Boston, 1870–1930* (Chicago: University of Chicago Press, 1980).

92. NYNCH, biennial report, 1917–18, 18; annual reports, 1923, 13, 14; 1929, 8, 29.

93. NYNCH, annual report, 1910, 8.

94. NYNCH, annual report, 1911, 2.

95. Walsh, *Sisters of Charity,* 100–101.

96. Ibid., 98; Francis Cardinal Spellman, *The Foundling* (New York: Charles Scribner's Sons, 1951).

97. Walsh, *Sisters of Charity,* 96.

98. New York Foundling Hospital, *Leadership into the 21st Century: 1999 Annual Report of the New York Foundling Hospital* (New York: New York Foundling Hospital, 1999), http://www.nyfoundling.org (accessed March 23, 2007).

NOTES TO CHAPTER 7

1. The National Abandoned Infants Assistance Resource Center defines the risks of abandonment as "the presence of drugs and/or HIV in the family," National Abandoned Infants Resource Center, http://aia.berkeley.edu (accessed February 8, 2007). In terms of infant abandonment, these ailments were to the twentieth century what sexual stigma and female underemployment were to the nineteenth.

2. For the absence of current-day record-keeping on foundlings, see "Boarder Babies, Abandoned Infants, and Discarded Infants, December, 2005," Abandoned Infants Assistance Resource Center, http://aia.berkeley.edu (accessed February 8, 2007).

3. "Mayor Giuliani and Brooklyn District Attorney Hynes Announce 'Baby Safe Haven'," press release, New York City Administration for Children's Services, December 21, 2000.

4. Thomas Crampton, "Three Abandoned Newborns Saved in a Day of Luck and Kindness," *New York Times,* February 25, 2004.

5. Administration for Children and Families, Department of Health and Human Services, Statistics, "Abandoned Babies—Preliminary National Estimates," http://www.acf.hhs.gov/news/stats/abandon.htm (accessed February 8, 2007).

For the New York City figure, see Cara Buckley, "Safe-Haven Laws Fail to End Discarding of Babies," *New York Times,* January 13, 2007. Various authors have put these figures in perspective by noting that in 1991, 21,600 babies had been left behind in hospitals. This number rose to 30,800 in 1998. See Cynthia Dailard, "The Drive to Enact 'Infant Abandonment' Laws—A Rush to Judgment? *Guttmacher Report on Public Policy* (August 2000): 1–11; Barbara Whitaker, "Death of Unwanted Babies Brings Plea to Help Parents," *New York Times,* March 6, 2000.

6. Patrick T. Murphy, "Helping Parents Choose Wrong," *New York Times,* June 27, 2000. Even though infant abandonment has become rare, between 1999 and 2007 forty-seven states passed "safe haven" laws that make it legal to abandon a baby at a specified site. Well intentioned as these are, there is a debate about how well conceived they are and how effective they have been. See Buckley, "Safe-Haven Laws Fail to End Discarding of Babies"; Dailard, "The Drive to Enact 'Infant Abandonment' Laws."

7. Faye Dudden, *Serving Women: Household Service in Nineteenth-Century America* (Middletown, CT: Wesleyan University Press, 1983), 1; David M. Katzman, *Seven Days a Week: Women and Domestic Service in Industrializing America* (New York: Oxford University Press, 1978), 44.

8. Dudden, *Serving Women,* 240; Katzman, *Seven Days a Week,* viii, 44.

9. Kriste Lindenmeyer, *A Right to Childhood: The U.S. Children's Bureau and Child Welfare, 1912–46* (Urbana: University of Illinois Press, 1997), 253.

10. Lindenmeyer, *Right to Childhood,* 47; Emma O. Lundberg and Katherine F. Lenroot, *Illegitimacy as a Child Welfare Problem* (Washington, DC: United States Department of Labor, Children's Bureau, 1920), 8.

11. Lindenmeyer, *Right to Childhood,* 50; Linda Gordon, *Pitied But Not Entitled: Single Mothers and the History of Welfare, 1890–1935* (New York: Free Press, 1994).

12. Molly Ladd-Taylor, *Mother-Work: Women, Child Welfare, and the State, 1890–1930* (Urbana: University of Illinois Press, 1994), chap. 5; Lindenmeyer, *Right to Childhood,* 152–57; Theda Skocpol, *Protecting Soldiers and Mothers: The Political Origins of Social Policy in the United States* (Cambridge, MA: Harvard University Press, 1992), chap. 8.

13. Ladd-Taylor, *Mother-Work,* 138, 147–49.

14. For this view, see Gordon, *Pitied But Not Entitled.*

15. Homer Folks, "The Foundling," in *Transactions of the Fifteenth International Congress on Hygiene and Demography* (Washington, DC, 1912), 88–89.

16. Sara Josephine Baker, *Fighting for Life* (New York: Arno Press, 1974), 120–21; Charles-Edward A. Winslow, *The Life of Hermann M. Biggs: Physician and Statesman of the Public Health* (Philadelphia: Lea and Febiger, 1929), 214–15.

17. Abraham Jacobi, *The Raising and Education of Abandoned Children in Europe, with Statistics and General Remarks on that Subject* (New York: Bellevue Hospital Printing Office, 1870), 10–11, 41.

18. Volcker Hunecke, "The Abandonment of Legitimate Children in Nineteenth-Century Milan and the European Context," in *Poor Women and Children in the European Past,* ed. John Henderson and Richard Wall (London: Routledge, 1994), 118.

19. Folks, "The Foundling," 88–89.

20. Paul Gilje, "Infant Abandonment in Early Nineteenth-Century New York City: Three Cases," *Signs* 8 (Spring 1983), 589–90.

21. Michael Grossberg, *Governing the Hearth: Law and the Family in Nineteenth-Century America* (Chapel Hill: University of North Carolina Press, 1985), 271–72.

22. Adoption overtook institutionalization for unwanted children in the 1940s, see Viviana Zelizer, *Pricing the Priceless Child: The Changing Social Value of Children* (New York: Basic Books, 1981), 190.

23. For urbanization, see Arthur M. Schlesinger, *The Rise of the City, 1878–1898* (New York: Macmillan, 1933); Federal Census, Table HS-2, "Population Characteristics: 1900–2002, http://www.census.gov/statab/hist/HS-02.pdf (accessed August 17, 2007).

24. Daniel Scott Smith and Michael Hindus, "Premarital Pregnancy in America, 1640–1971: An Overview and Interpretation," *Journal of Interdisciplinary History* 5 (Spring 1975): 537–38; Margaret S. Usdansky, "Single Motherhood: Stereotypes vs. Statistics," *New York Times,* February 11, 1996.

25. Rickie Solinger, *Wake Up Little Susie: Single Pregnancy and Race before Roe v. Wade* (New York: Routledge, 1992), 6–7.

26. Joan Jacobs Brumberg, " 'Ruined' Girls: Changing Community Responses to Illegitimacy in Upstate New York, 1890–1920," *Journal of Social History* 18 (Winter 1984): 246–72; Solinger, *Wake Up Little Susie,* 103–47.

27. Charles Meigs, *Obstetrics: The Science and Art* (Philadelphia: Lea and Blanchard, 1849), 615–16, as cited in Russell Viner, "Healthy Children for a New World: Abraham Jacobi and the Making of American Pediatrics" (Ph.D. diss., Cambridge University, 1997), 166.

28. Anne Bradstreet, "In Memory of My Dear Grandchild Elizabeth Bradstreet, Who Deceased August, 1665, Being a Year and Half Old," in *The Norton Anthology of American Literature,* ed. Ronald Gottesman et al. (New York: W. W. Norton, 1979), vol. 1, p. 52.

29. "The Foundling Asylum: A Glimpse into Its Workings," *New York Tribune,* June 10, 1883.

30. Gerald T. Koeppel, *Water for Gotham: A History* (Princeton, NJ: Princeton University Press, 2000); "Sickness and Health," in Judith Walzer Leavitt

and Ronald L. Numbers, eds., *Sickness and Health in America: Readings in the History of Medicine and Public Health* (Madison: University of Wisconsin Press, 1985), 3–10; Richard A. Meckel, *Save the Babies: American Public Health Reform and the Prevention of Infant Mortality, 1850–1929* (Baltimore: Johns Hopkins University Press, 1990); Julie Miller, "To Stop the Slaughter of the Babies: Nathan Straus and the Drive for Pasteurized Milk in New York City, 1893–1920," *New York History* 74 (April 1993): 158–84; Samuel Preston and Michael Haines, *The Fatal Years: Child Mortality in Late Nineteenth Century America* (Princeton, NJ: Princeton University Press, 1991), 208–9.

31. Bureau of the Census, *Historical Statistics of the United States: Colonial Times to the Present* (Washington DC: U.S. Government Printing Office, 1975), 57; press release, National Center for Health Statistics, Centers for Disease Control, February 11, 2004, http://www.cdc.gov/nchs/pressroom/04news/infantmort.htm (accessed August 17, 2007).

32. New York Metropolitan Board of Health, annual report, 1866, 10; New York State Department of Health, *Vital Statistics of New York State 2000* (Albany, NY, 2000), 87; press release, "Citywide Infant Mortality Rate Reaches Low, But Racial and Geographic Disparities Persist in Certain Communities," New York City Department of Health and Mental Hygiene, December 12, 2002, http://www.nyc.gov/html/doh/html/press-archive02/pr1081212.shtml (accessed September 24, 2007).

33. On the continuing high death rate of illegitimates see Lundberg and Lenroot, *Illegitimacy,* 28.

34. "Naming City Waifs," *New York Times,* August 23, 1900; "Future of Foundlings, Infants No Longer Named for Chance Localities," *New York Times,* June 28, 1903.

35. "Ashcan Baby Finds a Home in Fifth Avenue," *New York Herald,* Sunday magazine, December 26, 1909; "Name 1923 Foundlings, Miss Hooper Directs Choice of Titles for 20 Infants," *New York Times,* December 20, 1922.

36. Sylvia D. Hoffert, *Private Matters: American Attitudes toward Childbearing and Infant Nurture in the Urban North, 1800–1860* (Urbana: University of Illinois Press, 1989), 177–80.

37. "Institution Life, I, Foundling Asylum," *Illustrated American,* May 18, 1890, 310; NYNCH, annual report, 1911, 11; "Abandoned to the City's Care," *New York Herald,* January 14, 1895. See also "Has Baby-Adopting Fallen Out . . . Some Foundlings," *New York Herald,* March 27, 1904; E. Wayne Carp, *Family Matters: Secrecy and Disclosure in the History of Adoption* (Cambridge, MA: Harvard University Press, 1998).

38. "Denied She Had Any Daughter, Was Mrs. Marcella Edwards Miss Guthrie or a Bellevue Hospital Waif?" *New York Herald,* March 15, 1893.

39. "Unbalanced Man Shoots Two Nuns . . . Crazed by Secret of His Iden-

tity," *New York Herald,* July 18, 1902; "Shoots Sisters of Mercy, Former Waif There Invades Foundling Asylum," *New York Tribune,* July 18, 1902. See also "Told of Her Birth Girl Goes Insane: Knowledge That She Was a Foundling Kept from Miss Van Pelt All Her Life," *New York Times,* March 26, 1912.

40. Oscar Wilde, *The Importance of Being Earnest,* in *The Plays of Oscar Wilde* (New York: Random House, 1988), 369.

41. "A Satchel Full of Baby," *New York Herald,* March 22, 1889.

42. Historical Scrapbook, School of Nursing Records, New York Weill Cornell Medical Center Archives.

43. "Ashcan Baby Finds a Home in Fifth Avenue," *New York Herald,* December 26, 1909.

44. NYIA, annual report, 1887, 19.

45. Herman Melville, *Billy Budd,* in *Billy Budd and Other Tales* (New York: New American Library, 1961), 16. Thanks to Martin Miller for reminding me that Billy Budd was a foundling.

46. From the *New York Times*: "Baby Boy Found in Subway," October 14, 1921; "Foundling in Phone Booth," August 27, 1922; "Newborn Found in Garbage by Building Superintendent," November 11, 1994; "Woman Arrested after Newborn Is Found Dead in Trash," April 3, 1999; "Baby Is Found Dead in Trash on Broadway," October 12, 1999; "Single Mother Is Charged with Leaving Infant in Lot" (Hackensack, New Jersey), February 10, 2000; "Helping Parents Choose Wrong" (dumpsters), June 27, 2000; "Baby Found Abandoned at Subway Station," August 29, 2000.

47. "Abandons Baby by Ruse," *New York Times,* February 3, 1927.

48. "Newborn Girl Abandoned," *New York Times,* August 12, 1996.

49. For the "Pill," see Andrea Tone, *Devices and Desires: A History of Contraceptives in America* (New York: Hill and Wang, 2001), 203–59.

50. Stigmatization of illegitimacy certainly did not begin in the early nineteenth century, but it did reach a height then; see, for instance, Barbara Welter's discussion of "purity," in "The Cult of True Womanhood: 1820–1860," *American Quarterly* 18 (Summer 1866): 150–74. Between the 1960s and the 1980s, even as stigma eroded, the single mother remained enormously controversial. Examples include the furor that raged over Daniel Patrick Moynihan's *The Negro Family in America: The Case for National Action* (Washington, DC: U.S. Department of Labor, Office of Planning and Research, 1965), or Ronald Reagan's pronouncements about "welfare queens." But in the twentieth century the issues, having to do with race and the expenditure of federal funds on welfare, were entirely different from the ones that seemed important in the nineteenth century.

51. See, e.g., Matthew Purdy, "Newborn Found in Garbage by Building Superintendent," *New York Times,* November 11, 1994; Randal C. Archibold,

"Dignity for the Tiniest Victims: Paramedics Arrange Funerals for Abandoned Infants," *New York Times,* December 7, 1999.

52. Thomas Crampton, "Three Abandoned Newborns Saved in a Day of Luck and Kindness," *New York Times,* February 25, 2004.

Index

Page numbers in italics refer to illustrations. The letter t following a page number denotes a table; n denotes a note.

Vanderlyn, John, 52, 93
Viner, Russell, 292n4
Virchow, Rudolph, 177

Wald, Lillian, 237, 237
Walker, Virginia C., 212, 218
Webb, Mrs., 34–35, 195–96, 302n45
West, Benjamin, 92, 93
Wet nurses: African-American, 64–65;
used by the almshouse, 7, 50, 61–69,
161; children of, 110, 139–40; in
Europe, 19–20, 22, 181, 263n56; at
the Infant Department, 162, 163–66;
Italian, 215–17; used by the New York
Foundling Asylum, 137–38, 141–42,
194; used by the Nursery and Child's
Hospital, 112; in private homes, 139–
40; at the Randall's Island Infant Hospital, 170; rural, 19–20, 22, 181, 188–
89, 194. *See also* Baby farmers; Dry
nurses

Wheel (device for abandoning babies), 18,
135–36, 180, 230
Wharton, Edith, 143; *Age of Innocence,*
201; *House of Mirth,* 221–22
White House Conference on the Care
of Dependent Children (1909), 213,
230
White, Sarah (foundling), 31, 68–69
Wiebe, Jacob, 195
A Winter's Tale (Shakespeare), 16
Women: charities formed by, 110–11,
176, 223–24; legal status of in the
nineteenth-century United States,
111
Women's Prison Association, Isaac T.
Hopper Home, 157–58
Women's rights, movements for, 154–55,
156, 239
Wynne, James, 108–9

York, Laura (foundling), 236–37, 237

About the Author

Julie Miller is a social historian of the nineteenth-century United States. In 2006–7 she was a Bernard and Irene Schwartz Postdoctoral Fellow at the New-York Historical Society. She teaches at Hunter College of the City University of New York.